Early Chinese Revolutionaries
Radical Intellectuals in Shanghai and Chekiang, 1902–1911

Mary Backus Rankin

Harvard University Press
Cambridge, Massachusetts

Second printing, 1974
Preparation of this volume has been aided by a grant
from the Ford Foundation.
Library of Congress Catalog Card Number 76–115479
ISBN 0-674-22001-3 (cloth)
ISBN 0-674-22004-8 (paper)
Printed in the United States of America

Contents

For
Anne Converse Backus

The 1911 Revolution in China has recently become a popular subject of analysis by students of Chinese history. Its position in modern Chinese history is still being reinterpreted, but it was unquestionably a crucial event in China's struggle to find a new political system, to modernize her society and economy, and to achieve a new world role. The name 1911 Revolution is in a way unfortunate, because it immediately poses the question of whether the changes it wrought were sufficiently profound to be termed revolutionary. The resulting semantic complications can be more interminable than illuminating. Although I am inclined to believe that the events of 1911–12 by themselves do not justify the name revolution, the changes they produced were enough to ensure that the old Confucian order could not be resurrected again. The 1911 Revolution irrevocably committed China to search for new values, systems, and institutions. Thus it was the opening phase of a prolonged period of change, the cumulative effect of which was certainly revolutionary. Partly because 1911 did not bring quick solutions, understanding the aims and attitudes of radicals of that day becomes crucially important. Many of the same problems and issues shaped left-wing politics throughout the next four decades.

In this book I have approached the 1911 Revolution through the "student" radicals in a particular part of China. The result falls part way between local history and a topical case study. The localities, Chekiang and Shanghai, do not fit neatly into the usual regional divisions because one is a province and the other a unique metropolis in a neighboring province. Nonetheless, close ties did exist between the two areas, particularly within the revolutionary movement, and in combination they present an excellent opportunity to study the other facet of my concern: the aims and behavior of the radical intellectuals. This group was unusually important in these places. However, allowing for such special local conditions as the relative modernization and commercialization of Shanghai, the strong scholarly tradition in Chekiang, and the secondary importance of the army in Shanghai (and in Chekiang during the early phase of the revolutionary movement), I believe that much said about the radical intellectuals here can be applied to their activities in the rest of the country.

Concentration on Chekiang and Shanghai in itself indicates skepticism about the orthodox Nationalist interpretation of the 1911 Revolution, which affirms the leadership of Sun Yat-sen and the Revolutionary Alliance and stresses those places where Sun was most active—South China, Tokyo, and overseas Chinese communities. The evidence would indicate that there was no effective central revolutionary leadership, no united party, nor any main line of development. Understanding must come from correlating patterns of activity within regions of China rather than from following the history of emigré professional revolutionaries.

Two assumptions underlie the interpretations in this book: that the basic aim of the 1911 Revolution was modernization, closely tied to nationalistic attitudes; and that students and intellectuals formed the core of the revolutionary movement, which was a political phenomenon distinguishable from the Revolution itself. As an attempt at a modernizing revolution, the 1911 Revolution was one of the first twentieth-century national upheavals staged to usher in a new era of progress toward the benefits enjoyed by the stronger and richer West. This orientation raises numerous questions about the relationships among revolution, tradition, and modernization. Was revolution the most appropriate way for the 1911 radicals to pursue their goals or would they have been more effective if they had worked through existing nascent modern institutions, thereby avoiding disintegration that retarded national regeneration? Could such reformism have produced significant changes, and produced them fast enough to allay frustrations that lead to revolutionary demands? Were traditional forces so strong a barrier in China that modernization could only be achieved in conjunction with a violent social revolution, such as the one begun by the Communists in 1949? What aspects of tradition were antithetical to modernization, which ones could be rechanneled to promote change, and how did residual traditional influences color activities and organizations believed to be modern and new?

Emphasis on the central role of the young intellectuals implicitly distinguishes between the revolutionary movement and the Revolution in 1911. Constitutionalists, army officers, and others had the power to dominate the Revolution. However, here I have discussed them largely in terms of their relations with the revolutionary intellectuals, who were also important as catalysts before 1911 and as the pioneers of twentieth-century radical Chinese politics. The intellectuals' central role in the revolutionary movement, narrowly defined, is hardly suprising in a country where only a small minority had the knowledge to perceive and articulate, however superficially, the problems facing China. Radical proponents of modernization were found most readily among youths who received their education when values were already changing, new subjects were being taught, and new ideas being acknowledged. They were no longer committed to the old ways. They were profoundly concerned but had little influence over events, and so they suffered most intensely the frustrations that psychologically predisposed some toward radical solutions.

Since the radical tendency of Chinese student politics continued through the Republican period, understanding the 1911 radical intellectuals provides a foundation for understanding subsequent Chinese revolutionary history and some of the attitudes of Communist Party leaders. Their history should also give some insight into attitudes and frustrations of intellectuals in other countries seeking modernization. The spread of student dissatisfaction to many Western countries during the 1960's gives additional relevance to the 1911 radicals. In part their story provides perspective on the current American scene. If short hair and business suits seemed so outrageous in China in 1900, are long hair and sandals really so bad here and now? It also may aid in understanding contemporary American student behavior despite all the differences of time, situation, and culture. The radical political orientation of the Chinese students, their uncompromising moralism and attraction to simple solutions uncomplicated by too much factual analysis seem very familiar today. So does their anger at the system and their determination to provoke a confrontation with it. Individual students in China often did not remain radicals for many years, but the radical tendency in the schools persisted as long as the basic causes of dissatisfaction were not remedied. This may be the essence of the lesson that the 1911 student radicals have for the United States today.

This book began as a thesis at Harvard University, and I am deeply grateful to Professor John K. Fairbank for aid and advice at all stages. He forbore with many years of slow and distant progress, and his practical, patient encouragement has been an essential ingredient in the completion of this book. The entire manuscript was read by my parents, Louise Laidlaw Backus and Dana C. Backus, and the first two chapters by Linda Reed, all of whom provided helpful comments. E-an Zen periodically gave much needed aid in translating otherwise obscure passages. I would like to thank the staffs of the Harvard-Yenching Library, The Library of Congress, and The Hoover Library for a variety of assistance. Gladys Shimasaki did an excellent and appreciated job of typing.

The preparation of the manuscript and my postdoctoral research was assisted by two generous grants from the Joint Committee on Contemporary and Republican China of the Social Science Research Council and the American Council of Learned Societies. I would also like to thank Yale University Press for permission to use passages from my article "The Revolutionary Movement in Chekiang: A Study in the Tenacity of Tradition," which appears in Mary C. Wright, ed., *China in Revolution: The First Phase, 1900–1913.* The frontispiece cartoon, originally published in *The People's Cry (Min-hu pao)*, no. 2 (May 16, 1909), is from the Kuomintang Central Executive Committee, Committee for the Compilation of Materials on Party History, ed., *Min-hu jih-pao* (Taipei, 1969), p. 12, and is reprinted by permission of the Historical Archives Commission of the Kuomintang.

Finally, I appreciate the support of my husband, Douglas Rankin, who has long had to contend with otherwise useful bookcases filled with indecipherable books, stacks of paper all about the house, and lamentable inattention to things non-Chinese.

Washington, D.C.
October 1969

Early Chinese Revolutionaries

The sun is setting with no road ahead,
In vain I weep for loss of country.
. . . .
Although I die yet I still live,
Through sacrifice I have fulfilled my duty. . . .[1]

So wrote the revolutionary heroine Ch'iu Chin to a friend during the second week of July 1907. Five days later her premonition was realized when she was beheaded at the execution ground of Shaohsing prefectural city in the province of Chekiang. When she sent this letter, Ch'iu must already have heard of the failure and execution of her cousin and collaborator, Hsü Hsi-lin, in a nearby province. Her own plans for a rising in Chekiang were about to be discovered, and all her hopes for deliverance of both self and country smashed. In the face of certain disaster she decided to continue with as much as possible of her original scheme. Even when she heard that government troops had arrived from the provincial capital she refused to flee. Her only forces were a handful of students, and with their help she resisted briefly before the soldiers captured her. The presiding official at the interrogation was the hostile Manchu prefect, one of her intended victims. Under torture she confessed to little. Nonetheless, alarmed officials quickly executed her before further troubles could arise.

Ch'iu Chin's tragic end dramatized the dilemma of student revolutionaries at the beginning of the twentieth century in China. They were propelled by a great sense of urgency to act to save the country before it was finally appropriated by the imperialist powers and its people sunk irretrievably in ignorance and decadence. They naively hoped that they could usher in a new era of national strength and individual freedom. Yet bright, vague dreams of a happy future were coupled with the reality of the students' present impotence. Radicals moved between exhilaration and despair. Lacking effective power or consistent methods, they were often driven to self-defeating, self-sacrificing acts. Like Ch'iu Chin, some traded their lives for a moral triumph which they were sure would be acclaimed in the future.

Student radicalism during the last decade of the dying Ch'ing dynasty can be viewed in the context of the history of Chinese reaction to the Western presence in their country, dating back to the 1840's.[2] The revolutionaries who intended to overthrow the dynasty and establish a republic had been preceded by a train of thinkers who had sought ways to strengthen the country. The earliest modernizers wished only to adopt Western military technology. Before long a number of men also began to promote general industrialization, and eventually some realized the importance of administrative and political innovations. In 1898, under the impact of China's recent humiliating defeat in the Sino-Japanese War, a group of scholars and officials, in collaboration with the young emperor, tried to introduce sweeping reforms. Their brief period in power showed that men outside the government could take political initiative and that support for modernization was no longer limited to a few exceptional individuals. At the same time, their early failure seemed to show that change under that particular government was impossible. Two years later, reactionaries in the court made a final effort to obliterate all that was foreign and new when they supported the superstitious and xenophobic society known as the Boxers in an effort to kill or drive out all Westerners. The shock provided by the suicidal court policy during the Boxer Rebellion and the humiliation of having Western troops occupy Peking was followed by a new push for reform. This combination of events turned the radicals of the day more firmly against the government while, at the same time, offering them new freedom of action. Greater freedom in its turn brought new strains in relations with a government, most of whose officials were simply unable to understand the import of the radical movement. The next step was revolution, and by 1903 radicals who five years ago would have taken up the cause of the weak, but reformist emperor were vilifying older reformers for their continued support of the monarchy. The official examinations, the traditional means of recruiting and binding men into the political system, were abandoned when controlled reform became government policy after the fiasco of the Boxer Rebellion. On the other hand, before government constitutional reforms could offer new political roles to the educated classes, opposition to the foreign Manchu rulers of the Ch'ing dynasty and to their constitution were already basic tenets of radical groups. Institutions such as the provincial assemblies might never have appealed to the radicals, but they appeared just too late for the possibility to be tested. There were already growing numbers of students and scholars who believed that China could never be part of the modern twentieth century unless the government was overthrown.

The immediate beginnings of a Chinese revolutionary intelligentsia dated from the proliferation of modern schools teaching Western subjects and the new government policy after 1900 to encourage study in Japan. Modern schools brought together students and scholars already distressed by current events and interested in Western knowledge. Consequent excitement was intensified by fresh instances of Western imperialistic encroachment. The resulting burst of vehement radicalism almost immediately aimed at the overthrow of the Ch'ing government.

This kind of student politics was an innovation in China. It was not new for students to create disturbances or for older scholars to form cliques, but these groups had traditionally been related to immediate local interest, often self-interest, or to bureaucratic factionalism. Only now were students concerned with the full sweep of national policy. Now they believed they had a right to influence official decisions on such matters. These ideas came from their reading Western history and democratic political theory. The recent growth in communications—the press and the telegraph— gave added effect to their new-found ambitions. The whole radical movement was closely bound up with modernization in other spheres.[3] Modern schools formed its base and it developed most strongly in urban centers, particularly treaty ports, where modernization was more advanced than in the rest of China. The modernization and regeneration of China were the most compelling demands behind the radicalism of the students.

Once begun, radicalism grew wherever modern students congregated and "student circles" (hsüeh-chieh) developed—that vaguely defined stratum of students and quasi-students, scholars and teachers, booksellers, newspaper reporters, and hangers-on who regardless of age and exact occupation were associated with modern education and ideas. The general tone of the student circles was one of dissatisfaction and tremendous excitement. Its more radical elements were comparable to the nineteenth-century Russian intelligentsia in that they found inspiration in Western ideas, felt a certain gulf between themselves and the rest of their society, and were forced by their ideals into illegal political activity.

The Lower Yangtze provinces became the center of student radicalism shortly after 1900. This part of China had long been noted for its large numbers of scholars. Then in the latter half of the nineteenth century the treaty port of Shanghai became a focal point of modernization. These two factors combined to make the area one of prime importance in the development of the 1911 Revolution because the new student groups were a mainstream of the revolutionary movement. Sun Yat-sen, who has usually been regarded as the leader of the Revolution, does not play a large part in this story. His home province of Kwangtung, which was the focus of his activities within China, was outside of the economic and intellectual center of the country. Sun himself was a little too Western and international in his outlook to personify the new radical forces. His two early attempts at revolution in Kwangtung, in 1895 and 1900, had been largely isolated instances, and the idea of revolution did not gain impetus until it was linked with student radicalism, which offered a small but continuing base more closely tied to China's modernization.

This study concentrates upon the activities of the intellectual revolutionaries in two significant portions of the Lower Yangtze area, the city of Shanghai and the nearby province of Chekiang. It focuses mainly on the years 1902 through 1907, the period during which student radicalism made its greatest contribution to the revolutionary movement. This period can be further subdivided. The years 1902 and 1903 saw a distinctly revolutionary student movement grow from a less specific radicalism that was the heritage of the 1898 Reform Movement and the product of the distress over the Boxer Rebellion. By the end of 1902, the unfocused radicalism of students in new schools had already led them to clash with authorities. Student excitement continued to grow during the early months of 1903 until only a relatively minor provocation was necessary to push a segment of the student body into an open break with the government. The fortuitous timing of the Russian refusal to make a scheduled withdrawal of troops from Manchuria in March 1903 crystallized previous discontent into the revolutionary movement.

The Chinese students in Tokyo and in the modern schools of Shanghai led the way for their contemporaries elsewhere in the country. In Shanghai the Chinese Educational Association, the Patriotic School, and the newspaper *Su-pao* (*The Kiangsu Journal*) were the major institutions where the transition was made from reformism to radicalism to revolution. The new revolutionary movement was dramatized by the violently anti-Manchu articles in *Su-pao* during June 1903 and the consequent arrest and trial of six men associated with the paper.

The *Su-pao* trial was followed by a new phase. Revolutionaries gradually moved away from open verbal protests in the partially protected schools, press, and associations of the treaty ports and Tokyo. Instead they turned to direct violence and attempted to organize revolts in the interior of China. This new direction led to the founding of clandestine subversive organizations. In Shanghai the hypersecret Restoration Society (*Kuang-fu hui*) was established toward the end of 1904. Although this group originated in Shanghai, the interests of its members soon prompted some of them to return home to establish front organizations, make contacts with secret societies, and try to initiate revolution. Chekiang then became the most important locale of Restoration Society activities. The Ta-t'ung School in Shaohsing, Chekiang, was the chief of a number of front organizations in the province. From its activities came the risings of July 1907, the failure of which marked the end of this particular phase of the Revolution.

After 1907 there began a third period. during which the significance of the intellectual revolutionaries declined and different groups dominated the opposition to the government. This was partly the result of damage done to the always weak Restoration Society organization by the ill-timed risings in Chekiang and Anking. Relatively effective government control in Central China convinced the leaders of the Revolutionary Alliance (*T'ung-meng hui*), which had been established by Sun Yat-sen in Tokyo in 1905 and was now the major revolutionary party in the country, that risings could not succeed there.

More fundamental was the impact of the accelerating government commitment to institutional reform, particularly its acceptance of the principle of constitutional government. Self-government, educational, agricultural, and other associations and, after mid-1909, the provincial assemblies provided new employment for modern students and new channels for expressing demands for reform. The revolutionary movement lost momentum because alternative political outlets became available to radicals and reformers who had provided a reservoir of support for the professional revolutionaries. Opposition to the government broadened and altered. Railway politics and the timetable for constitutional government became major areas of dispute. The lead was taken by modernizing gentry, merchants, and scholars, members of the new army, and more moderate returned students in the provincial assemblies and other organizations. These people were active in the modernization of China, but their involvement was through legally and socially acceptable professional or entrepreneurial interests. They were more closely enmeshed in traditional social and political structures than the revolutionaries and lacked the radicals' romanticism, commitment to violence, and determination to obliterate existing mores and institutions.

The radical intellectuals were shoved toward the fringes of the political opposition. Many professional revolutionaries became émigrés, operating mainly in Tokyo, among overseas Chinese, or along the South China border. Revolutionaries who remained in China had to share the field of antigovernment propaganda with moderates, who became more effective once the government sanctioned groups to prepare the way for constitutional government. In Shanghai radical activities tended to become repetitious and routine. The radical intelligentsia continued to grow as a group, but many of its members were not steadily active politically. In Chekiang, away from the treaty ports, there were periodic meetings and visits, but little continuous revolutionary activity. The remaining local front organizations fitted so quietly into the scene that they compromised their revolutionary character. Secret society allies of an earlier period either became outright revolutionaries and left Chekiang or resumed their old ways, with little reference to the revolutionary movement. The new army units stationed at Hangchow were the most important new source of revolutionary strength. Officers who had been peripherally involved in the 1907 rising played an important part in planning the overthrow of the provincial government in 1911. However, in the intervening years they had acquired professional interests and the habit of military command, which set them apart from the intellectual revolutionaries who had dominated the Restoration Society risings four years earlier.

The romantic, radical trend in student politics, therefore, was an early phase in the development of the 1911 Revolution. It never died out, but it declined in significance after 1907, and the 1911 Revolution was not the result of the radicals' plotting. Although it represented a decisive break with the past, it did not usher in a period of rapid, continuing change. Nor did it lead to national strength and unity. Military rule, political fragmentation, and the persistent hold of tradition were a disappointment to many students. The incompleteness of the Revolution was symbolized by the "betrayal" of the new Republic by its first president, the ex-Ch'ing army officer, modernizer, and official, Yüan Shih-k'ai, who, after allying with the revolutionaries, promoted his own power interests instead of furthering their aims.

Nonetheless, the experience of the 1911 Revolution was a strong, fresh stimulus to student radicalism. This radicalism then developed into the intensified, Western-oriented intellectual ferment of the New Culture Movement, which began in 1915, and into the anti-imperialism of the May Fourth Movement, which took its name from demonstrations on May 4, 1919, against the awarding of German rights in Shantung to Japan at the Versailles Peace Conference. Left-wing movements and the early Communist movement followed in the 1920's. Protests against Nationalist government inaction against Japanese aggression in the early 1930's and opposition to Nationalist policies during World War II continued this trend in student politics. Finally, this political and ideological tendency contributed importantly to the Communist success in 1949.

When one tries to define the radicals of the 1911 period and pinpoint their relations with other groups one is frustrated by the lack of clear political distinctions. The 1911 Revolution was an early phase of a national regeneration movement in which doctrinal lines were not yet clearly drawn. The situation is further complicated because those people who called themselves revolutionaries neither exclusively made the Revolution of 1911 nor controlled it once it occurred. They tended to become lost in the confused political situation after the collapse of the dynasty, many were not consistently radical over a period of time, and almost all periodically shared political attitudes held by nonrevolutionaries. Attempts to define an ideological continuum from left to right based on European models require so many individual qualifications that they are not very useful. There were often no firm distinctions between revolutionaries and moderate scholars, merchants, gentry, and even some officials, all of whom were also concerned with the problem of how to modernize and strengthen China. The split between revolutionaries and constitutionalists, dramatized by the debates of the political exiles in Tokyo, was not as sharp in local instances back in China, where personal contacts and overlapping aims helped bridge the gap. The new Chinese intelligentsia was inherently less isolated than its nineteenth-century Russian prototype because its members lived in a society that honored students and scholars. Some revolutionaries had established scholarly reputations and many had acquaintances among gentry, merchants, and officials. Radical youths were from families in the elite stratum of society. Probably they came mainly from the lower and middle layers of this level, but they still might have access to men of influence. Even those radicals who were profoundly dissatisfied with the existing order, and unwilling to work peacefully for reforms within it, did not necessarily sever all their connections outside of the revolutionary movement. This behavior raises questions about the depth of their radicalism and the extent of their social alienation, for they sometimes appeared reluctant to sacrifice too much of their traditional privileged position. However, the seeming contradictions may perhaps be reconciled by allowing for the importance of particularistic, personal ties in Chinese society. Bonds between old friends, fellow students, teachers, and pupils, or fellow townsmen might persist despite newly developed ideological differences, particularly when these differences were largely matters of degree.

Revolutionaries and moderates might disagree on basic social questions yet still be in accord on many specific issues. In a particular case both might promote similar modernizing projects in education, agriculture, and industry. Then practical differences between individual modernizers often did not seem as acute as the gulf between all private advocates of modernization and local conservatives or government officials who, even when they favored controlled modernization, were suspicious of vigorous expressions of public opinion.

By 1911 radicals and moderates had grown closer together. Revolutionaries had gained publicity for their cause and achieved a certain romantic appeal. Otherwise, their use of violence had been notably unsuccessful and they may have become increasingly willing to look for allies outside their own circles. The moderates on their part were becoming more alienated from the government. Railway disputes directed their nationalism, combined with self-interest, specifically against the dynasty. Provincial assemblies brought disagreements with officials into the open. Although the aims and manifestations were different, some of the impatience felt by the revolutionaries was beginning to infect other groups.

All these factors helped make possible the initially broad coalitions which briefly headed the revolutionary governments. However, the area of agreement soon proved too small and the initial regenerative coalition was replaced by personal factions and military control. Then as the search for solutions to the problems of modernization deepened, ideological cleavages developed which eventually polarized into the political conflict between the Communist and Nationalist parties.

These splits were still in the future, however, and major divisions in Chinese politics during the first decade of the twentieth century revolved about different degrees in the development of nationalism and different concepts of social and political mobilization of the masses. These were the issues that dominated the intellectual environment in which students lived, and the issues that roughly separated conservatives, moderates, and radicals. The most conservative reaction to Western encroachment was xenophobic rejection, which was partly racial, but mostly cultural. This attitude had been reflected in most of the attacks on Western-inspired modernizers and in demands by the expositors of righteous criticism (ch'ing-i) for war to halt Russian and French imperialism during the 1870's and 1880's. The Boxer Rebellion and the support given to the Boxers by some members of the court and officials showed that such views were still influential in 1900. A still traditionalistic, but less strictly cultural and more nationalistic, view was taken by those willing to accept certain foreign methods to develop China's wealth and power while preserving basic Confucian values. They tolerated some foreign interference out of necessity, but looked forward to the day when China would be strong enough to throw the foreigners out. The phrase "Chinese learning for fundamental principles, Western learning for practical use" provided a theoretical rationale. Major modernizing officials of the end of the Ch'ing largely fell into this category.

A more decisive break with tradition was made by reformers or constitutionalists who were willing to abandon much of the past to achieve fundamental changes they believed necessary to make China a viable nation. Partly overlapping this group were merchants and gentry who undertook private modernizing projects in such spheres as railway building, mining, and textile manufacture. Their nationalistic intentions to strengthen China coincided with their private interest in profit, and they were less inhibited than government officials by the practical realities of foreign policy. They clashed with the government over acceptance of new foreign loans and granting of new economic concessions to foreigners. This type of conflict eventually turned them against the government, and remnants of traditional loyalty to the dynasty were replaced by nationalistic desire to save the country. The nationalism of such modernizers led them in a different political direction than did that of some constitutionalists who argued that the Manchu monarchy must be preserved because the confusion following a revolution would open the way for greater Western domination. By 1911 this was becoming an outdated position.

A further step was taken by those who opposed the Manchus as alien rulers. Because the immediate object of the 1911 Revolution was the overthrow of the dynasty, anti-Manchuism was enough to make someone who was quite traditional in other respects a member of the revolutionary movement. The revolutionary most famous for single-minded anti-Manchuism, Chang Ping-lin, was also skeptical of the good of importing Western social and political institutions. Some others were more willing to tolerate Westerners in the treaty ports than Manchus in Peking. Certain secret society leaders allied with the revolutionaries were attracted mainly by anti-Manchu propaganda. Sun Yat-sen was more anti-Manchu than anti-imperialist during this phase of his career.

A more clearly nationalistic line was taken by those who equally refused to tolerate either Westerners or Manchus. Nationalistic warnings against foreign encroachment pervaded the radical journals of the day. Many student revolutionaries turned against the Manchus more because of the dynasty's failure to defend China against the West than because of historically rooted racial antagonism. Rejection of all foreign power on Chinese soil then became a key to student radicalism.

The final step was the belief that the entire populace should be mobilized to strengthen the nation. Many student revolutionaries took this view.

However, they did not progress very far toward giving practical effect to this aim. Even the theory was qualified by despair at the ignorance of the masses and the implication that the educated radicals were the only ones who really knew how to rescue China. Before 1911, revolutionaries distributed pamphlets and contacted secret societies, but they did not proceed as far in mass agitation as did the student left during and after the May Fourth Movement of 1919. The Communists were finally most effective in uniting mass political participation and nationalistic goals.

A second major issue of the 1911 period was how much social change was desirable and how it should be reflected in the political structure. The traditional view was that political power was exercised by the court and a bureaucratic elite. They might seek the opinions of prominent gentry on the local level, but the final decisions were supposedly made by officials. National policy was the prerogative of the court and the bureaucracy. This attitude was held by most modernizing officials, even those who were ready to press for major administrative and economic changes. Many militarists and bureaucrats who held office during the Republic continued instinctively to suspect expressions of opinion by those outside the government.

During 1898, scholar-gentry reformers introduced the idea that policy initiative might come from without the bureaucracy. This beginning broadened into the constitutionalist movement. Modernizing scholars, gentry, and merchants began to form a new upper class related to the industrialization and modernization of China rather than to traditional criteria of office, examinations, and land. Constitutionalists sought institutionalized means of making upper- and middle-class opinion heard. A considerable number of returned students joined this group. Once assemblies were established, conflict developed with officials who were still suspicious of new forms of political expression. Constitutionalists turned against the government and by 1911 were willing to support its overthrow. They were ready to accept the end of the imperial system, but most would limit mass participation in government.

The radical students of the 1911 period called for equality of sex, age groups, and classes and believed in popular participation in government even though they did not clearly understand democratic institutions. Not all members of revolutionary parties shared these views, however. Some were skeptical of the value of Western democracy, and even the most egalitarian of the revolutionaries were more individualistic and antiauthoritarian than mass-oriented. The 1911 revolutionaries largely lacked the class orientation of nineteenth- and twentieth-century Western social democrats.

Student radicals of the late Ch'ing most strongly perceived inequities in the context of the traditional Confucian relationships—the social divisions that particularly affected them. Gaps between rulers and subjects, parents and children, elder and younger, or men and women seemed more oppressive and greater obstacles to freedom than did class barriers that historically could be bridged by talented and determined individuals. Therefore, the scope of the social radicalism of the 1911 generation was narrower than that of those revolutionaries who followed during the Republic, but within its limits the radicalism was intense enough.

Another spectrum, which reflects individual psychology as well as degree of modernization, may be based on attitudes toward normally accepted values of society. On one end were traditionalists who accepted the Confucian morality, the family system, and the desirability of passing the examinations and pursuing an official career. A new step was taken by men who had already achieved significant status under the old system and then began to promote Western education or industry. Further removed were younger men who sought a Western-style education and planned new careers in the army, education, industry, or government. Many of the students in Japan fell in this category, especially after the abolition of the examinations in 1905. Finally there were those whose hostility toward traditional society was so great that they were no longer willing to operate within it. They did not seek legitimate careers, but became professional revolutionaries. They might love China, but they passionately rejected existing social relations and values.

Not all individuals had reached consistent points in their thinking in different spheres and even the small number of professional revolutionaries was not a uniform group.[4] Surprisingly few of the revolutionaries were active for the entire 1903 to 1911 period. Some of the most romantically dedicated committed suicide or were killed during ill-judged risings. Less intense radicals might be deflected by serious study or the pursuit of a career. Others moved back and forth between active participation in the revolutionary movement and more passive, sympathetic radicalism, and some did not really lead very different lives than they might have as members of a nonconformist literary coterie a hundred years earlier. Certain other radicals who were not so opposed to the existing social order as to reject all legal constructive activity were diverted from the revolutionary movement by the opportunities created by the Ch'ing reform movement. These factors further obscured differences between revolutionaries and others and help explain the fairly large number of individuals who abandoned their radicalism after 1911.

Revolutionaries and moderates were linked by common concern with the modernization and strengthening of China and by their common membership in the educated classes. In contrast, there was no close contact between student radicals and the peasant masses. The traditional gap between the scholar and the laboring masses remained unbridged and thereby limited the degree and effectiveness of the students' radicalism. Despite efforts to enlist secret society support, the revolutionaries were not "going to the people" in the Russian populist sense. Their contacts were mainly with society leaders who were more skilled or educated than the average peasant and were closer to the students' social level. Revolutionaries felt no need to repay social debts and certainly did not believe that peasants embodied purer and better values than those held by the educated classes. Nor did they develop a peasant-based strategy the way the Maoist Communists did two decades later. They were not willing to invest many years in the countryside building their own organization on peasant discontent. Instead they tried to graft new institutions onto an unchanged village social structure.

Adoption of new Western-inspired ideas and goals actually may have initially moved the students farther from the peasants. Student concerns with individual freedom and national salvation were largely irrelevant to rural distress caused by food shortages, high rent, and taxes, or official corruption and harshness. These grievances could mainly be solved within the traditional framework. Modernizing changes, vital to the revolution-aries' hopes for national revitalization, were likely to immediately affect the peasants through still higher taxes, usurpation of land and buildings once used for more familiar purposes, new forms of corruption, and inter-ference with customary means of making a living. Radical intellectuals sympathized with the misery of the peasantry. However, their scale of priorities was different and their highly individualistic social rebelliousness was not attuned to peasant needs.

A problem separate from the definition of revolutionaries and objectives is how those people who called themselves revolutionaries organized to achieve their aims. Relevant to this question are the environments in which the revolutionaries operated, their organizational methods, and the in-fluence of external conditions on their behavior. Study of their movement in the differing milieus of Shanghai and Chekiang shows some of the effects of environment and sheds some light or relations between groups in adjoin-ing areas. Shanghai was the major Chinese center of urbanization, moderni-zation, and contact with the West. Opponents of the government found considerable protection in its International Settlement and French Concession. As a result, that city occupied a position in the Yangtze area similar to that of Tokyo vis-à-vis China as a whole. It was a source of radical ideas and organization and the locale of a radical press. Students experimented with bomb-making. Weapons might be illicitly purchased. Radicals from many provinces gathered there or fled there after local failures.

In the Chekiangese towns the limits on overt radical activity were much more severe. Radical literature was smuggled in, but not much was published. Revolutionary organization fragmented into small local groups. The typical unit was the revolutionary front, in which attempts to organize a rising occurred under the guise of legal, educational, or other activities. The revolutionaries had to deal with practical problems of handling relations with secret societies, local elites, and officials. In Shanghai they could simply proclaim their faith in revolutionary goals. In the Chekiangese towns they were forced to be more concerned with methods.

A somewhat symbiotic relationship between the movements in Shanghai and Chekiang points to the regional configuration of revolutionary activities in general. Radicalism grew most rapidly in the large cities, where there were many schools, and where modern books and newspapers were most readily available. To become an effective political force, however, the students had to move outside these centers to try to influence the political structure in towns and villages. Revolutionary groups concentrated in a number of treaty ports, particularly Shanghai, Hong Kong-Canton, and the Wuhan cities. Each was surrounded by a hinterland where revolutionaries normally kept in touch with the movement in the dominant city. Within the Shanghai orbit were much of the provinces of Kiangsu, Anhwei, and Chekiang. I have chosen to concentrate on Chekiang because the early revolutionary movement is best documented in that province and because there the Restoration Society intellectuals progressed furthest toward their goal of armed revolt. It seems probable that similar radial connections existed between the Shanghai movement and radical groups in Kiangsu and Anhwei and that the problems encountered by revolutionaries in Chekiang were also not unique.

The provincialism, or regionalism, indicated by such geographic groupings pervaded the revolutionary movement. It reflected differences in language and custom and the traditional feeling of special relationship with others from one's home area. Provincial ties were also evident in the student clubs in Tokyo and in such Tokyo publications as the periodicals *Tides of Chekiang, Kiangsu, Honan* or the pamphlets *New Hunan* or *New Kwangtung*. The first major revolutionary groups, the Society to Restore China's Prosperity (*Hsing-Chung hui*), the Society for China's Revival

(*Hua-hsing hui*) and the Restoration Society were essentially provincial organizations of Kwangtung, Hunan-Hupei, and Kiangsu-Chekiang respectively. This tendency continued in the Revolutionary Alliance, which, although a national party, exercised little control over provincial branches. Each of these developed in its own way and made its own alliances with other local groups. Such decentralization eventually contributed to the fragmented nature of the Revolution in 1911 and to the Revolutionary Alliance failure to establish a national government.

This provincialism, however, was neither exclusive nor in opposition to nationalism. Revolutionaries were strongly motivated by the goal of a strong, united modern China. They were bound together by membership in a common movement and there were numerous unsuccessful attempts to launch coordinate risings in several provinces. Personal animosities with provincial overtones developed out of the frustrations of an émigré situation and repeated failures. Even so, the provincialism within the revolutionary movement did not present the same threat to national unity as did that which emerged after the inconclusive Revolution of 1911, when provincial governments became dependent on regional military units. The resulting fragmentation was not the work of the radicals, but rather a testimony to their weakness relative to other groups.

Part of the revolutionaries' troubles lay in ineffectual organization. In general it can be said that their methods evolved less rapidly than their theoretical ideas. This lag does not belie their radicalism, but merely illustrates that it is easier to adopt new values than to devise new ways to give them practical effect in the face of considerable social inertia. The Chinese Communist Party is still wrestling with this problem today and it proved insurmountable for the early revolutionaries.

Revolutionaries were handicapped by the lack of models for oppositional politics in a society where political activity was theoretically integrated with the official bureaucratic structure. They knew something of Western organization, but this was outside their practical experience. The most influential precedents were the scholar-bureaucratic clique (*tang*) and the secret society. Heavy use of written propaganda also reflected the scholar's traditional reliance on the written word.

The clique by definition lacked permanence and had scant organizational structure outside the personal connections of its members. It offered little on which to base a modern party. Nonetheless, associations established by radical groups and the contentious tone which they often adopted were reminiscent of this traditional grouping. Radical schools and similar associations reflected the current trend of founding modern Western-style institutions. However, their style of operation paralleled that of the late Ming dynasty Tung-lin and other academies (*shu-yüan*) which traditionally had housed cliques. The same is true of the more inflammatory revolutionary literature. Radicals posed as embattled defenders of virtue and appealed to public opinion through dramatic denunciations. At times they virtually invited government suppression. Immediate defeat became moral victory in the long run.

Secret societies offered a more substantial model. From them revolutionaries borrowed some hierarchical schemes, esoteric rituals, and slogans and personal oaths. However, these served mainly as romantic window dressing and probably did more to enhance the radicals' self-image than to strengthen the party machinery. A more businesslike model of hierarchy was found in the modern army, but the loose coordination of revolutionary groups actually bore little resemblance to a military chain of command.

Although they were able to gain sympathy from some outside groups, the radicals were too disaffected from society as a whole to be widely influential. Few in numbers and without access to military force, they could not bring about the changes they passionately believed were essential for national survival and individual happiness. Their frustration, like that of the radicals in nineteenth-century Russia, led some to individual violence. If one were not effective, one might at least be romantic. Romanticism pervaded the activities of revolutionaries when they gathered together in such centers as Tokyo and Shanghai. There they might manufacture crude bombs and drink chicken blood to seal vows at secret meetings. Thus they bolstered their own sense of importance. But the audience was ingrown— limited to the narrow radical group in which they circulated. A few, however, were inspired to public acts of heroic self-sacrifice. Some were inspired by the Chinese popular heroic tradition. Others were also specifically influenced by Western anarchism. The revolutionary movement's martyrs were its most successful propagandists—again illustrating the element of moral suasion in the revolutionary appeal. However, this highly individualistic strain in the revolutionary movement contributed to the weakness of the party structure.

The picture of 1911 revolutionary organizations that emerges is one of transitional groups part way between traditional Chinese models and twentieth-century revolutionary political organizations in which a disciplined elite seeks mass support to overthrow the government. The very ideas of a revolutionary party and of politics as the proper concern of the whole populace were new and showed the influence of Western ideologies. The difficulties in realizing these ideas were not only the result of the political immaturity of the students, but also of China's great size and the unfavorable social and political environments in which the radicals had to operate. Revolutionaries were in effect organized in small local groups that often kept in touch with more important centers of revolutionary activity in the nearest treaty port or major city. After 1905 they had varying degrees of contact with the Tokyo Revolutionary Alliance, but attempts to coordinate activity were generally feeble. Because the organizations were secret and illegal, local groups inevitably tended to become discrete because of difficulties in maintaining contacts with one another and with higher party levels. The early Chinese revolutionary parties had no organization comparable to Communist parties, which offset this tendency to local autonomy with tight party discipline and a chain of command reaching up to a central committee.[5] Fragmentation was inevitable and the activities of local groups largely reflected the personalities of their own leaders and the exigencies of the immediate situation.

With few exceptions, the local environments hampered sustained revolutionary activity, as was varyingly illustrated by Shanghai and Chekiang. In Shanghai students were readily exposed to modern ideas and technology and enjoyed some political protection. These favorable factors were balanced by the probability that Western power would be used to crush any rising that occurred in that city. Freedom of expression was fostered, but limits were placed on subversive organization and activity.

In the towns and villages outside the treaty ports, the radicals were still more restricted, and the largely unchanged social environment also subtly influenced them toward traditional approaches not really suited to their aims. Because their small, weak groups risked destruction if discovered, the overt behavior of radical students who returned home to establish revolutionary fronts had to be similar to that expected of members of the educated classes. If they were successful in achieving community acceptance and access to funds and privileges, the traditional methods that they had to use tended to draw them back into the webs of social relationships from which they were actually trying to escape. The other side of the problem was that if they tried to defy accepted ways, they immediately aroused suspicion.

The strictly illegal part of revolutionary activities in the towns and countryside likewise had a strong traditional element. Organizations such as schools or militias under normal circumstances were used to bolster the existing political and social order. However, throughout Chinese history they had at times also been used by oppositional groups. The same was true of the revolutionaries' alliances with secret societies. These societies were often closely integrated with the local social structure. If not exactly legal, their existence was hardly secret. It does not seem to have been unusual for some local gentry, scholars, or merchants to maintain contacts with the societies that were useful in their private personal or business dealings. Dissatisfied members of the local elite might use such contacts to facilitate rebellion in times of disorder. Like earlier gentry and scholar rebels, the revolutionaries turned to the secret societies to provide the troops they lacked. This approach sometimes brought short-run organizational success, but did not come to grips with the problem of mobilizing a traditionally politically passive populace.

Away from the treaty ports the revolutionaries were thus forced into an ambiguous situation. Their ideas and aims were genuinely radical and as such were often at variance with those of allies whose support was essential for their continued existence. However, they lacked any equally new concepts of organization and behavior which might offer a way out of their dilemmas. The history of the radical intellectuals in Chekiang makes it fairly clear that those front organizations whose members allowed their radicalism to guide their actions were suppressed soon thereafter. Those which survived long enough to take part in the events of 1911 are less well documented, but they must have remained almost indistinguishable from genuinely moderate modernizing groups.

When considering the 1911 revolutionaries, with their many confusions, mistakes, and failures, it is well to remember that their real importance lies in their relevance to the future—not in their immediate political effectiveness. They were transitional figures between traditional scholar-rebels and twentieth-century revolutionaries. Control of the 1911 Revolution fell to other groups who shared the revolutionaries' disgust with the dynasty and accepted a republican political structure, but who had no enthusiasm for a thorough social and political reorganization. The 1911 Revolution, therefore, was not a complete revolution in itself, but the beginning of the revolutionary modernization of twentieth-century China. What the radicals of the day did was to introduce the whole idea of revolution and set the general style of left-wing student politics for the next forty years. Their combination of nationalistic, visionary dreams, institutional inexperience, and impatient radicalism was repeated in successive brief generations of students. The image of a revolutionary they established continued to exert a powerful appeal up to the time of the Communist victory. Such was its hold that even after 1948 the Maoist government has tried to keep it alive as a sustaining rather than an oppositional force.

2 Ideology and Morality: The Regeneration of China

The students who turned toward revolution in 1903 did not have any clear picture of the society they desired after the Manchu dynasty was overthrown. Nor did most have any well-thought-out philosophy to rationalize the aim of revolution. Their reactions were often highly emotional and full of youthful enthusiasm. They had rejected the traditional ways of China and despaired at the subservience of the Chinese people. Yet they were naively optimistic that once the revolution occurred it would bring a new era of national independence and individual liberty. Appropriately, one of the most influential revolutionary tracts was written by the eighteen-year-old Szechwanese Tsou Jung.[1] By virtue of his youth, his tempestuous but unstable views, his brief, dramatic political career and his mysterious death in jail, Tsou epitomized the spirit of the new student radicals. When he wrote *The Revolutionary Army (Ko-ming chün)* Tsou was strongly influenced by the democratic principles of the French and American revolutions, but the main impact of the book is that of a simple, prolonged call to revolt. The tone is set by the first paragraph:

> Sweep away thousands of years of despotism, cast off thousands of years of slavishness, exterminate the five million bestial Manchus, wash away the humiliation of 260 years of oppression and sorrow, cruelty and tyranny, turn the Chinese soil into a clean land and all the sons and grandsons of the Yellow Emperor into George Washingtons. Then we may rise from death and return to life, retrieve our souls; come out of the eighteenth layer of hell and ascend to the thirty-third level of heaven . . . and reach the highest honor, having one single great incomparable aim called revolution. Oh, how exalted is revolution! Oh, how supreme is revolution![2]

This idea of revolution which Tsou Jung and other youths found so compelling was without exact precedent in the Chinese tradition. There were elements in the old concepts which could quite easily be adapted to the service of a movement which sought fundamental and irreversible change. A dynasty was not considered inviolable. Evil rulers might lose the mandate of heaven. The people might then successfully rise against an oppressive government and overthrow it. The traditional lists of grievances—tyrannical rulers, corrupt officials, ruinous taxation, natural disasters aggravated by government mismanagement—could easily be compared with the complaints of the French Estates-General or the American colonists. Nevertheless, although the revolutionaries were quite willing to exploit traditional attitudes to gain support for their cause, they were aware that their movement differed from previous rebellions in Chinese history. On the whole they did not try to justify their departure by searching for past precedents. Unlike earlier reformers such as K'ang Yu-wei, the young radicals were iconoclastic enough to consider newness as an advantage. It did not have to be explained away, although it might sometimes be tactically expedient to disguise its extent.

The student revolutionaries were radicals and Westernizers[3] who owed a particularly heavy intellectual debt to more conservative reformers of the 1890's and early 1900's who had begun the work of making Western ideas available. Yen Fu popularized his interpretation of Herbert Spencer's Social Darwinism most effectively in his translation of and commentaries on *Evolution and Ethics* by Thomas Huxley, probably published in 1898.[4] Liang Ch'i-ch'ao's publications in Japan, *The Pure Criticism Journal (Ch'ing-i pao)* followed in 1902 by *The Renovation of the People (Hsin-min ts'ung-pao)*, helped introduce students to a wide variety of Western thinkers and details of Western political history.[5] By 1903 the ideas of the major Western liberal and revolutionary theorists were pretty well available in summary or translations and students in Japan had begun to publish translations themselves in such publications as *Translations by Chinese Students Abroad (Yu-hsüeh i-pien)*. Tsou Jung urged students to read Rousseau's *Social Contract*, Montesquieu's *Spirit of the Laws*, John Stuart Mill's *On Liberty*, Thomas Carlyle's *History of the French Revolution*, and the American Declaration of Independence.[6]

Two distinct problems emerge in considering the impact of Western ideas on the Chinese revolutionary movement. One concerns which Western writers and theories were most influential and how they were presented to the Chinese. Answers are to be found in studies of translations of specific Western works and in the writings of Liang Ch'i-ch'ao and other popularizers of Western thought. The second question with which I am concerned here is, What ideas did the students who read Liang and others absorb? These concepts were often loosely defined and not necessarily linked to specific Western philosophers. The general ideology of the radicals was a mixture of Western-derived thought, reactions to immediate issues, and conscious or unconscious traditional attitudes.

It may be possible to find a shift in the focus of revolutionary concern during the last decade of the Ch'ing. Before and during the Russo-Japanese War radical magazines were filled with discussions of nationalism, and after 1905 more space was given to combating the constitutionalist movement. However, I doubt that the general ideas motivating the revolutionaries changed greatly, and it would seem that this change was more marked in *The People's Journal* (*Min-pao*) in Tokyo than it was in revolutionary papers in Shanghai. Revolutionaries in Tokyo may have hesitated to attack Japanese imperialism publically, and writers in Shanghai had learned to curb anti-Manchu expressions. Such a factor may account for some of the differences. Nonetheless, the strong persistence of anti-imperialist themes in Shanghai revolutionary publications during the three years before the Revolution indicates that nationalism remained an important factor motivating radical politics.[7] There was even considerable continuity with the attitudes of the student radicals of the May Fourth Movement of the early Republic. Some of the same key ideas were current by 1903. Nationalism was a dominant theme. On the whole, it did not yet take the form of anti-imperialism in the Leninist sense. The Chinese themselves were considered as much to blame as Westerners for their country's weakness. Nor was there the disillusionment with Western forms of society and government which was later encouraged by the experience of World War I and the difficulties of trying to transplant democratic institutions to China. Science in 1903 particularly meant Darwinism and especially Social Darwinism, which, like Marxism-Leninism at a later date, promised a scientific explanation of the workings of politics and society. The parallel to the enthusiasm for democracy in the early May Fourth Movement was a somewhat vaguer commitment to freedom which was not very carefully worked out in institutional terms. Freedom meant both personal freedom for the individual and the freedom to develop abilities which would collectively enhance the strength of the country. That part of the revolutionary which was reacting against the authoritarianism pervading Chinese society kept running into his other, nationalist part.

The Environment: Beginnings of Radical Student Politics

The most significant early publications of the student radicals were written in Tokyo or Shanghai. The beginnings of the Shanghai revolutionary movement will be discussed in detail in the next two chapters. A brief look at the environment in which the Tokyo revolutionary literature arose is also relevant. Ideas and people moved quickly between Tokyo and Shanghai and students in the two cities reacted similarly to the same issues. Radicals in Tokyo enjoyed the greater immunity to Chinese government authority and it is not surprising that the greatest number of widely read periodicals and tracts originated in that city.

The revolutionary movement really emerged among the students abroad during 1903, almost simultaneously with its development in Shanghai. Earlier revolutionary organizations had remained apart from the main body of students. The Yokohama branch of the Society to Restore China's Prosperity, established in 1895, and the 1901 Kwangtung Independence Association (*Kuang-tung tu-li hsüeh-hui*) were mainly Kwangtungese provincial groups associated with Sun Yat-sen.[8] In late 1900 and early 1901 some of the survivors of T'ang Ts'ai-ch'ang's September rising in the name of the Society to Protect the Emperor (*Pao-huang hui*) fled to Japan, where they provided a new radical impetus. Several established the revolutionary *Chinese National* (*Kuo-min pao*) in the summer of 1901.[9] However, the Society to Protect the Emperor and the journals edited by Liang Ch'i-ch'ao were more influential than these early revolutionary groups. About 1900 there were probably fewer than a hundred Chinese students in Japan.[10] Even when the numbers began to increase after the Boxer Rebellion, most students were still just becoming acquainted with Western ideas. Few were ready to join particular parties.

The first organizations to include a large percentage of the Chinese students in Tokyo were traditionally modeled social groups, not political ones. The earliest was the Determination Society (*Li-chih hui*), established in 1900. Its successor was the Chinese Student Union (*Chung-kuo liu-hsüeh-sheng hui-kuan*), which was organized at the beginning of 1902 to help the growing number of students. This was a fraternal and service organization supported by monthly contributions from members and by funds from the Chinese minister to Japan. It maintained reading rooms, gave advice on such matters as lodging, and operated a Japanese language school.[11] Within the year provincial clubs were also formed. None of these groups was founded for political purposes. However, they could provide meeting places and leaders, and so they were drawn into any issue which generally excited the student body.

Increased political awareness led to a series of incidents that finally produced an irreparable gulf between many of the students and the Ch'ing government. The first clashes were provoked by older men long involved in the reform or revolutionary movements. The Chekiangese revolutionary Chang Ping-lin was responsible for the plan to hold a meeting on April 26, 1902 (the anniversary of the death of the last Ming Emperor), to commemorate the 242nd Anniversary of the Fall of China (*Chih-na wang-kuo erh-pai ssu-shih-erh nien chi-nien hui*).[12] A second major incident occurred in late July when a group of students demonstrated at the Chinese legation to protest the minister's decision to bar students without government scholarships from military preparatory school in Tokyo.[13] This demonstration was led by Wu Chih-hui, a Kiangsu scholar and teacher who had been a reformer since 1898 and would soon be one of the leaders of the early revolutionary movement in Shanghai.

These clashes cumulatively increased distrust between students and government authorities, personified by the Chinese minister to Japan, Ts'ai Chün. Within the student body lines were being drawn between the moderates and radicals—divisions which later became hardened in the constitutionalist and revolutionary parties. At the end of 1902 the Youth Association (*Ch'ing-nien hui*) was established. This was a revolutionary nationalist group modeled on Young Italy of the Italian unification movement. It was significant because it had a broader student basis than previous revolutionary societies and marked the rise of new radical figures. Its members came from several provinces, particularly in the Lower Yangtze basin. Many were students at Waseda University and had recently arrived in Japan with no previous political record.[14]

Growing student radicalism was further evidenced by two anti-Manchu speeches at the Chinese Student Union meeting to celebrate the 1903 lunar New Year.[15] The final break between government officials and the radicals came in the spring as a result of the highly emotional and nationalistic student reaction to Russian failure to complete the scheduled second stage in the withdrawal of troops which had occupied points in Manchuria during the Boxer Rebellion. The troops were to have been removed by March 26, but instead the Russian chargé d'affaires in Peking presented a list of seven new demands designed to ensure Russia's preeminence in the northeast.[16] This relatively minor incident became an important catalyst to the revolutionary movement because it occurred just after radical student groups had begun to form. News of the Russian demands appeared in a Japanese paper on April 28. The next day the Tokyo provincial clubs and Youth Association sponsored a general meeting attended by over five hundred students. This meeting approved the proposal to establish a Volunteer Corps to Oppose Russia (*Chü-O i-yung tui*). Participants cabled their intentions to Yüan Shih-k'ai and also decided to send two representatives to explain the students' views in person.[17]

Initially the students' nationalism was not directed against the Manchu court. Their first thought was to resist Russia, and they genuinely seem to have expected that the government would share their views.[18] The

Ch'ing government was faced, on a much smaller scale, with the same problem which plagued the Nationalist government twenty years later when students called for resistance to Japan. China was in no position to go to war with Russia, but it could hope for diplomatic support from the other powers in negotiations.[19] Bellicose students, therefore, were at best an embarrassment.[20] In addition, officials were predisposed to distrust students who were taking political initiative beyond their station and had already caused trouble.[21] Yüan Shih-k'ai refused to see the student representatives. Minister Ts'ai Chün asked the Japanese government to dissolve the Volunteer Corps, and both it and the Youth Association came to an end.

This was the last attempt the student radicals made to come to terms with the government. Once convinced that the Ch'ing would not resist foreign domination of China, they sought to save the country themselves by overthrowing the dynasty.[22] On May 11, almost immediately after the dissolution of the Volunteer Corps, a number of corps members established the Association for the Education of a Militant People (*Chün-kuo-min chiao-yü hui*). This group had a public facade, but actually was a highly secret revolutionary body.[23] It was an extremely amorphous group, but its members included some of the most active revolutionaries in the period before the founding of the Revolutionary Alliance. Most members returned to China or went to Southeast Asia to conspire against the government. The association was not significant for its practical effect, but because it marked a decisive commitment to revolution by a new portion of the student body.

In this atmosphere the number of student publications increased rapidly during 1903, when they included *Tides of Chekiang* (*Che-chiang ch'ao*), *Kiangsu, Hupeh Student Circles* (*Hu-pei hsüeh-sheng chieh*), *Translations by Chinese Students Abroad* and *Chihli Speaks* (*Chih-shuo*). Many of the periodicals were published by the provincial student clubs. Almost all were short-lived. A magazine which lasted as long as a year was a rarity. In that time the original founders might have left Japan or become deeply involved in other activities. Equally important was the chronic lack of funds. Publications were shipped to China, usually via Shanghai. They were distributed through radical organizations, bookstores, and newsstands, and copies were passed around among students in modern schools. The more popular periodicals might publish several editions of back numbers even after new issues were no longer being published. Despite general government disapproval, periodicals not specifically banned from the mails often sold surprisingly openly. Nonetheless, distribution was fairly difficult, haphazard, and presumably not usually very profitable.[24]

The Japan-based periodicals most relevant to the development of the Lower Yangtze revolutionary movement were *Tides of Chekiang* and *Kiangsu,* which were published by the provincial clubs of Chekiangese and Kiangsu students in Tokyo.[25] *Tides of Chekiang* was established in February 1903 and continued publication for ten issues. *Kiangsu* was started in April and also ceased after ten issues, not all in consecutive months, because of lack of funds.[26] The two periodicals carried similar types of articles on a wide range of modern subjects. They expressed similar ideas, although *Kiangsu* was the more radical.

Many of those connected with *Tides of Chekiang* had fairly recently come to Japan after studying or teaching in Hangchow. They included the editor Wang Chia-chü; Sun I-chung, one of the earliest Chekiangese radicals; Chiang Tsun-kuei, who became the second military governor of Chekiang in 1912; Chiang Chih-yu, a scholar who began by writing for Liang Ch'i-ch'ao's *The Renovation of the People,* subsequently taught at the Patriotic School in Shanghai, and later joined the constitutionalist movement; Hsü Shou-shang, described as a follower of Chang Ping-lin; and Chiang Fang-chen, who continued his military studies in Berlin and later became famous as a military modernizer during the Republic.[27] The Kiangsu group included such men as Chin Yü-liu, who in 1903 was a member of all the major radical organizations of Chinese students in Japan and in 1904 accompanied Huang Hsing to Hunan; Chang Chao-t'ung, also active in organizations in Japan; and Wang Yung-pao, who became an official and helped draft the Ch'ing constitution. The radical writer Liu Ch'i-chi contributed articles from China.

These groups were, in other words, fairly diverse, containing future constitutionalists as well as reformers and revolutionaries. Moreover, all those who joined the revolutionary movement were not necessarily settled in their views during the first half of 1903. Periodicals such as *Tides of Chekiang* and *Kiangsu,* which are inevitably classified as revolutionary in standard Chinese histories, actually did not print a great deal of inflammatory material. *Tides of Chekiang* in particular contains many articles which are reformist or at least politically neutral in tone.[28] Nonetheless, the problems of national regeneration dealt with in these periodicals were what served to excite the most radical students at the time and both periodicals contain articles in which the revolutionary implications are clearly obvious or openly stated.[29] Together with *The Revolutionary Army,* first conceived in Tokyo and written in Shanghai, and the slightly later tracts which the Hunanese revolutionary Ch'en T'ien-hua wrote in Tokyo, they provide a sampling of the views which propelled students toward revolution.

Elements of Student Revolutionary Ideology

Nationalism: The Motivating Force

Nationalism was the main ingredient which colored almost all aspects of the students' thought. How to save the country (*chiu-kuo*) from the inroads of Western imperialism was the great question of the last decade of the Ch'ing, and the warning that China was about to be sliced up like a melon (*kua-fen*) was one of the most frequent clichés in radical literature. Radical intellectuals were prepared to sweep away whatever in the old order seemed to stand in the way of national strength. The politically conscious scholar's old aim of saving a world centered about traditional Chinese culture (*chiu-shih*) was converted into the narrower goal of preserving the state. This goal transcended regional and provincial loyalties. Radicals might believe that their home province was particularly fitted to produce the heroes who would lead a national revival, or that local rehabilitation and self-government was an integral part of national regeneration. However, the provinces were part of the larger Chinese state; there was no contradiction between the whole and its components.[30]

The goals of nationalism required concrete steps to strengthen the country. However, the students, who lacked the means to enforce such measures, also saw in the ideology of nationalism a morality which in itself would contribute to the country's vitality. Nationalism was the great force sweeping the world. Beginning in Europe and then moving to the United States, it was finally spreading to Asia. Those who had previously tried to modernize China—the promoters of industrialization, the reformers of the 1890's, and the recent advocates of freedom and democracy—all were partly right, but they failed to grasp the root of their problems. In an era of nationalism China had to follow the trend of the times if she were not to be lost. Nationalism lay behind the unifications of Germany and Italy which turned them into great powers. China might also become powerful by following this road.[31] If she did not follow it she would surely be lost. The original nationalism of the major Western powers had been transformed into imperialism under the pressures of population growth and industrial expansion. Weak, traditionalistic states, whose people were not motivated by nationalistic concepts, would fall easy prey to the new forms of economic aggression.

To those who had come to place primary value on the nation rather than on the culture, China's history seemed a sorry picture. Chinese had failed to develop the national consciousness which had unified and invigorated the peoples of Western countries.[32] Revolutionaries made a fairly clear distinction between particularistic and universalistic concepts of loyalty. Tsou Jung, for instance, pointed out that France and the United States had no kings, but their people still worked hard to fulfill their duties to the country. The Chinese, however, were loyal to a particular dynasty and to the emperor, not to China. They, therefore, became slaves of an individual, not citizens of a country. From this point of view the great ministers of the nineteenth century—Tseng Kuo-fan, Tso Tsung-t'ang, and Li Hung-chang—were arch-villains. Out of loyalty to alien emperors they betrayed their country and killed their compatriots.[33] Such lack of patriotism served China ill in a competitive world, and the system which fostered it would have to be overthrown.

Race and Nation

Revolutionaries wedded traditional xenophobia and Sinocentrism to their new concepts of nationalism and Darwinian struggle. Racial themes that pervaded the 1911 revolutionary literature were partly propagandistic but also showed a genuine tendency to see the world in racial terms.[34] Thus they foreshadowed the extreme, racially tinged nationalism often expressed by the Communists after 1949. The subject of race appeared critically important to the 1911 radicals because of its relation to the development of the nation-state, which they accepted as the most vital form of political organization. They argued that the Chinese people under the Ch'ing dynasty were particularly removed from the government because the ruling house was of a different race. Of the various factors linking the inhabitants of a country—language, culture, history, geography—race was the most important. Nations were formed through racial struggles and, as a corollary, if a race were to survive it had to establish a nation. If there were two races in a country the unity between people and state would be destroyed. One race might be or become slaves and, therefore, have no relation to the state. One race might be assimilated or destroyed. Or it might develop racial consciousness and break away to form a new nation as occurred when the Austro-Hungarian empire split. Whatever happened, a racially divided country would lack internal strength and, at a time of rising, aggressive nationalism, was risking destruction.[35]

Revolutionaries believed this point was clearly illustrated by the effect of Manchu rule in China. Virtually all their publications enlarged upon the alleged inferiority of the Manchu race, the alleged viciousness of its conquest of China and exploitation of the Chinese people.[36] Revolutionaries often felt compelled to draw up detailed racial classifications of the peoples of the world.[37] The specifics of these schemes were not very important nor necessarily very accurate. Their main functions were to lend an aura of scientific authenticity to racial messages and to show that the Chinese and Manchus really were different peoples despite the embarrassing fact that the differences between them were considerably less than those between both of them and the white race.

Nonetheless, although an important figure like Chang Ping-lin might couch his revolutionary message chiefly in racial terms, the basic charge brought by most of the revolutionary intellectuals was that the Manchus had failed to protect China against Western imperialism. Lacking firm rapport with the populace, the government sought to buy off the powers. It did not care how much territory, money, or sovereignty it sacrificed as long as it could preserve itself by satisfying the foreigners' avarice.[38] The result had been a series of disasters, including the occupation of Peking by the Allied Expedition during the Boxer rising and subsequent Russian demands in Manchuria. Yet, the government deeply distrusted students who urged resistance to new encroachments.[39] The only solution was to rally the country under the slogans of nationalism. The first step would be to overthrow the Manchus. Then, after a modern government was established, it would be possible to expel the Westerners.[40]

This belief that meeting the threat of foreign imperialism was more important than revenge against the Manchus for old wrongs was forcefully expressed by the Hunanese revolutionary Ch'en T'ien-hua in his two widely read pamphlets, *A Bell to Warn the World* (*Ching-shih chung*) and *About Face!* (*Meng hui-t'ou*). In these works he elaborated at great length upon the threat from abroad; territorial, judicial, and economic concessions made to the Western powers; and the series of unsuccessful wars during the nineteenth century. He also told stories about alleged incidents of Western brutality toward Chinese and contempt for Chinese degeneration.[41] However, the first pamphlet in particular is remarkably free of invective aimed at the Manchus. Ch'en argued that the Manchus were weak and did not need to be feared any more, even though they had in the past conquered China and enslaved its population. In contrast the Western powers were rich and strong and would destroy China and the Chinese race if not resisted immediately.[42] If the Manchus genuinely reformed the government, eliminated all differences between Manchu and Chinese, and resolved to fight the foreign powers, it would be possible to cooperate with them.[43] However, the Manchus would not sincerely change their policies. They distrusted the Chinese and had fallen under the domination of the powers, who decided it would be easiest to let the Manchus remain as rulers of the Chinese and to control China by controlling them.[44] Since the government would not act, the Chinese population had to do so instead. Hatred for the Westerners had to be curbed and channeled so that Chinese might study them to discover why they were rich and strong. The country would be lost in about a decade, so immediate action was necessary. All groups—officials, soldiers, scholars, rich, poor, political parties, secret societies, women, and Chinese Christians—should contribute to the salvation of the country.[45]

About Face!, written somewhat later, was more specifically anti-Manchu than was *A Bell to Warn the World*.[46] Even so, the overriding aim was to save China from the West by mobilizing the country's wealth and power along Western lines of organization and by arousing the spirit of the people. The questions of the future political system and the fate of the Manchus tended to become lost in an emotional call to resist Western encroachment. Ch'en T'ien-hua's writings are unusual in the extent to which his anti-imperialism overshadows other questions, but his attitude is suggestive. Student revolutionaries vilified the Manchus and wrote of avenging wrongs done to ancestors. However, the traditional phrases had acquired a new meaning by their association with a budding nationalism. More real anger was felt over the Manchus' failure to insist upon the removal of Russian troops from Manchuria in 1903 than over the Manchu sack of Yangchow in 1645.

It is important to note that the revolutionaries usually stopped short of finding simple scapegoats for China's international problems. The imperialist powers were avaricious and the Manchus weak and unprincipled, but the Chinese themselves were also to blame. If they had not been indifferent to the humiliations visited upon them, the country would never have fallen so low. The revolutionaries' attitude toward the West was particularly complex. They deeply resented Western encroachment upon China, yet the West was also the source of their political ideas and revolutionary inspiration. There was an unstated hope that if China proved it had the right to join the civilized nations by carrying out a revolution the way Britain, the United States, and France had done, then perhaps the Western powers would respect her desire to be treated as their equal. This thought may be implied in the optimistic view of a postrevolutionary China taking a prominent place in the international order without engaging in any struggle to achieve this aim.[47] China's international problems would be solved internally, and the West, the source of freedom and democracy, would welcome the change. The students' anti-imperialism was still limited to reactions to concrete events and was not buttressed by a generally anti-Western or anti-capitalist philosophy.[48] Sun Yat-sen felt similar optimism shortly after the Revolution when he hoped that Western countries would invest large sums in the industrial development of the new China.

Social Darwinism: Acceptance of a Competitive World

Adoption of the principles of Social Darwinism to explain the workings of international affairs gave particular urgency to the problem of revitalizing China. The radicals' picture of the international order was far from the comfortable traditional confidence that the world was dominated by a civilized and revered Chinese empire. Events of the preceding half century had shattered the old serenity and now the new intellectuals raised the question of whether China would continue to exist at all. They saw a political world shaped by struggle between states and races, not one ordered by a paternal Middle Kingdom. In this struggle only the fittest would survive: the strong becoming progressively stronger and the weak weaker.[49] This theory seemed to explain the Western wars of the eighteenth and nineteenth centuries and the spread of Western domination in Asia and Africa. The material power of the major Western states was evident, and so were their national organization and constitutional governments. Since the struggle was inevitable and unrelenting, China had to choose whether she would follow the path which had made the West strong or whether she would move toward extinction. The examples of Poland and India, Vietnam and Africa indicated what would happen to a country that lost out.[50] It would cease to exist, or at best remain a hollow shell under foreign control. The law of the survival of the fittest condemned people ruled by foreigners to a decline.[51] They would become slaves, be unable to develop their natural abilities, and be ground down under the tyranny which the revolutionaries believed was an inevitable ingredient of foreign rule. In China this process had already begun. For two hundred and sixty years the Chinese had been slaves of the Manchus, and now that the Manchus had sunk under Western domination, Chinese had become slaves of slaves. In his emotional style Tsou Jung postulated a reverse form of evolution if the Chinese failed to reform themselves. They would sink still deeper into slavery, become apes, wild pigs, oysters, and finally become extinct.[52]

Such fears of racial extinction, which were to appear occasionally in the writings of many Chinese revolutionaries including Sun Yat-sen, seem wildly exaggerated when viewed from an objective distance. Nonetheless, they were a basic element in the reaction against the imperialism of another race. The expressions were hyperbolic extensions of the radicals' preoccupation with the struggle for existence and their determination to fight for survival. The poignancy of the racial fears of radical intellectuals who view themselves struggling against a different people are suggested by certain similarities between statements of the 1911 Chinese revolutionaries and black militants in the United States in the 1960's. The author of the secret declaration of principles of the Society for the Education of a Militant

People maintained that under continued Manchu rule someday Chinese "may vanish from the face of the earth." He affirmed that "even if our hopes for the future are doomed to failure, it is better to struggle to the death than do nothing," and concluded, "if we succeed we shall become citizens of an independent nation; if not we will be dead heroes in the cause of justice." At a news conference in Washington, D.C. after the assassination of Martin Luther King in April 1968 the militant black leader Stokely Carmichael replied to various questions that "Black people are not afraid to die. We die all the time. . . . We're not afraid to die, because now we're gonna (*sic*) die for our people. . . . White America has declared war on black people. . . . And black people are going to have to find ways to survive. The only way to survive is to get some guns. . . . Then we're going to stand up on our feet and die like men." Despite the differences in culture and circumstance both statements affirm the certainty of violent racial struggle, both convey the same relationship between individual sacrifice and group survival and declare violent death a more honorable course than passive submission that is really self-destruction.[53]

Although the idea of struggle for survival could be used in almost any context, the 1911 revolutionaries tended to apply it particularly in racial terms. A crisis was now imminent; the white race had already subjugated the black, red, and brown races, leaving the current struggle between the white and yellow races. In this battle the white race was superior in industry, military might, government organization, and the independent spirit of its people. Nonetheless, the example of Japan showed it was possible for the yellow race to rise. China had gradually been declining under oppressive imperial governments for two thousand years while other countries had been advancing. Yet, her earlier history was one of progress, so even she might progress again if the people would throw off the influence of ancient custom.[54] China was facing disaster; but the revolutionaries were proclaiming an urgent warning, not giving way to total despair. The natural laws of evolution were not impervious to human intervention. China's decline would result in extinction if unchecked, but the trend still was not irreversible. There was time for the Chinese to adapt to the conditions of the modern world if they would arouse themselves quickly. To find a way out of the intolerable future that China faced from evolution the revolutionaries abandoned science in favor of the voluntary exercise of individual wills and sought a substitute for material strength in moral regeneration.

The Remedy: Revolution and Violence

China's desperate position justified and even demanded the use of violence. With "the storm" upon them, "surrounded by tigers and wolves," how could the Chinese "wait upon events?"[55] Only the most drastic measures would revive the country. The first step would be to break the existing tyrannical system and overturn the old government. Destruction had to precede reconstruction; the poisonous mists had to be swept away before the clear sky could be seen.[56] A tyranny could never establish a republic nor an old-fashioned government mold a modern political system.[57] Since the eighteenth century the revolutionary tide had been rising throughout the world. Europe had been transformed by its national revolutions. Recent clashes between the government and radicals, such as the 1898 Reform Movement, T'ang Ts'ai-ch'ang's attempted rising in 1900, and the student unrest in 1903, showed that revolutionary potential existed in China as well.[58] It was even possible to find examples of individual revolutionaries in Chinese history despite the alleged lack of fundamental change and the slave-producing tyranny under which the people lived.[59] Now if the Chinese did not wish to remain slaves they had to sacrifice their lives and wealth to overthrow the government and drive out the Manchus. Only in this way could China become independent and a power in the world.[60]

The French and American revolutions were probably the most influential precedents. A more recent model was also found in Russian nihilism, anarchism, and extreme populism. "Nihilists" in Russia were produced by the shortcomings of the Russian government and officials. The desperate economic situation of the peasantry and the rottenness of the bureaucracy and judiciary aroused the anger of the Russian students. Their instinctive repulsion was reinforced by philosophies and ideologies from Western Europe. Then they accepted terrorism as the best method for overthrowing the tyrannical government.[61] Clearly some of the revolutionaries saw close parallels between the Chinese and Russian situations and believed that they should take the Russian terrorists as a model.

The revolutionaries' call for violence was closely linked to their dark predictions of China's future. Their sense of extreme urgency caused them to part company with constitutionalists who shared many of their other views. For several reasons the revolutionaries saw no remedy for China's problems in a constitution granted by the Manchu government. There was an emotional, nationalistic refusal to believe that a constitution conferred by a foreign ruler could end oppression. Closely related was the idea that a constitution was irrelevant to the problems of an ignorant, unawakened people faced with imminent disaster at the hands of Western imperialism.[62] If the Manchus simply gave the Chinese a constitution, the people would have no opportunity to develop the independent, nationalistic spirit essential for success in the modern world.

There was also skepticism that people and society would change without strong leadership from a dynamic government dedicated to reform. Revolutionaries saw little likelihood that the old government could be persuaded to change itself and its policies. For several decades concerned scholars had been founding newspapers, translating books, and sending telegrams without any effect.[63] Those constitutionalists who were impressed by the the progress Japan made after adopting a constitution failed to perceive that in Japan this step was preceded by reforms carried out in the early Meiji period by a small number of men. Only then was it possible to establish constitutional government. The lesson of the 1898 Reform Movement and the Boxer Rebellion was that the dynasty regarded reformers as its enemies. In the eyes of the court, constitutionalists who sought peaceful reform of the government were the same as revolutionaries. The lesson was plain. The old government had to be overthrown to make way for a new one that would take the lead in remolding China. Unlike the constitutionalists, revolutionaries were not willing to wait for slow change from below.

Finally, they argued that the situation had deteriorated too far to allow moderate reform from within. Even if the Ch'ing government could establish a constitution it could not retain the backing of the people. Given the current misery of the peasantry, the disorder of government finances, and the spread of racial ideas, free discussion would be impossible to curb once it had begun. Like the convening of the Estates-General in France, a Manchu constitution would lead to revolution.[64]

The National Political Order: Freedom and Democracy

The revolutionaries' argument with the constitutionalists revolved about the immediate need to overthrow the government. Ridicule of the constitutionalists did not imply opposition to parliamentary institutions after a republic had been established. Next to nationalism the radical writers stressed the ideas of freedom, equality, and political democracy which they derived from European writers such as Rousseau, Mill, and Montesquieu and the examples of the English, French, and American revolutions. The concern with liberty was twofold. Not only would it bring personal enrichment to the individual, but it was a way to help make China strong. Revolutionaries reasoned that China was sinking toward extinction because the people had been prevented by centuries of tyranny from assuming political responsibility. There were no political rights, no local self-government, and no opposing political parties. The Chinese people had little political awareness and ability because they lacked actual experience in government.[65] Exclusion from politics also dimmed their sense of nationalism. People naturally tended to love themselves and to place their own interests before those of the country. Only if a majority participated in the government would a majority have cause to be patriotic. Taxes and military service, for instance, would be given willingly if the people had a stake in the government, but were merely considered a form of oppression when they did not.[66] Selfish interests—a combination of Adam Smith's enlightened self-interest and the traditionally condemned selfishness of human nature—could be a basis for nationalism if people identified their individual advantage with that of the country. Representative institutions would foster a national consensus which would strengthen the state in struggles with others.[67] Conversely, a dictatorial government might even drive people of the same race to revolt. Thus the American colonies rebelled against British rule although the colonists were Englishmen themselves.[68]

Despite their preoccupation with strengthening the state, the radical intellectuals also felt a real emotional commitment to the values of freedom and equality. These they viewed in the light of their own personal struggles against the authority of parents, school officials, or government representatives. Students who left their homes to go to Tokyo or Shanghai sought individual independence as well as a chance to contribute to national salvation. The more individualistic aspects of democracy particularly appealed to them. Women's rights was already a fashionable cause in radical circles. The American Bill of Rights and similar documents exerted a powerful influence.[69] Very probably the still fairly weak concern with class equality and interest in social democracy was based more on the belief that individuals had the right to fully develop their personal abilities than on socioeconomic considerations.

The most immediate object of individualistic attack was the family system. Radicals had not yet developed a comprehensive antifamilial theory. However, in their own lives they had often rejected family restraints, and a number of critical articles on the family system appeared in their journals. The Western family, in which children are reared to become independent individuals and skilled, useful citizens was contrasted with the Chinese family, where the unlimited, lifelong demands of filial piety impeded both national consciousness and personal development.[70] China required a family revolution to free the individual before a political revolution to free the people as a whole would be possible. The position of the father was similar to that of the ruler, and the family served as a model for an authoritarian monarchy.[71]

The Chinese family, political system, and social order all had discouraged the people from developing a spirit of self-government. Tyranny had permeated the entire country. The emperor was the sole political master of the empire and government policy represented his personal ideas. Under this system the populace suffered all the miseries of oppression, for the government was run solely for the benefit of a minority. As long as it prospered, the ruling group did not care if it sacrificed the interests of the people. There was little hope of redress and the government put forth all its power to suppress any who tried to resist.[72] The common people were bled by corrupt officials, landlords, and local bullies. They were oppressed by taxes, but no laws protected their interests.[73]

Radicals made frequent use of the word "happiness," which they borrowed from such liberal phrases as "life, liberty and the pursuit of happiness." The vague promises this term held out required no real definition. It implied a thorough contrast with the misfortunes of the present and fitted the intellectuals' optimistic view of a postrevolutionary future. The increasing numbers who enjoyed ever higher levels of happiness was a measure of progress. When only a few monopolized the store of happiness available in a country, the resulting tyranny made rebellion inevitable.[74] The fates of Charles I of England, Louis XVI of France, and Alexander II of Russia all indicated the rise of popular power in the West. Because the government was now in their hands, peoples in the West enjoyed a greater degree of happiness than did the Chinese. When political leaders were subordinate to the common people, government policy was in accord with popular ideas and its aim was the greatest happiness of the greatest number. The people of the country were "citizens not servants, masters and not slaves."[75]

After popular rights and freedom had been wrested from the government, political leaders in Europe and America drew up constitutions to guarantee that liberty could never be suppressed. Under genuine constitutional government the strong, wise, or noble were prevented from taking advantage of others. Fathers could not exploit their sons, nor rulers their subjects, masters their servants, husbands their wives. "Therefore individuals' rights and freedom are protected and the peace of society secured."[76] Radicals had considerable faith in the rule of law provided the laws followed rather than preceded a revolution.

They did not, however, give serious consideration to the problems of establishing and maintaining the future political institutions. Instead they tended to borrow wholesale those parts of the Western political record which were in accord with their enthusiasm for democratic rights and liberties. This tendency is illustrated by the sixth chapter of *The Revolu-*

tionary Army. Tsou Jung's new central government would be headed by a president and vice-president chosen from among the heads of the provincial assemblies. All in the country would be citizens and have the duties of loyalty to the state and the payment of taxes. Males would be required to give military service. All would enjoy the rights of life, liberty, equality of sexes and classes, freedom of speech, press, and thought. If the new government became oppressive the people would have the right to rebel, although they should not do so in protest of minor shortcomings. The new country would be a free and independent republic, having complete equality in diplomatic intercourse with other countries. Its constitution and laws would follow the model of the United States.

The act of revolution was more real and had a more compelling appeal for the radical intellectuals than did the ordering of the still unobtainable future society. So much in the current society had to be swept away that the revolutionaries' imagination centered upon the destruction of the old.[77] They believed that the institutions and attitudes which made the West strong had largely sprung from revolutions. If China were not to be doomed she had to adopt this method. Then the desired institutions might follow of their own accord. The revolutionaries had to believe that institutions could be freely transferred from one country and civilization to another. It took much sad experience after 1911 before they realized all the difficulties involved.

Revolutionary Education and Morality

Only part of the solution to China's problems could be achieved through institutional change. Moral reeducation of the people was equally necessary. Preoccupation with educational questions stemmed from the traditional high regard for learning which revolutionary students and scholars still shared. Behind it lay a certain distrust of the masses, reflecting the traditional gulf between scholar and peasant. Early revolutionaries also anticipated left-wing social critics of the Republican period (such as the writer Lu Hsün), whose concern for the Chinese masses led them to bitter indictments of the people's superstitions, ignorance, and apathy and of the customs which produced these attitudes.[78]

Education was to contribute to the new China in two ways. First, there was an obvious need for educational improvement if the Chinese people were to acquire the skills necessary to compete in a modern, industrialized world. Universal education in Europe had produced enlightened, skillful, and patriotic populations. Countries possessing such a populace had become strong and taken the lead in the struggle for existence, whereas

China had fallen behind because she did not.[79] One author went so far as to claim that the fates of the countries of the world would ultimately be controlled by the outcome of the "educational struggle." Military battles and industrial, commercial, and agricultural competition might superficially seem more important. Basically, however, their outcome was governed by the levels of education in the countries involved.[80]

Radicals understood the importance of a modern technical education and sought it themselves in the new schools. However, this method alone would bring change much too slowly to prevent the destruction of China that they believed was immanent. Moral reeducation was to provide the necessary shortcut. The revolutionaries had rejected the specific traditional Confucian morality, but they retained the idea that morality was a primary ingredient of learning.[81] Liang Ch'i-ch'ao's theories were extremely influential. Revolutionary literature abounds in indictments of the superstition, degeneracy, and ignorance of the Chinese, and the phrase "renovate the people" is used over and over again. However, unlike the moderates, radicals saw moral revival as an accompaniment to revolution, not a substitute for it. Renovation required political leaders who would seek to guide the people toward change and a new system whereby people outside the government might influence officials to provide enlightened leadership. Blaming the fall of the country solely on the worthlessness of the people was like blaming the fall of a dynasty on the revocation of heaven's mandate. In each case the individual was likely to consider matters beyond his influence and give up trying to change them.[82]

In pre-1911 revolutionary literature, moral indictment of the Chinese was often related to two pairs of opposing terms: civilized and barbaric and slaves and citizens. The former was used almost in contradiction of the traditional view of a civilized China surrounded by lesser barbarians. Revolutionaries still referred to Manchus as barbarians in the old sense. However, for many the word civilization no longer had the same cultural connotation. They defined it in relation to the new values of progress, national strength, and political liberty. The path to civilization was that traveled by Europe and the United States in the eighteenth and nineteenth centuries. The French and American revolutions were civilized because they led to freedom and equality for all, but left to their own devices the Chinese masses would follow the superstitious, pointlessly destructive, barbaric model of the Boxer Rebellion.[83] Chinese were barbaric because they followed ignorant superstitions, accepted foreign rule, lived under a tyrannical government, and were oppressed by harsh laws.[84] The word was seldom closely defined and often came close to being a catch-all condemnation for all that the radicals disapproved of in Chinese society. This attitude toward tradition paved the way for the iconoclasm of the New Culture and May Fourth movements of the early Republic.

The same was true of the contrast between slaves and citizens. Chinese were barbaric partly because of the subservience that had been fostered by centuries of education in the virtues of loyalty and filial piety. Citizens were able to govern themselves, had independent spirits, and enjoyed the happiness of freedom. Slaves had none of these attributes, but were willing to allow others to govern them and to copy all their masters' mores.[85] This highly inaccurate description of the cultural relations between Chinese and others had mainly an emotional value. It expressed some of the radicals' rejection of traditional morality and was intended to shock the reader into realizing the desperate situation.

Once the disease was diagnosed it could be cured. Slavery was more the result of the psychological characteristics of the people enslaved than the superior force of the conquerors. Indians would not be slaves of the English, nor Annamese slaves of the French, nor Chinese slaves of the Manchus if they were not willing to submit.[86] Through the right kind of education people could be taught patriotism and their sense of personal freedom could be developed. The old contempt for the soldier could be replaced by a new militancy.[87] If the masses could be made to desire change, then China might not have to wait until the general level of knowledge had been raised before it could begin to compete successfully with the rest of the world. Physical fitness, nationalism, and revolutionary zeal were all bound together in a philosophy that foreshadowed Communist emphasis on sports and gymnastics after 1949.

These attitudes toward education represented an early attempt to deal with the persistent twentieth century problem of mobilizing the traditionally politically passive Chinese populace. Radicals realized that without active popular support they would be powerless to give effect to their ideals. A revolution required a great leader like Washington or Napoleon, but even more important, it required countless unhonored Washingtons and Napoleons ready to sacrifice their lives.[88] The radical intellectuals did not, however, believe the masses had the initiative or the capacity to grasp their political role spontaneously. Instead, the intellectuals were sure that they had a clearer understanding of affairs that entitled them to lead and educate the people. They were the heaven-appointed (t'ien-chih), able to comprehend and strive for the needs of the people without being led astray by selfish considerations. This confidence was widespread in radical circles, anticipating Sun Yat-sen's concept of the foreknowers who were to guide China through the formative stages of the Republic.[89] Later the same attitude contributed to the idea that intellectuals in the Communist Party should lead the revolution. The belief that the people could not change themselves and had to be guided and remolded from above had authoritarian implications not yet clear to the 1911 radicals who tended to relate such concepts as citizenship to liberal definitions of individualism and nationalism. Nonetheless, the tendency to approach China's problems this way—a tendency encouraged by a desire for haste and by the tremendous difficulties attending forced modernization—led in different directions than the slower educational processes envisaged by reformers and liberals.

The search for quick solutions and popular support thus blurred the line between objective impartation of knowledge and the dissemination of propaganda. In practice many of the schools established by revolutionaries offered little solid education, either traditional or Western. Political discussions and military drills filled much of the students' time and interest. This was a point that separated revolutionaries from reformers and even resulted in disagreement between the most radical and the more cautious revolutionaries. The question of whether correct attitude might be a substitute for concrete knowledge and real power persisted into the Republican period. Since 1947 the Communists have explored the problem at length in the debates over whether it is more important for people to be red or expert.

Radical Psychology: Ch'iu Chin and Heroism

Even in the more intellectual aspects of their ideology the radical intellectuals displayed inconsistencies which can be partly attributed to the emotional strains of transition between old and modern ways. They were torn between hope and fear for the future. Angry rejection of much of the Chinese tradition and excitement over the new Western theories led to exaggerated attacks on Chinese character and society. At the same time the radicals loved China and never totally rejected their inheritance. Romanticism and bright dreams of the future were partly an escape from the iconoclastic logic of their theories. The past also had meaning, and from the beginning many revolutionaries found in parts of Chinese history sources of pride and identification.

Continuity with the past was facilitated by the numerous subsidiary traditions within the general Chinese culture. Buddhism, Taoism, and popular fiction all offered variant patterns of behavior upon which iconoclasts could draw. One concept which had great influence in radical circles was the traditional hero. The hero stood outside the proper Confucian order, but his image was nonetheless deeply rooted in popular imagination. Young students were most readily introduced to this concept by reading such novels as *The Romance of the Three Kingdoms* (*San-kuo chih yen-i*) and *All Men Are Brothers* (*Shui-hu chuan*). Although too unruly and disruptive for orthodox sanction, the hero in his way embodied certain Confucian virtues such as loyalty and uprighteousness. There was an affinity between the virtuous censor who courageously attacked misdeeds at court and the man who turned to arms to defend what he believed to be right.

The student radicals were particularly drawn to the model of the more active and warlike heroes.[90] From impotence and frustration was born a revolutionary romanticism in which students became adventurers (*hsia*) pursuing updated goals. Some also added Western anarchist theories and heroes to the traditional concept. The heroic ethic required a moral elevation and emotional intensity which combined well with youthful idealism. "Passionate and sensitive, the heroes possess outstanding gifts of personality and talent and the resolution to behave on a level higher than that of the sages and the wise. They are kind and generous and refuse rewards; for duty and ideal they sacrifice their dearest and closest attachments." The traditional hero is a lonely, isolated figure. "But this anguish does not stop him any more than other obstacles or conditions do: driven by passion and faith, he gives himself entirely to his goal, resolved to persevere against all odds. Death itself does not deter him. Thus he knows no failure: his venture succeeds on a moral plane...."[91] This description of the ideal traditional hero could be used almost without qualification to describe the ideal revolutionary and it explains much about the revolutionaries' actions and the nature of their influence. Many of the early student radicals did seek to sacrifice themselves for their cause and the success which they attained was largely moral. They were the devoted defenders of a new morality of country, freedom, science, and progress. The Ch'ing dynasty was corrupt, oppressive; its rulers were ancient barbarian enemies now destroying China to preserve their feeble hold on power. The pages devoted to vilification of the dynasty may perhaps be partly explained by the need to establish it as evil and the Manchus as traditional villains. Once a moral dichotomy had been established, the revolutionaries became the defenders of virtue—leaders of a righteous revolt against a despotic government.

Tsou Jung, who died in jail, was one of the prominent early revolutionary martyrs in Central China. Another was Wan Fu-hua, who was jailed after an unsuccessful assassination attempt. Wu Yüeh was killed while trying to assassinate the imperial commissioners leaving to study foreign constitutions. Ch'en Tien-hua[92] committed suicide, and Hsü Hsi-lin and Ch'iu Chin made virtually suicidal attempts to lead uprisings aimed at overthrowing the government. Ch'iu Chin was intimately connected with the Lower Yangtze revolutionary movement and has become one of the heroines honored today by both Communists and Nationalists. She has also left behind a fairly considerable volume of writings so that it is relatively easy to gain a picture of the motives which governed her career. Like all unusual individuals she was not altogether typical of the general group to which she belonged. Being a woman set her apart and probably resulted in her having an unusually strong sense of loneliness, isolation, and fighting against desperate odds. She also had a more thorough classical education and seemingly a deeper appreciation of Chinese history and culture than some of the somewhat younger intellectuals whose other attitudes she shared. However, Ch'iu was sufficiently typical of the more ardent and impatient revolutionary intellectuals so that a study of her ideas may help illuminate the course of the entire movement.

Ch'iu Chin unquestionably possessed a brilliant and forceful personality—the product of considerable intelligence and talent, an unusual upbringing, and the accident of living at a time when greater individual liberty was becoming possible. She was born in 1875 or 1877 into a scholarly Chekiangese family, some of whose members held low official position.[93] Both parents were exceedingly indulgent to their oldest daughter. She was tutored with her elder brother and acquired a good knowledge of the classics, history, and poetry. Ch'iu also evidently liked to picture herself in the role of a knight-errant (*yu-hsia*). She read swashbuckling novels, learned to ride a horse and use a sword, and she was proud of her ability to drink huge quantities of wine. This upbringing was poor preparation for Ch'iu's marriage in 1896 to Wang T'ing-chün, the son of a wealthy merchant of Hsiang-t'an, Hunan.[94] There was little scope for Ch'iu's pastimes in the conservative, substantial Wang family and her conventional husband was small consolation. Although they soon had a son and later a daughter there was slight affection in the marriage. At the Wang's home Ch'iu wrote poetry and was unhappy.

An important change in Ch'iu's life came when her husband purchased an official post in Peking. There she was fairly free to pursue her own activities. During these years she became a friend of several talented women, particularly the calligrapher Wu Chih-ying, whose husband was an associate of Wang. Had Ch'iu lived at another time she might have continued to find an outlet in poetry, scholarship, and friendships. However, new ideas were now in the air and new possibilities were opening up. Ch'iu was influenced by the 1898 Reform Movement and witnessed the humiliation of Western troops entering the capital during the Boxer Rebellion. She became an advocate of women's rights and became filled with ambition to save the country. When she returned to Peking again after a year or two back in Hunan she was still more distressed by her confined and seemingly meaningless existence.[95] By late 1903 Ch'iu had resolved to leave her family to study in Japan and she arrived in Tokyo during the spring or summer of 1904.[96]

Ch'iu attended the normal school of the Aoyama Vocational Girls School in Tokyo. However, most of her time must have been devoted to other activities. As a Chekiangese married to a Hunanese, she became an active member of both provincial clubs.[97] She actually seems to have been closer to the Hunanese group, particularly Liu Tao-i, who in 1906 was executed for revolutionary activities in Hunan. She, Liu, and eight others formed a rather amorphous society of radicals called the Ten Men Corps (*Shih-jen t'uan*).[98] Ch'iu's other activities included membership in the Encompassing Love Society (*Kung-ai hui*),[99] a society of women progressives, and writing for the *Vernacular Journal* (*Pai-hua pao*), published by a radical subsidiary of the Chinese Students Union.[100]

Emersion in student politics quickly led the already disaffected Ch'iu to enthusiastic support of the revolutionary movement. With a characteristic flair for the dramatic she bought a short sword which she often carried. In her spare time she studied marksmanship and bomb making. During the fall of 1904 Ch'iu joined the Yokohama branch of the Triads, a small group composed mainly of student revolutionaries rather than traditional secret society types.[101] However, the experience must have been useful to her when she began to work with various Triad offshoots in Chekiang. On a trip home the following spring she met a number of important revolutionaries in Shanghai and Chekiang including Ts'ai Yüan-p'ei and Hsü Hsi-lin. Then in early August she joined the Revolutionary Alliance in Tokyo and was appointed party head for Chekiang.[102]

A second critical point in Ch'iu's career came at the end of 1905 when she joined the agitation against the more stringent regulation of Chinese students in Japan announced by the Japanese Ministry of Education in late November.[103] She was one of a group of thirty or forty who returned to Shanghai early in 1906.[104] This action marked the end of Ch'iu's pursuit of education and the beginning of her career as a professional revolutionary. Probably shortly after her return she joined the Restoration Society, then the main revolutionary organization in Kiangsu and Chekiang.

Ch'iu Chin holding short sword. *Ch'iu Chin shih-chi* (Shanghai, 1958).

Ch'iu Chin in Western men's clothing. *Ch'iu Chin shih-chi* (Shanghai, 1958).

For a time after returning to China, Ch'iu seems to have been undecided about what to do. First she taught at the Hsün-ch'i Girls School in Huchow, which had been founded by the Chekiangese revolutionary Ao Chia-hsiung. There she became fast friends with the headmistress, Hsü Tzu-hua, but she was too radical for the school's trustees and many of the students and she left when summer vacation began.[105] Back in Shanghai she experimented with explosives[106] and helped raise funds for the radical Chinese Public Institute (*Chung-kuo kung-hsüeh*).[107] That fall she traveled about Chekiang helping to organize a rising scheduled to coincide with the one planned by the Revolutionary Alliance in Hunan. Disappointed when plans had to be cancelled, she briefly returned to her feminist interests by establishing the *Chinese Women's Journal* (*Chung-kuo nü-pao*) in Shanghai during January 1907.[108] The next month she left to assume the leadership of the revolutionary Ta-t'ung School in Shaohsing.

During the last six months of her life, Ch'iu's individual history is inseparable from the broader history of the revolutionary movement in Chekiang and will be considered later in that context. From her personal point of view these months fulfilled her previous aspirations. She was finally engaged in an enterprise which, if successful, would alter the course of Chinese history. In pursuit of both cause and fame she rigidly followed her plans to the very end. For her the end was execution in Shaohsing on July 15, 1907.

In Japan, Ch'iu adopted the additional name of the Heroine of Chien Lake (*Chien-hu nü-hsia*) after the lake near her family's home outside of Shaohsing, Chekiang. The choice was a highly revealing one which tells a great deal about her aspirations as well as her general picture of what a revolutionary should be. Ch'iu came to the revolution as a poet, not as a theorizer or a politician. Her ideology reflected the current individualism, nationalism, and anti-Manchuism of the radical students, specifically colored by her own romantic style. Although a radical modernizer who consumed the fashionable Western ideas, she never gave up interest in Chinese history and traditional literature. In her writings Rousseau and Poland exist side by side with the Duke Lu Yang and the ancient state of Ch'u.[109]

Ch'iu was above all an individualist of extremely strong will. Otherwise it would never have been possible for her to break with her past by going to Japan, and her success in doing so underlined her conviction that sufficient determination would overcome all obstacles.[110] Yet this same success saddled her with a burdensome loneliness and uniqueness. Even her early poems are filled with melancholy[111] and the difficult step that she took in going to Japan intensified this strain. Ch'iu was accepted to a remarkable degree by other revolutionaries and even secret-society members, but a woman revolutionary was still something of a curiosity. In addition she had to contend with opposition from her family, to whom she had always been close. Her mother was willing to support her, but her two brothers disapproved of her activities.[112] Although proud of her determination and self-reliance she felt that her decision had been bitter as well as necessary.[113] After 1904 she seems to have hovered between exaltation over her new freedom and despair over the slowness and difficulty of realizing her ideals.[114] It then became imperative for her to prove to herself and others that her decision had been right.

Ch'iu's individualism and romanticism, her modern aspirations and historical loyalties combined in the theme of the hero, which dominated both her writings and actions. Her view of the free and equal future society remained visionary. In contrast she had many specific ideas about the type of person who would lead the way. The country was defenseless and the people asleep in their ignorance. They had to be awakened, protected, and guided by heroes who understood the danger and were ready to sacrifice themselves for the benefit of their lesser compatriots. Like many of the other student revolutionaries of her time, Ch'iu anticipated the idea of the foreknowers later popularized by Sun Yat-sen. Probably her belief in self-sacrifice was influenced by the Buddhist concept of the Bodhisattva.[115] She also admired heroic-tragic figures in Western history such as the guillotined Madame Roland (Lo-lan fu-jen), the Russian populist Sophia Perovskaya, Napoleon, and the Polish revolutionaries.[116] However, she was mainly following the Chinese heroic tradition. The traditional hero and the revolutionary were combined into one image and it was this role which Ch'iu Chin especially aspired to play.

The romantic hero was a subject which lent itself to poetic expression and it is in Ch'iu's poems that this concept most strongly emerges. Her earlier poems foreshadowed this development with such themes as the chrysanthemum—proud and sorrowful, alone possessing the bravery and will to withstand the autumn winds.[117] When she turned toward the revolutionary movement, Ch'iu entered a world of dragons and tigers, clouds and raging seas, where only the brave might prevail.

> Ascending to heaven mounted on a white dragon,
> Crossing the hills astride a savage tiger.
> Angry shouts summon the winds and clouds
> And the spirit dances, flying in all directions.
> A great man in the world

> Must commune with heavenly spirits,
> And look after those other sons of pigs and dogs
> Who are beneath his company.[118]

Those who walked in this world included some of the great figures of Chinese history and historical fiction: the founder of the T'ang dynasty, Li Shih-min, and his rival Hsiang Yü; the famous adversaries of the Three Kingdoms period, Liu Pei and Ts'ao Ts'ao; and Ching K'o, who was executed after unsuccessfully trying to assassinate the ruler of Chin.[119] Such a hero is bold, open-hearted, and supernaturally strong and fierce.[120] He "is ashamed to decay like grass and wood." Fearless of the enemy ". . . he would incessantly pour forth his crimson blood to save his brothers. His thoughts, instructive to others, well forth from a splendid flowered tongue and are transformed into hundred-foot waves. . . ." Unconscious of self, in a crisis he would not hesitate to sacrifice his life.[121]

This was the sort of person whom Ch'iu aspired to be. She wished "single-handedly to rescue the ancestral country." Her ambition could not decay. At the "war drums sound" fury welled up in her heart.[122] She had turned her back on wealth and honor to requite her ancestors.[123] The only reason, then, to preserve her life was so she could sacrifice herself for her country. Though the present road was difficult she might later find honor—her "blood" after death might still turn to "jade."[124]

With her sword in hand, Ch'iu might be filled with the exhilarating conviction that she could realize her ambitions. Yet from 1900 on she was plagued by a nagging sense that her life was passing by and she had not made her contribution to the world. During the planning for a rising in Chekiang in 1907 her desire for a hero's fame, her belief that such a goal could be achieved through self-sacrifice, and her sense of urgency[125] came together and pushed her toward a death which she might easily have avoided by simply taking the trouble to escape before it was too late. At the end, Ch'iu's reaction was highly individualistic. There was no thought of preserving herself or her organization for subsequent attempts to advance the cause. It was better to go to a noble death. The sincerity of her actions might then bring her honor and win sympathy for the revolution. Both resulted, but Ch'iu was not to be there to try to ensure that her vision of the future was the one that was realized.

The wedding of the kind of psychology personified by Ch'iu Chin to the ideology of the revolutionary intellectuals sometimes produced political action more violent and radical than the revolutionaries' ideas alone seemed to require. Social and political changes being demanded by the revolutionaries were not so very different from those asked for by constitutionalists. Nor was their rejection of tradition absolute. However, many revolutionaries did desperately desire modernization and believed, with partial justification, that those controlling government and society wanted only to preserve their old positions and the old ways. The frustration of seeing reform efforts repeatedly engulfed by social and institutional inertia, while the imperialist threat seemed to intensify, led them to denounce the government fiercely, to seek to destroy it, and on occasion to destroy themselves in protest. The revolutionary act had a psychological value apart from its success or failure, for it enabled its perpetuators simply and dramatically to transcend the discouraging present and link themselves to their vision of the world to come with the purity of their intentions unsullied by compromise.

It was worthwhile to risk all to combat the existing enemy. China's problems were blamed on the Manchu Ch'ing dynasty, and many revolutionaries facilely assumed that if the dynasty were eliminated genuine modernization would quickly follow. They desired a cataclysm that would release dynamic forces within China. Particular ideologies were less important for the time being than was achieving a sense of movement. Therefore, revolutionaries emphasized destruction over construction, and men of quite basically different attitudes could cooperate on the immediate goal of overthrowing the government. Western-derived ideas had begun to stimulate political action at this stage of China's development, but divisions on the basis of specific ideologies were still vague and secondary to generally shared hopes for the future.

3 Beginnings of Revolutionary Activity
in Shanghai I:
Leadership and Institutions

Radicals first began to seek ways to implement their new theories and romantic dreams in the large cities. Urban centers were more effective incubators than smaller towns even though modern ideas rapidly spread to wherever new students were found. The Shanghai environment was the most favorable of all, and during 1902 and 1903 that city was almost as important as Tokyo in the development of the revolutionary movement. Radical intellectuals first organized in significant groups within China in Shanghai and there they defiantly proclaimed. their revolutionary intentions.

Shanghai had been a center of Western influence in China for fifty years. It offered examples of Western trade, finance, and industry. Western reformers, such as the missionary Timothy Richards, helped make Western ideas available through translation of books on Western history, science, and geography. Under the management of Richards and other missionaries, translations by the Society for Diffusion of Knowledge (*Kuang-hsüeh hui*) influenced Chinese reformers after 1887. Two years later the missionary-managed *Globe Magazine* (*Wan-kuo kung-pao*) was revived and again began to print its translations and suggestions for reform.[1] Daily contacts with foreigners increased Chinese knowledge of the West and also resulted in irritations and humiliations which fostered nationalism.

Once radical ideas had begun to develop, the Shanghai administrative divisions offered particular advantages to opponents of the Ch'ing government. Besides the part of the city under Chinese jurisdiction, Shanghai was divided into an International Settlement (basically Anglo-American) and a French Concession. The former, in particular, was important as a political refuge. It was governed by its own Municipal Council, elected by property renters within the Settlement, and subject to the general supervision of the consular body. Foreign residents of both the International and French sectors enjoyed extraterritoriality. Partly out of conviction and partly to eliminate as much Chinese jurisdiction as possible, some of the same legal protection was extended to Chinese residents of the foreign concessions. In the International Settlement a Mixed Court, presided over by a Chinese magistrate and a British assessor or an American representative of the United States consul-general, considered criminal charges brought against Chinese by foreigners and mixed civil cases in which a foreigner was the plaintiff. Cases involving only Chinese were to be tried by the magistrate alone, but all warrants for arrests had to be countersigned by the senior consul-general and executed by the municipal police. The powers of the court gradually became more specific and the scope of the foreign assessor's authority increased. By 1902 no Chinese resident of the Settlement could be arrested and removed by Chinese officials without a preliminary hearing before the Mixed Court. The check afforded by the Municipal Council and the foreign assessor on Chinese judicial procedures could be important in political cases. The policy of the Western community was to give asylum to political refugees as long as they did not disturb the peace of the Settlement or use its territory for active plotting to overthrow the Chinese government.[2] Purely verbal attacks on the government were generally tolerated as an exercise of the right to free speech.

Attracted by these opportunities, dissidents tended to congregate in the International Settlement. Shanghai was one center of the Reform Movement from 1896 to 1898 and the two important reform papers, *The Chinese Progress* (*Shih-wu pao*) and *Straight Talk* (*Ch'ang-yen pao*), were published there. In 1900 T'ang Ts'ai-ch'ang carried out the initial organization for his Hankow revolt in Shanghai. He also persuaded many prominent Chinese modernizers to join in forming a National Association (*Kuo-hui*) to consider how to rescue China from her difficulties. This group contained such major reformers as Yen Fu and Yung Wing and also a number of men who later were involved in or influenced the *Su-pao* case: Chang Ping-lin, Lung Tse-hou, and Shen Chin. Because of the diverse political views of its members, the society did not accomplish much and dissolved after the failure of T'ang's rising.[3]

The educated populace of Shanghai was unusually aware of political events. Mass meetings were frequently held to criticize government policies. Such was the meeting held by gentry, merchants, and students to protest the rumored deposition of the Kuang-hsü Emperor after the collapse of the 1898 Reform Movement. Over 1200 signatures were affixed to a telegram sent to the Ch'ing court.[4] Another example, which foreshadowed events of 1903, was a meeting in May 1901 to protest the ratification of the treaty with Russia after the Boxer Rebellion because it might lead to the loss of Manchuria.[5]

Against this background of political activity and awareness the revolutionary movement emerged as distinct from the reform party in 1902 and 1903. As in Japan, student protest against authority and nationalistic protest against foreign encroachment were main instruments of radicalization. The major organizations reflected the intellectuals' orientation toward education and journalism: The Chinese Educational Association (*Chung-kuo chiao-yü hui*), The Patriotic School (*Ai-kuo hsüeh-she*), and the newspaper *Su-pao* (*The Kiangsu Journal*). Leading figures included men such as Chang Ping-lin, Wu Chih-hui, Ts'ai Yüan-p'ei, and *Su-pao* owner Ch'en Fan, all of whom had been reformers before turning to revolution. To these were added a younger group of revolutionaries who came to politics after the failure of the 1898 Reform Movement and the Boxer Rebellion. Such youths as Tsou Jung and Chang Shih-chao, the editor of *Su-pao* during its last fateful month, were often more extreme, romantic, and uncompromisingly nationalistic in their views than were the older radicals.

The arrest and trial of Chang Ping-lin, Tsou Jung, and others connected with *Su-pao* was the most dramatic single event in the history of the revolutionary movement in Shanghai during these years. Consequently, the *Su-pao* case is often discussed out of context as though it was the chief example of revolutionary activity. Actually, the radical articles in *Su-pao* were the culmination of a year's developments. Arrests were precipitated as much by activities of students at the Patriotic School and the series of public protest meetings in Chang's Garden as they were by the anti-Manchu articles in *Su-pao*. The same people were involved in all these aspects and one event influenced the development of others. *Su-pao* was certainly important, but it was far from the entire story.

Legacy of the Reform Movement: The Chinese Educational Association

The problem of suitable textbooks for new courses became acute once the number of schools teaching modern subjects began to increase after the Boxer Rebellion. Translations of Japanese texts were frequently used, but they were not really adequate for the needs of Chinese students. There was a sudden boom in the publication of modern books and translations of Western works. In Shanghai the Commercial Press (*Shang-wu yin-shu-kuan*), the Bookshop for Diffusion of Knowledge (*Kuang-chih shu-chü*), the National Studies Association (*Kuo-hsüeh she*), the Shanghai agency for the *Renovation of the People,* and other firms specialized in this field, but the demand was far from met. The Chinese Educational Association was established in the spring of 1902, partly in response to this situation and partly as a blind for other activities. Its stated purpose was to improve the quality of textbooks available in Chinese schools. In fact it became a gathering spot for revolutionaries in the Lower Yangtze area.[6] These two aspects of its activities were linked by the belief that needed changes could not occur until youths had absorbed new knowledge and a new set of moral values. A new type of education emphasizing Western learning and a nationalistic spirit was thus a necessary basis for either reform or revolution.

The society was established in late April or early May with headquarters in the International Settlement.[7] The young organization suffered from financial difficulties, had few members, and did not accomplish much during the first few months. It did not become important until the fall of 1902 and then it developed along lines rather different than had originally been planned. There is little evidence that much progress was ever made toward the original aim of editing new textbooks.

The original founder and first president was Ts'ai Yüan-p'ei, who was joined by a number of other scholars and students in Shanghai such as Chiang Chih-yu, later a member of the *Tides of Chekiang* group in Japan and after that a member of the constitutional party, Lin Hsieh, who took part in the 1911 Revolution in Fukien, the liberal scholars Yeh Han, Wang Chi-t'ung, Chiang Wei-ch'iao, and Wang Te-yüan. Invitations to join and work for the group were sent to progressive friends of its members who were outside Shanghai.[8] The original nucleus was augmented by Chang Ping-lin, who returned to Shanghai from Japan shortly after the association was founded, the Buddhist monk Huang Tsung-yang, and Wu Chih-hui when he returned from Japan in August.

Ts'ai, Chang, Wu, and Huang were the most important members of the group. In their different ways they were the leaders of Shanghai radical circles at the crucial time when the revolutionary and reform movements separated. A brief survey of their early careers, therefore, may help explain how this transition occurred. Ts'ai and Chang were natives of Chekiang and the other two were natives of Kiangsu. They were all in their later thirties in 1903. Wu and Huang were born in 1865, Ts'ai in 1867, and Chang in 1868. Each came from a family wealthy enough to educate its sons, even though each family was not necessarily rich. Ts'ai's father was the proprietor of a local bank and an uncle held a low examination degree. Despite financial difficulties after his father's death in 1877, Ts'ai's education continued under his uncle and a series of local scholars.[9] Chang Ping-lin came from a wealthy, scholarly family whose fortunes had declined somewhat after officers of the loyal Hsiang army appropriated part of the family lands before the Changs could return after fleeing the Taiping rebels. His grandfather had amassed a large collection of Sung, Yuan, and Ming dynasty first editions. His father was a poet, and Chang himself received an excellent classical education.[10] Wu Chih-hui was brought up by his maternal grandmother after his mother died when he was five. He was educated by a series of private school teachers and in academies in Kiangsu. Besides classical texts Wu also studied economics, politics, history, writing seal characters, and English.[11] Huang Tsung-yang's education was the least conventional. He was most devoted to studying poetry and ancient character texts. He frequented a Buddhist monastery near his home, where he must have acquired much of his early knowledge.

Ts'ai Yüan-p'ei had received the *chin-shih* degree in 1890 at the early age of twenty-three. He then held a series of government appointments as Chief Historiographer of Shanghai and then Chekiang, Hanlin Bachelor and Hanlin Compiler, second class.[12] Wu Chih-hui also passed the government examinations, becoming a *chü-jen* in 1891. He failed the *chin-shih* examinations the next year, however, and never held an official post. Chang Ping-lin tried once to pass the district examinations, but failed. He never tried again, preferring to devote himself to literary and historical studies rather than an official career. Huang Tsung-yang never attempted to study for the examinations; instead he became a Buddhist monk when he was nineteen, taking the name of Wu-mu shan seng (the monk of Wu-mu mountain).[13]

All four men were noted for scholarly or artistic talents and Ts'ai, Chang, and Wu all taught before their involvement with the Patriotic School. During 1900 and 1901 Ts'ai Yuan-p'ei was superintendent of the Chinese and Western School (*Chung-Hsi hsüeh-t'ang*) in Shaohsing and had short-lived connections with a number of other schools in Chekiang. In 1901 he was invited to join the faculty of a special course of studies just being established for older scholars at the Nan-yang Public Institute, one of the foremost modern schools in Shanghai. Wu Chih-hui taught at the Pei-yang Public Institute in 1897–98 and then in the fall of 1898 moved to the Nan-yang Public Institute, where he taught for three years. Chang Ping-lin was the most famous classical scholar of the group. He studied the *Spring and Autumn Annals* and the *Tso-chuan* commentary under the guidance of the Chekiangese scholar Yü Yüeh at the famous academy *Ku-ching ching-she* in Hangchow.[14] Soon thereafter he began his political career, but he also taught briefly at the Ch'iu-shih Academy in Hangchow, the Ch'eng-cheng School in Shanghai, and the missionary Tung-Wu College in Soochow.[15] Huang Tsung-yang continued to study after he became a monk and also began to paint in an attempt capture the essence of Buddhist teachings. He eventually became well-known for his accomplishments and developed a wide acquaintance among scholars of his generation including Chang, Wu, and Ts'ai.

All these men were influenced by the Sino-Japanese War, the 1898 Reform Movement, and the Boxer Rebellion. Ts'ai Yüan-p'ei began to study Western science and history after China's defeat by Japan because he was convinced that Japan's military superiority lay in that country's greater degree of Westernization. He was not active in the Reform Movement, but he sympathized with the reformers, particularly T'an Ssu-t'ung. Disillusioned with the government after the anti-Reform coup in September 1898, he resigned his position to devote himself to education. Wu Chih-hui began to promote a variety of reformist causes such as vernacular literature, abolition of foot-binding, and abandonment of the stylized "eight-legged essay" form required in the official examinations. Early in 1898 he met K'ang Yu-wei and presented a reform memorial to one of the censors in Peking. He left the Peking area just before the beginning of the hundred days of reform, however, and was not involved in the events of the summer. Two years later Wu was profoundly disturbed by the news of the Allied Expeditionary Forces' capture of Peking during the Boxer Rebellion. His initial reaction was to propose to give arms and military training to the students at the Nan-yang Public Institute, where he was then teaching, so they might form the nucleus of a national army.

Huang Tsung-yang's connection with current events was more remote, but he did study Western works as well as conventional scholarly and religious subjects. In contrast, Chang P'ing-lin began his political career as a reformer in 1895 when he joined the Society for Self-Strengthening (Ch'iang-hsüeh hui) established by K'ang Yu-wei. A year later Chang was invited to join the staff of the reformist publication *The Chinese Progress,* which was then being organized in Shanghai with Liang Ch'i-ch'ao as editor. In 1898, when the Reform Movement was flourishing, Governor-General Chang Chih-tung summoned him to Hupeh. At that time Chang Ping-lin mainly agreed with reform leaders on political issues but disagreed with their reinterpretation of Chinese tradition. He could not accept K'ang Yu-wei's idea of transforming Confucianism into a modern Western-style religion, and he later saw Buddhism as the means to develop the people's moral capacities. Chang also believed in the authenticity of the *Tso-chuan* commentary on the *Spring and Autumn Annals,* which he had especially studied.[16] He therefore rejected the reformers' arguments in favor of the *Kung-yang Commentary,* a long ignored apocalyptic work which might be used to justify social change. Influential reformers soon persuaded the governor-general to dismiss him and Chang returned to Shanghai, where he served briefly as an editor of *Straight Talk*, a reform paper established to combat *The Chinese Progress* by Wang K'ang-nien, who had had a personal falling out with K'ang and Liang.[17] After the anti-Reform coup in September, Chang returned to Chekiang and then fled to Taiwan. From that time on he supported himself by journalism or teaching while following a radical political career.

The backgrounds of these four men were similar, but their temperaments were quite diverse and they became revolutionaries at different times and in different ways. Chang Ping-lin was the first to join the revolutionary movement. His family had kept alive some of the hatred of the Manchus which existed at the time of the conquest. When he was a child his grandfather told him stories of famous scholars who refused to serve the Ch'ing. Later Chang read of Manchu cruelties in the *Tung-hua lu* and the collection of writings by Ming loyalists, *Anecdotes of the End of the Ming* (*Ming-chi p'i-shih*). This background didn't immediately turn Chang against the dynasty, but it may have influenced him not to seek an official career. In 1898 he was still ready to accept Manchu rule. After fleeing to Taiwan he supposedly wrote his first revolutionary article, approving Sun Yat-sen's activities and urging K'ang Yu-wei and Liang Ch'i-ch'ao to forsake the dynasty.[18] However, he also published an article "On Guest Emperors" (*K'o-ti lun*) in Liang's *Pure Criticism Journal* in which he argued that the Chinese should recognize the Manchus as "guest emperors" as in the past they had invited foreigners to be high ministers.[19] Not long afterward he finally repudiated reformist views and called for revolution in the essay "Correcting the Error of Guest Emperors" (*K'o-ti k'uang-miu*).[20] Before mid-1900 Chang had cut off his queue and openly declared himself against the regime. That summer he joined the National Association in Shanghai, but he soon withdrew because he rejected the association's support of the emperor. After T'ang Ts'ai-ch'ang's revolt failed, Chang's name was again among those to be arrested. He first went to Soochow and then fled to Japan, where he openly advocated revolution.

Chang became a revolutionary when his childhood anti-Manchuism was reinforced by the experiences of the failure of the 1898 Reform Movement and the Boxer Rebellion. Without resentment of Western imperialism his anti-Manchuism would probably have taken no more radical form than refusal to accept government office. As it was, he became noted for vitriolic racial views. His revolutionary style was influenced by his brilliant and irascible personality. Chang was a nonconformist who cared little for other's opinions.[21] In debate he had a sharp tongue and he wielded a sarcastic pen. He wrote anti-Manchu tracts in such an uncompromisingly high style that they were more admired than read by young revolutionaries who had a less thorough classical education than he.[22] The very real abilities that Chang brought to the service of the revolution were partly offset by an unfortunate tendency to make enemies among his associates and the enthusiasm with which he carried on his protracted feuds.

In contrast to many of the other revolutionaries Chang was never greatly attracted by Western ideas and political institutions. Examples from Western history in his early revolutionary tracts were mainly used to buttress his racial argument.[23] He also referred to many figures and incidents in Chinese history which did not usually appear in revolutionary literature.[24] Chang shared some of the nationalism of the younger students and he blamed the Manchus for subservience to Westerners.[25] However, his nationalism retained a large cultural element. Thus he tried to discourage students at the Patriotic School from studying English, which he said would make them slaves of foreigners.[26] When looking for a moral basis for the new China he rejected both Western religion and the officially sanctioned Confucianism in favor of Buddhism, a traditional but unorthodox mode of thought.

Later, as editor of *The People's Journal* (*Min-pao*), Chang wrote numerous articles in that journal in which he formulated views on economics, political democracy, and other issues raised by Sun Yat-sen's "Three Principals of the People."[27] In 1902 and 1903, however, his writings consisted mainly of attacks on the Manchus and on constitutionalists for continuing to support the dynasty. The most celebrated presentation of these themes was in his "Letter Disputing K'ang Yu-wei" (*Po K'ang Yu-wei shu*), published in *Su-pao* during June 1903. Here Chang goes to great lengths to argue the racial differences between Chinese and Manchus, the cruelty of the Manchu conquest, and the continued humiliation and oppression of the Chinese. There is a good deal of cultural bias and traditional Chinese contempt for steppe "barbarians" in Chang's definition of race. Thus he saw the Chinese as a single people even though they had once been divided into distinct groups. The groups had been assimilated, but the Manchus by definition were unalterably different and inferior.[28] The Kuang-hsü Emperor was made the symbol of Manchu decadence. Ludicrous in his subservience to the empress-dowager and criminally ineffectual in his inability to defend even the Manchu homeland from foreign encroachment, the emperor was totally unfit to govern the country.[29]

Chang's quarrel with the constitutionalists stemmed from their different reactions to the failure of the 1898 Reform Movement. His theoretical premises again were based on his racial views. Racial differences irreconcilably divided peoples so that it was impossible for two races to share equally and amicably in a government. Current proposals for a constitutional monarchy would, therefore, only perpetuate Manchu domination.[30] Chang selected K'ang Yu-wei as the chief villain among the constitutionalists and portrayed him with the same polemical unfairness as he did the Kuang-hsü Emperor: K'ang was seeking to convince the Manchus of his loyalty so he might receive office and increase his personal wealth and position.[31]

Overthrow of the Manchus was more important to Chang than repulsing Western imperialism and he rejected the constitutionalist argument that revolution would lead to division of China among the Western powers by arguing that Manchu rule was equally foreign. Even a few decades of fragmented independence would be better than none at all.[32] Chang had little faith in Western representative government,[33] but over a Manchu monarchy he favored a democratic republic. The important point was to get rid of the Manchus. This could only be done by enlisting broad mass participation in a violent struggle through which the people would be educated to break their habitual acceptance of Manchu rule. The call for struggle may reflect some influence from Social Darwinism, but Chang's particular model was more traditionalistic. He was encouraged by the contemporary Kwangsi secret society rebellion, which he believed demonstrated that popular revolution was possible in China. It also showed that the people had learned the lessons of earlier risings and were groping toward a democratic revolution which would be more advanced and thorough than previous upheavals.[34] Chang's narrow racism was not typical of the revolutionary intellectuals, but he was influential because of the single-mindedness of his basically simple message and because of the clear distinction he drew between the constitutionalist and revolutionary movements at a time when the two were just beginning to separate.

Ts'ai Yüan-p'ei, who played an equally prominent role in the early revolutionary movement, was a very different personality. Whereas Chang was intolerant and aggressive, Ts'ai was broad-minded and humane. He was generally interested in history and culture as well as in classical interpretation and acquired from the Confucian tradition faith in the basic goodness of individuals. As a teacher after 1898 he became increasingly committed to promoting Western ideas and fostering individual freedom. By 1900 he had become an advocate of academic freedom and women's rights. He continued to develop these views at the Nan-yang Public Institute in 1901 and 1902, where he spoke out in favor of democratic liberties.[35]

Ts'ai was also a patriot and by 1902 he evidently doubted that either the government or traditional Chinese society could realize the values of nationalism and freedom. In November 1902 he sided with the students who withdrew from the Nan-yang Public Institute and helped them organize the Patriotic School.

Although Ts'ai was a leader of radical and revolutionary groups in Shanghai for the next four years, it can be argued that he was actually drawn into the revolutionary movement by the logic of his association with the more fervent radicals in the Patriotic School. Among the revolutionaries Ts'ai was distinguished by his tolerance and rationality. These traits showed plainly in an article entitled "Explaining Enmity to the Manchus"[36] which appeared in *Su-pao* during March 1903. In it Ts'ai argued that there were no practical racial distinctions between Chinese and Manchus and that the only important privileges Manchus still retained were control of the throne and the right to half the government posts. The reason for the struggle against them was, therefore, to end the tyranny of minority over majority. This purely political question tended to become muddled because even those Chinese most familiar with Western thought were unconsciously influenced by outmoded traditional contempt for barbarians. Moreover, revolutionaries sometimes intentionally disguised Western ideas of democracy with anti-Manchu talk to avoid offending potential allies who still held to Confucian values. In reality the revolutionaries' "racism" was not the same as traditional ideas of race, but this difference was not readily apparent. Ts'ai saw democracy in the twentieth century as a river whose flow could not be stopped. The real enemies of the Manchus, therefore, were those who sought to preserve their minority privileges. They were following policies which would lead to the same sort of disastrous blunders as were committed by French nobility before 1789.

This analysis is a good deal more acute than were the views held by many of Ts'ai's colleagues, but it is hardly rousing revolutionary literature. Ts'ai remained more a scholar than an activist even when calling for the overthrow of the government. Like many radical intellectuals Ts'ai closely linked the concepts of education and revolution. However, he was probably atypical in giving greater weight to the inherent value of education as a way to individual self-realization and freedom. For him it was not simply a vehicle for propaganda and a means to national enlightenment and strength. Ts'ai was admired for his learning and liked for his good nature, but he was never an effective revolutionary leader. As head of the Restoration Society his leadership became nominal because members preferred to follow more dramatic and active younger men. Eventually Ts'ai chose education over revolution and went to Berlin in 1907 to study philosophy and learn more of the West. During the Republic he was to use this experience to be of considerable service to China—but as an educator not as a revolutionary.

Wu Chih-hui, like Ts'ai Yüan-p'ei, did not fully become a revolutionary until after the founding of the Patriotic School. During his three years of teaching at the Nan-yang Public Institute, Wu had begun to identify more closely with the students than with the faculty. In 1901 he went so far as to advocate that the teachers and administrators meet with students to formulate policy.

Soon after, in the spring of 1901, Wu went to Tokyo and entered the Higher Normal School (*Kōtō shihan gakkō*). Although he received some financial aid from the Nan-yang Public Institute, he was somewhat unusual at that time because he did not have a government scholarship. The decision to go to Japan was prompted by disapproval of the policies of the new Nan-yang director,[37] but also probably indicated growing concern over China's weakness. Wu was still decidedly not revolutionary, however, and while in Japan he refused to meet Sun Yat-sen because he disapproved of Sun's political views.

After several months in Japan, Wu made one more attempt to follow a conventional career. At the end of 1901 he was invited by a friend who was a personal secretary (*mu-yu*) of the governor-general of Kwangtung and Kwangsi to come to Canton to help establish a university there. The governor-general was then very old and the government was really directed by his son and a group with whom Wu became acquainted. He could have taken this opportunity to follow an official career, but he was repelled by the maneuvering and corruption involved. Therefore, he returned to Japan in the spring and reentered the Higher Normal School. This time Wu had his first really serious clash with government authority over the admission of nonscholarship students to the Chinese Students Military Preparatory School. He was forced to leave Tokyo and go back to Shanghai, where he joined the Chinese Educational Association.

Wu's ideas, like those of many of his contemporaries, were rapidly evolving at this time, so it is difficult to define them at any given point. When he returned to Shanghai in August 1902, he made a speech at the meeting called to consider how to respond to the restrictions on private students desiring to enter military schools in Japan. In it he castigated government decadence and rottenness and the loss of national rights.[38] He was not necessarily definitely committed to revolution at that time, however. The personal characteristic which had been most evident in his activities during the previous two years was a strong intolerance toward conventional authority, which eventually led him to anarchism and a sweeping rejection of tradition. This trait enabled him to fit easily into the atmosphere of the Patriotic School. Under the influence of the increasing radicalism of that group, Wu evidently became a revolutionary by early 1903. His biographer dates this event from a meeting in February at which *Su-pao* was formally accepted as the organ of the Patriotic School. Wu made a revolutionary speech there.[39] He also cut off his queue about this time although he had previously defended it. During the next few months Wu was one of the most radical speakers at the weekly meetings of the Patriotic School group in Chang's Garden.

Despite strongly held views, Wu's revolutionary bent remained highly theoretical and intellectual—more adapted to study and written polemics than to organization, fighting, and fund raising. He fled from Shanghai to Hong Kong in July 1903 to escape arrest for his connection with *Su-pao*. From there he sailed to England, arriving in the late fall.[40] During the next three years Wu lived and studied in London. In 1906 he moved to Paris, where he lived with a number of radical Chinese students. Together they formed the World Association (*Shih-chieh she*), which acquired a printing press and in 1907 began to publish the anarchist journal *New Century* (*Hsin shih-chi*).[41] In 1909 Wu went back to London and did not return to China until after the Revolution. During his years in Europe, Wu became a convinced anarchist. He also maintained connections with Sun Yat-sen and the Revolutionary Alliance and carried on a feud with Chang Ping-lin which had originated in Shanghai in 1903. After the Revolution, Wu resisted offers of official positions for a time because of his anarchist convictions. He did, however, join the Kuomintang, which he served in various capacities. Eventually he was classified as a member of the party's right wing at the time of the split with the Communists in 1926.

Because of his religious vocation, Huang Tsung-yang was the most anomalous of the four leaders of the Educational Association. The details of his life are less readily available and it is unusually difficult to ascertain his views. Although he associated with revolutionaries, he was not politically active himself and was not a member of a revolutionary party. He was a formidable associate because he enjoyed the patronage of Lo Chia-ling, the Sino-French wife of a wealthy Jewish merchant in Shanghai named Silas A. Hardoon (Ho-t'ung).[42] Lo Chia-ling was a devout Buddhist, so Hardoon built the Ai-li Gardens, which contained a Buddhist hall, for her use. Subsequently he added a school for monks and invited Huang to head it. Both husband and wife greatly respected Huang and generally followed his advice. This influence enabled him to persuade them to make large donations to causes he favored. Huang evidently was moderate in his suggestions, but his access to Hardoon's wealth could not but raise his stature in radical circles.

In the Educational Association, Huang played the role of organizer, chief fund raiser, and conciliator. After the arrests in June 1903, Huang stayed in Shanghai and worked for the acquittal of the defendants. After the first phase of the trial he went to Japan, where he lived near Sun Yat-sen. Huang made friends with a number of Chinese merchants there and when the revolutionary journal *Kiangsu* was about to close he was able to raise funds to allow it to continue a little longer. He also donated a sum to help finance one of Sun's visits to overseas Chinese communities.

In 1904 Huang returned safely to Shanghai, where he lived in the Ai-li Gardens and devoted himself to scholarly and religious pursuits. He played no political role except for a brief time during 1911. Then he helped persuade the Restoration Society revolutionary Li Hsieh-ho to retire to Woosung and not contest Ch'en Ch'i-mei's claim to be military governor of Shanghai since the gentry and merchants favored Ch'en. Huang also persuaded Ho-t'ung to donate a large sum to the military government which Li established at Woosung.

After 1911 Huang retired again to a Buddhist life, although he maintained old friendships such as the one with Chang Ping-lin. His religious attitudes paralleled his secular views, for he evidently favored a less strict regimen than did some of his more traditional brothers. In 1916 he was bypassed for abbot of the famous Chin-shan monastery in Kiangsu because he had worn lay dress and had a political record. Three years later he left to restore and head the Ch'i-hsia monastery near Nanking, which had been destroyed during the Taiping Rebellion. When he died in 1921 at the age of fifty-six he was greatly respected and left many disciples.[43]

Huang Tsung-yang's interest in the Educational Association and the Patriotic School stemmed from concern over imperialist encroachment and the belief that youth must be reeducated to save China. Education was to foster the independent spirit and nationalistic dedication that would transform slaves into citizens.[44] Huang was one example of the connection between Buddhists or Buddhism and the revolutionary movement.[45] Corrupted forms of Buddhism had for centuries been associated with secret societies and their rebellions. However, revolutionaries were more interested in Buddhism as an intellectual and moral system. Intellectuals had traditionally found in Buddhism an escape from the Confucian system that dominated conventional society. Student radicals had likewise rejected traditional society and found in the revolutionary movement an alternative morality and sense of identification. Although they and the Buddhists moved in largely different worlds there was perhaps a psychological similarity between the two groups, which resulted in mutual sympathy if their paths happened to cross. Both were apart from the mainstream of Chinese life. It was also easy to draw parallels between the self-sacrifice, willpower, and compassion of the bodhisattvas and the similar traits demanded of radicals who were going to save China and revitalize the people.[46]

This look at the leading members of the Chinese Educational Association casts doubts on claims that it was originally established as a revolutionary front.[47] Other sources refer only to the stated aim of improving the quality of textbooks in the belief that better Western-oriented education was vital for the salvation of China.[48] It seems to me that at the beginning this latter statement was closer to the truth. All four of the leaders were deeply concerned about the future of China and after the events of 1898 and 1900 had lost, or almost lost, faith in reform, but had not quite taken the next step. It was first the impact of the addition of a larger number of younger radical students organized in the Patriotic School and second the agitation against Russian Policy in Manchuria which turned the association into a mainly revolutionary group. The Educational Association was a transitional body, important because it was in existence to take the lead when events outside its control radicalized the political atmosphere.

Toward Revolution: The Patriotic School

The first important change in the nature of the Educational Association occurred with the founding of the Patriotic School in November 1902. The initial proposal that the association establish a school had been made in August at the meeting to welcome Wu Chih-hui after his expulsion from Japan.[49] A loose organization was formed at that time to assist Chinese studying in other Asian countries, and delegates were selected to make representations to the Japanese government. Some attending the meeting believed that even so students would still be freer to receive the education they wanted in a sympathetically operated school in China.[50]

The Ink Bottle Incident

Nothing came of the proposal at that time, but three months later the Educational Association was prompted to action by the withdrawal of over a hundred students from the Nan-yang Public Institute.[51] This school had been established by the prominent modernizing official Sheng Hsüan-huai in 1896 in accord with the theory of "Chinese learning for fundamental principles, Western learning for practical use."[52] Both foreign and Chinese instructors were employed. The student body was divided into a middle school of six forms, an upper school, and a special course for those who had already passed the government examinations but wished to supplement their traditional knowledge. Graduates of the upper school might enter Sheng's Railway or Economics schools.[53] The Institute was one of the leading modern schools in China and was one of the first to send students to study in Japan.[54]

Until 1902 the president of the school was the American sinologue Dr. John C. Ferguson, who was a personal friend of Sheng and assisted in many of his projects.[55] The Chinese director was Ho Mei-sheng, a cousin of Sheng Hsüan-huai and a noted essayist and calligrapher. When Ho died in 1901 he was succeeded by Chang Chü-sheng, a modernizer who encouraged students to read such "new books" as the translations of Yen Fu. Chang soon resigned because of conflict with Ferguson, who did not approve of the new trends of thought among the students. The principal at the time of the withdrawals was the more conservative Han-lin scholar Wang Feng-tsao. Thus at a time of rising student unrest the administration had not developed a consistent policy toward the new radical ideas. Liberal and conservative faculty members also feuded with one another.[56]

The students were affected by the most progressive current ideas: first, the 1898 Reform Movement, next the movement to protect the emperor, and then after 1900 the new patriotism and the ideas of Western political philosophers. Such traditional anti-Manchu works as *Anecdotes of the End of the Ming, A Bitter History (T'ung-shih),* and *A Record of Ten Days at Yangchow (Yang-chou shih-jih chi)* circulated among the students. Liang Ch'i-ch'ao's *Renovation of the People* was much read after it began publication. The students were given to political discussions and the Student Association held weekly meetings in Chang's Garden. So young a group could hardly be expected to arrive at powerfully thought out conclusions. Discussions were generally rather vague. The students' views were not uniform and they were not sure what they wanted, but those who set the trend in 1902 were probably most influenced by the ideals of the French Revolution. Liberty, equality, and fraternity were in the air.[57]

In this atmosphere conflicts over curriculum and discipline developed between students and faculty. Teachers of Chinese refused to allow students to read *The Renovation of the People* or translations of Rousseau for their classes. Students in turn disliked such standard works as the *Collected Statutes of the Ch'ing Dynasty (Ta-Ch'ing hui-tien)* and *A History of the Imperial Military (Sheng-wu chi).* They also protested such restraints on their behavior as seating of a faculty member at each table to keep order during meals.[58] The important issue for the students was freedom to read and discuss what they pleased,[59] but the explosion occurred over a trivial incident of student tampering with an ink bottle belonging to the Fifth Form Chinese teacher, Kuo Chen-ying. Kuo was a conservative *chü-jen* who had forbidden the reading of new books and was very unpopular among the students. When he asked the student sitting nearest his desk who was responsible, the student replied that he did not know. Kuo then gave him a major demerit (three of which would result in expulsion). A few days later he was questioned again and accused by Kuo of being responsible. Then he and two other members of the class were expelled for being disrespectful to their teacher.[60]

That evening Fifth Form students held a meeting to protest the expulsions. Before the meeting an announcement from the principal's office was posted accusing the students of advocating rebellion and threatening the entire Form with expulsion if the meeting was held. In reply the Fifth Form decided to resign and, on returning to their dormitory, started to pack their belongings. However, representatives of other Forms persuaded them to wait and appeal to the principal. The next day, November 15, a student strike was called and representatives went to call on the principal, but he refused to see them. A mass meeting was then held at which the students decided that each Form would send a delegation to present their views to the president. He, too, refused to see them, but he sent a subordinate to request that they go back to their dormitories until a solution could be worked out the next day. The students agreed to go, but they stipulated that a representative should meet with them at 10:00 the following morning. When no one had arrived by early afternoon on November 16, the Fifth Form students walked out.[61] Joining them were many members of other Forms, a few older students from the special course, and a handful of liberal faculty members. Most significant among these was Ts'ai Yüan-p'ei. Ts'ai had sympathized with and encouraged the students from the start. After their withdrawal he was to prove an even more valuable ally.

The school's administration had obviously blundered, the more so since the students' demonstrations had been orderly and dignified throughout. They had, according to one report, behaved with more restraint than certain of the conservative faculty members.[62] Since the dispute had originated in a manifest display of pettiness by one of the teachers, the students' protest found a good deal of support outside the school. Wang Feng-tsao offered his resignation as principal and Sheng Hsüan-huai himself appealed to the students to return. About one-third did so, but the majority declined.[63]

I have described this incident in some detail because the students' behavior and the issues involved are quite typical of the rash of similar incidents that occurred during late 1902 and 1903 in modern schools scattered throughout China. Individually these affairs often were not greatly important, but taken together they show widespread student dissatisfaction at that time. Those who withdrew from school were forced to find another school or find an occupation. If they founded a new school of their own, their rebelliousness was institutionalized and nourished rather than being dissipated in a single incident. This course was also followed in a number of other cities, but the Patriotic School established by the Nan-yang students was the best known institution of its type and made the greatest contribution to the development of the revolutionary movement.

The Patriotic School

Almost immediately after the withdrawal, steps were taken to provide new facilities for those students who wished to continue their education in Shanghai. Ts'ai Yüan-p'ei, as a member of the Educational Association, was a key figure in working out the arrangement. The students determined to establish a school and appealed to the Educational Association to aid it by supplying teachers, funds for the school and for study abroad, and by helping finance and write articles for a student paper. Progressive bookstores were requested to donate textbooks and supplies.[64] Within three days the Patriotic School was more or less operative. Ts'ai Yüan-p'ei was chosen principal with Wu Chih-hui as his assistant,[65] and a three-story house was rented in the International Settlement. The Educational Association offices were moved to the ground floor and the top two floors were occupied by the school. Classes were held on the second floor and the top floor was used as a dormitory for students without relatives in Shanghai.[66]

The establishment of the Patriotic School led to a reorientation of the Educational Association. It had already become directly involved in teaching a month before when a number of members established the Patriotic Girls' School (*Ai-kuo nü-hsüeh-hsiao*). This school lent its name to the Patriotic School, but it was otherwise a secondary undertaking. After November the main functions of the Educational Association were connected with the operation of the Patriotic School. The two organizations remained separate entities. However, most students became members of the association and a number of the original members of the association taught at the school.[67]

The first effect of the Patriotic School was to greatly increase the need for money. The Educational Association had already received a donation from Huang Tsung-yang's patron, Lo Chia-ling. Huang now approached her again and received a considerable sum, 10,000 yuan according to one source.[68] Ts'ai Yüan-p'ei obtained another sizable amount from K'uai Kuang-tien, a liberal expectant taotai who was serving under the governor-general in Nanking.[69] With these and other lesser donations it was possible to start the school. Operating expenses were kept as low as possible. Student allowances were very small and those with family in the area did not receive any financial help.[70] Teachers held other jobs and served without pay, with the possible exception of a Western woman who taught advanced English courses.[71] The school's financial problems were alleviated when it became linked with *Su-pao* early in 1903. Members of the school wrote articles for the paper in return for a monthly donation of a hundred yuan.[72] Money remained a problem, however. In the spring of 1903 Huang Tsung-yang was elected president of the Educational Association in place of Ts'ai Yüan-p'ei. Some members felt that because he was a Buddhist he would not be suitable, but Wu Chih-hui overcame these objections by pointing out that Huang was their most successful fund raiser. Unfortunately, after his election he did not succeed in bringing in any more large sums.[73]

Despite financial uncertainties the Patriotic School flourished. The nucleus of students from the Nan-yang Public Institute was increased by youths who withdrew from other schools. The largest addition was a group who came to Shanghai in May 1903 after resigning from the Nanking Military Academy (*Nan-ching lu-shih hsüeh-t'ang*).[74] Initially the Patriotic School students invited other groups who withdrew to join them. With these additions the school had to rent more space for classrooms and locate an empty lot where students could drill.[75] Expansion strained the school's limited resources. During the spring it announced several times in *Su-pao* that it was full and hoped that students who withdrew from schools in other cities would found their own institutions or at least wait until the Patriotic School had a chance to expand gradually before coming to Shanghai.[76] It is hard to say how many students actually attended the school. At its height there were well over a hundred.[77]

In addition to genuine scholars and students, the school and associated organizations also attracted a number of people of lower social status who became attached in a variety of capacities. These men were literate, but they could not be considered members of the scholar class. They were of a type frequently attracted to the secret societies. One such person was Ch'ien Yün-sheng, a vagrant from Chinkiang who was a secret society member with a criminal record which eventually forced him to flee to Shanghai. He had already met and worked for one of the radical reformers in Chinkiang. In Shanghai he attended the meetings in Chang's Garden and claimed to be a member of the Triads sent by Sun Yat-sen to raise money and foment revolution. Ch'en Fan trusted him and Ch'en's daughter employed him on the *Women's Journal* although other prominent members of the group were strongly suspicious of him. In Chinkiang, Ch'ien had become a Christian to try to evade the law. There he was a "rice Christian." In Shanghai he was probably a "rice revolutionary."

A somewhat more respectable character was a colorful Kwangtungese named Hsü Ching-wu. Hsü was commonly known by the nickname of Great King of the Prostitutes (literally wild chickens—*Yeh-chi ta-wang*) because of his lurid newspaper stories about prostitution. In 1903 Hsü wrote for *The Gaiety Journal* (*Fan-hua pao*) and also specialized in selling revolutionary literature in his bookshop and in various teahouses along Foochow Road. On Sundays he and his daughter gave revolutionary speeches in one of the local parks. After the Patriotic School and Patriotic Girls' School were established, they worked for those organizations.[78]

The organization of the school's administration and curriculum reflected the temper of the students. They had left their old schools to gain greater freedom and were in no mood to submit to another strict regimen. Now they wanted to control their own affairs, discuss current politics and "advanced theories," display their patriotism, hold meetings, and do a little studying in between. Discipline was a particularly touchy question. Those in charge were usually students themselves and so were accorded only limited authority. In addition, they were not supposed to use harsh language toward trouble makers, but to rely on gentle remonstration and persuasion. The student body was divided into groups of twenty or thirty, each of which elected a head. These groups debated questions of rewards or discipline. Really serious offenses might be debated by an assembly of the whole school. Unruly students might receive major demerits or be expelled after they had accumulated three.[79] However, it was not as simple a matter as at the Nan-yang Public Institute. Administration also was in the hands of the students, and officers were kept to a minimum. There was a president, an executive secretary, an inspector of students, and a treasurer.[80] Under this system very little "tyranny" was practiced.

Teaching arrangements for the more conventional courses were rather loose. The school was divided into a regular and upper division of two years each. The formal curriculum called for the study of ethics, mathematics, science, Chinese literature, geography, history, English, and gymnastics during the first two years. In the third year students took moral philosophy, mathematics, biology, Chinese literature, psychology, logic, Japanese, English, and gymnastics. The fourth year was to be devoted to mathematics, chemistry, Chinese literature, sociology, principles of nationalism, economics, government, law, English, and gymnastics.[81] It seems doubtful, however, that all these courses were taught. By far the best instruction was offered by older scholars from the Educational Association such as Ts'ai, Wu, Chang, and Chiang Wei-ch'iao. For the rest, the school relied on whomever it could get. Students who were at all qualified also taught some courses like English and mathematics,[82] but they were hardly able to conduct satisfactory classes. The problem of maintaining a competent faculty coupled with the amount of time the students spent on military drill and extracurricular political activities meant that the educational level of the school was rather low. One student left for Japan because he believed that in Japan he could study as well as work for the revolution. At the Patriotic School he found no time for study.[83]

Most of the students were mainly interested in precisely those activities which interfered with their academic studies. For the first time they were completely free to discuss Western political theories and demonstrate their patriotism and love of liberty. A school publication, *Student World* (*Hsüeh-sheng shih-chieh*), brought their ideas into print.[84] The Educational Association, including Patriotic School students after November, held weekly meetings in Chang's Garden to discuss current topics. After the lunar New Year these gatherings were formalized under the name of a debating society and the content of the speeches became increasingly radical.[85]

Military drill, which was part of the school's curriculum, was also time-consuming. Besides the initial courses at the school, the Educational Association established a physical-education association on March 15. Members were supposed to obtain additional recruits and eventually to return to their homes to train others. Thus the movement for physical education would spread from Shanghai to the interior of the country and begin the creation of a militant citizenry. About a hundred students initially signed up for the physical-education course.[86] Probably most, but not necessarily all, were from the Patriotic School. It is not clear what happened to this group; it may have been lost in the more extreme agitation against Russia which was soon to occur. It is, however, interesting to note that even before they were incensed by the new Manchurian developments the radicals' nationalism was leading them to think in terms of directly mobilizing the masses. Such work did not have to be coupled with revolutionary agitation, but it was unlikely to be approved by the government and could very easily become subversive. After the beginning of the anti-Russian agitation, student military activities intensified. The initial lack of instructors was remedied when the students from the Nanking Military Academy arrived. In May a more formal student army was organized on the model of the Volunteer Corps in Tokyo. It, too, soon took the name of Association for the Education of a Militant People.[87]

The complex of radical student groups was completed by the Patriotic Girls' School, which outlasted the Patriotic School to provide a link between the organizations of 1902–03 and the Restoration Society. This school was founded on October 24 by members of the Educational Association interested in women's education. Chiang Chih-yu, who later became a constitutionalist, was the first principal. Among the other sponsors were Ts'ai Yüan-p'ei, Huang Tsung-yang, the Fukienese radical Lin Hsieh, and Ch'en Fan.[88] The first students were female members of the families of the founders. Most of them were mature women with family duties and so many dropped out. Before long only about ten remained. A change came when Chiang left for Japan and was succeeded as head of the school by Ts'ai Yüan-p'ei. Ts'ai moved the school to a new location near the Patriotic School and opened the enrollment to all girls qualified to enter. Many of the teachers at the Patriotic School also taught at the Girls' School. Ch'en Hsieh-fen, the daughter of the *Su-pao* publisher, was active in its administration.[89] Under this stimulus the number of students began to expand and the school provided girls with some of the same sort of patriotic and democratic fare available at the Patriotic School.[90] Ch'en Hsieh-fen also published the *Women's Journal* (*Nü-pao*, also referred to as *Nü Su-pao*), a short-lived female counterpart to her father's paper, which advocated women's rights and women's education.[91]

The Patriotic School soon became a model for similar ventures elsewhere. Members of the Educational Association were sent to organize branches in Chekiang and Kiangsu. One was founded at Ch'ang-shu and another at T'ung-li in Wu-chiang district. This latter branch most closely copied the prototype at Shanghai. There was a subsidiary Youth Association, which was a quasi-school open to boys ten to sixteen years of age. Military drill and calisthenics were taught by a physical-education association. In addition there was a debating society. Girls could pursue similar studies in the Ming-hua Girls' School.[92] Independently established schools also followed the pattern pioneered by the Patriotic School. Among these were the later Mutual Assistance Primary School (*Li-tse hsiao-hsüeh-hsiao*) in Shanghai, the Central Kiangsu Public Institute (*Wu-chung kung-hsüeh*) in Soochow, and the school founded by students who withdrew from Chekiang College in April 1903.[93] In May, Anking students founded a

Patriotic Society (*Ai-kuo hui*) and announced their desire to cooperate with the Patriotic School.[94] A group that withdrew from the T'ao-hua ling Middle School in Hupeh consciously followed the example set by the Nan-yang Public Institute malcontents and founded another Patriotic School.[95]

The Patriotic School's appeal to restless students was obvious enough. As much a society as a school, it offered unusual freedom and ample time for philosophical discussions or political demonstrations. There the radicals attempted to put their educational theories into practice. Modern subjects dominated the curriculum. Military drill and physical education were to foster the skills and attitudes needed by a militant citizenry. The aim of developing an independent, pioneering spirit overshadowed considerations of academic excellence.[96] Of course, as a practical matter the educational import of the school was negligible, but its political contribution was considerable. The radicalizing influence of its environment on both students and teachers was almost immediate.

Su-pao: The Acquisition of an Organ of Propaganda

Early in 1903 the institutional complex about the Patriotic School was completed by the agreement whereby teachers and students wrote articles for the newspaper *Su-pao* in return for a monthly donation. This arrangement had distinct advantages for both sides. The school needed money and a means to answer its conservative critics.[97] Ch'en Fan, the owner of *Su-pao,* already had connections with the school. One of the students was his nephew[98] and Ch'en also had previously been friendly with major members of the Educational Association. Now he acquired a talented writing staff and an entrée into the new market being created by modern students.

When *Su-pao* first appeared there was no suggestion of the radical climax which was to come in 1903. The paper was founded as a trade journal in 1896 by Hu Chang, who named his Japanese wife as owner. This stratagem allowed him to enjoy the legal advantages of extraterritoriality by registering the paper with the Japanese consulate. *Su-pao* had close connections with Japanese officials and was in effect the Shanghai organ of the Japanese government. Despite these advantages, it suffered from indifferent management and had a checkered career punctuated by a number of lawsuits. In 1899 it was bought by Ch'en Fan.[99]

Ch'en was a native of Hunan who later moved to Kiangsu.[100] He was a reformer who held a *chü-jen* degree and became involved in revolutionary activities almost in spite of himself. In 1903 he was forty-three years old and, therefore, a good deal older than most of the students with whom he worked.

His desire to modernize and strengthen China was undoubtedly sincere and once he became committed to the revolutionary movement he remained loyal to it. In his personal habits, however, he seems to have been relatively conservative. Among other things he kept concubines, which was hardly in accord with radical morality.[101]

Ch'en had a rather unlucky life. He first became disillusioned with the Ch'ing government as a result of personal misfortunes. His elder brother was sentenced to life imprisonment for his part in the 1898 Reform Movement.[102] Shortly after that Ch'en was dismissed from his post as magistrate of Ch'ien-shan district, Kiangsi, because of an attack on missionaries in the area under his jurisdiction. Angry and disgusted with the vicissitudes of official life, Ch'en moved to Shanghai intending to promote modern education to save China. The Boxer Rebellion was a further shock which helped to push Ch'en in a radical direction. It is not clear whether he went to Japan at any time in 1901 or 1902, but his name appears as one of the eight founders of the Hunan Translation Society, which began to publish *Translations by Students Abroad* in late 1902. This magazine contained translations of Japanese and Western works which the editors believed would be helpful in building a strong China.[103]

When Ch'en bought *Su-pao* he first published writings of Liang Ch'i-ch'ao and K'ang Yu-wei and called for protection of the emperor against the empress-dowager and for the establishment of a constitution. He was assisted in operating the paper by his brother-in-law Wang Wen-p'u, his son, and his daughter, who was also a competent essayist. Ch'en began to move toward a more radical position at the end of 1902 when his paper published an article entitled "Student Tides" (*Hsüeh-chieh feng-ch'ao*) which supported the position of the Nan-yang Public Institute students.[104] After *Su-pao* became the organ of the Patriotic School its articles followed the trend of student politics in Shanghai that spring. The final shift to an openly revolutionary position in June was not Ch'en's idea, but he condoned it and from then on was associated with the revolutionary movement.[105]

During the spring of 1903 *Su-pao* became the newspaper of the new student circles in China. Its interests and influence were not limited to Shanghai, although it particularly recorded student activities in that city. It also carried news about modern schools in many parts of China. Most of the reports concerned Kiangsu or Chekiang, but items can be found about schools in at least nine other provinces. At least occasional issues of the paper must have reached many cities,[106] for students in widely scattered schools looked to the paper to represent their views. Letters were received from as far away as Hunan, Hupeh, and Peking.

Su-pao made a special point of reporting student strikes and describing examples of "decadence" (*fu-pai*) in conventional schools. It presents a fascinating chronicle of student unrest during the spring of 1903 which shows that dissatisfaction was widespread and that students throughout China were disturbed by the same general problems. The most frequently mentioned complaints were faculty refusal to permit free discussions of current events or prohibitions against reading "new books" and unfair punishment or expulsion of students. There were also an equal number of accusations of general "tyranny," conservatism, and corruption.[107] Other complaints were incidental. What modern students everywhere wanted was more personal freedom and a genuine modernization of the content of education.

Editorials and other articles likewise represented advanced student views and contain the same general ideas found in all radical student publications in 1903. There are the familiar themes of the Darwinian struggle for existence, the imperialist threat to national existence, the ignorance and barbarism of the Chinese people, and the call for self-sacrifice to build a strong China. Chinese are urged to promote modern education, industrialize the country, strengthen the armies, honor military virtues and physical exercise, and promote women's rights and equality in general. The *Su-pao* articles during the spring of 1903 contain few surprises. If there is any particular characteristic of the paper's message, it is an unusual emphasis on the role of education in regenerating China, which reflects the concerns of the Educational Association. This preoccupation appears in the large number of news items about modern schools and in articles on educational theory as well. Particularly during February and early March one finds articles valuing education for its own sake as well as for its political significance.[108]

It is difficult to distinguish any decisive trend toward radicalization in *Su-pao* during the spring before the sudden change that occurred when Chang Shih-chao became editor on June 1. Scattered calls for revolution appeared throughout the spring, but so did articles proposing long-term reformist solutions and criticisms of anti-Manchuism.[109] Before June the specifically political message of *Su-pao* was unclear. One reason why this was so was caution: anti-Manchu statements in speeches made in Chang's Garden were usually omitted to avoid trouble.[110] Another was that the *Su-pao* editors before June were less radical than the most extreme members of the Educational Association. However, a more basic reason why *Su-pao* avoided attacks on the government through most of the spring was perhaps that the distinction between reform and revolution was still ambiguous to many intellectuals. The political implications of the general radicalism in student circles were not yet fully clear.

Although the possibilities were not immediately realized, the institutional ingredients for an irrevocable break with the government existed once *Su-pao* became linked with the Patriotic School. Radical attacks made only at local meetings might have been overlooked by the Ch'ing government, but they could not be ignored when they began to appear in print in June in a daily which found its way to modern schools in many cities and towns. The path which was to lead to the arrests at the end of June was open and we may now turn to the events which formed the immediate background of the open proclamation of revolutionary intent.

During the spring of 1903 the Educational Association, Patriotic School, and *Su-pao* operated in an atmosphere of growing unrest. These three organizations played a leading role in attacks on Ch'ing policy, but they by no means manufactured the discontent. There was a more complex interaction whereby events pushed the radicals toward an openly revolutionary stand while, at the same time, participation of the Patriotic School group in general protest meetings and demonstrations raised the intensity of opposition. The result of the spring's activities was the *Su-pao* case, which dramatized the break between the radical intellectuals and the government.

The Meetings in Chang's Garden

Nationalistic distress over China's foreign position which welled up at that time was expressed most sharply in a series of public meetings at the merchant and newspaper promoter Chang Su-ho's Garden (commonly called simply *Chang-yüan* in Chinese sources) in late April and May. The grounds of this park contained halls suitable for large audiences and the garden had been a favorite spot for political gatherings for several years.[1] The major meetings in the spring of 1903 were called in response to two situations: first, the rumor that Kwangsi Governor Wang Chih-ch'un had requested French aid to suppress a persistent rebellion in his province and, second, the revelation of additional Russian demands in Manchuria. Moderates as well as revolutionaries participated in the agitation, but in the end the latter emerged as a separate and militant group. The meetings had marked influence on both the radical shift in *Su-pao*'s policy and the Chinese government's determination to check the antidynastic trend in student circles.

The trouble began about April 22 when natives of Kwangtung and Kwangsi living in Shanghai heard rumors that Governor Wang had requested a loan and troops from the French in Indochina in return for mining and railway concessions.[2] The alleged request was prompted by a secret society rebellion which spread throughout Kwangsi in 1902 and 1903. The fluid situation produced by dissolving and reappearing bands was extremely difficult to control and Wang was in trouble with the Peking authorities because of his failures.[3]

About the same time as the news came from the south a telegram was sent to the Chinese Educational Association from students in Japan also telling of Wang's intentions.[4] Merchants in Shanghai telegraphed Cantonese merchants in Saigon and Hanoi and received from them confirmation that Governor Wang had signed, or was about to sign, an agreement. On the evening of April 23 a meeting of Kwangsi natives was held at their Kweilin Club. They sent telegrams to highly placed fellow provincials, such as the vice-presidents of the Boards of War and Public Works, the governor of Szechwan, and the governor-general designate of Kwangtung and Kwangsi, asking their help in stopping Wang's plan.[5]

On April 25 notices were posted calling for a meeting of natives of the Liang-Kuang provinces in Chang's Garden later that day. These notices told of Wang's plans and stated that once French troops entered Kwangsi the province would not be returned intact to China. The meeting attracted a crowd of three hundred to five hundred gentry, merchants, and students[6] who filled a large hall at the garden. The chairman was Lung Tse-hou, a scholar from Kwangsi and a follower of Liang Ch'i-ch'ao, who was to play an important role in the meetings.[7] Speeches were made by both reformers and radicals, including some members of the Educational Association. Many talks were patriotic, but fairly moderate in tone. One speaker called attention to the behavior of foreign troops in 1900 and to the Russian troops currently in Manchuria. A second man dwelt on the general danger of inviting foreign troops into a country, giving the example of the Britons who were conquered by Picts and Saxons after the Saxons had been asked to help against the Scots. Another denied that the situation was similar to the 1860's, when the British gave aid against the Taiping rebels, and a Hunanese announced that he was ashamed of the way his fellow provincial, Governor Wang, was selling out the country.[8] Certain suggestions, such as the proposal that the empress-dowager retire on a pension for life,[9] were unlikely to gain much good will in Peking. As a group the Educational Association speakers warned that all Chinese must oppose the arrangement with the French, for it presaged the division of the entire country. Wu Chih-hui drew a picture of Wang calling in French troops to save his own position when unable to suppress a determined rebellion against official repression. The most radical proposal was a call for training militia throughout China. Banks should contribute funds and students take the lead in organizing forces. This suggestion anticipated ideas that were behind the student armies organized against Russia a few

days later.[10] At the end of the meeting a telegram was sent to Peking protesting Wang's action as a precedent which would give the powers a lever for
demands on China and asking that Wang be dismissed from office.[11]

The meeting broke up about 6:00 P.M. The next day a second meeting
was held at the Kwangtung Guildhouse. This one was also well attended
and attracted some of the wealthier and more prominent Chinese who
had hesitated to attend the more public demonstration at Chang's Garden.
Lung Tse-hou was there, but the Educational Association held its annual
meeting that same day, so its members could not attend. At this second
meeting it was resolved to telegraph other areas to ask for support. Strikes
and boycotts were proposed to bring an end to the agreement with France
and secure Wang's dismissal.[12]

This agitation in Shanghai and elsewhere obtained its immediate objective.
French troops never were invited into Kwangsi and Wang was dismissed
and his rank reduced.[13] Among the intellectuals in Shanghai the question
of Wang held the center for only a few days. It served as a prelude to the
more radical demonstrations which immediately followed against the new
Russian moves in Manchuria. The anti-Wang demonstrations had been
initiated and mainly financed by gentry and merchants. A considerable
number of students took part, but the Educational Association did not
contribute toward telegraphic expenses.[14] The meetings were patriotic
and agitated, but on the whole they were directed against Wang rather
than the central government which the participants sought to influence.

Many of the same people, notably Lung Tse-hou, took part in the anti-
Russian meetings. However, students formed a high percentage of the
audience, and the leadership was more in the hands of the radicals. It
would be a mistake to consider the anti-Russian movement a revolutionary
inspired demonstration. The first anti-Russian meeting was summoned
by a merchant, who also paid its expenses, and reformers and constitutionalists were among its leaders.[15] A large segment of the informed populace
was disturbed by the government's Manchurian policy. As in Japan the
Shanghai protests were spontaneous and, at first, not necessarily antigovernment. However, the radicals quickly abandoned any thought of
influencing Ch'ing policy. Before the anti-Russian demonstrations there
were revolutionaries at the Patriotic School and in the Chinese Educational
Association. After the beginning of May the groups can be called genuinely
revolutionary organizations.

The first anti-Russian meeting was held in Chang's Garden on April
27. The majority of the audience and most of the speakers were students
or teachers from modern schools. There were also some men of substantial

wealth present, as demonstrated by the donation of a diamond ring worth over a thousand Mexican silver dollars when subscriptions were called for at the end of the meeting.[16] A telegram was sent to the Wai-wu pu which declared that "if the government consents to the Russian demands it will on the one hand abandon its sovereignty in internal affairs and on the other invite great bloodshed from abroad." The people, it affirmed, would reject such a treaty. A second telegram was sent to the ambassadors of the foreign powers saying that even if the government should consent to the Russian demands, the Chinese people would never recognize the agreement. Russia, not China, would be responsible for revived hostility and any ensuing attacks on foreigners.[17]

At the end of the meeting a committee was established to plan further meetings and raise funds. It was first called the Committee of the Four Social Classes (*Ssu-min tsung-hui*), but this name was changed to Citizens' Committee (*Kuo-min kung-hui*) at the second mass meeting on the Manchurian question. The new name was intended to emphasize the aim of awakening the spirit of citizenship in China's subservient people so they might enjoy their natural rights and play their part in safeguarding the nation.[18] The organization planned to establish a council hall where people could discuss current affairs.[19] Feng Ching-ju, then manager of the reformist Bookshop for Diffusion of Knowledge, was the principal founder of the society. Among the other leaders were Tsou Jung, Ch'en Fan, Huang Tsung-yang, Ts'ai Yüan-p'ei, and Lung Tse-hou.[20] It was at first a heterogeneous body of revolutionaries, reformers, and those who could not be classified in either group. Many of the major figures were members of the Educational Association, but they did not take the initiative in establishing the committee and the initial expenses were paid by the constitutionalist agency for *The Renovation of the People*. Radicals and moderates were still cooperating.

On April 30 a second mass meeting was held under the chairmanship of Ts'ai Yüan-p'ei. About twelve hundred people attended, a sizable percentage coming from the Patriotic School and the Yü-ts'ai School, another modern school in Shanghai. A number of girls from the Patriotic Girls' School were also present. This meeting was perhaps more militantly patriotic than the first. After the reading of the procedural rules two verses of a patriotic song were sung. Ts'ai Yüan-p'ei then read a telegram from students in Tokyo telling of their plans to form a Volunteer Corps and asking for support in Shanghai. Lung Tse-hou rose and asked whether they could remain idle while the Tokyo group had shown its patriotism. He proposed that all who agreed should go outside the hall and salute the students in

Japan. Most of the assembly followed him outside and lined up in rows facing northeast, where they bowed in the direction of Japan. Upon returning they drafted a reply to the students in Tokyo and another telegram to Peking offering military volunteers. A committee was selected to raise funds for a corps.[21]

After these meetings a Volunteer Corps was established on the model of the corps in Tokyo. Most of its members were drawn from the physical-education association of the Educational Association and from students at the Patriotic and Yü-ts'ai schools.[22] The corps had more enthusiasm than formal organization and daily drills helped keep student excitement at a high pitch.

Under the pressure of growing radicalism the cooperation between reformers and revolutionaries, which had still existed during the anti-Russian meetings, came to an end. The first rift in the Citizens' Committee occurred almost immediately over the question of establishing a Volunteer Corps.[23] The final break came in June, when Lung Tse-hou suggested changing its name to the Citizens' Association for Parliamentary Government (*Kuo-min i-cheng hui*) with the aim of demanding a constitution from the Ch'ing government. Revolutionaries on the committee could not agree to this proposal and withdrew. The entire Patriotic School group divorced itself from the committee, which gradually dissolved.[24]

The students followed their own path and the Patriotic School sponsored its own public meetings.[25] About this time students also began to make their first contacts with secret societies outside Shanghai. Chang Shih-chao and others traveled along the Yangtze distributing revolutionary literature.[26] This significant departure was, however, cut short by the arrests at the end of June. The revolutionaries still mainly engaged in open propaganda and verbal attacks on the government and these reached a climax in *Su-pao* during the month of June.

Publication of Defiance: *Su-pao's* Radical Period

The enthusiastic radicalism of the students at the Patriotic School even infected more moderate members of the group. Among these was Ch'en Fan, who on May 27 took the decisive step of requesting Chang Shih-chao[27] to edit his paper. Chang was the most able of the students who had come to the Patriotic School from the Nanking Military Academy. He was a sworn brother of Chang Ping-lin, Tsou Jung, and Chang Chi[28] and thoroughly shared their revolutionary views. According to Chang Shih-chao, Ch'en was not aware of how extreme Chang's views were when he offered him the job as editor. Ch'en, he believed, wanted to advocate the current trends of progressive thought among the intellectuals to further increase the circulation of his newspaper, but was not in favor of all-out revolution. Chang had attracted Ch'en's attention by writing articles suitable for this purpose. According to Wu Chih-hui, Ch'en also thought Chang would make a likely husband for his daughter, but Chang afterwards denied knowledge of any such motive. Whatever Ch'en's intentions, he was in for a rude shock. Chang's first act as editor was to draft an article entitled "All Chinese Authorities Are Revolutionaries" (*Lun Chung-kuo tang-tao chieh ko-ming-tang*). Early next morning Ch'en called on Chang, who was still in bed, and angrily let him know that the paper could not publish such material because it would bring trouble with the government.[29] However, that evening Ch'en told Chang he could have a free hand. Chang immediately took advantage of this permission and from then on *Su-pao* was operated as a revolutionary journal. Ch'en had been right, it did bring trouble with the government.

Chang Shih-chao called upon some of the most radical members of the Educational Association, who obliged him with a series of articles so extreme that it is surprising, even considering the journal's protected location in the International Settlement, that it was able to continue for another month. The revolutionaries could not resist the temptation to carry out a traditional moral crusade. Not only did the government have to be destroyed, but it had to be constantly told how and why it was to be destroyed. *Su-pao* sought to write a revolution into being. In the end it achieved some propagandistic success, but only at the expense of the closing of the paper and the Patriotic School. The *Su-pao* case was the first example of what was to be a persistent pattern in the course of the Lower Yangtze revolutionary movement. The intellectual revolutionaries, often at great personal sacrifice, gained publicity for their cause, but at the cost of destroying their institutional base.

Like the later Ta-t'ung School in Chekiang, the Educational Association–Patriotic School–*Su-pao* combination recalls the late Ming dynasty Tung-lin Academy that gave its name to the movement that sought to combat eclectic and iconoclastic philosophical tendencies among the literati and the decay of political morality at the court.[30] The parallel is not one of purpose, but of style, technique, and choice of institutions from which to operate. The Tung-lin partisans were one of the most famous examples of the moralistic, generally conservative expressors of righteous criticism (*ch'ing-i*) who appeared throughout Chinese history whenever segments of the literati and officialdom believed the integrity of the Confucian order was in danger.[31] The revolutionaries had a different message, but they, too, were convinced of their moral superiority and sought to expose the evil degeneracy of their opponents. Unlike the Tung-lin group, most revolutionaries believed that sweeping institutional changes were necessary, but they still devoted much space to combating what they thought was the moral decline of the Chinese. They also were drawn to attack quixotically antagonists stronger than they. The Tung-lin Academy achieved permanent moral fame, but, in the relatively static atmosphere of the Ming, it had no lasting political effect after its destruction by the eunuch Wei Chung-hsien. The revolutionary intellectuals, too, won moral recognition and in a period of change their movement was not blocked by individual defeats. They did, however, gradually deplete their resources so that the movement in many places was eventually controlled by sympathizers whose aims were only partly the same as those of the original revolutionary group.

Student revolutionaries found it harder to discard the Confucian temperament than the Confucian ideology, and this observation points to the persistence of a general literati oppositional style in Chinese politics. This style was characterized by moralistic criticism, frequent immoderation, and personal vilification of opponents. It had traditionally been encouraged by such factors as a political theory that called for government by virtue, absolute imperial rule that even at its most tolerant discouraged stable political groupings, and the twin influences of palace politics and Confucian particularism that encouraged personal factions. The old habits continued after Chinese political life began to change in the late nineteenth century and in the twentieth century. They were reflected in frequent libels published by the press, in the charges hurled by the revolutionaries and other opponents of the Ch'ing dynasty, and in the quarrels among politicians during the Republic. The savage condemnations of opponents of Mao Tse-tung during the cultural revolution are also in line with this tradition.

Whatever the other drawbacks of this approach, it could produce effective propaganda. The June *Su-pao* articles, Tsou Jung's *The Revolutionary Army*, which *Su-pao* reviewed,[32] and Chang Ping-lin's "Letter Disputing K'ang Yu-wei," which was published in the paper, together formed a body of literature marking the emergence of a revolutionary movement in Shanghai. All were basic reading for modern-minded students. The unusually violent and uncompromising material printed in *Su-pao* during its last month made other radical journals of the day seem relatively tame. The provocative contents of articles were enhanced by printing words and phrases such as "revolution" and "oppose the Manchus" in boldface.

No possibility of compromise with the government was admitted. Although *Su-pao* joined in publishing rumors in early June that the two representatives sent from Tokyo by the Volunteer Corps to Oppose Russia to see Yüan Shih-k'ai were to be executed, the paper, perhaps with some benefit of hindsight, was strongly critical of their mission. Why after developing revolutionary and nationalistic spirits should the students contradictorily oppose the Russians instead of the Manchus and beg favors from their enemies? Since Manchuria was the domain of the Manchus it was not the business of Chinese to try to protect it when the Manchus themselves failed to do so. If the student representatives were accused of being rebellious and threatened with execution for their pains, they had only themselves to blame. They should not have tried to help the Manchus, thereby inviting a certain rebuff.[33]

This rigid attitude was extended to the reform movement as well. The radical organizations in Shanghai had members who could still be more properly classified as reformers rather than revolutionaries, but they did not set the tone at *Su-pao*. Some attacks went beyond the usual objections to the hollowness of a constitution granted by a tyrannical and foreign government, impugning the sincerity of the reformers themselves. K'ang Yu-wei was described as being willing to compromise with the Manchus because he was greedy for honors and office.[34] One article even hinted that if he assumed office, as it was evidently falsely rumored he might, he might be in danger of assassination.[35] Much more moderate and reasoned attacks on the reformist position were also published[36] and a plea was even made for cooperation between constitutionalists and revolutionaries in opposing the Manchu government.[37] The burden of the *Su-pao* articles, however, was to open a gulf between revolution and reform.

In keeping with the paper's generally uncompromising tone, a considerable number of articles directly advocated killing Manchus. This approach sometimes took the form of praise of anarchism. Russian tyranny nourished the terrorism of the nihilist party. In Russia the nihilists succeeded in bringing about reforms, and the Chinese should awake and borrow their method of assassinations.[38] More often articles simply exhorted Chinese to murder Manchus. Four hundred million Chinese should be able to slay the emperor as easily "as pushing over a rotten tree."[39] "Only when we have finished killing the Manchus will we stay our hands."[40] Such statements, of course, added to the inflammatory potential of the paper and figured in the charges brought against the defendants in the *Su-pao* trial.

The flamboyant radicalism and anti-Manchuism of some of the *Su-pao* articles probably did not mean that the Shanghai students were more militant than those in Tokyo or elsewhere. The explanation may partly lie in the combination of the journalistic talents of Chang Shih-chao and the influence of Chang Ping-lin, who was a master of anti-Manchu invective.[41] The atmosphere at the Patriotic School and the *Su-pao* offices encouraged unrestrained expression which found its way into print. Other articles directly reflected the students' élan and sense of importance. They saw themselves as leaders initiating China into a new age. They were "the primary motive force of the entire country and the mothers (*sic*) of the progress of civilization."[42] Students in Paris, Vienna, and Berlin were credited with having overthrown governments during the nineteenth century. Students had created the worldwide revolutionary tide.[43] Chinese students should not do less, and it was precisely because they were forsaking this vanguard role that the student representatives from Japan were criticized for trying to offer their services to Yüan Shih-k'ai. In the end this euphoria contributed to the downfall of both *Su-pao* and the Patriotic School.

The End of the Beginning

Strains Within the Revolutionary Camp

Perhaps under the stress of uncertainties created by *Su-pao*'s constant trumpeting of revolutionary intentions, antagonisms among the radicals suddenly welled up in June, leading to a split between the Educational Association and the Patriotic School in the middle of the month. There had, for some time, been disagreements between two groups in the Educational Association. The more extreme wished to use the association and the Patriotic School as frankly revolutionary organs. Among those who held this dominant view were Chang Ping-lin and Wu Chih-hui, but Ts'ai Yüan-p'ei was their chief spokesman. Others, headed by the Chekiangese scholar Yeh Han, believed that it was more important to concentrate on education. They were convinced that the people's knowledge had to be broadened as a prerequisite for any more specific steps in the resurrection of China. Revolutionary activities unquestionably got in the way of learning and, therefore, ought to be curbed.[44]

This conflict between the goals of politics and learning was to be repeated several times in the various schools established as revolutionary fronts. It was really inherent in the choice of schools for this purpose, if only because it was necessary to make some pretext at offering a regular education for the sake of appearances. Nor could the revolutionaries treat education with complete cynicism, for their own ideology gave it an important place in the regeneration of China. Therefore, their schools inevitably attracted some students, teachers, and donors who were modernizers but who neither regarded education as synonymous with political propaganda nor believed it should be subordinated to revolutionary goals. Still other aspects of this problem became clear when the revolutionaries attempted to use schools as a political base outside the protection of the treaty ports; this development will be considered later as part of the history of the Ta-t'ung School in Chekiang. For the moment it is enough to point out that this problem was present from the beginning.

What really lay behind the break was a somewhat different conflict between the young students at the Patriotic School and the older scholars of the Educational Association. The students as a whole were a more militant group, and even those members of the Educational Association who were definitely revolutionaries had arrived at their views in a different way and had a much firmer grounding in traditional learning and culture than did their young protégés. The students, true to their rebellious record, resented what seemed to them to be the older scholars' interference in their affairs even when they were agreed on principles.

The basic issue was whether the school or the association would dominate.[45] Friction came to a head over a number of relatively minor points. Most important was the allocation of funds. Since the school had begun to receive a monthly donation from *Su-pao* it had become the wealthier organization. The students felt that the Educational Association was diverting funds that were rightfully theirs for its own purpose. Of course, some of the original association members were contributing articles to *Su-pao* in their capacity as teachers at the school and therefore thought that since they were helping to earn the money they had a right to influence how it was used. Perhaps related to this argument was a controversy between the students and the Educational Association over alleged irregularities in the accounts of the bookseller and propagandist Hsü Ching-wu, who was "business manager" of the Patriotic School. Lastly, personal conflicts envenomed the situation. Chang Ping-lin felt strongly that the association should be the dominant group. He had no sympathy with the students' position and in the end believed that the association should found a new school. Wu Chih-hui just as strongly took the part of the students. The two men began to dislike each other intensely and finally would not even attend meetings together.[46]

Ts'ai Yüan-p'ei and Huang Tsung-yang tried to act as mediators, but without effect. On the evening of June 12 an acrimonious meeting between students and representatives of the Educational Association took place. Chang Ping-lin declared that the school must be subordinate to the association and a student representative replied that without the school the association would have no place to carry on its activities. After more argument Ts'ai Yüan-p'ei walked out of the meeting in disgust. More walkouts followed. The next day Ts'ai announced that he was exasperated with both sides and was planning to go to Tsingtao, then a German concession, to improve his knowledge of that language in preparation for study abroad.[47] Despite efforts to dissuade him, Ts'ai left on June 18, and the next day the Patriotic School and the Educational Association formally split.[48]

There is no way of telling what the final outcome would have been because within two weeks the school had been closed by government officials and the Educational Association seriously depleted. Had the revolutionaries remained united they still would have been unable to prevent the closing of their organizations. However, a more cohesive group might have salvaged more after the arrests. The Chinese government was not in a strong position in the case and rapidly weakened itself further by the sort of mishandling that seemed almost invariably to characterize its attempts to crush revolutionaries. It was able to check the movement in Shanghai as much as it did because the revolutionaries themselves were divided and uncertain of their goals.

Government Response

Officials watching student circles in 1903 must have viewed the developments with growing alarm. Unrest was obvious, and even if most students were not revolutionaries they were radical enough for conservative officials to suspect they might be. Aside from their activities in Japan and Shanghai, students were already beginning to move out from those two centers into the interior of China. Moreover, in January some members of Sun Yat-sen's Society to Restore China's Prosperity had taken part in a rising in Canton. Finally, the peasant and secret society rising in Kwangsi was proving extremely difficult to quell, and few members of the government were clearly aware of distinctions between this traditional type of rebellion and the nascent revolutionary movement.[49] Not surprisingly, important officials argued that subversive ideas among the students had to be stamped out before they became uncontrollable. Government suspicion and confusion was summed up in a telegram from Peking to the provincial governors and governors-general. Students in Tokyo had formed a revolutionary party. The court feared that students returning to China would attempt a rising like T'ang Ts'ai-ch'ang's in 1900. Even if members of the Tokyo Volunteer Corps were sincere in their stated aim of defending China against

Russia they might upset the country's international relations as had the Boxers three years before. The whole movement was unfathomable (*p'o-tse*) and was best suppressed.[50]

Minister Ts'ai Chün in Japan and Commissioner of Trade Lü Hai-huan in Shanghai were particularly diligent in warning just how dangerous the students were. Ex-Governor Wang Chih-ch'un understandably felt no great affection for the students in Shanghai. He and his friends, who included Commissioner Lü, put pressure on the government to punish his critics.[51] These men all had influence, but the primary mover behind the *Su-pao* case was Tuan-fang, then acting governor-general of Hunan, Hupeh, and Kiangsi provinces.[52] Part Chinese and part Manchu, a reformer, and an extremely able administrator, Tuan-fang was one of the outstanding figures of the last decade of the Ch'ing dynasty.[53] He had taken part in the 1898 Reform Movement but had escaped punishment, and after 1900 he became a leader of the Manchu reform efforts. From 1901 to 1909 he held a series of governorships and governor-generalships in the Yangtze provinces. In these positions he promoted modernization of education, industry, and government administration. He was also one of the five special commissioners sent abroad to study Western political systems and make recommendations on the establishment of constitutional government in China.

Tuan-fang's philosophy was similar to the moderate reformism of Chang Chih-tung, who sought to introduce institutions responsible for Western strength and prosperity while preserving traditional Chinese culture. As a moderate, an official, and a Manchu he regarded revolution as an anathema and had little patience even with more innocent expressions of public opinion. He used all his considerable abilities to keep control over the radical students. His secret police and informers penetrated the revolutionary movement. He played a role in combating all the major revolutionary efforts in the Yangtze area through 1908 regardless of whether or not they occurred in areas under his jurisdiction. Consequently, he was thoroughly feared and disliked by the revolutionaries. In the end they had their revenge. Tuan-fang was sent to Szechwan in 1911 as acting governor-general to suppress opposition to the central government's railroad construction plans. Before he reached the provincial capital the Revolution broke out at Wuchang and he was murdered by mutinying soldiers under his command. Until then he had been a formidable opponent, however. His opposition was one important cause behind the lack of revolutionary success in Central China before 1911. The opening round took place in 1903.

Officials first seriously became alarmed about events in Shanghai at the time of the anti-Wang and anti-Russian meetings. At the end of May, Trade Commissioner Lü wrote the Manchu Kiangsu Governor En-shou that the "so-called enthusiastic youths" meeting in Chang's Garden were plotting revolution under the guise of protesting French and Russian acts.[54] After *Su-pao* began publishing revolutionary articles, the Patriotic School was watched by Chinese government spies and on June 11 an agent provocateur tried to induce Wu Chih-hui and Ts'ai Yüan-p'ei to address a meeting outside the International Settlement where they could be arrested by the Chinese police. [55] As a result of pressure on the International Settlement authorities, Wu Chih-hui was summoned to the police station for questioning six times during late May and June. Each time he was asked whether arms were hidden at the school.[56]

Not all the local and provincial Chinese officials wished to move against the Shanghai radicals, a factor which was eventually to be a great help to the revolutionaries. The governor-general of Kiangsu and Anhwei, Wei Kuang-tao, was a modernizer whose grandson was studying in Japan. Wei was perfectly loyal to the dynasty, but he was inclined to take a lenient view of student activities. He had also advised the Grand Council to resist Russian demands firmly, so he at least partly shared the views expressed at the meetings in Chang's Garden. Certain expectant officials, such as T'ao Sen-chia, Yü Ming-chen, and K'uai Kuang-tien, all of whom evidently had Wei's confidence, had personal ties with the radicals. K'uai had donated money to the Patriotic School. T'ao was a friend of Ts'ai Yüan-p'ei's and went to the Patriotic School several times to urge Ts'ai to modify his speeches so as not to alarm Peking.[57]

Under pressure from his subordinates, Lü Hai-huan and En-shou, and from Tuan-fang and Peking, Wei Kuang-tao finally had to act. Even so he was suspected of being too lenient by many other officials.[58] The case was at best difficult to handle because arrests could only be made with the agreement of the foreign consular corps and the Shanghai Municipal Council. Chinese officials, therefore, had to persuade skeptical Western authorities that the men they wanted had committed crimes that warranted their arrests. The first approaches were made by Lü Hai-huan, who initially requested the arrests of Ts'ai Yüan-p'ei, Wu Chih-hui, and the two students (who were in Shanghai at this time) sent from Japan to see Yüan Shih-k'ai. On a second occasion Lü asked for the arrests of Ts'ai, Wu, Huang Tsung-yang, and Feng Ching-ju. Both times he was refused by the Municipal Council. Therefore, Expectant Taotai Yü Ming-chen was sent from Nanking to work with Shanghai Taotai Yüan Shu-hsün to persuade the council to make arrests.[59]

The Chinese government weakened its position at the outset by stressing the allegedly subversive character of the mass meetings in Chang's Garden during late April.[60] In reply the Municipal Council unsympathetically pointed out that many of the charges made at these meetings, for instance the accusations against Governor Wang Chih-ch'un, had been widely made in the press and even by officials, so it was unfair to select men who had attended the meetings for punishment.[61] The council was evidently more amenable to the argument that the articles being published in *Su-pao* were treasonable. It remained firm, however, on two points. The arrests were to follow the usual International Settlement procedure of swearing out a warrant signed by the senior member of the consular body, and the prisoners were to be tried by the Mixed Court.

In the end the two taotais had to agree. A warrant was issued for the arrest of Ch'en Fan as owner of *Su-pao;* Chang Ping-lin, Tsou Jung, and Lung Tse-hou as rebels who wrote *The Revolutionary Army;* and Ch'ien Yün-sheng, Ch'en Chi-fu, and a nonexistent Ch'en Shu-ch'ou as "editors" of *Su-pao.* In justification the warrant cited a telegram from Kiangsu Governor En-shou in which he ordered the Shanghai Taotai to make arrests at the Patriotic School, "which gathers together unruly fellows to seduce them to discuss revolution, a situation tantamount to rebellion. . . ." It also referred to a telegram from Governor-General Wei ordering the arrest of those connected with *Su-pao* and the closing of the paper as the most "insolent" and "heedless" among those in Shanghai.[62] Although not mentioned, the Chang Garden meetings were still undoubtedly a major factor prompting the arrests. Lung Tse-hou was not a revolutionary and had no part in either *Su-pao* or the Patriotic School. He had, however, taken part in T'ang Ts'ai-ch'ang's rising in 1900 and called attention to himself by his prominent part in the meetings.[63]

The exact circumstances of the arrests were to become the subject of conflicting and acrimonious accounts among the revolutionaries, and the record is further confused by initial government misinformation about the identities or roles of those arrested. Two points seem clear, however. The Taotais Yüan Shu-hsün and Yü Ming-chen were reluctant to carry out their orders and none of the important figures would have been arrested if they had not been willing to be taken into custody.

Yüan Taotai, who throughout the case was caught between his superiors' orders and the realities of foreign power in Shanghai, may just have felt that the job was impossible on the terms Peking desired. Yü Ming-chen deliberately sought to subvert government policy because of personal friendships and his moderately reformist views. He provides an early example of the outside sympathizer who aided the revolutionaries without becoming involved in their movement. During the Sino-Japanese War, Yü had served in Taiwan and had played a part in the short-lived Republic of Taiwan organized by patriots on the island who had hoped to forestall cession to the victorious Japanese. After the Republic of Taiwan failed he retired to Nanking with the rank of expectant taotai. He refused to accept a regular administrative position; but he did become director of the Nanking Military Academy, a post he held at the time of the *Su-pao* case. His son had studied in Japan, where he had met Wu Chih-hui. The younger Yü was also a friend of Chang Shih-chao and evidently engaged in some revolutionary work.[64] Yü himself knew Ts'ai Yüan-p'ei and Wu Chih-hui. Chang Shih-chao, before his withdrawal, had been an outstanding student at the military academy and had received a prize awarded by Yü as director.[65]

Chang Shih-chao's name was not included among those to be arrested, although as editor of *Su-pao* he would have been a logical choice. It seems clear that he was excluded because of the previous teacher-student relationship between himself and Yü.[66] Ts'ai Yüan-p'ei had left Shanghai for Tsingtao before the arrests, so he was not a problem for Yü. However, Wu Chih-hui had been on the government's blacklist for some time and could not be overlooked. Instead he was warned beforehand. On June 28 Wu received an invitation from Yü Ming-chen's son to join him for dinner at a certain restaurant. When Wu arrived he found Yü instead of his son. During the course of the meal Yü contrived to show him the warrant with his name and the others' names on it.[67]

The next day Chinese and Western police jointly raided the premises of *Su-pao,* the Patriotic School, and *The Women's Journal,* the paper published by Ch'en Fan's daughter. The minor figures were arrested first and Ch'en Fan's son, Ch'en Chung-i, was seized under the impression that he was his father. Ch'en Fan himself was later recognized but not arrested, a lapse which he interpreted as another warning from Yü Ming-chen. He and his daughter then hid at the home of Chang Shih-chao's father-in-law (the son of a Ch'ing general)[68] until they could get passage to Japan. That evening Chang Ping-lin readily went with the police when he was discovered at the Patriotic School. Lung Tse-hou voluntarily surrendered on the 29th or 30th. At first Tsou Jung hid at the house of a Western missionary, but he then gave himself up at a police station on July 1 at the urging of his sworn brothers, Chang Ping-lin and Chang Chi.[69]

After July 1 the original Patriotic School complex was broken up. The school had to close and on July 7 *Su-pao* was closed by order of the Mixed

Court.[70] Some Educational Association members including Lin Hsieh, Huang Tsung-yang, and Chiang Wei-ch'iao stayed in Shanghai to help the prisoners or carry on the more moderate activities of the Educational Association. Wu Chih-hui left for Hong Kong and then went to England. Many others fled to Japan and some returned home, where at least a few, such as Ao Chia-hsiung in Chekiang, promoted revolution.[71]

Publicity for Revolution: The *Su-pao* Case

If Chang and Tsou hoped to use the trial for antigovernment propaganda they succeeded brilliantly. This achievement was not so much because of their own performances, for they occupied the witness stand only briefly, but because of the long argument between the Chinese government and the Western authorities. The *Su-pao* case dragged on for almost eleven months while Chinese and foreigners argued over whether the prisoners should be tried before the Mixed Court or in Nanking and what sentence they should receive. As negotiations continued interminably the Chinese government appeared both unreasonably vindictive and ridiculously ineffectual.

Chinese authorities saw the *Su-pao* case as the most important of a series of blows aimed at the radical intellectuals. Conservatives at Peking were reported to be urging the closing of all modern schools and condemning study in Japan for producing revolutionaries.[72] These extreme views could not prevail. However, a number of important reformist officials, including Chang Chih-tung and Tuan-fang, considered the time ripe to crush subversive tendencies among the students. New efforts were made to ban progressive and radical literature from the schools.[73] Police surveillance increased. Students returning from abroad were particularly suspect—sometimes with good reason—because in the wake of the anti-Russian agitation a number came home to spread patriotic and republican ideas. During the summer a large number of arrests were reported in the Yangtze provinces, especially Yangchow and Shanghai. Most of these reports turned out to be spurious rumors, but their existence indicated the tension between intellectual and government circles.[74]

The general government aim of disciplining student radicalism was not unreasonable from its point of view, but officials were often immoderate or indiscriminate in implementing this policy, which thereby was discredited in liberal as well as radical circles. The worst blunder was the execution of Shen Chin in Peking at the end of July. During the 1898 Reform period Shen had joined reform groups in Hunan, where he met the reformist leaders T'an Ssu-t'ung and T'ang Ts'ai-ch'ang. He became especially intimate with the latter, whom he followed to Japan and Shanghai. Shen helped T'ang plan the Hankow rising in 1900. When it failed he fled to Shanghai and then went north to Tientsin. He reached Tientsin at the time the Allied Expeditionary Force was occupying that city during the Boxer Rebellion. There he became friendly with a number of Western officers who were unaware of his political views. The exact nature of Shen's activities in the Peking-Tientsin area from 1901 to 1903 are rather vague. He evidently supported himself by newspaper work and single-handedly sought antigovernment recruits. He did not keep in touch with other radicals or revolutionaries, and it is also not clear whether he was promoting revolution or restoration of the power of the Kuang-hsü Emperor. Finally his activities attracted attention. He was betrayed by an acquaintance and on July 19 was arrested, reputedly at the order of the empress-dowager. Shen was secretly interrogated, and on July 31 he was beaten and strangled to death in prison without trial.

In the background of this incident were palace negotiations on the Manchurian question, which had aroused public fear that a corrupt court would give in to Russian demands. There were rumors of a secret treaty. Shen, who was working as a reporter for a Japanese paper, was strongly anti-Russian. His articles were often biased and probably calumnious. On July 27 the Tientsin papers carried his report of the text of an alleged secret agreement on Manchuria. The court was furious over this interference with efforts to reach a compromise with Russia and it was widely believed that this was the real reason for his death.[75] Government frustration over the *Su-pao* affair was also suspected to have been behind the hasty punishment.[76] Strong public reaction resulted. A protest meeting was held in Shanghai. Laudatory articles about Shen Chin appeared in the radical and reformist press and the Western-language press also reacted unfavorably.[77] Some of the Chinese officials realized that their chances in the *Su-pao* case had been hurt.[78]

Initially, at least, not all the Shanghai press was favorable to the prisoners. Several Chinese papers criticized revolutionary views and the moderately reformist *The News* (*Hsin-wen pao*) especially ridiculed Chang Ping-lin's refusal to leave the sanctuary of the International Settlement.[79] With the passage of time and especially after the Shen Chin case, public opinion became more favorable to the prisoners. Some of the general reasons for this sympathy, aside from the ever-present foreign concern to uphold the principles of extraterritoriality, were summed up by the *North China Herald*. The principles behind the case could be interpreted as government conservatism versus popular demands for reform. The

Su-pao articles were childish radicalism, but no real threat to the government. The Western legal distinction between political and other crimes would be violated by surrendering the prisoners to Chinese authorities. Finally, there was the persistent conviction that the meetings in Chang's Garden as much as the *Su-pao* articles precipitated the arrests—in other words, that the defendants were being tried for nationalistic and reformist views as well as for their revolutionary pronouncements.[80] At least some Chinese moderates had been impressed during the spring by the sincerity, though not the practicality, of the students who called for war with Russia. They doubted that the students were rebels and believed that the government had greatly overreacted to the "menace" of a couple of hundred unarmed youths returning home to arouse the nation against foreign imperialism. They shared the radicals' nationalism and during the *Su-pao* case were further appalled at the picture of the Chinese government humiliating itself by unsuccessfully bringing all its resources to bear to extradict six men, and try to destroy them, for no reason other than to assuage official anger.[81]

The details of the trial and the negotiations between Chinese and foreign authorities have been treated elsewhere and will only be briefly summarized here.[82] Once they had committed themselves to the prosecution of the *Su-pao* prisoners, government officials believed that rebellion would be encouraged if they did not punish them severely as an example to others. Death was thought the only appropriate sentence for Chang and Tsou. Since the Mixed Court could not be trusted to impose this penalty, the primary object was to transfer the prisoners to Nanking for trial by a Chinese court. A supporting consideration was that the case would set a precedent for handling any future trials of political prisoners. If the Mixed Court was allowed to try the prisoners it would remove the International Settlement even further from Chinese sovereignty. Rights "usurped" by the foreigners would be difficult to win back in the future.[83] Conversely, the Shanghai Municipal Council and the British consul particularly wished to exclude Chinese government jurisdiction from the International Settlement, although they also thought the death penalty was much too harsh a sentence and believed they were upholding higher principles of justice. The Municipal Council was in a fairly weak legal position when it insisted that the Mixed Court had jurisdiction over the case, but it had a strong bargaining point. The prisoners were in its custody.

After the two opening hearings before the Mixed Court on July 15 and 21, the case was adjourned indefinitely until the diplomatic questions could be settled. A majority of the Shanghai consular corps disagreed with the

British consul and favored extradicting the prisoners.[84] The decision was referred to the ambassadors in Peking and eventually to the home governments. Although the initial balance was unfavorable to the prisoners, it became more favorable the farther the level of decision-making moved from Shanghai. Democratic home governments, especially the British and American, gave greater weight to general considerations of free speech and treatment of political prisoners. While the question was still pending, the execution of Shen Chin cast grave doubts on Chinese judicial procedures. On August 5 the British cabinet announced that the prisoners should not be transferred. This really decided the issue because Britain was the dominant foreign power in the Yangtze Valley. The French and American governments followed suit before the end of the month.

Negotiations still dragged on, however, as Chinese authorities offered various concessions in hope of still gaining their main point.[85] The officials, particularly Governor Wei, were loathe to show weakness which would expose them to attacks from conservatives. They were, nonetheless, aware that there was no longer hope of extradicting the prisoners. Finally, the trial was reopened before the Mixed Court on December 3, with the addition to the bench of the Shanghai Magistrate, a Chinese official of higher rank than the Mixed Court Magistrate. None of the testimony of the next two days made any difference in the outcome. The facts were well-known, and the British assessor, who held the real power in the court, had already decided that Tsou and Chang should receive light jail sentences and the other four prisoners be released. Those four were released in December, but the case reached a deadlock again when the British assessor refused to accept the sentence of life imprisonment imposed on Chang and Tsou by the two Chinese judges.[86] Decision was again referred to Peking, but by this time the Chinese government position was extremely weak. All negotiators were tired of the case and, faced with the increasingly real possibility that the Municipal Council might simply release the prisoners, the Chinese authorities gave in to avoid further embarrassment. At the end of May 1904 the Mixed Court sentenced Chang to three years' imprisonment and Tsou to two. Sentences were computed from the time of arrest, so both had already served almost eleven months.[87]

One of the ironies of the *Su-pao* case is that although it is a famous landmark of the revolutionary movement, the issue of revolution was never clearly brought out in the trial itself. The most striking point about the indictment presented by the government is the traditionalistic manner in which it viewed the prisoners' alleged crimes. There is no discussion of the Western-inspired political ideas which motivated the students. Instead about a quarter of the specific passages cited are objectionable because of some direct insult to the emperor: failure to elevate the characters of his name, the use of the taboo personal names of the Kuang-hsü, Kang-hsi, and Ch'ien-lung emperors and various less technical insults such as calling the emperor a "criminal before heaven" and a "low wretch." Chang Ping-lin was especially inventive of this type of invective and most passages of this sort were written by him. Other passages contained insults to Manchus in general, calling them "pig-tailed barbarians," "nomadic herdsmen," "thieves," "aliens," "sons of wolves," "stupid as donkeys or pigs." Almost all the others cited are direct calls to overthrow or kill the Manchus. Only the opening paragraph of *The Revolutionary Army* with its call to sweep away tyranny, cast off slavishness, and turn all Chinese into George Washingtons, embodies many of the themes which were basic to the ideology of the student revolutionaries. The accusations partly reflected the government's English lawyer's advice that the Municipal Council was most likely to agree to arrest the defendants if they were charged with slander.[88] However, they may also indicate that officials were still puzzled by the aims of the revolutionaries and the nature of the revolutionary movement. Like rebels throughout Chinese history, the defendants' crimes were seen as lèse majesté and intent to overthrow the dynasty. The whole complicated question of reform and revolution is ignored.

Chang Ping-lin and Tsou Jung had allowed themselves to be arrested to dramatize the revolutionary cause, but they had no chance to testify at length until December, when the case was already stale news. Then they both followed the line of defense worked out by their lawyers: they had written the articles cited in the charges as private expressions of opinion with no intention of publishing them to incite the country to rebellion.[89] Chang was composed, sarcastic, and witty on the stand, but he mainly restricted himself to answering the specific accusations against him.[90] Tsou wavered somewhat and maintained that he had now abandoned the ideas expressed in *The Revolutionary Army* for socialism.[91] Neither testimony taken alone would have been enough to rally support to the revolutionary banner. Rather it was the history of the case as a whole that had the impact.

The suspense of the long drawn-out trial and the harsh penalty originally contemplated by the Chinese government won sympathy for the prisoners. Among the radical students, Chang and Tsou became heroes. Readership of *The Revolutionary Army* and the "Letter Disputing K'ang Yu-wei" boomed. During the trial a spate of literature about the case appeared, beginning with Chang Ping-lin's reply from jail to his critics on *The News*, which was published in *Su-pao* on July 6.[92]

Before the excitement had entirely died down it was revived all over again when Tsou Jung died in jail in April 1905. The nature of his illness was not clear. Conditions in the Mixed Court jail were notoriously bad and there was a high mortality rate, particularly among Western prisoners.[93] However, Chang Ping-lin's picture of his life there, though austere, is not brutal. He did not have to perform unduly hard labor and, although restricted in the visitors he received and the type of books he was allowed, he was able to write articles for the radical Chinese Daily (*Chung-kuo jih-pao*) in Hong Kong during his imprisonment. Tsou received similar treatment, but he did not adjust well to prison life and became increasingly upset as the months passed. His mental condition may have led to a general physical breakdown or he may have contracted tuberculosis. By the time he received medical attention it was too late to save him.[94] The rumor immediately circulated in student circles that Tsou had been poisoned at the wish of the Manchu government.[95] Rumors that Chang Ping-lin, too, would be poisoned arose as the end of his term approached.[96] When Chang's prison term did expire on June 29, 1906, the Revolutionary Alliance sent a representative to Shanghai to arrange for his passage to Japan. When he arrived in Tokyo he received an enthusiastic welcome at a meeting attended by perhaps two thousand students.[97] With that demonstration the *Su-pao* case was closed as a direct revolutionary influence.

The effect of the case on radical organizations in Shanghai was less happy. Shortly after the arrest of the *Su-pao* defendants, the members of the Educational Association, Patriotic School, and *Su-pao* scattered. Yet the protection afforded by the International Settlement was sufficient to prevent a complete debacle. Some of the old group soon reassembled to found new organizations. Therefore, it cannot be said that the *Su-pao* case checked the revolutionary movement more than momentarily. Possibly the advantage of the resulting publicity outweighed the organizational reverses.

The trial did, however, alter the nature and direction of the revolutionary movement. First of all, it widely advertised the distinction between the revolutionary and the reform, or the constitutionalist, movements. The Educational Association was not a purely revolutionary organization nor were the Chang Garden meetings the exclusive work of revolutionaries. The Patriotic School's pupils, like students in Japan, became more revolutionary as they went along and are hard to characterize at any one moment. Even *Su-pao* during the last month continued to employ men with views considerably more moderate than those of Chang Shih-chao. The Ch'ing government did not clearly distinguish between revolutionaries and followers of Liang Ch'i-ch'ao, and in early 1903 the distinction could not have been clear to many radicals. After *Su-pao* had underlined the revolutionary position, after *The Revolutionary Army,* the *Letter Disputing K'ang Yu-wei,* and the specific literature about the *Su-pao* case had been widely read, there could be little doubt that there was a difference. *Su-pao* was not wholly responsible for this development. A similar evolution took place in Japan at the same time, largely because of the Manchurian question. However, *Su-pao* certainly made a significant contribution. This separation of revolutionary and constitutional partisans did not end the interaction between revolutionaries and more moderate reformers. Nonetheless, the revolutionary movement matured and became distinct and the *Su-pao* case helped show the way.

Part of the process was the change from an open to a clandestine movement and a related shift in emphasis from propaganda to directly seeking to overthrow the government by assassination or through a rising. Sun Yat-sen had followed this course since 1895, but, except for T'ang Ts'ai-ch'ang's rising in 1900, the intellectuals in the Yangtze Valley did not turn to violent means until after 1903. The *Su-pao* group attempted to win their goal by lectures and demonstrations. After that course failed, the revolutionaries tried a new tack. By the end of 1904 the revolutionary movement (*ko-ming tang*) in the Lower Yangtze was more like a combination of traditional Chinese secret society with modern revolutionary party and less of a traditional loose clique of men of similar outlook and aspirations—less of a *tang* in the Tung-lin sense. Yet, again it will be seen that certain elements of the original approach continued to have a fatal attraction for the radical intellectuals.

The Chinese government's handling of the *Su-pao* case was something less than a brilliant success. It not only failed to quash the radical movement by making an example of the prisoners, but it lost more prestige internationally and at home. Especially notable were the number of officials, particularly Yü Ming-chen, who disagreed with and deliberately sabotaged the government's policy. In later incidents, also, revolutionaries were to receive aid, sometimes unintentional but at other times deliberate, from men holding official rank. These men were usually not revolutionaries themselves but reformers who found that, at least in specific instances, they had more in common with the revolutionaries than with the government's policies. By exacting harsh penalties, often hounding minor figures and bungling efforts at publicity, the government tended to alienate a wide spectrum of public opinion ranging from mildly reformist to radical. Men who were not in sympathy with the revolutionaries, but who saw them being punished for holding views which moderates largely shared, were likely to take alarm and increasingly lose confidence in the government. In the *Su-pao* case Tsou and Chang admitted they were revolutionaries although the others did not. Still, at least the English-language press kept returning to the point that it believed that the anti-French and anti-Russian agitation was a basic reason behind the arrests. Many prominent men in Shanghai shared the concern on these points and hardly would have been likely to believe that such activities warranted the death penalty. Thus the government lost even more sympathy than the revolutionaries gained.

5 The Urban Revolutionary Environment: Continued Activity in Shanghai

During the eighteen months from the beginning of the *Su-pao* case to the end of 1904, revolutionary activity continued in the Shanghai area in a somewhat lower key. Three currents intertwined to produce the next significant advancement of the movement. First, there were a number of short-lived schools and newspapers which succeeded in keeping alive the traditions of *Su-pao* and the Patriotic School. Second, radical and nationalistic sentiments continued to develop among the student body as a whole, aside from the influence of specifically revolutionary groups. Finally, Shanghai was affected by the general shift in the revolutionary movement toward active attempts to overthrow the government. Shanghai became a transfer point for returning students and for weapons and literature, a place to raise funds, and a relatively safe and convenient spot for revolutionaries from several different provinces to meet and lay plans. All these activities culminated in the formation of the first general revolutionary party in the Lower Yangtze area, the Restoration Society, in the late fall of 1904.

The Legacy of the *Su-pao* Period

After the Patriotic School closed, the Patriotic Girls' School was kept alive by certain of the less flamboyant members of the Educational Association, such as Chiang Wei-ch'iao and Chung Hsien-ch'ang, who did not flee Shanghai. It was, however, in severe financial straits with less than 150 yuan a month for expenditures. At the end of 1903 Ts'ai Yüan-p'ei returned from Tsingtao and made the school his revolutionary headquarters. He became its director and in the spring of 1904 was also elected head of the Educational Association. Ts'ai attached great importance to these two organizations as meeting places for revolutionaries and a way to spread propaganda. While he headed the school, the chemistry of bomb-making and the principles of nihilism and the French Revolution were taught along with conventional subjects. With this new stimulus, the organizations enjoyed a brief resurgence. The Patriotic Girls' School moved to a new location to accommodate its expanded student body. It added a special short course for married women and opened for the new term on March 11. Later that spring the Educational Association offered evening courses in language, science, and mathematics for those interested in a modern education who had to work during the day. Many of the faculty were drawn from members of the association, but other scholars also taught there.

Internal troubles began almost immediately, however. That spring the feminist reformer Chang Chu-chün arrived in Shanghai. She persuaded Ts'ai Yüan-p'ei to establish a handicrafts course at the Patriotic Girls' School to foster women's economic independence. Chang was invited to help found the course, but after a month she enticed most of the students and teachers to a new girls' school under her direction. This defection was a severe blow from which the Patriotic Girls' School did not fully recover. It remained Ts'ai Yüan-p'ei's revolutionary headquarters until he left Shanghai, but it never became an important institution. In 1907 and 1908 it again enjoyed a brief revival. This time, however, it was partly supported by government funds and was no longer a revolutionary front. In the winter of 1908–09 the school was closed and the building was auctioned off. By this time the remnants of the Educational Association had also dispersed. Only a few members remained in Shanghai and the society had lost any revolutionary significance.[1]

Another attempt to carry on the traditions of the Patriotic School was made by the brothers Liu Chi-p'ing and Liu Tung-hai, who established the Mutual Assistance Primary School in February or March of 1904. The aim was to develop revolutionary talent by teaching radical ideas and military drill. Classes were held in Liu Chi-p'ing's house and revolutionaries such as Ch'in Yü-liu, who had been active in radical student societies in Japan, were invited to teach. The school was disbanded within a few months, but a number of its students, with the encouragement of Ts'ai Yüan-p'ei, organized the Youth Study Association (*Ch'ing-nien hsüeh-she*). This group survived until the end of the year, when it was implicated in Wan Fu-hua's attempt to assassinate ex-Governor Wang Chih-ch'un and was closed by the authorities.[2]

As in the first half of 1903, newspapers as well as schools were among the main revolutionary organs. The first successor to *Su-pao* was *The China National Gazette* (*Kuo-min jih-jih pao*), which opened in late July. Many staff members had been part of the Educational Association-Patriotic School group. Chang Shih-chao returned from Japan and he was joined by Chang Chi, Lin Hsieh, Liu Shih-p'ei (Liu Kuang-han), and a few former students at the Patriotic School. Ch'en Fan gave some aid from Japan.

The publisher was Lu Ho-sheng, a Kwangtangese who had grown up in Hong Kong. He had attended the British Naval Engineering School (*Hai-chün kung-ch'eng*) there and then worked for some years for Western papers in Shanghai. On the strength of his connections, *The China National Gazette* was registered with the British consulate so it might enjoy the full protection of extraterritoriality.[3]

Although the members of its staff were genuinely radical, *The China National Gazette* was a very pale reflection of its predecessor. It neither conveyed the excitement of student circles, as had *Su-pao* during the previous spring, nor echoed the inflammatory revolutionary denunciations in *Su-pao* during June. The paper carried news of the *Su-pao* case, criticized the government on specific issues, called for an end of monarchial rule at home and of humiliation abroad. The standard ideas in radical student publications were all present, though stated much more cautiously. Thus an article denouncing Chinese willingness to accept foreign rule mentioned the Ch'i-tan, Jurchen, and Mongol dynasties, but said nothing of the Manchus.[4] The paper also frequently reprinted articles from English-language Shanghai papers. This was a convenient way both to criticize the government safely and to gather news with a small reportorial staff. However, it is unlikely that this practice would have been approved at *Su-pao* during June. Much of the change can probably be attributed to the lessons of the *Su-pao* case. It is also possible that some of the initial élan of the group had disappeared. The atmosphere of the Patriotic School could not be re-created and the remaining members of the group were prepared to go about their revolutionary business more quietly and soberly.

Despite the *Gazette*'s relative moderation, the Chinese government sought to close it. It could forbid the sale of the paper outside of Shanghai,[5] but was unable to suppress it in the International Settlement. However, the paper's staff accomplished the government's purpose for it. Lu Ho-shen and some of the others became involved in a complicated and bitter personal quarrel which led to a suit in the Mixed Court.[6] Ch'en Shao-pai, the Kwantungese revolutionary associate of Sun Yat-sen who headed the *Chinese Daily* in Hong Kong, came to Shanghai to mediate. He and others finally reconciled the two sides. The suit was dropped, but by then the financial backers had withdrawn support and the paper could not continue.[7]

Although it survived no more than a few months, *The China National Gazette* was of some significance in maintaining the continuity of the revolutionary movement in Shanghai. It brought together again people who had been active in the previous organizations. Some of its staff were also responsible for founding other minor radical publications in Shanghai. Lin Hsieh established *The Chinese Vernacular Journal (Chung-kuo pai-hua-pao)* in the fall of 1903, and in 1904 Ch'en Ch'ü-ping edited *The Twentieth Century Stage (Erh-shih shih-chi ta-wu-t'ai tsa-chih).*[8]　•

The place of *The China National Gazette* was taken by *Warnings on Russian Affairs (O-shih ching-wen).* Tension in Manchuria mounted during the fall of 1903, and early in 1904 Russian troops moved into Fengtien province as a prelude to the Russo-Japanese War. Anti-Russian sentiments, particularly among student groups, reached new peaks in major centers such as Shanghai, and a number of small associations were founded to discuss the Manchurian situation. Ts'ai Yüan-p'ei, Liu Shih-p'ei, and others established an Association of Comrades to Resist Russia *(Tui-O t'ung-chih hui)* in the International Settlement during December 1903. For two months this group published *Warnings on Russian Affairs,* which concentrated almost exclusively on the Manchurian issue. This paper focused upon Russian imperialism all the nationalistic themes prevalent in radical publications during the past year. In a long series of articles it appealed to numerous groups and classes to play their part in saving the country. The editors linked nationalism to opposition to the dynasty by pointing out the failures of Ch'ing foreign policy. Antidynastic sentiments were more subtlely presented than they had been in *Su-pao*, however. Copies of the paper were distributed in teahouses and restaurants to try to reach people who did not ordinarily purchase radical literature. After the actual outbreak of war between Japan and Russia the original objectives were broadened to general opposition to imperialism, and on February 26, 1904, the paper appeared under the new name of *The Alarm Bell (Ching-chung jih-pao).* From the beginning *The Alarm Bell* warned that Japan ultimately would become as predatory as Russia. It continued to denounce all instances of imperialistic encroachment and also printed articles on such subjects as education, constitutionalism, and official corruption that were common in radical journals. On January 28, 1904, *The Alarm Bell* printed a translation of a Japanese article that purported to describe secret German plans for control of Shantung. Protests by the German consul led the police to raid the paper's offices at the end of March. Liu Shih-p'ei was forewarned and fled, but five minor functionaries were arrested. Two of them received jail sentences of six months and a year respectively after a trial on charges of sedition, and the other three were released. But the paper's offices were permanently closed.[9]

The Alarm Bell was a particularly apt example of the significance of nationalism in the growth of the revolutionary movement. Like *The China*

National Gazette it helped bridge the gap between the *Su-pao* period and the founding of the Restoration Society. A number of its staff had been connected with the Patriotic School or the Educational Association. Others had worked for *The China National Gazette, The Twentieth Century Stage,* or *The Chinese Vernacular Journal.* This confusing welter of names is significant because it indicates a growing nucleus of men in Shanghai who came mainly from the Lower Yangtze provinces and whose main energies were devoted to promoting radical and, in most cases, frankly revolutionary causes.[10] The schools and papers that they used as their organs were not, however, strong enough organizations to surmount the various problems of internal jealousies, financial stringency, and official hostility. They served as a means to keep the revolutionaries together and as channels for radical propaganda, but they were hardly serious threats to the dynasty.

The receptive audience provided by students in the conventional modern schools in Shanghai was a considerable advantage to the narrowly revolutionary organizations. There was always a market for revolutionary publications, which were made available to the student population through such bookstores as the Mirror of Today Bookshop (*Ching-chin shu-chü*), the Eastern Continent Bookshop (*Tung-ta-lu t'u-shu-chü*), and the National Studies Association. The most influential works were still *The Revolutionary Army*, the writings of Ch'en T'ien-hua, and well-known compilations like *The Soul of Huang-ti* (*Huang-ti hun*) and *A Record of the Su-pao Case* (*Su-pao an chi-shih*). A number of those employed on revolutionary papers and periodicals published their own radical pamphlets, so there was a considerable body of revolutionary literature which originated in Shanghai.[11] Progressive ideas were also spread through the "new theater," which presented plays on topical subjects.[12]

Revolutionary literature was, of course, not the only influence on the average modern student who was still exposed to a mixture of revolutionary, reformist, and simply nationalistic views. The experiences of Hu Shih, prominent liberal, scholar, and language reformer during the Republic, are suggestive of influences on and reactions of politically interested youngsters. Hu relates that when he entered school in Shanghai in 1904, his elder stepbrother gave him a case of "new books" which were mostly essays by Liang Ch'i-ch'ao. These seemed very radical at the time. Later he and another student borrowed and copied a volume of *The Revolutionary Army,* which also made a great impression and helped inspire Hu to leave the school before the end of the term to avoid being examined by the Shanghai Taotai.[13] At the next school he attended, Hu was introduced to the theory of evolution through the works of Yen Fu. The students applied these ideas to the international scene and concluded that China's successive defeats proved the urgent need of reforms that would fit the country for survival in the struggle for existence.[14] Even after being introduced to other writers, Hu continued to find Liang Ch'i-ch'ao a source of inspiration. He was particularly influenced by the concept of renovation of the people with its attendant connotations of national loyalty, individual rights and freedom, self-government, progress, economic independence, self-reliance, and the inculcation of a private morality and sense of duty.[15] Although he was abandoned by the very radical students, Liang retained his popularity among most of the students because he articulately presented ideas of liberty and regeneration that greatly appealed to youths beginning to break with traditional culture.

Hu Shih also stresses the influence of *The Eastern Times* (*Shih-pao*), another nonrevolutionary but progressive paper, established in 1904 by Ti Ch'u-ch'ing. Ti was a *chü-jen* from Kiangsu who had joined the 1898 Reform Movement and had been involved in planning T'ang Ts'ai-ch'ang's rising, after which he fled to Japan. He was a friend of K'ang Yu-wei and Liang Ch'i-ch'ao, who together provided almost one-third of the initial financial backing for the paper. *The Eastern Times* then competed with the two other major Chinese-language papers in Shanghai, *Shen-pao* and *The News* (*Hsin-wen pao*). Both these papers were foreign owned and Ti believed correctly that there was room for a paper presenting a purely Chinese progressive view. Its general policy was constitutionalist, but it took a strongly anti-imperialist stand on international issues that was very satisfying to all students. *The Eastern Times*'s strong support of the anti-American boycott of 1905 increased its circulation, and it soon became one of the most widely read publications in Central China.[16]

In 1904 the great topic of the day was the Russo-Japanese War. News of the conflict crowded other issues from both the radical and reformist press. Student sympathies strongly favored Japan, as did public opinion in general. The Ch'ing government's proclamation of neutrality only stirred up more anti-Manchuism.[17] The generally radical and nationalistic intellectual environment set the stage for an attempt in November to assassinate Wang Chih-ch'un, the ex-governor of Kwangsi, who was then living in Shanghai. This case again illustrated the intermingling of nationalistic and revolutionary motives. It underlined the growing attraction which violence had for the radical intellectuals. By accident it also came very close to publicly revealing the extent to which Shanghai had become a meeting point for professional revolutionaries in Central China.

Wang Chih-ch'un had been unpopular in radical circles since the exposure of his plan to use French troops to help suppress the Kwangsi rebels in 1903. He was known to be an admirer of Tsar Nicholas II and favorably inclined toward Russia. Some believed he favored an alliance with that country and probably wrongly suspected he was engaging in negotiations aimed at winning Russian favor by giving her strategic rights in Manchuria.[18] Anti-Russian and nationalistic sentiments, therefore, found in him a logical target.

Wan Fu-hua, who attempted the assassination, was somewhat older than most of his associates and had only been briefly involved in the radical movement. He was from Ho-fei in Anhwei, had studied in Hunan and then came to teach in Shanghai in 1903 at the age of thirty-eight.[19] A close friend and fellow villager was an ardent revolutionary and influenced Wan to join the revolutionary movement. He met and associated with some of the major radical figures in Shanghai,[20] but except for his one day of glory does not seem to have played a very active role. Other revolutionaries knew and presumably approved of his intention to assassinate Wang, but the actual attempt was carried out by Wan alone.[21]

Once he had decided to kill Wang Chih-ch'un, Wan spied on his victim's house, but he found that it was well guarded and that Wang only left home with a large retinue. Therefore Wan faked a dinner invitation from a friend to lure the governor out on November 19. Wang was deceived, but when he arrived at the appointed time and found his friend was not at the restaurant he became suspicious and started to leave. Wan was waiting for him near the bottom of the stairs with a borrowed gun. The first shot misfired because he had forgotten to release the safety catch. Before he could fire again Wan was overpowered by the governor's servants and was arrested.[22]

This incident was also widely publicized by *The Eastern Times* and other papers and greatly agitated the students in Shanghai, who generally sympathized with Wan.[23] The advantage which the publicity may have given the revolutionary cause was almost offset by the accidental involvement of some of the major revolutionary leaders. Three weeks before Wan's attempt, Huang Hsing and others had fled to Shanghai from Changsha when plans for a rising there had been discovered by the authorities. A careless remark to the police by a mutual acquaintance, who was questioned after visiting Wan in jail, led to the arrest of several members of this group, including Huang Hsing.[24] Their true identities were never discovered and eventually all were released except Wan and one man who had been carrying a pistol. Thus a serious blow to the revolutionary movement was avoided. Wan himself was tried before the Mixed Court despite efforts by the Chinese government to have the case transferred to the Chinese courts.[25] He was sentenced to ten years at hard labor and disappeared from the public scene.[26] His vain effort was both a late echo of the 1903 demonstrations and a forecast of things to come. Assassination attempts and similarly self-sacrificing acts were to play an important part in the revolutionary history of the next few years.

The Restoration Society

By the end of 1904 the formation of a secret revolutionary organization in Shanghai was, if anything, overdue. A nucleus of professional revolutionaries had worked with one another for some time. They drew support from the students in the modern schools and enjoyed a tolerable degree of safety in the International Settlement. For about two years radicals returning from Japan had bolstered the numbers of revolutionaries in China, and since the end of 1903 some returned students had seriously been organizing for the armed overthrow of the government. Huang Hsing had founded the Society for China's Revival in December 1903, and Chekiangese revolutionaries had begun to organize the secret societies in that province during 1904. Shanghai was already a central point. Huang Hsing had bought arms and ammunition there for his planned rising in Hunan.[27] After he was forced to flee Changsha he began making new arrangements in Shanghai for a second attempt until his plans were changed by his arrest following Wan Fu-hua's assassination attempt.

All this activity pointed to the need for a more effective and secret organization in Shanghai. The existing schools, newspapers, and associations were not broadly based. They were plagued by internal dissension and, most important, they were intended to dispense propaganda and were not suited for action. Since they were trying to draw attention to the revolutionary cause they invited official notice which would have been disastrous had their members actually been plotting a rising against the government.

The Shanghai organizations, beginning with the Chinese Educational Association, formed one group of antecedents of the Restoration Society. Additional impetus came from revolutionaries returning from Japan during 1904 and one thread runs via Chekiangese students in Tokyo back to early radical activity in Hangchow. A number of members of the Society for Education of a Militant People formed an assassination corps in Tokyo during 1903. In 1904 the Hunanese student Yang Yü-lin and other associates inclined toward anarchism came to Shanghai, where they continued experiments in bomb-making. They invited Ts'ai Yüan-p'ei to join the group.

The Educational Association member, Chung Hsien-ch'ang, was welcomed for his knowledge of chemistry and other Shanghai radicals also became members.[28] They knew of Huang Hsing's plans for a rising in Hunan and did what they could to help him.

Yang Yü-lin did not stay long in Shanghai and was not permanently interested in that part of China. More important on the local scene was the founder of the Shanghai branch of the assassination corps, Chang Ping-lin's son-in-law—the Chekiangese revolutionary Kung Pao-ch'üan. Kung's role in the Shanghai revolutionary scene can be traced back to the fall of 1903 when about ten members of the Chekiangese students' provincial club in Tokyo decided to form a revolutionary group which would organize a rising against the Ch'ing government as well as just disseminate propaganda.[29] Some of the students already belonged to the Society for Education of a Militant People and told their plans to Kung Pao-ch'üan and Wei Lan, another Chekiangese member of the society. They also made contact with T'ao Ch'eng-chang, who had just come to Japan and who had met Kung in 1902.[30] In December 1903 or January 1904 a second meeting was held and T'ao and the others attended. There they decided that T'ao and Wei should go to Chekiang and Anhwei to make contacts with secret societies. Kung went to Shanghai and two other students went to Changsha to make connections with Huang Hsing and the Society for China's Revival.

After Kung Pao-ch'üan organized his assassination corps in Shanghai he kept in contact with T'ao Ch'eng-chang. By fall T'ao had progressed far enough in the organization of the secret societies to come to Shanghai for consultations with other revolutionaries. After he arrived he and Kung discussed organizing a party along lines the Tokyo group had originally contemplated in Tokyo. Aside from Chang Ping-lin, who was still in jail, Ts'ai Yüan-p'ei was the best known revolutionary in Shanghai. T'ao hesitated to approach Ts'ai because of the latter's high scholarly reputation. Therefore Kung and Ts'ai carried out the negotiations to establish the Restoration Society and it was agreed that Ts'ai would personally invite T'ao to join.

The Restoration Society was founded in November or early December.[31] The new organization probably retained much of the atmosphere of the assassination corps and was initially conceived as a highly secret association. Recruits were introduced by a member of the group. Upon joining they took a blood oath to be faithful to the revolutionary cause. One old member recalls that he swore to "restore the Chinese race and recover our mountains and rivers, to devote myself to the country, and to retire after completing my service." Members were not supposed to know others in the society until they received orders to carry out a joint task.[32]

However, from the beginning the Restoration Society was never able to maintain any high standards of discipline or exclusiveness. Not all those who worked closely with party members joined the society.[33] In other cases, members such as Wu Yüeh pursued their own schemes without making any attempt to integrate them with revolutionary plans of the organization as a whole. Although it was the major revolutionary society in the area, the Restoration Society was never able totally to embrace and control the revolutionary movement in the Lower Yangtze.

One problem was a lack of strong, unified leadership. Ts'ai Yüan-p'ei was no more than the nominal head of the society. He was respected for his learning and his character. He had been prominent from the beginning of the Shanghai revolutionary movement and had wide connections in radical circles.[34] However, he had no contacts with secret societies in the provinces and seems to have been temperamentally poorly suited for the practical aspects of fund raising, making alliances with nonintellectuals, and working out the detailed organization for a rising. Members did not look to him for authority in the party.[35] The real leaders were T'ao Ch'eng-chang and Hsü Hsi-lin. Because they already had contacts in Chekiang, the center of Restoration Society activities almost immediately shifted away from Shanghai. T'ao had organizational ability and a good sense of practical possibilities. However, his prudence, his thorough classical education, and his somewhat narrow revolutionary views tended to set him apart from the more radical returned students in the society. By 1907 he had largely withdrawn from an active part in the planning in Chekiang. Hsü Hsi-lin, on the other hand, was popular and much admired for his revolutionary ardor.[36] In the end, though, it was this trait which led him into the extremely ill-considered attempt which precipitated the failure of the party's plans. Ch'iu Chin, the third major figure in the party, played a role in Chekiang only after T'ao and Hsü had left and she, like Hsü, was more zealous than careful. Although there was no power struggle for control of the Restoration Society, quarrels developed among the leaders, for instance between T'ao and Hsü, partly because of personality differences and partly because of disagreements over tactics.

Many of the rank-and-file members of the Restoration Society were young intellectuals from Chekiang, Anhwei, and Kiangsu, and most had studied in Japan. There was a small Tokyo branch which seems to have mainly consisted of Chekiangese students.[37] Many of the first members came from the group which had been active in Shanghai since the *Su-pao* period.[38] With a few exceptions they do not seem to have been among the most active members of the party. They stayed in Shanghai while the most important work was being carried on in Chekiang and probably continued to follow much the same pursuits as they had before. In Chekiang some recruits were found among students in Hangchow and in the new army. A particular effort was made to ally with secret societies and to persuade secret society leaders to join the Restoration Society. During the first half of 1907 Ch'iu Chin attempted to enroll secret society members into the party on a large scale.[39] In addition at least a few members were gentry or merchants.[40] Generally their main contribution was to supply funds. Finally, it should be noted that several women played significant roles. Besides Ch'iu Chin, her friend the poetess and educator Hsü Tzu-hua was a member. More important than Hsü were the Yin sisters, Jui-chih and Wei-chün, who continued party work in Shanghai through the Revolution.

The beginnings of the Restoration Society were entwined with the assassination corps and assassination and anarchism played a persistent role in the party's history. Assassination promised an easy way for a still weak movement to publicize the revolutionary cause and shake the government. It also gave individual romanticists a chance to demonstrate their own faith and courage against strong odds. A sketchy acquaintance with theoretical anarchism was a further influence. By the end of 1903 at least one translation of a Western tract on anarchism had been made by Chang Chi. The revolutionaries were familiar with Russian nihilism and admired such Russian political figures as Bakunin and Sophia Perovskaya. Chin I's translation of a Japanese work about the Russian terrorists appeared in 1904 under the title of *The Blood of Freedom* (*Tzu-yu hsüeh*). Student magazines and newspapers published articles on anarchism and nihilism and Yang Yü-lin's pamphlet *New Hunan* (*Hsin Hu-nan*) also discussed the Russian nihilists.[41] One Restoration Society member, Liu Shih-p'ei, was later a founder of the anarchist-inclined Society for the Study of Socialism in Tokyo in 1907 and his wife, Ho Chen, is said to have been involved in an assassination plot.[42] Even such basically traditionalistic figures as Chang Ping-lin and T'ao Ch'eng-chang were interested in anarchism as a possible postrevolutionary form of government.[43]

Anarchism appealed to radical intellectuals who had been exposed to Western ideas, but who actually had had only limited contact with the West and consciously or otherwise retained many traditional values. It promised an egalitarian, utopian future society without the need of understanding and assimilating the complicated, alien Western democratic institutions. However, the chief appeal was anarchism's straightforward promotion of violence. To most students it was almost synonymous with assassination.

The most striking anarchist inspired assassination attempt by a Restoration Society member was made by Wu Yüeh in Peking. Wu was a younger son of an educated but poor family of T'ung-ch'eng, Anhwei. His mother died when he was seven and he was brought up by two elder brothers. Because the family was impoverished, his father gave up pursuit of an official career to go into trade. However, he made sure that his sons had a chance to study. Wu enjoyed history and ancient literature, but disliked practicing the eight-legged essay for the official examinations and after several years he turned from these studies to modern subjects. First he tried to enter the language school at the Kiangnan Arsenal in Shanghai, but failed. Then he went north and entered the Pao-ting Higher School with the aid of the recommendation of a family friend. There he was first introduced to radical ideas. Under the influence of Tsou Jung's *The Revolutionary Army* and the Russian occupation of Manchuria he became a nationalist. Through reading Liang Ch'i-ch'ao's works he became a constitutionalist, but after gaining a wider knowledge of radical literature Wu was converted to the idea of revolution and turned against Liang for misleading him. He gradually built up acquaintances among revolutionaries, including Ch'en T'ien-hua and Yang Yü-lin. Yang visited the Pao-ting School several times during 1904 and 1905 and established connections with a group of radical students there, including Wu. It was Yang who introduced Wu into the Restoration Society as well as instructing him in the use of explosives. News of Wan Fu-hua's assassination attempt and an attempt in Honan to kill the influential Manchu vice-president of the Board of Finance, T'ieh-liang, inspired the Pao-ting group, but they had to give up the idea of assassinating T'ieh-liang as too difficult. Encouraged by Yang, Wu then made plans to kill the five imperial commissioners being sent abroad to study foreign constitutions. Wu intended to throw a bomb at the commissioners at the railway station as they were about to start their journey. However, the bomb exploded prematurely, killing Wu while the commissioners escaped.[44]

Wu left a group of writings behind him, including his "Personal Introduction" (*Tzu-hsü*) and several letters explaining his motives. In these he argued that the Chinese had been debased by their historic indifference to whether they were ruled by foreigners. Although at present they were slaves, Chinese might wipe out this humiliation by revolution.[45] The first step was to drive out the Manchus before resisting the Western countries.[46] Wu's final aim was a strong, reconstructed, and peaceful China, but he felt the Chinese had suffered so long under foreign tyranny that only drastic and violent remedies could relieve their condition.[47]

Wu was also aware of the difficulties which uninfluential students faced in trying to rouse the country. Looking for a short cut, he found it in assassinations. The Manchus could be eliminated either by assassinations or revolution. The latter method required mass participation, but the former method could be carried out by individuals. At present China was in the period of assassinations. The country was not ready for revolution, but assassinations, evidently pictured as catalysts to rouse the populace, could usher in the revolutionary stage.[48] Wu called upon the students not to fear death, but to adopt the ways of the Russian nihilist party.[49] He himself would be emancipated by a heroic death instead of waiting to be carried off by sickness in his old age.[50]

The concern with anarchism and nihilism displayed by members of the Restoration Society was not highly theoretical. They were attracted by the simplicity of assassination as a revolutionary technique and similarities which they discerned between their own situation and that of the revolutionary intelligentsia in Russia. These aspects could easily be related to the traditional Chinese concept of the hero. Some figures, such as Ch'iu Chin, were mainly influenced by traditional ideas, whereas others like Wu Yüeh were more directly swayed by Western theories. However, it is often difficult to disentangle the influences of these two strains. Taken together they had a strong bearing on Restoration Society activity.

One final point to be considered in connection with the Restoration Society is its relations with other revolutionary organizations. The accepted picture of the society has been colored by the feud that developed between it and the Revolutionary Alliance in 1910. However, during its early years its members cooperated with fellow revolutionaries in other parts of China and Japan. Before the Restoration Society was even founded T'ao Ch'eng-chang and other Chekiangese revolutionaries had hoped to rise in support of Huang Hsing's Changsha attempt in November 1904. Contact with Hunan was maintained through two Chekiangese students who went to Changsha for the purpose and taught at the Ming-te and Industrial schools there.[51] Huang also kept in touch with Ts'ai Yüan-p'ei in Shanghai, who further contributed to coordinating plans in the two provinces, but Huang's failure temporarily ended chances for cooperation.[52]

The establishment of the Revolutionary Alliance in August 1905 led to new opportunities. None of the Restoration Society leaders were present at the founding of the Revolutionary Alliance,[53] but some members in Tokyo joined shortly thereafter. Ts'ai Yüan-p'ei was designated to found and head the Shanghai branch of the Revolutionary Alliance and many Restoration Society members then joined. T'ao Ch'eng-chang did not join until he went to Japan in 1906, but then for a time he worked in the Revolutionary Alliance and was associated with *The People's Journal*. Ch'iu Chin became a member of the Revolutionary Alliance in Tokyo immediately after it was founded and was put in charge of building the party in Chekiang. She did not join the Restoration Society until she returned to Shanghai several months later.[54] The only major holdout was Hsü Hsi-lin, who never joined the Revolutionary Alliance and disavowed Sun Yat-sen in his confession after assassinating En-ming. Hsü's attitude probably reflected provincialism and the kind of snobbishness that Sun often inspired in North and Central China intellectuals who were not as Westernized as he. A more immediate reason may have been that the first convenient opportunity which Hsü had to join the Revolutionary Alliance was when he went to Japan in 1906. At this time he quarreled with T'ao Ch'eng-chang over future strategy. T'ao joined the Revolutionary Alliance and Hsü returned to China to pursue his own plans, rejecting any further association with his former colleague.[55]

In Shanghai, Ts'ai Yüan-p'ei actively headed the local branch of the Revolutionary Alliance for less than a year. Because of his plans to go to Germany he wished others to assume his responsibilities. Therefore, in the spring of 1906, Kao Chien-kung[56] was sent from Tokyo to take charge of a Kiangsu branch of the party which would incorporate the Shanghai branch. As a first step Kao established the Steadfast Conduct Public Institute (*Chienhsing kung-hsüeh*) to serve as a revolutionary front in the same way as Ts'ai Yüan-p'ei used the Patriotic Girls' School as his headquarters for the Restoration Society. Kao and a number of other revolutionaries taught there, including such veterans of Shanghai radical organizations as the writer Liu Ch'i-chi, who had started as a student at the Patriotic School, and Ch'en Ch'ü-ping, who had served on *The China National Gazette*. Among the textbooks used were *The Soul of Huang-ti,* the Chinese translation of Carlyle's *French Revolution,* and Chang Shih-chao's *T'ang-lu ts'ung-shu*. Liu Ch'i-chi edited the radical *Revival Journal* (*Fu-pao*) there and the proofs were sent to Tokyo for publication.[57] Revolutionary literature shipped from Japan was collected at the school before being taken to bookstores for distribution. Some of the first students were drawn from those who returned from Japan in early 1906 in protest against the new regulation of Chinese students in Tokyo. They were a thoroughly radical group who, with representatives of the Chinese Public Institute, took part in such projects as welcoming Chang Ping-lin from jail and laying a memorial tablet to Tsou Jung.

The first meeting of the new party bureau was attended by Ts'ai Yüan-p'ei and Liu Shih-p'ei along with some thirty others, indicating a harmonious transition from the old party organization. In 1907 the Revolutionary Alliance in Shanghai, like the Restoration Society, was gravely affected by the failures in Anking and Chekiang. The Steadfast Conduct Public Institute dispersed and party headquarters dissolved. Organizational work remained at a minimum for the next two and a half years.[58]

The Steadfast Conduct Public Institute and the Kiangsu Revolutionary Alliance are not mentioned in histories of Restoration Society activities in Chekiang or Shanghai. Neither is there evidence to indicate that there was rivalry before 1910 and there certainly was some overlap in membership. It seems possible that most rank-and-file members of the Restoration Society did not significantly distinguish between the two organizations, for both were engaged in revolutionary work. The Restoration Society, unlike the Society to Restore China's Prosperity and the Society for China's Revival, probably remained a separate organization because at the time the Revolutionary Alliance was founded the Restoration Society leaders, in contrast to Sun Yat-sen and Huang Hsing, were having considerable success in building up a revolutionary organization in their own provinces. Therefore, they were not in Japan to join in establishing the Revolutionary Alliance and, not having this initial stake in the new organization, saw no reason to dissolve their old one, which was then doing well. Although provincialism may have been a factor, there is little indication of unwillingness to co-operate with revolutionaries from other areas.

T'ao Ch'eng-chang maintains that the Restoration Society rank and file in the interior of Chekiang knew nothing about the Revolutionary Alliance.[59] This is possible because they were exposed to only a local range of the party's interest. Among the leaders the situation was somewhat different. In 1906 the Restoration Society played a part in the general quickening of revolutionary activity in the Yangtze area which followed the organization of the Revolutionary Alliance. Both the Restoration Society and the Revolutionary Alliance recruited members among students and among the army in Hangchow and the two groups then founded a joint organization.[60] Ch'iu Chin traveled about Chekiang organizing a rising which was scheduled to take place three days after the rebellion encouraged by the Revolutionary Alliance in Liu-yang and Li-ling districts of Hunan and P'ing-hsiang district, Kiangsi.[61] Because the "P'ing-Liu-Li" rising failed so quickly, there was no opportunity for the Chekiang revolutionaries to rise in their turn.

After this failure and the numerous arrests of Revolutionary Alliance members which followed in the Middle Yangtze region, possibilities for cooperation again narrowed. Revolutionary Alliance leaders were convinced that government control in Central China was too strong and shifted their attention to Kwangtung and the southern border. The Restoration Society was at first unaffected and continued with its plans. Before the date set for the rising in Chekiang in 1907, Ch'iu Chin sent a representative to Tokyo to ask the Revolutionary Alliance for provisions and military supplies. Huang Hsing, who was then in Hong Kong, returned to Japan when he received the request, but Ch'iu Chin was executed before he could be of any assistance.[62] The Restoration Society was badly broken down by the failure in Chekiang. Some members continued to work in the Lower Yangtze provinces. Many others fled to Japan and because the Restoration Society had no appreciable organization abroad, its members worked for the Revolutionary Alliance.[63] In this new situation, personal and provincial antagonisms developed, and in 1910 Chang Ping-lin and T'ao Ch'eng-chang reconstituted the party to oppose Sun Yat-sen and the Revolutionary Alliance. The two groups then competed for funds and membership in Tokyo and among the overseas Chinese in Southeast Asia. There was also rivalry between the two party branches in Shanghai. Nonetheless, this phase seems to have had relatively little bearing on contemporary events in the Lower Yangtze area, but belongs instead to the history of activities of and dissensions among the revolutionaries overseas.

After the Revolution the Restoration Society briefly reemerged as a local political force in Shanghai and Chekiang. However, it was unable to compete successfully with the Revolutionary Alliance and other groups in the political power struggles which followed the Revolution. The final blow was the assassination of T'ao Ch'eng-chang early in 1912, after which the society evaporated.

The Restoration Society made its major contribution to the revolutionary movement from 1905 to mid-1907. In these early years the chief contrast between it and the Revolutionary Alliance was that the Restoration Society was a local organization founded in China which had developed a fairly pervasive revolutionary network in the areas upon which it concentrated, particularly in Chekiang. The Revolutionary Alliance, established in Japan, drew supporters from all of China, but its connections in any single place tended to be more superficial. After the Restoration Society had suffered a major defeat it was the more vulnerable organization. It had no base to fall back upon except the International Settlement in Shanghai, which had its limitations as a refuge. When the Revolution succeeded in 1911, the Revolutionary Alliance was stronger, better known, and better able to compete successfully with the Restoration Society for political position, even in the latter's old strongholds of Chekiang and Shanghai.

Continuing Character of the Shanghai Movement

Until the end of 1904 the Shanghai revolutionary movement evolved steadily, but for the next six years it remained fairly static. There was more activity from 1905 through mid-1907 than there was for two or three years after the Chekiang and Anking cases. However, the revolutionaries' occupations did not vary greatly. They continued to experiment with explosives. Both the Restoration Society and the Revolutionary Alliance operated revolutionary fronts. Radical journals, bookstores, and schools appeared and disappeared. Revolutionaries took part in a number of general public meetings, demonstrations, and boycotts. No really important change occurred until the Central China Bureau of the Revolutionary Alliance was founded in early 1911. Therefore, I will not attempt to describe all the groups in detail, but will concentrate on a few of the more significant or analytically useful points.

Before the collapse of the Restoration Society in Chekiang (and the slightly earlier failure of the P'ing Liu-Li rising in Hunan and Kiangsi), Shanghai was still important as a meeting point for revolutionaries in Central China. Major party leaders made periodic trips to the city. For a time after the Restoration Society was first established, its members met in a back room of the Jen-ho Coal Company, managed by a sympathetic merchant named Wang Lien who was also a party member. The revolutionaries soon came to fear that they would be discovered by one of the many people who visited the building in the normal course of business. To ensure greater privacy they established the Association of Chekiangese Students in Shanghai (*Che-chiang lü-Hu hsüeh-hui*), which posed as a scholarly bookselling and publishing organization. This association continued as a Restoration Society organ through 1907. It was directed by local Restoration Society members, including Wang Lien. In 1907 a man who had briefly headed the revolutionary Ta-t'ung School in Chekiang became an officer of the Shanghai establishment. Besides serving as a meeting place, the association forwarded correspondence. Code words were used to refer to the Restoration Society and to identify the writer as a party member. Messages might be couched in such terms as an order for books and school equipment.[64] Most of the contacts were with Chekiang. However, the Chekiangese revolutionaries also tried to keep in touch with the Revolutionary Alliance in Hunan and much of this contact seems to have been via Shanghai.

After 1907 Restoration Society activities were mainly carried on by the Yin sisters, who fled from Shaohsing to Shanghai after the Ta-t'ung School was closed. They ran a bookstore as a cover for meetings and correspondence and sometimes helped other revolutionaries in financial straits. In 1910 when Chang Ping-lin and T'ao Ch'eng-chang revived the Restoration Society T'ao asked the sisters to take charge of the daily work of the Shanghai headquarters, which was named the Jui-chün Study Society in their honor.[65]

After the Steadfast Conduct Public Institute closed in 1907 the Revolutionary Alliance had no party headquarters in Shanghai until Ch'en Ch'i-mei arrived from Tokyo a year later and established a party meeting place at the T'ien-pao Inn.[66] There he planned a major meeting of Chekiangese revolutionaries in the summer of 1909, which was broken up shortly after the participants arrived in Shanghai because Liu Shih-pe'i informed the police and the Chekiangese secret society leader and revolutionary Chang Kung was arrested. After that Ch'en found a new location for his headquarters. He and the Yin sisters knew of one another's activities, but after the Restoration Society and Revolutionary Alliance became competitors abroad there was also rivalry between the two groups in Shanghai. Ch'en Ch'i-mei tried to persuade the sisters to go to Southeast Asia so there would be no one to supervise Restoration Society activities in Shanghai. He also at least once intercepted funds intended for their headquarters.[67]

Journalism and education continued to play a leading role on the Shanghai radical scene.[68] Perhaps the most interesting of the minor radical organizations in Shanghai during this period was the Chinese Public Institute (*Chung-kuo kung-hsüeh*), which was founded in 1906 by students returning from Japan in protest against the more stringent regulations imposed by Japanese education authorities.[69] Its origin and original purpose was strikingly like the Patriotic School, but it lasted longer. To continue to operate it had to make certain compromises which the Patriotic School had avoided by its early demise. Some of the Chinese Public Institute's problems had been incipient in its precedessor, and its history throws some additional light on the Patriotic School.

The decision to establish the school was made in January or February and a building was rented at Woosung that spring. By then, however, the agitation over the Japanese regulations had died down and many had returned to their studies. The school had trouble finding students and raising funds. Officials suspected it as revolutionary, and potential merchant and gentry backers thought the Western-dressed youths in charge were rather outlandish. It was rescued from its difficulties by the suicide of one of the founders, who drowned himself in the Whampoa River and left behind a note saying he was dying because the school was dying. The resulting publicity brought more donations and classes continued.

The students were a radical group, many of whom wore Japanese dress and cut their queues. More time was given to political activity than to study and standards were not very high. Japanese teachers were hired for some courses, such as advanced algebra and natural science, and students who knew Japanese translated. Certain other courses, physical education, for example, were taught by students themselves. There was also a group of more traditional teachers, but they did not set the tone.

The school had connections with members of both the Restoration Society and the Revolutionary Alliance. *The People's Journal* was easily available and students going home for vacation would smuggle copies into the interior inside pillows. More ardent students might put pressure on others to cut off their queues and join one of the revolutionary parties.

Initial organization followed democratic principles which placed the students in complete control of school policy. A senate of the heads of classes elected the administrative officers, mainly from among the student body. Senate meetings were often stormy and sometimes broke up in disagreement.

The system was far from efficient and became more difficult by the end of 1906 because newly enrolled students were beginning to outnumber the original group. The early basis for unity no longer existed. Moreover, the school was badly in need of funds and those responsible for administration felt it necessary to adopt a more conventional structure in the hope of attracting official and additional private aid. Therefore, ten prominent citizens, including the gentry-industrialist Chang Chien, were invited to become trustees in the spring of 1907. They chose a superintendent. The senate was abolished and all administrative officers were chosen by the older authorities.

These changes brought about strong protests from the students, who organized the Society of Friends of the School (*Hsiao-yu hui*), which bickered with the new authorities for a year. In the fall of 1908 matters came to a crisis when the society adopted a new set of regulations. The superintendent then forbade any further meetings and expelled two student representatives. In retaliation the student body struck. More expulsions followed. The faculty and one of the trustees tried to mediate, but both the students and the administration were too aroused. After about a week of tension the majority of the students resigned in response to the latest administration attempt to break the strike.

Within ten days the departing students managed to raise a little money, rent a building, and establish a New Chinese Public Institure. They started with a student body of 160 or 170 and were able to attract many of the teachers from the old school. The head of the board of trustees was Li P'ing-shu, another Shanghai gentry-merchant who developed connections with the revolutionary movement and was to play a role in 1911.

The new school had a great deal of spirit and very little money. Students often had to contribute funds for rent and other expenses. By the end of a year it had more students than the Chinese Public Institute and a debt of 10,000 yuan. Li P'ing-shu and others sought to reconcile the two institutions because of the new school's financial problems. At the end of 1909 agreement was reached and a merger effected. All those who wished to return to the old school were allowed to do so and it assumed responsibility for the new school's debts. Many of the students were disappointed and were unwilling to return. The decision had been made, however, and from its radical beginning the Chinese Public Institute ended up in the hands of more moderate and conventional leaders.

This progression was not unique in the history of revolutionary front organizations and indeed in microcosm paralleled the history of the Revolution as a whole. Nor did it mean that the school was entirely divorced from radical politics. Li P'ing-shu, one of its trustees, came to have close connections with the Revolutionary Alliance leaders in Shanghai. Chang Ch'eng-yu, a Hupeh student at the school in 1911, was the organizer and leader of the Shanghai Dare-to-die Corps at the time of the Revolution and recruited some of his force from the student body. What the history of the school does illustrate is that first, the distinction between modernizing and revolutionary institutions was often rather tenuous and that, second, militantly radical concerns often had to compromise with respectability if they were going to retain the financial backing to operate for long. Some funds raised by revolutionary leaders abroad were turned over to local groups which had good connections with the central party. However, these were mainly used for secret party activities and for risings. There was not enough money to support all front organizations and non-party radical institutions. They had to rely on whatever local sources they could find and these were often not revolutionary.

The first important radical periodical to be established in Shanghai after the founding of the Restoration Society was *The Struggle* (*Ching-yeh hsün-pao*), published by a study society of the same name. Its first issue appeared in the fall of 1906. The editor of the journal was a Hunanese student, Fu Hsiung-hsiang, who was or soon became a member of the Revolutionary Alliance. Fu was a writer who joined the radical literary

Southern Society in 1909.[70] Another staff member was Hu Shih, then an iconoclastic student at the Chinese Public Institute. The stated aims of *The Struggle* were to advance education, arouse the people's spirit, reform society, and promote freedom. Its real purpose was to propagate revolutionary ideas. Most of the members had been to Japan and many were students at the Chinese Public Institute. The paper was written in a vernacular style and advocated a common spoken language based on the Peking Mandarin dialect. After the first ten issues, publication stopped, recommencing during the spring of 1908. During the second phase Hu Shih was in charge of editing the paper and wrote many of the articles. He had a free hand to write what he wished and at that time began to develop ideas on superstition, social immortality, and written use of the vernacular, for which he was to become noted after the Revolution.[71] Thus, although *The Struggle* was reputed to be a revolutionary organ many of its articles were not political and many of the ideas it contained could easily have been accepted by constitutionalists or other progressively minded Chinese—another example of overlap between reform and revolutionary circles.

The most influential revolutionary papers were the series published by Yü Yu-jen, beginning with the *Shen-chou Daily*, established in the spring of 1907. Yü was a Shansi native who fled to Shanghai when the Shansi governor branded him as a revolutionary for publishing a collection of verses entitled *The Chamber Half-way between Laughter and Tears* (*Pan-k'u pan-hsiao lou shih*).[72] After deciding to venture into newspaper publishing, Yü went to Japan to raise funds and joined the Revolutionary Alliance at that time. The Hunanese revolutionary Yang Yü-lin joined him in founding the paper, which employed a number of other revolutionaries and had the support of such major figures as Chang Ping-lin. Chang Chien was one of its backers—another instance of his connection with radical groups before 1911.[73] Although theoretically a revolutionary organ, the *Shen-chou Daily* suggested its views with circumspection. Opposition to the dynasty was expressed by such guarded devices as dating with cyclical characters instead of reign years.

Yü Yu-jen left the paper after less than a year when a fire destroyed its offices. Yang took charge until he left to study in Britain late in 1908. Others continued to publish the *Shen-chou Daily* until 1927 and it was briefly revived in 1936.[74] It remained a radical publication and gave editorial support to later revolutionary organs published by Yü.[75] However, it was in the mainstream of the revolutionary movement only during its first year.

After a little over a year Yü Yu-jen returned to publishing in Shanghai with the establishment of *The People's Cry* (*Min-hu jih-pao*) on May 15, 1909. Like the *Shen-chou Daily*, *The People's Cry* and its successors avoided direct attacks on the dynasty. Nevertheless they were in constant trouble with the authorities. The editors of *The People's Cry* defined the paper's mission as awakening popular consciousness and expressing popular complaints, particularly on questions of official malfeasance and foreign encroachment. They launched into a series of sharp attacks on government and official shortcomings in Shensi and other provinces. The message of the articles was enhanced by some savage cartoons depicting official exploitation and duplicity. The result was four lawsuits in the Mixed Court. At the instigation of the Kansu-Shensi governor-general, the Shanghai Taotai accused Yü of misappropriating funds from the Kansu Famine Relief Society, of which Yü was a member. Yü was arrested on August 3 and three slander suits against the paper followed. *The People's Cry* had provided office space for the Kansu collection and assumed an undefined role in the fund raising. The account books were badly confused and there was a discrepancy of over two thousand dollars between what the paper had publicly reported had been collected and the actual amount forwarded to Kansu. Much of this difference was the result of overly optimistic estimates of sums to be raised by the sale of benefit tickets. Probably no intentional embezzlement had occurred, but the affair had been badly mismanaged and Yü agreed to pay the difference owing. The slander charges were also justified by strong language and unsubstantiated accusations against the officials concerned. However, the libels in *The People's Cry* were probably no worse than frequently appeared in other Chinese papers. There is no doubt that Chinese officials were out to close *The People's Cry*, and they succeeded. The paper ceased publication after August 14. The trial continued through early September when Yü was released from jail, but he was expelled from the International Settlement.[76]

Soon he was back to found a thinly disguised successor, *The People's Sigh* (*Min-hsü jih-pao*) on September 13. This time the paper was registered with the French consulate for additional safety, but invited foreign displeasure by a strongly anti-imperialist stand. Before long it was in difficulty for attacks on Japanese encroachment in Manchuria. The Japanese consul brought pressure on the Shanghai Taotai, who asked the Mixed Court to close the paper. The police shut down the paper on November 19 before the court had considered the case. The two hearings that followed were presided over by the Chinese Magistrate, the Japanese vice-consul, and the Japanese Mixed Court assessor. Each time the paper's lawyers protested the biased composition of the bench, the Japanese consulate tried to evade the issue. Before any actual trial was held a verdict was suddenly handed down December 29 permanently closing *The People's Sigh* and stipulating that the printing press should not be used to publish another paper.[77]

The People's Cry had closed under a cloud, but the arbitrary treatment of *The People's Sigh* aroused wide sympathy in reform and radical circles. Large protest meetings were held in Nanking and Shanghai. Students in Tokyo petitioned the censorate to memorialize the throne on behalf of the paper. Students in Peking also held a meeting.[78] Support came, too, from the reformist Chinese press and English-language papers. *The Eastern Times,* the *Shen-chou Daily, The Eastern Miscellany,* and the *North China Herald* all criticized the conduct of the Chinese officials and the Mixed Court.[79] The Chinese government had again mishandled a case and appeared in an unfavorable light.[80] Moreover, the revolutionaries were not permanently silenced, for on October 11, 1910, Yü Yu-jen and the same general group established *The People's Stand* (*Min-li pao*). This time they managed to stay out of serious trouble and the paper continued to be the main organ of the Shanghai revolutionaries until the fall of 1913, when it supported the unsuccessful anti-Yüan Shih-k'ai Forces during the Second Revolution.

During these years from 1906 to 1910 there were two significant developments in Shanghai. One was mainly of historical importance for the events of 1911: the formation of a new group of revolutionaries who were to play the major role in the Shanghai Revolution. These men were members of the Revolutionary Alliance and looked to Ch'en Ch'i-mei for political leadership. Many served on the staff of one or several of the papers published by Yü Yu-jen, and Ch'en himself worked as a reporter for *The People's Stand*. In 1911 they worked with Sung Chiao-jen, T'an Jen-feng, Lü Chih-i, and others newly arrived in Shanghai. This was largely a different group from those who had begun their radical activities in Shanghai before 1906 or 1907.[81] Among its more prominent members were Fan Kuang-ch'i from Anhwei and Ching Yao-yüeh of Shansi, who were to become important members of the Central China Bureau, and the writer and journalist Wang Chung-chi.[82]

Ch'en Ch'i-mei was indisputably the dominant figure, and he did much to shape the course of the Shanghai Revolution.[83] He was the son of a merchant of modest means from Huchow, Chekiang. As a child he was apprenticed to a pawnshop in a neighboring town. After five years he escaped this life and in 1896 began to study English at the Chinese and Western Academy (*Chung-Hsi shu-yüan*) in Shanghai. During the next two years he continued Western studies at the Chin-ling Language School. Then he obtained a government scholarship for military studies at the Chinese

Students' Military Preparatory School (*Seijo gakkō*) and Army Officers' Academy (*Shikan gakkō*) in Tokyo. He graduated from the latter in 1902, just before radical ideas became widespread among the Chinese students in Japan. Despite his military training Ch'en was not ready to settle down to an army career and spent the next few years in a variety of miscellaneous activities. He became an accountant in a silk shop in Shanghai. Then he studied physics. In 1905 he helped organize the anti-American boycott in Changsha. In 1906 he was back in Tokyo studying police and military methods. During these years Ch'en evidently became increasingly nationalistic and radical. He joined the Revolutionary Alliance while in Tokyo in 1906 and thereafter found his niche as a party organizer. Shanghai became his special sphere, but because he was Chekiangese he also had some influence in the revolutionary movement in that province. In 1911 he skillfully consolidated his position as military governor of Shanghai with the aid of both merchant-gentry and secret society Green and Red Gang allies. He also helped plan the Hangchow revolution and played significant parts in organizing the Chekiang-Shanghai army which captured Nanking and in establishing the provisional national government at Nanking at the beginning of 1912.

Ch'en was a professional party politician who stands out among the Shanghai radicals as being more manipulative, more of an organizer, and less of a romantic idealist than many. His talents would have been useful to the Kuomintang during the Republic, but he unfortunately was caught in the general collapse of revolutionary forces after the first few months of 1912. Ch'en disapproved of the North-South Accord and refused to serve in Yüan Shih-k'ai's government. He soon was forced to resign as Shanghai military governor and was preparing to go abroad when the assassination of Sung Chiao-jen began a new series of struggles between Yüan and the revolutionaries. Thereafter Ch'en made three unsuccessful attempts to seize control of Shanghai from militarists allied with Yüan, in the fall of 1913 as part of the "Second Revolution," in December 1915, and in April 1916. On May 18, a month after the last attempt, he was assassinated. During this period Ch'en was closely associated with Sun Yat-sen and joined the Revolutionary Party (*Ko-ming tang*) in Tokyo in 1914, but he preferred to concentrate on his old base in Shanghai rather than to adopt Sun's strategy of focusing on Kwangtung and southwest China. Later his nephews Ch'en Li-fu and Ch'en Kuo-fu carried on his party role as Kuomintang organizers closely associated with Chiang Kai-shek.

Ch'en's group developed its own connections with merchant and gentry liberals who gave financial support—chiefly for publishing ventures before 1911. Among these were Shen Man-yün, from Wusih, Kiangsu, who was assistant manager of the Hsin-ch'eng Bank. Shen sought Yü Yu-jen's acquaintance after reading articles in his papers. He donated funds to *The People's Stand.* In 1911 he contributed to the Shanghai military government and was minister of finance.[84] Shen introduced Yü to two other useful individuals, Wang Chen and Li P'ing-shu. Wang, who was originally from Wu-hsing, Chekiang, was apprenticed to a Shanghai bank when he was fifteen. At twenty-three he became manager of the Tien-yu Trading Company and went on to an extremely successful business and philanthropic career in Shanghai. He was assistant finance minister of the Shanghai military government in 1911 and one of the trustees of the Bank of China, established right after the Revolution. During the Republic he held various other public economic or financial positions.[85] Li P'ing-shu was perhaps the most important of the revolutionaries' outside connections. He had been magistrate of Sui-ch'i district in Kwangtung during the Sino-French war. There he had organized militia and repelled the French, but was dismissed after the treaty was signed. Afterward he was proctor at the Kiangnan Arsenal, a leader of self-government groups, and chairman of the Shanghai City Council.[86] He was also connected with the Chinese Public Institute and was acquainted with Ch'en Ch'i-mei and a number of other Revolutionary Alliance members. Somewhat further removed was Chang Chien. Chang's main activities were industrial and educational promotion in his native Nan-t'ung district and his leadership of the Kiangsu constitutionalists and the provincial assembly. However, he did have some contact with the Shanghai radical scene through his association with the *Shenchou Daily* and the Chinese Public Institute. After the Wuchang rising he decided that China's best hope lay in a republican government and joined Ch'en Ch'i-mei and other revolutionaries in early efforts to form a provisional national government.[87]

The Revolutionary Alliance group was fortunate in finding one source of funds within their midst. Chang Jen-chieh came from a family of wealthy silk merchants of Wu-hsing district in Chekiang. He had received a good modern education with the expectation that he would eventually carry on his father's business. To broaden his experience he became an economic attaché at the Chinese embassy in Paris after previously purchasing the title of expectant taotai. In Paris, Chang became a theoretical anarchist and finally managed to convince the Chinese student radicals in France to accept him despite his official post and wealthy background. In 1903 Chang founded companies in Shanghai, Paris, and London which traded very profitably in tea, silk, and curios until about the time of World War I. When not managing his business affairs Chang promoted anarchist and generally revolutionary causes. He was one of the founders of the anarchist World Society in Paris in 1906 and provided most of the funds to finance its journal *New Century*, which began publication the next year. After 1906 Chang spent much of his time back in China, particularly in Shanghai, where he had a branch of his curio company and where he also headed a branch of the World Society. He joined the Revolutionary Alliance in Hong Kong in 1907 and after that contributed heavily to party finances. He also helped support Yü Yu-jen's newspapers. After the Revolution he raised funds for the Shanghai military government and the projected northern expedition in January 1912. Later he joined the Kuomintang. He was close to Chiang Kai-shek and during the second half of 1926 was acting chairman of the standing commission of the Kuomintang Central Executive Committee. After the Northern Expedition was completed he served as chairman of the National Reconstruction Commission and as governor of Chekiang.[88]

The other major development was really the continuation of a process begun in the 1890's: the emergence of a definable intelligentsia in the Shanghai area. It consisted of intellectuals who in varying degrees were associated with the revolutionary movement or the radical schools and press. Some were members of a revolutionary party. Others just sympathized with most revolutionary views while their main interests were more literary or educational than narrowly political. Many spent much of their time away from Shanghai. However, regardless of their place of origin, they had friends and intellectual ties in Shanghai and kept returning to that city. They were united by a common attraction to social change and intellectual innovation. Although they might bicker among themselves they were in a sense a community separate from the rest of society. They had their own special causes, like the memorial meeting held for Tsou Jung after his death in the spring of 1905[89] and the welcoming of Chang Ping-lin from jail by members of the Restoration Society, Revolutionary Alliance, and Educational Association the following year.[90] Such projects often seem to have interested the radicals more than some of the important movements going on around them. The anti-American boycott, which was a major event in Shanghai during the last six months of 1905, is scarcely mentioned in revolutionary histories even though some of the students who took part in the demonstrations must have had connections with revolutionaries. Nationalistic agitation had made its chief contribution to revolutionary development during 1903. Now nationalism was becoming more deeply ingrained in other groups. The radicals were able to look on the anti-Russian demonstrations as a family affair, but they had no such proprietary interest in the boycott and probably would have had difficulty dealing with many of the merchants whose cooperation was necessary to make an embargo work.

The organization which came closest to symbolizing the Shanghai intelligentsia was the Southern Society (*Nan-she*). This radical literary society was consciously modeled on the Revival Society (*Fu-she*) of the late Ming dynasty, a literary group which for over ten years was a national political force.[91] Liu Ch'i-chi, Ch'en Ch'ü-ping, and Kao Chien-kung first planned the Southern Society in 1907, but it was not actually established until November 1909. At the beginning there were only a few dozen members, but these grew to over a thousand during the Republic.[92] The Southern Society was a very loose grouping of intellectuals and it met irregularly. The largest number of members came from Kiangsu. Chekiang was a poor second, and Anhwei, third. It was thus a predominantly Lower Yangtze group, but there were at least a few members from most of the other provinces. The founders came from the group of revolutionaries who had been most active in Shanghai during the period from 1904 to 1907. A few, such as Liu Ch'i-chi and Lin Hsieh, had been students at the Patriotic School. Many of this group were no longer actively participating in Shanghai radical politics.[93] The Southern Society also included members who worked for the papers published by Yü Yu-jen and such members of the Revolutionary Alliance's Central China Bureau as Ch'en Chi-mei, Sung Chiao-jen, and Lü Chih-i. The society provided a link between early and later revolutionary activity in Shanghai and between party and nonparty radicals.

Significantly it was not a political group. It seems to have been characteristic of many radical intellectuals not to remain politically active for extended periods. This was one reason why Sun Yat-sen, with his many years of party work, had few rivals who could dispute his claims to revolutionary leadership. This factor was related to and contributed to the overlap between a general radicalism derived from both modernizing and nationalistic attitudes and reformist and revolutionary politics. It also contributed to the weakness of the revolutionary movement because many radical intellectuals were not temperamentally inclined to the practical political activity needed to give effect to their views.[94] Some illumination of the kind of life led by the new intelligentsia is provided by the biography of the poet Su Man-shu. Su himself was not entirely typical because he was more apolitical than many of his radical friends and also because he was a Kwangtungese. However, he was an adopted member of the Central China radical intellectual circles and his history is suggestive of characteristics of the intelligentsia as a group.

Su was born in Yokohama, the son of a Cantonese comprador of a tea company and a Japanese maid.[95] He received his early education in his father's native village. Then he studied English in Shanghai and returned to Yokohama to enter the Ta-t'ung School in 1898. In 1902 and 1903 he studied first at the preparatory school for Waseda University and then at the Military Preparatory School (*Shimbu gakkō*). He refused to sign the manifesto of the Meeting to Commemorate the 242nd Year of the Fall of China,[96] but he joined the Youth Association, the Volunteer Corps to Oppose Russia, and the Society for the Education of a Militant People. Later in 1903 Su returned to China. He served briefly on the staff of *The China National Gazette* in September and October before going south to Hong Kong, where he stayed at the offices of the radical *Chinese Daily*. He refused to return home on the death of his father, but became a Buddhist monk for three months in the winter of 1903–04. Then he briefly stayed again at the *Chinese Daily* and returned to Shanghai later that spring. For the next several years Su traveled about the Yangtze Valley, northern Chekiang, and Japan. He visited in Shanghai, Wuhu, Nanking, Changsha, Hangchow, and Tokyo. During this time he wrote and taught. Su was primarily a poet and a painter, but he preferred the society of radicals. He was in Changsha periodically during 1904–1906, when the Society for China's Revival was active in Hunan, and while there he taught at the radical Industrial and Ming-te schools. In Wuhu he taught at the similar Wan-chiang Middle School. In Tokyo in 1907 and 1908 he associated most closely with the loosely anarchist group which published the *Journal of Natural Law* (*T'ien-i pao*) and contributed both to that magazine and *The People's Journal*. In the fall of 1909 he followed the path taken by many other Chinese radicals, to Southeast Asia, where he taught overseas Chinese in Java until returning to Shanghai in February 1912. After the Revolution, Su continued to write, teach, and associate with radical friends. He traveled between Tokyo and the same cities in Kiangsu, Anhwei, and Chekiang until illness forced him to remain in Shanghai for the last year before his death in May 1918. While in Tokyo he wrote two articles for *The Republican Miscellany* (*Min-kuo tsa-chih*), the organ of Sun Yat-sen's Revolutionary Party. He also played some small role in the "Third Revolution" against Yüan Shih-k'ai in 1916, but his activities were still mainly nonpolitical.

Su Man-shu may have been an extreme case, but a number of points about his life have a wider application. He cut himself off from traditional ties of place and family, which for him were already weak because of his mother's lowly position and foreign citizenship. All the new intellectuals were forced to make some sort of break with the past, which in Su's case was symbolized by refusal to return home when his father died. Although he was a southerner, Su spent most of his adult years in the cities of Central China or in Tokyo. These places were evidently more congenial to the life he had adopted, and Shanghai was one of the cities to which he most frequently returned. Su had rejected conventional Chinese society and in an earlier period he would probably have found his niche in Buddhism (which he tried briefly) or as part of some literary coterie. In the early twentieth century he escaped into the new radical circles. Despite his constant travels, his existence was not really rootless. He had his own circles of associates and his own itinerary which repeatedly returned him to the same places on a well-established circuit. Su must have enjoyed himself thoroughly and, paradoxically, regardless of the new milieu in which he moved, he did not personally lead a very different life than he might have before the revolutionary movement had ever begun. He was simultaneously traditional and modern.

The new intelligentsia, of which Su was a part, overlapped the revolutionary movement but was not identical with it. I would suggest that many other radical intellectuals, even some who were members of the Revolutionary Alliance, were touched only lightly by the practical aspects of revolutionary work. Their radicalism lent itself to a literary career and semi-Bohemian life more than to party activity. Like intellectuals all over the world they were hard to organize and discipline. A loose, nonparty group like the Southern Society more accurately reflected their tendencies than did the Revolutionary Alliance. The Shanghai branch of the Revolutionary Alliance and in 1911 the Central China Bureau most effectively carried on the organizational impulse begun in that area in 1904 by the Restoration Society. It should be remembered, however, that party activities were carried on by only a small percentage of the Shanghai radical intellectuals and that it was alliances with other classes and groups—merchants, police, soldiers, local groups—which brought success during the actual Revolution.

The intellectuals in Shanghai as a group remained divorced from political power and separate from conventional society. In the last decade before 1911 the city became well-established as the gathering place for the new intelligentsia. It continued to be prominent in radical trends during the Republic. However, Shanghai attracted dissatisfied intellectuals precisely because it was atypical of the rest of China. There they found congenial company, but they had limited means to influence developments elsewhere. Individual radicals kept returning to Shanghai, but when they wished to make an attempt to overthrow the government they usually left the city for their home towns or provinces.

Shanghai's contribution to the 1911 revolutionary movement lay in its relatively favorable environment, which allowed it to become a regional center. The Shanghai movement had more continuity and vitality than those in the provinces because it enjoyed the protection of the International Settlement and because modernization that had initially stimulated radical ideas was furthest advanced there. Radicals from many provinces were attracted to Shanghai, and some of their organizations had more than purely local significance. Radical influences spread out from the city to give impetus and a little cohesion to revolutionaries throughout the Lower Yangtze provinces. Even so, revolutionaries in Shanghai did not really dominate the movement in the surrounding area any more than those in Tokyo controlled revolutionaries in China as a whole. More radicals concentrated in Shanghai than elsewhere in the country and they could express their views more freely. If the government collapsed they had a reasonable chance of seizing power in the city, but their ultimate fate depended on what happened in the rest of China.

The environment in which the revolutionary movement developed in Chekiang was in marked contrast to that of Shanghai and the resulting movement was significantly different. Before the immediate events of the Revolution in 1911, when attention focused on seizing the provincial capital of Hangchow, there was no real center of revolutionary activity. Ningpo was evidently not important enough either as a treaty port or an intellectual center to have more than local significance. Hangchow was a center of early student radicalism. Later the new army units stationed in its environs attracted party organizers. However, it could not compete with Shanghai as a radical center and did not dominate revolutionary activities elsewhere in the province.

Much of the work was done in the smaller cities, towns, and villages, which were less directly affected by Western-inspired changes. There revolutionaries established front organizations and sought alliances with local illegal groups. This sort of activity was more directly subversive than much of that engaged in by students in Shanghai. Moreover, revolutionaries were more vulnerable to arrest away from the International Settlement. Greater circumspection was necessary and radicals only occasionally displayed the flamboyance and articulation which characterized the Shanghai scene. Despite the difficulties, those who seriously hoped to organize an armed rising had to leave the shadow of Western power in Shanghai and go where they could find recruits to fill the ranks of their "revolutionary armies."

In Chekiang the intellectual revolutionaries originally found two bases on which to build their antigovernment movement. One was the traditional anti-Manchuism and current economic unrest of the secret societies. The other was local students and scholars throughout the province who had been influenced by modern ideas. Before students began to return home to spread propaganda from Shanghai and Tokyo in late 1903, radical ideas had penetrated many of the towns, at least on a small scale. Older scholars had also been influenced by the impact of the Sino-Japanese War and the Boxer Rebellion. Though

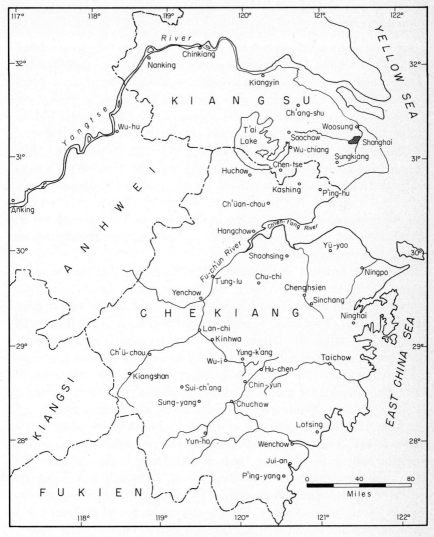

Chekiang and Vicinity

generally more moderate than the students in the new schools, some among them became proponents of reform and were willing to give limited support to radical colleagues.

Secret Societies

When revolutionaries approached the secret societies they were seeking contacts with an illegal element in Chinese society which nonetheless played an important and often openly recognized role on the local scene. Most secret societies in the province were related to the Triad Society (*Hung-men, San-ho hui,* and so forth), which had originated in Chekiang and Fukien in resistance to the Manchu invasion and were deeply entrenched in the area. In Chekiang the Triads remained militarily powerful through the middle of the K'ang-hsi period. A leader named Chang Nien-i established a rebel center at Ta-lan Mountain in Yü-yao district, eastern Chekiang. He then succeeded in uniting with rebels in the western part of the province and with the bandits and salt smugglers on Poyang and T'ai lakes. However, his rebellion was suppressed about 1707 and his followers scattered about Chekiang, Kiangsu, and Kiangsi.[1]

The Triads persisted in Chekiang after this failure, but they were no longer a relatively unified, actively antidynastic group. The total number of members gradually increased during the Ch'ing, but they were divided among many small societies. New groups evidently made use of the general Triad rituals, ranks, and terminology. These were part of the dominant secret society tradition in the area and had obvious advantages in attracting recruits and maintaining solidarity among members. However, societies were often founded for purposes which had little to do with the original Triad aims. Unless bands were recruited among an itinerant group, they might be limited to a small part of the province. Members of the lower classes found security in the fraternal ties and protection offered by the societies. Individuals higher on the local social scale might use leadership of a society to enhance their personal power, both legal and illegal. As long as no unsettling conditions arose, a society might exist quite peacefully for many years. It could not be officially sanctioned, but its existence might be well known and tolerated by local authorities who found it advantageous to cooperate with society leaders whose local influence was often greater than theirs. Since the societies were still illegal, however, they tended to become involved in criminal activities profitable to their members. When government control weakened, societies would foment or give leadership to local unrest. Expansion by vigorous bands might either bring conflict with other groups or result in cooperation and alliances. Boundaries between admitted bandit bands, secret societies of long standing, and semiprivate gangs were not aways very clear. Nor were legal and illegal organizations always distinct. Militia raised to keep order, for instance, might shift to banditry or rebellion. The term secret society used here actually covers a variety of illegal or quasi-legal organizations which had affiliated themselves with the locally dominant Triad tradition. A detailed study of local social conditions should reveal that societies were an integral part of the local society in which they played varied and important roles. Revolutionaries who looked for allies among them were seeking a short cut to local influence by gaining the cooperation of already established, potentially disaffected groups.

In Chekiang the mid-nineteenth-century Taiping Rebellion brought a revival of secret society militancy and anti-Manchuism. The many existing groups did not unite, but weakening government control resulted in the emergence of a number of new, independent societies which fell into the general Triad category.[2] The unsettling effects of the Taiping Rebellion were reinforced by the economic and social dislocations which attended and followed it. The rebellion left large areas of uncultivated land, particularly in northern Chekiang. Some was reclaimed by former owners, but many had been killed or were long delayed in returning. Much vacant property was, therefore, settled by immigrants (k'o-min) from other parts of Chekiang and from other provinces, especially Kiangsu and Honan. The influx of new settlers, vagrants, and disbanded soldiers (who often were not natives of the province) resulted in disturbances and frequent banditry. Conflicts over property rights and conflicts because of cultural and linguistic differences inevitably developed between immigrants and the remaining natives of a district. Immigrants often behaved in a high-handed manner and resorted to force against competitors for property. On the other hand, because they were a disruptive element, officials treated them unsympathetically.[3] Therefore, there were legitimate grievances on both sides. Feelings ran high, often with bloody results, as in 1883 when immigrants in two districts of northern Chekiang were massacred by the old inhabitants.[4] The situation was analogous to the tension between the Hakka and the native inhabitants of Kwangtung, which was one of the factors behind the Taiping Rebellion. Such disruptions favored the recruitment of secret society members, and when the revolutionaries began to seek adherents in Chekiang they believed that an area with a large number of immigrants was a favorable place to work.

Reinforcing the special effects of the Taiping Rebellion were the usual late dynastic problems of official corruption and exactions and poor harvests with attendant famines—phenomena made worse by the slow recovery of the province from the Taiping devastation.[5] On top of all was the xenophobic reaction to Western encroachment. Ningpo never became a really major treaty port and the Hangchow harbor was dangerous to shipping, so eastern Chekiang never had as much contact with Western traders and businessmen as did the areas about Shanghai, Canton, or along the banks of the Yangtze River. However, missionaries were at work throughout the province, bringing the usual intercultural problems with them. Attacks on missionaries were frequently associated with the history of the secret societies.

The societies that the revolutionaries contacted were the Chung-nan Society, the Crouching Tiger Society (*Fu-hu hui*), the White Cloth Society (*Pai-pu hui*), the Double Dragon Society (*Shuang-lung hui*), the P'ing-yang Society, the Dragon Flower Society (*Lung-hua hui*), and the Chekiangese salt smugglers.[6] All were Triad splinter groups and most had been founded during or after the Taiping Rebellion. There are no accurate accounts of the number of members. The larger societies may have numbered ten or twenty thousand. Groups of that size often broke up into branches of about three or five thousand members.[7] It is impossible to say how much control was exercised over branch leaders, but the general picture of fragmentation is very clear. Often a new society would split off from an old one, headed by a particularly dynamic member of the parent group. The general situation seems to have been one of flux, with some societies persisting over a long period and others coming and going. The fortunes of any one society might also vary. At times it might become almost extinct, only to revive under new favorable circumstances.

The Chung-nan was a strong society, older than the others, which had been brought from Hunan to Kiangsi and from Kiangsi to Ch'ü-chou, Chekiang, and Kienning, Fukien. It was the forerunner of a number of other societies in Chekiang, including the Double Dragon, the Dragon Flower, and the Crouching Tiger.[8] The original leader in Chekiang was Ho Pu-hung. His lieutenant was a former member of Tseng Kuo-fan's Hunan army, who resigned after the Taiping Rebellion and settled in Kinhwa. One of the branch leaders was an ex-soldier named Liu Chia-fu, a native of southwestern Chekiang. Liu had fled to Fukien after creating some disturbance while still in the army. In Fukien he joined the Chung-nan Society. Among his chief followers were a boxer and an elementary school teacher who practiced arts to acquire supernatural powers and who believed himself fated to be the assistant of a king.

In the summer of 1900 Liu took advantage of the confusions created by the Boxer Rebellion to start a rising of his own. He progressed as far as his home town of Kiangshan in Ch'ü-chou and then, on the advice of one of his lieutenants, paused several days to take steps appropriate for one who was challenging the dynasty. He changed his name to Lo p'ing-kuo-wang, established a court ritual, and held a feast for his officers. Meanwhile, a subordinate went north to Kinhwa and Yenchow and made alliances with secret societies in those prefectures. Liu then moved against the prefectural capital in Ch'ü-chou. The rebels' approach was used by a group in the city to foment a riot aimed at the reformist district magistrate and local Christians. Soldiers roamed the city freely for several days, uncurbed by the taotai and other conservative officials. The magistrate and his family were killed as were foreign missionaries and Chinese converts in the city. This rioting was followed by a vigorous defense of the city and Liu failed to capture it. Government troops from Chekiang and other provinces attacked the forces he had left to guard the towns he had already taken. Liu fled and died somewhere in Kiangsi or Fukien. Some of his followers joined or formed other Chekiangese secret societies and later had contacts with the revolutionaries.[9]

One of the Chung-nan offshoots, the Crouching Tiger Society, was established in Taichow.[10] Its head was Wang Hsi-t'ung, a holder of a *hsiu-ts'ai* degree from Ninghai district in that prefecture. Wang founded the society in order to expel Westerners and during 1900 and 1901 and again in 1903 he instigated a series of missionary cases in the Ninghai area. The revolutionary organizer T'ao Ch'eng-chang claimed that after 1903 or 1904 there was a general reduction of missionary cases in Chekiang because revolutionary propaganda had succeeded in converting Wang and other anti-Christian xenophobes to anti-Manchuism. Perhaps T'ao was over-optimistic in his assessment, for in 1905 there again were attacks on Roman Catholics in the Ninghai area, indicating that the conversion of the Crouching Tiger Society may not have been complete. Some of the change which T'ao believed occurred may have been another example of the sort of anti-dynastic, anti-Christian ambiguity in secret society attitudes which was evident early in the Boxer Rebellion before the anti-Christian strain became dominant. In Chekiang the evidence suggests that as dissatisfaction increased and became more political, xenophobic opposition to Western Christianity was transformed into opposition to Manchus as foreign rulers.

The Double Dragon Society (sometimes called the Ten Thousand Cloud Society) was also related to the Chung-nan Society. Its leader, Wang Chin-pao, was from a poor family. His father had been a boxer and served for some years as a guard at the house of a wealthy man named Huang in Sungyang, Chuchow prefecture, in the interior of Chekiang. Later his father traveled about Fukien and Kiangsi, giving boxing lessons. Wang traveled with him as a youth and thus was introduced to secret societies in the areas they covered. After 1894 his father became infirm and settled down in Sungyang, working as a watchman for local businesses. Wang, who was also a boxer, became a guard at the house of his father's former employer. Huang urged Wang to form a society because he wished to seek revenge for some personal grievance. Wang, therefore, undertook to organize a branch of the Chung-nan hui. To recruit members, he took advantage of the local annual autumn river festival known as Double Rapids (*Shuang-t'an*) at which the farmers in the district gathered, feasted, and engaged in mock battles. The name Double Dragon echoed the festival's title. Huang bribed the underlings of the corrupt local prefect, so no attempt was made to interfere with the society's recruitment and other activities. Wang proved a very popular organizer and within a year or so there were an alleged twenty thousand members, divided into branches in all ten districts of Chuchow. These were organized in accordance with a poem devised by Wang, each branch being designated by one, two, or three characters from the poem.

When the revolutionaries began to make contacts with the secret societies in 1904, they were introduced to Wang by the leader of the Dragon Flower Society. Wang then made plans for a rising, which he called off when warned that government officials had heard of his intentions. However, the provincial government offered a reward for him and Wang, then age twenty-five, was betrayed by an acquaintance. The society was carried on by his subordinates and remained strong for at least several more years.[11]

The White Cloth Society dated back to the time of the Taiping Rebellion. It probably originated about 1860 in militia organized in Jui-an, Wenchow prefecture, by the younger brother of the well-known official and Sung scholar Sun I-yen. Two years earlier the Gold Coin Society (*Chin-ch'ien hui*) had sprung up around P'ing-yang to the south. This group attracted a considerable following and unsuccessfully attempted a rising in 1861. Evidently the Sun family developed the militia, under the name of the White Cloth Society, as a counterbalance. When Tso Tsung-t'ang's troops approached Hangchow in 1864, the Suns thought it prudent to disband the militia and they forbade the society to propagate its ideas in Hangchow.[12]

The society did not die out, however, because some of its members emigrated from Wenchow to Chuchow and Yenchow, taking the remnants of their organization with them. In Yenchow the White Cloth Society eventually found a leader in P'u Chen-sheng, a senior licentiate by seniority (*sui-keng sheng*) from a wealthy and generous family in T'ung-lu. The versatile P'u was skilled in medicine, physiognomy, and astronomy—abilities which probably served him well as a secret society leader. He held an official or quasi-official position as general director of immigrants (*k'o-min tsung-tung-shih*) for six districts south and southwest of Hangchow. Because of his efforts on their behalf, he became very popular with the immigrants and thus gained control of the White Cloth Society.

On the pretext of protecting the countryside against bandits in the wake of the Boxer disturbances, P'u organized society members into militia during 1901 and 1902. These were united in a possibly secret hierarchy of military units with P'u as commander-in-chief. During the summer of 1902 trouble erupted between Catholic converts and the rest of the populace. Some years before an Earthly Lord Religion (*Ti-chu chiao*) had been organized in opposition to the Catholics (*T'ien-chu chiao*) and during 1902 it gained in importance. There was possibly some overlap between adherents of this sect and the White Cloth Society. Evidently there was also rivalry between the society and the Catholics. White Cloth Society members sold cloth tickets bearing the seal of the society and other devices which guaranteed protection to the purchasers. Officials were slow to prohibit this practice and Catholics sometimes took the initiative in reporting holders to the magistrate of T'ung-lu district, which was the center of the unrest. P'u on the other hand attracted support among the populace opposed to the Catholics.

His real purpose was to oppose the government, however. When officials had difficulty restoring order, P'u seized on this opportunity to start a rising late in 1902. He told the officials that his militia would suppress the Catholics. Then he sent a secret warning to the missionaries and told his followers not to wantonly destroy churches because the real fault lay with the officials, not the missionaries. Rice for provisions might be taken from the Christians, but they were not to be harmed and no other plundering was allowed. P'u's forces were relatively well disciplined and were well received in the villages. When government soldiers sent against him killed and plundered indiscriminately, support for P'u's rising broadened. From Ch'ü-chou, Chuchow, Fukien, and Kiangsi he also received aid from other secret societies that had stirred up trouble in their own areas to divert government troops. P'u marched on Yenchow, but, when the local troops were reinforced from the provincial capital, he could not stand against the superior government numbers. He led his remaining followers to hide in the mountains. Because of his popularity with the local people, the Ch'ing officials had difficulty tracing him. By offering rewards and using many spies they eventually located and surrounded his troops. P'u held out several days, but he saw that he couldn't escape and that the government troops were plundering the villages. Therefore, he surrendered on the condition that his followers would be treated leniently. Gentry from six districts in Yenchow petitioned on P'u's behalf and the governor feared that his execution would precipitate another rising. So P'u was imprisoned and his son executed in his stead. Followers repeatedly tried to release him from jail, but P'u always refused. However, he remained in contact with secret society circles and was to help T'ao Ch'eng-chang by giving him letters of introduction to secret society leaders. In the spring of 1907 he died in jail at the age of sixty-three.[13]

Another and much smaller group whose origins were also related to the post-Taiping immigration was the band formed by the brothers Kao Ta and Kao K'uei. It was a strong bandit force, but not the only one of this type. It is mainly of interest as another example of the effect of the disruption of the Taiping Rebellion and of the interrelations between banditry, secret societies, and, later, the revolutionaries. The Kao brothers had moved from Taichow to Kinhwa to cultivate abandoned fields. There they ran into difficulties with the yamen underlings and fled to the mountains, where they organized a bandit band. It became strong enough to be a worthwhile ally and the Chung-nan Society leader, Liu Chia-fu, sent an emissary to the Kao brothers. They eventually reached agreements with several of the secret societies. Because of these connections they were introduced to the revolutionaries, frequented the Ta-t'ung School, and were finally killed while aiding a Dragon Flower Society group in an anti-Ch'ing rising in 1907.[14]

The two societies which had the closest relations with the revolutionaries were the P'ing-yang and the Dragon Flower. The P'ing-yang Society was strongest in Chenghsien of Shaohsing prefecture. Shaohsing also became the headquarters of the revolutionaries, so it was natural that contacts should have developed. In addition the society's leaders had much in common with the radical students. The founder was Chu Shao-k'ang, the son of a wealthy doctor, who had passed the examinations for the *hsiu-ts'ai* degree at an early age. He originally founded the society about 1900 to gain revenge on a bandit and an unsavory member of the local gentry who had killed his father. After meeting the revolutionaries Chu worked very closely with them until the movement fell apart in mid-1907. Even after this time he maintained contacts and after the Revolution held a number of military posts, reaching the rank of lieutenant general. His chief assistant was

Wang Chin-fa, who was a military graduate under the old examination system and had also studied at the radical Ōmori Physical Education Association in Japan. Upon returning home he sought to organize militia for use as a revolutionary army. He was a friend of Chu, who entrusted him with much of the management of the society. Wang's relations with the revolutionaries were even closer than Chu's. After 1907 he aided T'ao Ch'eng-chang abroad in Japan and later in Southeast Asia. Thus he became more closely identified with the revolutionary movement than with the secret societies. In 1912 he was assassinated during the power struggles that followed the Revolution.

The Dragon Flower Society was also a young group founded in 1900 or 1901. The organizers chose its name to take advantage of previous local rumors that true peace in the empire would only be achieved by expelling those who were not members of the "dragon-flower society." This was the time of the Boxer Rebellion and probably the "dragon" and "flower" referred to China. The slogan was, therefore, antiforeign and antimissionary, but the society does not seem to have been actively anti-Christian at the time it was contacted by the revolutionaries.

The society had about twenty thousand members divided into separate branches in each district where it flourished. These were mainly in Kinhwa, but there were also branches in Taichow, Chuchow, and Shaohsing prefectures. Each branch had one head as well as four assistants in charge of affairs in the north, south, east, and west subdivisions of the district. At least once, in 1903, one of the branches engaged in a minor war with a local bandit.

The Dragon Flower leaders were Shen Yung-ch'ing and his two assistants, Chang Kung and Chou Hua-ch'ang. These three seem to have been more or less equal, maintained separate headquarters, and had their own especially trusted assistants. All had been members of the Chung-nan Society and Shen and Chang had each been a member of another secret society before that. Shen joined the Hundred Sons Society (*Pai-tzu hui*) and then the Chung-nan Society, of which he became a chief lieutenant. After the death of the Chung-nan head he established his own society. Shen's headquarters were in a general store and his personal assistant was a former soldier. Chang Kung had established the Thousand Men Society (*Ch'ien-jen hui*) before joining the Chung-nan Society. After the founding of the Dragon Flower, his main contact points were first a theatrical company and then a teashop. The theatrical company served as a convenient blind, enabling Chang to travel about the prefecture giving speeches and winning converts. His closest assistant was a good boxer who had held a variety of jobs. Chang first saw him when he was a cashier for a troupe of players and persuaded him to leave his employment and join the Dragon Flower Society.[15]

Shen was a member of a wealthy local family, but he had once been imprisoned for bribery. There is no information about Chou Hua-ch'ang's background, but Chang Kung, like the P'ing-yang Society leaders, had much in common with the revolutionary intellectuals. His father was a teacher and Chang received a traditional education. In 1900 he and Chiang Lo-shan, who was to become one of the society's branch leaders, studied at the Tzu-yang Academy in Hangchow. There they were among those who promised T'ang Ts'ai-ch'ang's younger brother that they would support T'ang's Hankow uprising. When T'ang's rising failed, Chang returned to his secret society activities. Nonetheless in 1903 he took and passed the traditional examinations for the *chü-jen* degree. After the *Su-pao* case, he and the other Kinhwa natives, including one former member of the Han-lin Academy, founded a newspaper called *Collections of the New* (*Ts'ui-hsin pao*) to spread radical ideas in the interior of the province. The paper was read by students in Chekiang schools and came to the attention of the Manchu prefect of Yenchow when a copy smuggled into the prefectural school was discovered. Before orders to close the paper had been transmitted to Kinhwa, Chang had been warned by revolutionaries in Hangchow and the offices were moved to a new address.[16] These activities were very similar to those of the intellectual revolutionaries, and Chang worked closely with the Restoration Society when it became active in Chekiang. After Ch'iu Chin's execution Chang fled to Shanghai. He continued revolutionary activities and was finally arrested and imprisoned in 1909.[17]

It seems possible that Chang initially turned to the secret societies because at the time they were the most readily available organizations through which he could express his dissatisfaction. He had much in common with the revolutionaries, had known some during their student days in Hangchow, and had he begun his political activities a few years later he might have directly joined the Restoration Society. A considerable basis, therefore, existed for cooperation even though Chang also must have been less influenced by Western ideologies and more attracted to traditional means of power and prestige, such as a *chü-jen* degree, than were most of the student members of the Restoration Society.

The final group with which the revolutionaries developed important contacts were salt smugglers, who were prominent in Chekiang, Kiangsu, Kiangsi, and Anhwei, particularly in the area between Hangchow Bay and T'ai Lake.[18] Their origins can be traced back to boatmen, smugglers, vagrants, and urban unemployed in ports along the Yangtze River and the Grand Canal during the early eighteenth century. Many local groups sprang up and these were further organized by three leaders during the Yung-cheng reign. They volunteered to escort the grain transport ships, then badly plagued by robberies, to Peking. After successfully completing the voyage, they were rewarded and again given this commission. Their gang then expanded along the grain transport routes. Members in the Lower Yangtze area were controlled by Pan Ch'ing, who had once been a Triad, but had established his own Brothers and Elders (Ko-lao hui) gang in rivalry to the Brothers and Elders Society leader who then controlled smuggling in the area. From the name of this founder, the society was called P'an-men and Ch'ing-chia, or Ch'ing-pang. It was commonly referred to as the Green Gang (also pronounced ch'ing-pang). When the grain tribute system was finally abolished in 1901, boatmen among gang members lost their jobs and the gangs turned more openly to salt smuggling and other crime. Membership became more diverse and the Green Gang became a major power among urban lower classes. Probably the later Shanghai gang of the same name was a descendant of the original group. There was a branch centered in Taichow and Wenchow of eastern Chekiang. Another particularly formidable branch in the early 1900's operated in the general area of T'ai Lake and had organized vagrants and criminals throughout southern Anhwei, southern Kiangsu, and northern Chekiang.

The organization and names of the smuggling groups originated in the organization of the grain transport and the names of ships and docking points en route. Their rituals and esoteric terminology differed from those of the Triads. Although their rituals provided a certain common bond, the salt smugglers were definitely not a unified group and battles were sometimes fought between rival gangs. Besides salt smuggling, strong gangs engaged in large-scale piracy against merchant and government ships on the lakes, rivers, and canals, raided shops and wealthy homes, and attacked local military posts. The larger groups were relatively well equipped with boats and rapid-firing guns and were strong enough to give serious trouble to the government troops.

Although there is little biographical information about the smugglers, presumably most of them were marginal members of society. The two leaders of a major rising in northern Chekiang during 1907–08, Yü Meng-t'ing and Hsia Chu-lin, illustrate this point.[19] Both were originally from Anhwei. Yü was a boxer who had no taste for respectable occupations in farming or trade. When he was eighteen years old he went to Hangchow and joined the government forces led by Tso Tsung-t'ang that had re-captured that city from the Taiping rebels. Then he entered a naval force. When the force was disbanded he drifted about northern Chekiang and southern Kiangsu for a year, finally ending in jail for opening a gambling house. After his release he went to Chen-tse on the Kiangsu-Chekiang border, where he found numerous salt smugglers. Yü led one of the bands in a successful raid on a rival group and was chosen leader as a result of this exploit. Because of his ability to prevent unrestrained plundering by his men and his Robin Hood-like practices of robbing the rich and protect-ing the poor, Yü became very popular. Ch'ing officials considered him to be a clever and able leader. When he finally was captured he was offered a position in the army and only after he refused was he executed.

Hsia did not learn any trade in his youth. When somewhat older, he became addicted to gambling and was always stirring up trouble. To escape the authorities he changed his name and joined the prefectural antisalt smuggling forces. However, his identity was discovered and he fled to Ningpo. There he evidently engaged in smuggling, for in retaliation the government seized his family property. Angered, Hsia returned to the T'ai Lake area and embarked upon a large-scale smuggling career. He was considered less intelligent and more vicious than Yü, but he managed to assemble a strong band and cause much trouble for the officials. He was finally killed in battle with government forces in 1908.

The large number of societies in Chekiang suggest pervasive dissatisfac-tion throughout the province. Almost all the groups contacted by the revolutionaries had been founded relatively recently, indicating a surge of discontent during and following the Taiping Rebellion. Even without prompting from the revolutionaries, several groups moved from their original functions to rebellion against the government.

The unrest expressed through the secret societies did not represent the grievances of one particular class. Because of lack of biographical data it is difficult to generalize about the social composition of societies. Most of the rank and file had to be drawn from the usual assortment of peasants, small tradesmen, and vagrants. The one particular group from which a large number came were the immigrants. Most of the leaders about whom we have any information were ex-soldiers, pugilists, or educated men, some of whom held examination degrees. Local merchants also often found society membership useful and sometimes held important positions.[20]

A significant number of the more important society members were essentially déclassé in terms of traditional social divisions. They were drawn from the most able of those who did not fit into the conventional class structure or pursue respected occupations.[21] Other leaders came from middle levels of the local social structure. They were scholars, merchants, or lower gentry, or at least they had enough education to plausibly pretend to be. Some were traditional members of the local elite who turned to the secret societies for a variety of reasons: opposition to the government, desire for personal revenge, and hostility to Christianity. They used societies as a well-established institutional device to gain ends which could not be achieved through the legal social and political structure.

Chekiangese secret societies may have had an unusually large number of gentry or near-gentry leaders compared to societies in other parts of China. There was no one dominant society in Chekiang, and the resulting fragmentation and overlap between secret societies and more strictly personal gangs may have encouraged scholar-gentry involvement because they could easily found and lead their own groups without having to accept a subordinate position in a larger hierarchy. Probably Chekiangese conditions were not uniquely different, however. Even though there were only a few inclusive societies in some provinces, actual activities were in smaller groups, whose leaders might behave very independently. Where societies were organized along trade routes, there was presumably relatively more merchant and less gentry leadership. Elsewhere degree holders and locally prominent landlords were also active in secret societies—at least periodically and under the right conditions—as shown by the situation in Shantung during the Nien rebellion of the 1850's and 1860's.

In Chekiang a bridge between traditional society leaders and the revolutionary students was created by a transitional group of scholars who had started to turn to the secret societies about 1900. If a revolutionary party had existed in the province they might have joined it directly, but secret societies were still the only institution available to organize against the government. It seems significant that a number of leaders of the two societies that cooperated most closely with the revolutionaries had already been exposed to "modern," Western views. When radical intellectuals began to return to organize in Chekiang about 1904, they found potentially discontented elements of the populace already organized in relatively politically minded groups. Equally important, they were able to approach the educated society leaders, particularly the transitional segment, from the basis of fairly similar backgrounds and certain shared attitudes. There was no distinct barrier between secret societies and intellectual circles.

Intellectual Circles

Besides being an area of widespread secret society activity, Chekiang was an intellectual center long noted for its scholars, academies, and libraries. After the Sino-Japanese War, a developing interest in reform among gentry and officials was especially evident in the promotion of modern education. Thus Western ideas began to be more widely diffused among students, paving the way for the iconoclastic restlessness which would lead some to revolutionary ideas half a decade later.

Hangchow was the first center of modern thought. There such papers as *A Journal for Setting the Age in Order* (*Ching-shih pao*), published during the fall of 1897, helped spread Western ideas.[22] "Modern schools" founded by progressive gentry to teach Western as well as traditional Chinese subjects included the Ch'iu-shih Academy, founded in 1897, and the Yang-cheng Academy, established two years later. The gentry education movement was also evident outside the provincial capital. The prominent scholar and educator Sun I-jang, son of Sun I-yen, was said to have helped found over three hundred primary and middle schools in the southeastern prefectures of Chuchow and Wenchow during the latter half of the 1890's. In Shaohsing the Chinese and Western School (*Chung-Hsi hsüeh-t'ang*) offered Western language even though the teaching of Western ideas was discouraged.[23]

Private promotion of education was reinforced after the Boxer Rebellion when, in 1901, the government called for the establishment of a national school system that would teach some modern subjects. The practical results of this policy change were not always very striking. Often existing academies were transformed into new official schools by simply changing their names and providing them with government funds. Thus in Hangchow in 1902 the Tzu-yang Academy became the Ch'ien-t'ang District School, the Yang-cheng Academy was transformed into Hangchow Prefectural Middle School, and the Ch'iu-shih Academy became Chekiang College.[24] Not all the modern government schools, especially newly established ones, offered a very sophisticated introduction to the West or even a very satisfactory education of any kind.

From 1901 to 1903 three such schools were established by the magistrates and prefects in the town of Kashing. In 1903 all the students in the prefectural middle school were studying English, but there was no foreign instructor at the school.[25] Student disappointment in the school's courses and teachers led to a sharp drop in applications for admission during 1903.[26]

However, the new schools were still sufficient to interest students in modern knowledge and the government education program probably further encouraged private initiatives in education among members of the local elite. During 1903 educational associations were established by scholars and gentry in a number of prefectures to compile statistics on education, found schools, and consider textbooks and teaching methods. These associations were probably composed mainly of moderate reformers. However, they sometimes also had connections with radicals. The Shaohsing Educational Association was first organized by Shaohsing natives in Shanghai, and Ts'ai Yüan-p'ei was one of its officers.[27]

The spread of modern ideas after the mid-1890's led an increasing number of young men to develop a serious interest in current events that predisposed them toward radical theories. Some traveled to Hangchow, where they met in schools and reformist associations. One of the first groups to be organized was the Chekiang Society (*Che-hui*), which was founded in 1899 or 1900 to discuss current problems.[28] Its members came from all parts of the province and included a number of individuals who later played radical or revolutionary roles in Chekiang or among the Chekiangese students in Japan. Wang Chia-chü edited the radical journal *Tides of Chekiang* in Japan in 1903. Chiang Fang-chen also became part of the *Tides of Chekiang* group, later continued his military studies in Germany, and during the Republic was well known as a military educator and advisor to Wu Pei-fu, Chiang Kai-shek, and other army commanders. He was accompanied to Japan by another member, Chiang Tsun-kuei, who joined both the Restoration Society and the Revolutionary Alliance, became an officer in the new army, and was the second military governor of Chekiang after the Revolution. Sun I-chung also studied in Japan and returned to Hangchow to found the radical *Vernacular Journal* (*Pai-hua pao*) in 1903. Ch'en Meng-hsiung studied abroad and on returning to Chekiang was involved in the revolutionary movement and established a progressive girls' school in Wenchow. Ao Chia-hsiung and Chang Kung were to become prominent among the second-level subversive leaders in the province. The Chekiang Society was thus a transitional, reformist organization, symptomatic of the growing concern over China's future which was soon to push some of the reformers toward revolutionary ideas.

The subversive potential of this incipient discontent was shown as early as 1900 when T'ang Ts'ai-ch'ang's younger brother visited Hangchow. Antigovernment feeling had recently been inflamed by the execution of two Chekiangese officials in Peking for advocating suppressing the Boxers.[29] Some students, including a number at the long-established Tzu-yang Academy, promised support for T'ang's planned rising in Hankow. They never took any action, however, because T'ang failed too quickly.[30]

The chief center of early radicalism in Hangchow was the Ch'iu-shih Academy. Its faculty and students included many who became active in the revolutionary or constitutional movements, and it supplied many of the first Chekiangese students to go abroad to study in Japan. Very possibly, acquaintances developed in this school contributed to the cooperation of revolutionaries and constitutionalists in 1911. Such men as the scholar Sung P'ing-tzu and Ch'en Fu-ch'en, the future president of the Chekiang Provincial Assembly in 1911, lectured there, reinterpreting the Confucian classics to justify modern reformist ideas.[31] Chang Ping-lin had also briefly given anti-Manchu lectures in 1898 before fleeing to Taiwan to escape arrest when the Reform Movement collapsed.[32] Chang was a friend of Ch'en, who had warned him that he was in danger of being arrested.[33] Nearby, on the same street, was the Military Preparatory School (*Wu-pei hsüeh-t'ang*), later the Military Primary School (*Lu-chün hsiao-hsüeh-t'ang*), to which the first revolutionary ideas in the Chekiang army can be traced. Contact between the students in the two schools helped foster the growth of radical attitudes.[34]

Radical tendencies in the school finally resulted in a clash with government authorities. In 1901 Sun I-chung, a young radical from Hangchow, lectured on Chinese literature. During the summer vacation a progressive student literary society offered a course in modern subjects for which Sun wrote an essay, "On Abolishing the Queue" (*Tsui-pien wen*). One or two students changed the straightforward term "this dynasty," which Sun had originally used, to "the bandit Ch'ing" (*tsei-Ch'ing*). News of the manuscript in this form passed through a series of people until it reached the provincial governor. The school's reformist director, Ch'en Han-ti, fought the charge of disrespect for the dynasty and the governor evidently did not want to press the case too far. In the end he was content with a perfunctory inspection trip to the school, followed by a second visit and lecture against sowing discord between Chinese and Manchus.[35]

The Ch'iu-shih Academy was untouched, but Sun I-chung could no longer remain in Hangchow. At the invitation of the gentry T'ao Chün-hsüan, he moved to the Tung-hu Industrial School (*Tung-hu t'ung-i hsüeh-hsiao*) in Shaohsing, bringing his radical ideas with him.[36] More important, Sun and a number of associates soon went to study in Japan, where they joined revolutionary organizations such as the Youth Association. The *Tides of Chekiang,* in particular, was staffed by former students at the Ch'iu-shih Academy.[37]

Intellectuals in Chekiang were influenced by the same issues and displayed attitudes similar to those of their counterparts in Japan and Shanghai. As in Shanghai, concern over Russian encroachment in Manchuria was evident as early as the spring of 1901, when a meeting was held in

Hangchow to urge opposition to Russian designs. Gentry, literati, and merchants signed a petition to the Chekiang governor and telegrams were sent to other governors and governor-generals.[38] The timetable of student radicalization was also similar to that in Shanghai. Students began to go to study in Tokyo in still small but significant numbers during 1902.[39] Those who stayed behind had, if they wished, access to at least some of the radical newspapers and periodicals being published in Tokyo and Shanghai by early 1903.[40] Student unruliness became a problem for school authorities in Chekiang during the spring of 1903 at about the same time as student strikes proliferated in other parts of China.

The major incident was the withdrawal of virtually all the students at Chekiang College in the spring of 1903. Possibly not all the students were happy about the conversion of the Ch'iu-shih Academy into a government school the previous fall.[41] Discontent increased because the president relied heavily on the advice of an unpopular inspector and real trouble began during opening exercises on March 4, 1903. While the provincial governor was inside the school buildings a student tried to look inside his empty sedan chair and was kicked away by one of the bearers. Angry students demonstrated, demanding punishment of the offender, and they were not satisfied with the governor's claim that a beating had been administered to the bearer after he returned to the yamen. When they threatened to strike, the college president refused to support the students further and threatened expulsions. Frictions between the students and administration continued, finally resulting in the dismissal of six students on April 13. The director adamantly refused to listen to protests of student representatives and four days later the student body walked out, forcing the temporary closing of the college.[42] The withdrawing students were familiar with the example of the Patriotic School in Shanghai. Some telegraphed Wu Chih-hui and Ts'ai Yüan-p'ei asking them to come to Hangchow and help found a new school.[43] Ts'ai and Wu could not leave Shanghai, but Lo Chia-ling, the chief financial supporter of the Patriotic School, reportedly sent 500 yuan to the Hangchow students.[44] A New People's School (*Hsin-min shu*) was established within a week. Soon thereafter some of the students established the Determination School (*Li-chih hsüeh-t'ang*), which combined with another student-established school late that summer to form the Chekiang Public Institute (*Liang-Che kung-hsüeh*), which was closely modeled on the Patriotic School.[45] This withdrawal was followed very shortly by withdrawal of some of the students at the Ch'ien-t'ang District School when the administration refused to expel a homosexual student.[46] Then on April 28 over fifty left the Baptist missionary Hui-lan Academy protesting the "tyranny" of the president, pressure to join the church, bad food, and the expulsion of a fellow student.[47] There was at least some similar unrest in schools outside of Hangchow. At the Hsiu-shui district school in Kashing about ten students were expelled and some others withdrew after demonstrating against the "humiliation" of a visiting Westerner being allowed to strike the school's bell.[48] Another indication of ferment was the founding of debating societies and student associations to practice military drill.[49]

The indigenous intellectual turmoil, which by 1903 seems to have penetrated many of the towns of Chekiang, had two important effects for the development of the revolutionary movement. First, it inspired students to go to study in Shanghai or Japan, whence some returned as dedicated revolutionaries. Second, when radical students began to return in significant numbers late in 1903 and during 1904, they found people who already shared or at least partially sympathized with their views. One of the students who withdrew from Chekiang College was Ma Tsung-han,[50] who a few years later accompanied Hsü Hsi-lin to Japan and finally helped him assassinate Governor En-ming. The presence of students like Ma helped pave the way for the organization of revolutionary forces.

This potential support in the modern schools and secret societies determined the direction of the early revolutionary movement in Chekiang. Schools represented the beginnings of change that fostered the growth of radical ideas. Revolutionaries had to utilize and accelerate this trend if they were to win significant support among the educated classes. Secret societies related to longstanding sources of discontent that revolutionaries had to exploit if they were to gain the popular following necessary to upset the traditional power structure. The third major target of revolutionary infiltration in China as a whole, the new army, was organized relatively late in Chekiang. One does not find, therefore, the immediate intermeshing of military officers and radical intellectuals such as occurred in Hupeh. Initially the schools and societies were the most promising source of recruits. They also provided the immediate institutional models for revolutionaries to copy. Radicals often chose to found schools as their front organizations. The type of men who led or joined secret societies were the revolutionaries' rural allies. The kind of activities secret societies engaged in, their methods of recruitment, and their organizational forms all influenced revolutionary practices.

There is some indication that the secret societies in Chekiang had begun to change slightly in the late Ch'ing. The P'ing-yang Society and the Dragon Flower Society, in particular, attracted some leaders and members who were aware of national problems and questions of modernization. On the whole, however, the societies seem to have remained "primitive rebels," protesting only immediate wrongs and oppression,[51] insofar as they were rebels at all. It would require very strong leadership to turn them into a mass base for the revolution the radicals desired.

During the four years of 1904 to 1907, the Chekiangese revolutionaries made a sustained effort to penetrate both the illegal (secret societies) and legal (schools and militia) institutions in local social and political structures. Their plans were national in scope and radical in intent. However, when the revolutionaries moved into the provincial towns and villages they had to operate in an environment where the traditional pull was much stronger than in Tokyo or Shanghai and where immediate causes of unrest were usually limited and local. Tensions, therefore, more easily developed between the modern and traditional elements in the revolutionaries' own psychologies and between their modern goals and the compromises forced upon them by the need to conform superficially to local standards. A study of their methods illuminates the opportunities that existed for revolutionary work and also the difficulties in maintaining the sense of purpose essential to a front organization while escaping detection until the planned rising took place.

The revolutionaries' activities during these years fall roughly into three periods. During 1904 and 1905 they established contacts with secret societies and founded schools or other organizations. The establishment of the Ta-t'ung School in Shaohsing marked the culmination of this phase. During 1906 the leading revolutionaries turned to other projects, dissensions arose, and the Restoration Society organization in Chekiang threatened to disintegrate. Toward the end of 1906 a new impetus was provided by plans for a rising (which proved abortive) to support the Revolutionary Alliance revolts in Hunan and Kiangsi. The momentum thus generated led directly into the final phase of planning for a major rising in Chekiang led by Ch'iu Chin in cooperation with Hsü Hsi-lin in Anking. Failure in July 1907 was followed by sporadic secret society risings during the rest of the year, but these were scattered and anticlimactic, without significant effect.

The Revolutionary Leadership

The most outstanding revolutionaries in Chekiang were T'ao

Ch'eng-chang, Hsü Hsi-lin, and finally, Ch'iu Chin. Ch'iu Chin's life has already been discussed. Hsü Hsi-lin, who was a distant cousin, had a quite similar personality and history.[1] He was born in 1873 in Tung-p'u village about fifteen miles from Shaohsing, the eldest son of a large family. His father was a well-to-do merchant from a respected local clan. He also had some ability as a Sung scholar and hoped that his son would follow a traditional scholarly and official career. Hsü Hsi-lin was a bright but obstinate boy, and relations with his conservative father were often strained. When he was about twenty years old Hsü passed the examinations for a *hsiu-ts'ai* degree. He was more interested in subjects such as mathematics, astronomy, geography, and agriculture than in classical studies, however. To the disappointment of his father he did not continue to work toward an official career. Instead he acquired some familiarity with Western literature and began searching for a new role in life. He taught at the Shan-yin district school and despite the opposition of conservative gentry was active in promoting local welfare and reform projects. During the Boxer Rebellion he sought to organize militia with the arguments that the court was not benefiting the country and officials could not be relied upon to defend the people. When he met with more resistance, Hsü decided to quit his home village.

In 1901 Hsü was appointed to teach mathematics at the Shaohsing prefectural school. There he impressed the prefect, who adopted him as a protégé. According to one report Hsü spent a good deal more time cultivating this official contact and operating a bookstore which sold texts to the school than he did in teaching mathematics. While in Shaohsing, Hsü was further exposed to Western ideas and tried to reprint old copies of *The Renovation of the People* and other "new books."[2] During the summer of 1903 he accompanied a Japanese teacher at the prefectural school to the Osaka Exposition. He then went to Tokyo, where he evidently did not enroll in a school, but lived among the Chinese students for a few weeks or months. While there he met T'ao Ch'eng-chang and Kung Pao-ch'üan, and his radicalism was deepened through the influences of the anti-Russian agitation and the *Su-pao* case.

Hsü returned home a very modern young man who freely expressed his opinions, thereby completing his alienation from his father. He did not immediately attempt any revolutionary activity, but by then he was certainly extremely radical. After resigning his position at the Shaohsing prefectural school he and a friend founded the Je-ch'eng Primary School to teach military drill at Tung-p'u. He also continued his bookstore with the aim of influencing students toward modern ideas by selling "new books" to the schools. Neither project was a success. The bookstore failed and the school was temporarily closed after Hsü raised a storm of rumors and indignation by hiring a military band from Nanking to aid in teaching drill to the students. Hsü then began to make acquaintances among the secret societies and at the end of 1904 journeyed to Shanghai, where he joined the Restoration Society.

Having joined the Revolution, Hsü wanted action and chafed under Ts'ai Yüan-p'ei's relatively tame leadership. In February 1905 he returned home and began to make further contacts with secret societies in Shaohsing and Kinhwa prefectures. In June of that year he also took part in gentry-inspired agitation against Roman Catholics in Shaohsing who were alleged to have acquired property without adequate compensation.[3] That summer he was visited in Shaohsing by other revolutionaries and began the main part of his revolutionary career, which will be described in this and the following chapter.

Relatively little written by Hsü has survived,[4] so it is difficult to gain a clear picture of his personality. Evidently he was a person of some ability and intelligence who could favorably impress the Shaohsing prefect and later Anhwei Governor En-ming. He also had a compelling, uncompromising nature which attracted many of the younger members of the Restoration Society. As a revolutionary leader he was distinguished by a persistent preoccupation with assassination. He was extremely determined, but his desire for dramatic action, perhaps spiced by some egotism, was not balanced by sound judgment. When he finally reached a position where he could realize his intentions, he displayed an extraordinary and fatal lack of common sense.

T'ao Ch'eng-chang was a very different personality.[5] He was born in 1878 in Kuei-chi district of Shaohsing prefecture. His family had lived there a long time and evidently enjoyed gentry or near-gentry status. T'ao received a good classical education, but also developed a fondness for "new books." He was gradually converted to the idea of racial revolution. Resentment of the privileged status of bannermen contributed to the development of T'ao's anti-Manchuism and it seems probable that traditional influences played a large part in his revolutionary views.

At the time of the Boxer Rebellion, T'ao traveled to Peking in the hope of assassinating the empress-dowager. He also traveled in Fengtien and Inner Mongolia to determine the possibilities of rebellion. In 1901 T'ao again went to Peking, but he found no opportunity for action and returned home. The next year he went to Japan, where he entered the Preparatory School for Chinese Students (*Seika gakkō*). T'ao desired a military education and sought to enter the Chinese Students' Military Preparatory School. However, the supervisor of Chinese military students in Japan, Wang Ta-hsieh, was suspicious of T'ao and prevented his admission. When T'ao's uncle, then an official in Peking, came to Tokyo on a mission he and Wang devised a plan whereby T'ao was admitted to the school. Then during summer vacation his uncle invited him to Peking and tried to persuade him to follow a career there. When T'ao refused and returned to Japan he found that his name had been erased from the school records. T'ao evidently remained in Japan for a time and returned periodically during 1903. He eventually met and gained the confidence of Chekiangese radicals in Tokyo and in late 1903 agreed to return to Chekiang to organize secret societies as a revolutionary force.

During 1904 and 1905 T'ao was the most important revolutionary figure active in Chekiang. He left the Restoration Society group centered in the Ta-t'ung School a year before it was destroyed in mid-1907. After 1907 he joined in another effort to unite the secret societies in five Lower Yangtze provinces during 1908 and 1909. Most of the time, however, he spent abroad in Japan and Southeast Asia. He was one of the Revolutionary Alliance members who protested against Sun Yat-sen's leadership, and in January 1910 he and Chang Ping-lin revived the Restoration Society to compete with the Revolutionary Alliance for members and funds in Southeast Asia. Because he was away from China so much, T'ao was out of touch in Chekiang and did not return until after the Revolution had occurred in that province in 1911. He was a member of the senate, which served as a provisional legislative body for the military government, and he helped organize the Chekiangese army, which took part in the revolutionaries' attack on Nanking. He was never able to control the political situation, however. In January 1912 he was mysteriously murdered in a hospital in the French Concession at Shanghai. At the time Ch'en Ch'i-mei and T'ao were competing to control the revolutionary movement in Kiangsu and Chekiang. Chang Ping-lin and other Chekiangese charged that Chiang Kai-shek, then Ch'en's lieutenant, was responsible for T'ao's death. Although the accusation has never definitely been proven, it is almost certain that Chiang was responsible for T'ao's death, following the orders of Ch'en Ch'i-mei.

T'ao was much more conservative and cautious than Hsü Hsi-lin or Ch'iu Chin. Information about him is scarce, but he seems to have been less influenced by new Western ideas than Ch'iu or Hsü. The regulations he drafted in an effort to unite the secret societies (which will be discussed in the next section) rely heavily on classical quotations and allusions and show little appreciation of Western political philosophies. Very probably his views were similar to those of Chang Ping-lin, with whom he was able to cooperate for several years.

Although T'ao was an excellent organizer and sensible strategist, his different temperament set him somewhat apart from many of the other Chekiangese revolutionary intellectuals. The unfortunate result was that T'ao's efforts eventually became rather isolated and ineffectual and the movement in Chekiang was deprived of his steadying influence. It was Ch'iu and Hsü rather than T'ao who shaped the climax of the Restoration Society activities in Chekiang.

Development of Secret Society Contacts

Revolutionaries directed their first efforts in Chekiang toward the secret societies. The initial problem was to gain introductions and establish personal relations with secret society leaders. Without the confidence of those men it would be impossible for the students to make use of the secret society organizations. Much of the groundwork was done by T'ao Ch'eng-chang and another returned student, Wei Lan; both spent a good part of 1904 traveling about Chekiang talking to potential allies.

Late in 1903 T'ao obtained an introduction to the Crouching Tiger Society leader, Wang Hsi-t'ung, but upon reaching Taichow he found that Wang had gone into hiding elsewhere. After this unsuccessful beginning T'ao met Wei Lan, who had just returned from Japan. Together they went to Shanghai and conferred with Ts'ai Yüan-p'ei at the beginning of 1904. Then they returned to Hangchow, where they stayed at the offices of the Hangchow *Vernacular Journal*. This paper was then being edited by Sun I-chung and its offices served as an early contact point for the revolutionaries in Chekiang. Sun was acquainted with the White Cloth Society leader P'u Chen-sheng, who was in jail in Hangchow. He introduced T'ao and Wei to P'u, who gave them a list of names and introductory passes to those places where his society was strong. With this help they succeeded in making contacts during a tour of the province. Roughly speaking, the two traveled upriver from Hangchow as far southwest as Ch'ü-chou. Then they turned east toward the coast, making contacts in the prefectures of Chuchow, Wenchow, and Taichow. This route enabled them to cover much of the province, except for the Ningpo area, where for some reason these revolutionaries do not seem to have been active. En route they paused for a couple of months in Wei Lan's native place, Yün-ho in Chuchow. There Wei established a school at which T'ao taught while Wei and a relative traveled about the prefecture. In the late spring T'ao returned to

Shanghai and then spent the summer in Hangchow at the *Vernacular Journal* offices writing a revolutionary tract entitled "A History of the Ebb and Flow of the Power of the Chinese Race" (*Chung-kuo min-tsu ch'üan-li hsiao-ch'ang shih*). Meanwhile Wei Lan successfully made contact with many more secret society members, including the leaders of the Dragon Flower, Double Dragon, and Crouching Tiger societies.

In the fall T'ao Ch'eng-chang again returned to Shanghai, where he discussed plans with Huang Hsing and Ts'ai Yüan-p'ei for a rising on the empress-dowager's seventieth birthday. T'ao and Wei Lan then returned to Chekiang to mobilize the Dragon Flower and Double Dragon societies in the western part of the province. Part of the revolutionary forces were to march from this base into Kiangsu to Nanking and on toward Changsha and others were to occupy the northern and eastern parts of Chekiang. At the last minute T'ao called off the plans when he saw a report of Huang Hsing's failure in a Shanghai paper. By then local authorities knew trouble was afoot and the rewards they offered led to the assassination of the Double Dragon Society leader, Wang Chin-pao. After this setback T'ao Ch'eng-chang left Chekiang for about six months, first going to Shanghai, where he joined the Restoration Society, and then to Japan, where he renewed relations with other revolutionaries there.[6]

Organizational and Propaganda Techniques

Although T'ao's and Wei's work with the secret societies in 1904 ended in frustration, their contacts provided a foundation for future organization and indoctrination. The Chekiangese societies were so fragmented that it was necessary to impose some order on them if they were to be an effective fighting force. Revolutionaries, therefore, devised intermediate organizations, which were part way between the traditional societies and the revolutionary party. Within this general method they followed two different approaches. One was to preserve as much of the traditional society organization as possible and to emphasize ideas which were close to the conventional secret society attitudes. The other was to bring society members into a revised revolutionary party and to attempt to convert them to the attitudes of the student revolutionaries. In keeping with his more traditionalistic bent, T'ao Ch'eng-chang favored the former approach whereas Ch'iu Chin later adopted the latter manner.

An example of T'ao's technique has been preserved in the regulations he devised for a new secret society which he hoped would unite the other groups.[7] T'ao adopted the name Dragon Flower Society for his organization, but it is not to be confused with the genuine secret society with the same name. It has generally been believed that he wrote the regulations in 1904 or 1905. However, it is very possible that they were not written until 1908, when T'ao and other revolutionaries were seeking to unite the societies of Kiangsu, Chekiang, Fukien, Anhwei, and Kiangsi.[8] Since the regulations were almost certainly never put into effect, their date is not really important. They are, however, significant as an indication of T'ao's approach, which probably did not change greatly over the years.

T'ao took great pains to show that his new system meant no sharp break with secret society practices. He drew upon a mixture of traditional secret society and bureaucratic forms which he blended into a military organization. The field command was divided into five armies, each headed by a grand commander. Below the commander were nine grades, ranging down to rank-and-file members. T'ao based his titles on T'ang and Ming dynasty official titles and was also careful to equate each of them with the corresponding Triad and smugglers' terms.[9] Traditional slogans, passwords, and ceremonies of the various societies were to remain unchanged. Provisions for recruitment, promotion, and punishment also followed the old forms and T'ao even went so far as to promise that posthumous titles and honors would be awarded for particularly meritorious service when the new dynasty was established.[10]

T'ao's ideological appeal to the secret societies, preserved in an essay preceding the specific regulations of his Dragon Flower Society, also followed traditional lines. In it he drew heavily upon the Chinese classics and history, with relatively little discussion of Western ideas. As a first step T'ao did seek to revise the traditional attitude toward rebellion. In doing so he set forth a transitional view of efforts to overthrow the government which rejected the orthodox theory of rebellion, but failed to assimilate the Western concept of revolution. T'ao denied that the emperor received his mandate from heaven and could only be overthrown if heaven withdrew it—an act independent of any human will.[11] This theory had been devised by scholars at the demand of later emperors who did not want anyone to rebel against them. A true interpretation of the classics, according to T'ao, showed that the ancient sages believed the emperor derived his right to rule from the people and if they were dissatisfied they might overthrow him. Rebelling (*tsao-fan*) was thus tantamount to breaking the emperor's mandate (*ko-ming*).[12] T'ao was forced to resort to some laborious selections and contrived interpretations to justify this view from passages in the Confucian classics.[13] After reviewing the classics T'ao moved to a historical discussion. Here his most pertinent point was the association of rebellion with opposition to barbarian rule. He emphasized the cruelty of the Manchu invasion and the harshness of their subsequent rule and, like many of the other revolutionaries, described the Taiping Rebellion as the first temporary break in the darkness of Manchu tyranny.[14]

T'ao's interpretations are highly suspect from a scholarly point of view, but they were based on a thorough knowledge of the classics and followed the conventional Chinese practice of justifying new ideas by finding them in the past. When he turned to discussion of the postrevolutionary Chinese state, however, T'ao showed that he had not progressed further to acquire new images based on Western ideas. T'ao demonstrated that he was aware of the discontent of the countryside by giving special consideration to economic questions. However, his solutions of common land ownership, light taxation, small armies, and sufficient food and shelter for all[15] are merely a composite of utopian goals of traditional visionary reformers and programs generally pursued by a new dynasty anxious to pacify the countryside.

T'ao's treatment of political institutions was even more superficial. Like all revolutionaries he strongly distrusted the Manchu constitutional movement, but he went beyond attacking proposals for constitutional monarchy to display a general distrust of constitutions.[16] He evidently failed to appreciate the relation between some form of constitution and republican government. China was to be a republic, but T'ao seems to have conceived of this political form more in moral than in institutional terms. An emperor would no longer be able to run the government for his private interests and the evils resulting from the inevitable debasement of a hereditary ruling house would cease. Able and popular governors, reminiscent of the exemplary legendary emperors Shun and Yao, would result. Then it would not matter how the government was organized. It might be headed by a president, a citizens' council, or have no head in accord with the principles of anarchism.[17] Western-inspired political forms were not sufficiently meaningful to T'ao that he thought it important to choose among them.

All these ideas could be fitted into traditional secret society patterns of thought. On one point only did T'ao directly oppose the attitudes of some of the society's potential members. He specifically enjoined them to protect foreign lives and property if they did not want Westerners to aid the dynasty. "It must never be misunderstood that the Manchus are our enemies and the Westerners are our friends."[18] Thus he sought to persuade the secret societies to abandon their opposition to Christianity in favor of opposition to the dynasty and to narrow their xenophobia to anti-Manchuism. He never states what the attitude toward Westerners might be once the immediate enemy was overthrown.

As part of a more general propaganda offensive the revolutionaries sought to reach all classes and all parts of the province with revolutionary literature.[19] T'ao, Wei Lan, and Ao Chia-hsiung each wrote their own tracts. In addition many thousands of the better known revolutionary works were imported during 1904 and 1905. Tsou Jung's *The Revolutionary Army* and Ch'en T'ien-hua's *About Face!* were the most popular. Copies of Chen T'ien-hua's *A Bell to Alert the World* and numerous periodicals published by student groups in Japan were also extensively used. In places where society members assembled, such Shanghai revolutionary newspapers as *The China National Gazette* and *The Alarm Bell* were made available. Secret societies, especially the Dragon Flower Society, as well as the student revolutionaries aided in dispersing literature[20] which was evidently used to attract recruits to the societies as well as to the revolutionary party.[21]

Most of the Restoration Society radicals probably preferred to bring secret society members into the revolutionary party and to try to convert them to the students' outlook rather than devise an organization on the model of the Triad societies. In 1907 when Ch'iu Chin assumed the leadership of the Ta-t'ung School and began to plan for a rising, she sought to unite the secret societies by bringing all members into the Restoration Society. Although this effort occurred after the initial period of revolutionary organization in Chekiang, it is worth considering here as a contrast to T'ao's approach.

Ch'iu organized the Restoration Society into sixteen grades designated by one or two characters from a short poem she composed which reflected the party's anti-Manchu aims. This was a traditional device, but Ch'iu also provided alternative, "modern" designations by the letters of the English alphabet.[22] The choice of this kind of organization was obviously influenced by the need to accommodate the secret society hierarchy, but she did not specifically equate the party ranks with those in the societies. The regulations for a Restoration Army (*Kuang-fu chün*), which Ch'iu wrote about the same time, also show an effort to give a modern and revolutionary stamp to a group composed mainly of secret society and militia members.[23] Military ranks were derived from the modern Japanese army with the addition of a number of titles and somewhat altered terminology.[24] The first character of the compound meaning "restoration" (*kuang*) was written in white moons on the back of the "soldiers'" black uniforms, and the army's white banner was decorated with the character *Han*, meaning Chinese.

In a preface to the regulations of the Restoration Army, Ch'iu Chin characteristically stressed the need for individuals to risk death for the cause of revolution and the preservation of the race. She went on to say that China had reached a critical point under the twin pressures of Manchu tyranny and Western aggression (for which the Manchus were partly responsible). A long history of slavish subservience to the Manchus had only debased the Chinese character. Constitutional proposals were not remedies, but merely devices to increase Manchu power at the expense of the Chinese. The time, therefore, had come to wipe out more than two hundred years of humiliation by overthrowing the dynasty and establishing a new empire (*ti-kuo*), ruled by Chinese. Presumably, because this piece was aimed mainly at the secret societies, no mention is made of a republic. The emphasis is racial, not political. However, in another shorter proclamation intended to be read to the army, Ch'iu covers much the same ground and also calls for the establishment of a republic.

Ch'iu's organizations still contained many old elements, but she had moved farther from the Triad tradition than had T'ao, who undoubtedly had a deeper knowledge of and sympathy with the secret societies. Although Ch'iu had been briefly exposed to Triad ritual in Japan, her interests and knowledge were more in the realm of modern army organization and her attitudes were more typical of the radical, nationalistic students who had been to Japan. Thus instead of quoting the classics to justify rebellion, Ch'iu echoed Tsou Jung and Ch'en T'ien-hua. Instead of being deeply interested in ways of improving the lot of the peasantry, she called for individual sacrifice to prevent a Darwinian extinction of an unfit Chinese race.

Ch'iu Chin and T'ao Ch'eng-chang chose two possible approaches to the problem of influencing secret societies. Both, however, chose to approach the rural populace through the secret societies and so remained within the traditional framework of political power. Chinese Communist writers have presented the revolutionaries' approaches to the secret societies in terms of a partial alliance between petit bourgeois intellectuals and peasants forming the basis of the 1911 Revolution.[25] However, the secret societies were not class organizations, and many of the revolutionaries' closest contacts were with the more educated elements. The radical intellectuals before 1911 fell somewhere in between gentry of scholar rebels, who had traditionally cooperated with secret societies when it suited their purposes, and the Russian populists or the Maoist wing of the Communist Party, who, in different ways, were directly concerned with peasant grievances. Dissatisfied members of the educated classes traditionally made common cause with secret societies from time to time. Such association in the mid-nineteenth century is recorded in a verse repeated at initiation meetings that has been preserved in a gazeteer of T'ung-ch'uan prefecture in Szechwan.[26] The Taiping rebels, who had many characteristics of a secret society or sect, had a number of educated men among their leaders besides Hung Hsiu-ch'üan.[27] The Nien rebels, a remnant branch of the White Lotus Sect, were joined by a number of lower gentry. Many of their leaders were drawn from prominent members of the large clans—men of wealth and local influence, even those who did not hold degrees.[28]

When the revolutionaries sought to use the secret societies as troops, they were still close to the old mold. It is instructive to compare T'ao Ch'eng-chang's and Wei Lan's tour of secret societies in 1904 with an expedition of members of the Peiping-Tientsin Student Union in January 1936 to awaken the rural masses of northern Hopei to the Japanese threat. In 1936 the students sought to bypass the local elites and speak directly to the villagers. However, the peasants received them indifferently and only in the schools did the crusaders find a warm welcome. To remedy this situation most of the students accepted radical proposals to combine nationalistic slogans with economic propaganda against rents and taxes. This new approach successfully aroused peasant interest until the agitators were intercepted and sent home by the authorities.[29] In 1936 student groups, who were influenced but not controlled by Communists, were anxious to speak to the rural lower classes directly and were willing to adjust their techniques to realize this end. Before 1911, student revolutionaries were mainly interested in winning over the leaders of traditional illegal groups who might then urge their followers to join the revolutionary forces.

The student revolutionaries of 1911 and the peasants lived in different worlds and neither was entirely in sympathy with the other.[30] At the end of the Ch'ing there were numerous riots to protest modern innovations such as schools, education, self-government, and other associations or similar reformist institutions which peasants only saw as imposing additional burdens.[31] An example occurred south of Wenchow city during September 1904 when the prefect laid a tax of 60 cents a *mou* on orange groves to finance the cost of new schools. The orange growers destroyed the office set up to collect the new tax and a few days later a crowd set out for the city. On the way they were met by soldiers and persuaded to go home. Only one man was arrested and the tax was soon removed to assuage popular feelings.[32]

The revolutionaries, however, approved of new schools and other modern institutions. They were steps toward the regeneration of China and places where adherents or sympathizers might be recruited. They were not prepared to lead a purely peasant revolt against rents and taxes even though they might deplore the oppression of the masses. They saw themselves as "foreknowers" who understood that the vital immediate problems were to save, strengthen, and reform the nation and society as a whole. The new aims of the partly modernized revolutionaries set them apart from traditional rebels, but also limited their interest in local economic grievances of the lower classes. They sought to use, lead, and educate the people, but not to bridge the social gap and identify themselves closely with the attitudes and problems of the peasantry. Revolutionaries gained relatively easy entrance into the countryside, but the alliances they made never entirely committed either side.

Establishment of Legal Local Organizations

The difficulties in maintaining contacts and coordinating the activities of the secret societies underlined the revolutionaries' need to develop their own bases from which to spread propaganda, deepen relations with the secret societies, build up a party cadre, and provide some rudimentary training for a future revolutionary army. It would have been virtually impossible for an illegal subversive organization to carry on such activities in the Chekiang interior without being soon detected. Therefore, several of the revolutionaries, more or less independently, arrived at the idea of establishing schools, militia, and guilds as blinds behind which they could pursue their aims. The schools and other organizations were not intended merely to disseminate revolutionary propaganda, but to facilitate preparations for a rising. Thus there were two distinct types of revolutionary activity. One was to infiltrate schools in order to give lectures and spread propaganda which would win new converts. The other was to found an institution to throw a cloak of respectability over a subversive organization. In this case propaganda was played down to prevent discovery. In following this course of action the radicals were simultaneously taking advantage of opportunities afforded by the modernization movement and of the relative degree of freedom traditionally enjoyed by members of the local elite.

The most important of the front organizations established in Chekiang were the Wen-T'ai-Ch'u Guildhall, founded by Ao Chia-hsiung toward the end of 1904, and the Ta-t'ung School, which Hsü Hsi-lin established in the early autumn of 1905.[33] Although different from the hit-and-run tactics often employed by the Revolutionary Alliance, founding such organizations was not a unique method. Institutions such as schools and militia had traditionally been used from time to time by opponents of the government. Revolutionaries elsewhere in China also pursued this course. After 1909, revolutionaries (at least some of whom were members of the Revolutionary Alliance) in Shou-chou, Anhwei, used the local agricultural and educational associations as a base for their activities. This group was luckier in its timing and was able to play a major role in the Revolution in northern Anhwei in 1911.[34]

The times were particularly favorable for the use of schools and similar institutions by revolutionaries. The Manchu reform movement was well under way by 1904. At the beginning of that year the throne approved a new, more elaborate set of regulations for a modern school system. The following year the traditional examination system was abolished. The government was now thoroughly committed to overhauling the education system. It encouraged the establishment of schools by frequently rewarding local officials and gentry who contributed funds or founded a school.[35] In the spring of 1904 one Western traveler in Chekiang remarked that "every district city will apparently soon boast of a school where Western learning is taught."[36] Schools with a special curriculum were established as well as standard primary and middle schools. In 1905 Sun I-jang and others founded a chemistry school.[37] Schools emphasizing military training were not uncommon, especially during and after such international crises as the Sino-Japanese War. Many of these schools were ephemeral and teaching standards were low. However, the existence of the education movement meant that revolutionaries could establish front organizations without attracting unusual attention and often with official encouragement.

When revolutionaries sought to establish a respectable front organization they superficially joined the elite layer of local society and within limits had to conform to the accepted ways of doing things. As founders of schools and other institutions they were in the same category as reform-minded gentry, scholars, and merchants who formed part of the middle and upper level of local society. They had to contact and influence officials to gain permission to establish their institution and to be sure it was allowed to operate thereafter. Because revolutionaries usually founded front organizations in or near their home towns they often already had acquaintances that they could use to their advantage.

Common interest in and promotion of modernizing projects created bonds between revolutionaries and progressive members of the local elite. The Chekiang revolutionaries began their institutional projects with the interest and support of nonrevolutionary modernizers in the community. Radicals were thus able to use the liberals who could be deluded about the real aim of an institution that was in fact being used for subversive projects. However, the advantage was not entirely with the radicals. If a school declined as a revolutionary center, nonrevolutionaries might come to play a role in its management. This possibility was enhanced because the revolutionaries often had to rely on people outside their ranks for funds and support against suspicious officials if they were going to continue to operate for long in one place. A spectrum of revolutionary and progressive elements emerged within the educated class without any hard lines between them. On one end were the professional revolutionaries. Next were such men as Ao Chia-hsiung, who knew the professional revolutionaries and took part in some of the revolutionary organizations, but who did not entirely cut the ties with their traditional life and might or might not continue to be an active revolutionary until 1911. A somewhat similar intermediate group were founders of front organizations that never were really active. The radicals operating them then became practically indistinguishable from moderate reformers. One step further removed were the scholar, gentry, and merchant sympathizers who provided funds and protection to the revolutionaries, but did not personally play a very active role. A highly placed example was the Chekiangese governor's private secretary, Chang Jang-san, who on occasion helped the revolutionaries. Finally, there were progressive members of the local elite like Sun I-jang, who might be acquainted with some revolutionaries and who themselves were promoting similar modernizing projects. They and the revolutionaries could be brought closer together if local officials were clumsy in suppressing a revolutionary organization so as to appear to be needlessly persecuting respectable, though radical, citizens or indiscriminately threatening all modernizing ventures. Early instances of progressive support foreshadowed the later cooperation between those involved in provincial autonomy and constitutional movements and the Revolutionary Alliance.

An example of support for revolutionaries from progressive members of the local elite is found in the "Song of New Mountain" case, which dragged on from the summer of 1906 to the spring of 1907.[38] The defendant was Ch'en Meng-hsiung, a radical returned student who was a friend of Ao Chia-hsiung and had previously helped him in managing the Wen-T'ai-Ch'u Guildhall.[39] His most highly placed supporter during the affair was Sun I-jang. Sun's educational activities have already been mentioned several times. He was a man of eminent respectability and considerable influence in the province as well as in his home district. Although not a radical himself, he knew a number of radicals or revolutionaries, including Chang Ping-lin.[40] Sun was a member of the Eastern Chekiang school, which specialized in the study of historical documents and whose members believed that national affairs were the proper concern of the scholar. He had made a special study of the idealized Confucian description of the government institutions of the Chou dynasty, the *Rites of Chou* (*Chou-li*), which he analyzed as a constitution for the state. Sun distinguished between the underlying principles of government and the changing forms in which they were manifested. The basic laws underlying Eastern and Western, old and new systems were, he believed, the same. Thus the cream of the ancient political order collected in the *Rites of Chou* was essentially one with reasons why the present Western countries were wealthy and strong. Sun justified reform with the aid of this transitional philosophy and, although certainly not a revolutionary himself, had some sympathy for radical views.[41]

The background of the "Song of New Mountain" case began when Ch'en returned home to Lotsing in Wenchow prefecture during 1905. In 1906 he established the Ming-ch'iang Girls' School and he and a radical Buddhist monk established a Monks' and People's School (*Seng-min hsüeh-t'ang*). Radical literature, including Ao Chia-hsiung's "Song of New Mountain," was distributed at both schools. The monks also practiced military drill and aroused the anger of the district magistrate by disrupting a meeting of local students called as part of the official preparations for constitutional government. A scholar with a grudge against Ch'en's family took the opportunity to accuse Ch'en of being a member of the Brothers and Elders Society, establishing a political party with Ao Chia-hsiung, and teaching revolution in the girls' school. He produced a copy of "Song of New Mountain" as evidence. Government troops searched and closed the Ming-ch'iang School, plundering in the process. Ch'en was forewarned and had destroyed all copies of the song in the school beforehand. He fled to avoid arrest and made his way to Japan with the help of Sun I-jang, whom he had met previously. Some members of the local gentry telegraphed the Commissioner of Education's Office in Hangchow to protest the excesses of the troops in closing the school.

Ch'en eventually returned to Hangchow for trial because he feared that Ao Chia-hsiung and other friends would be arrested. The interrogation brought out no damaging evidence against him, and a deputy sent to Lotsing discovered that his accusers were not disinterested. Several of the Wenchow gentry, including Sun I-jang, guaranteed Ch'en. Among those from Kashing who spoke on behalf of Ao was the son of the former governor-general of Kwangtung and Kwangsi.[42] The result was that the case was dropped. The Lotsing Magistrate was transferred and the man who initially brought the accusation was punished for presenting false charges. Without the support of reformist members of the gentry community, however, Ch'en would hardly have fared so well.

The Wen-T'ai-Ch'u Guildhall

The timing and location of the legal institutions established by the revolutionaries were not the result of any predetermined plan but merely depended upon when and where a revolutionary happened to decide to pursue such a course. The first such attempt was the Wen-T'ai-Ch'u Guildhall. The founder of the guildhall was Ao Chia-hsiung, the son of a prosperous merchant family of P'ing-hu in northeastern Chekiang.[43] Ao had passed the district examinations at an early age and, following his father's wishes, studied tax accounting at the Hsiu-shui district yamen in Kashing prefecture. However, he disliked the work and soon resigned. Under the influence of the 1898 Reform Movement he went to Hangchow, where he became one of the founders of the Chekiang Society. In 1900 Ao moved to Kashing and embarked on a number of projects to promote local education, agriculture, and industry. With other scholars he established a Society to Study Agriculture and the Bamboo Forest Primary School (*Chu-lin hsiao-hsüeh-hsiao*). He also organized a local militia to help protect against the ever present smugglers and bandits and founded an elementary school which had as its main purpose the teaching of the method of preserving meats. Meat preservation was an important local industry and, moreover, Ao's father dealt in salt meats. During 1902 he gradually moved toward revolutionary ideas and at the beginning of 1903 went to Shanghai, where he attended the revolutionary Patriotic School. There he seems to have been one of the more prominent students and in the spring of 1903 was elected to two offices in the Educational Association.[44] He evidently was particularly close to Chang Ping-lin among the older scholars of the association.

After the *Su-pao* case Ao returned to Kashing, where he organized a debating society and an educational society which were to spread radical propaganda. Local officials closed the organizations almost immediately[45] and Ao left town to travel in southeastern Chekiang. He was one of the Chekiangese revolutionaries who planned to support Huang Hsing's rising in the fall of 1904.[46] The next year he returned to Kashing to found the Wen-T'ai-Ch'u Guildhall, which was briefly the center of revolutionary activity in Chekiang. Ao never identified totally with the revolutionary movement, however. He refused to join the Restoration Society. After the guildhall closed he maintained contacts with some of the revolutionaries, but no longer played an important part. He also remained in touch with secret societies, among which he probably had a large acquaintance. His last important political act was to persuade the salt smugglers who rose in late 1907 to bypass the city of Kashing and leave it unharmed. When in 1908 he was murdered at the age of thirty-four, it was unclear whether private enemies or political reasons were responsible. Ao remains an interesting but somewhat enigmatic figure. He seems to have been part revolutionary, part independent radical, and part disreputable lower gentry. His history again calls attention to the diverse natures of those who have usually been lumped together as revolutionaries.

Ao intended to use the guildhall to organize and finance militia that would serve as the basis for a revolutionary army. There were a large number of immigrants from the southeastern prefectures of Wenchow, Taichow, and Chuchow in the Kashing area. They had a general reputation for unruliness and, therefore, seemed likely material for a rising. To finance this undertaking, Ao proposed to obtain permission for the guildhall to act as tax collecting agent for the government. The people would pay taxes to the guildhall, thus avoiding the exactions of the yamen clerks. It would then allegedly turn the funds over to the government but actually would use them to buy military provisions and supplies. It would also serve as a center from which to organize the secret societies. If the plan failed, at least it would not cost anything. Ao called upon the local officials and gentry leaders and received their support by presenting the guildhall as a means to control the immigrants and keep peace between the immigrants and the original inhabitants. Ao himself put up the money to establish the organization sometime during October or November 1904.[47] Local gentry were legally prohibited from collecting and transmitting taxes, although it was not an uncommon practice.[48] Nonetheless, official approval of this plan seems a bit extraordinary and probably indicated weakening government control. The guildhall was really a gentry-type organization, but evidently it acquired semiofficial status by official approval of its function.

Ch'en Meng-hsiung helped Ao establish the guildhall. Among others who worked for it were a number of students and merchants originally from southeast Chekiang who could establish rapport with the immigrants. These students evidently had not studied abroad and at least some of the merchants had secret society connections. There was also a significant direct secret society element in the guildhall and very soon a number of the professional revolutionaries were added to the group. T'ao Ch'eng-chang, who had previously met Ao in Shanghai, came to the area to see Kung Pao-ch'üan. Kung brought T'ao to discuss plans with Ao and the two found themselves in substantial agreement on strategy. T'ao introduced Wei Lan, whom Ao accepted as director of the guildhall. Wei brought two of his relatives and some other revolutionary associates into the organization. After the newspaper *The Alarm Bell* was closed in Shanghai, Liu Shih-p'ei fled to Kashing and helped manage the guildhall for a few months.

The main work of the guildhall centered about strengthening contacts with secret societies and recruiting among the villages. Ao provided funds to enable the cadres to travel about northern Chekiang. There is little specific information about just how the villagers were approached or organized. Evidently, they were recruited to form militia and the guildhall was presented as a secret or quasi-secret society. Ao decided that the best way to attract recruits was through the superstitious, debased Buddhist-Taoist religion of the countryside. He therefore established an Ancestral Sect (*Tsu-tsung chiao*) complete with sacred texts, incantations to assure longevity, secret slogans and passwords, and chose a native of Wenchow to head the sect.

After the failure of the plans for a rising on the empress-dowager's birthday in 1904, the most active revolutionaries in the province and some of the secret society members who were closest to them moved to the guildhall. Their strategy was to establish contacts with secret societies in northern and western Chekiang and southern Kiangsu as well as to build militia composed of immigrants. The Chekiang salt smugglers were also sought as allies. The revolutionaries did not believe that Chekiang alone was an adequate base for revolution. Plans were laid for one army to march through Kiangsi to cut off the government troops in Hunan and Hupeh. The other was to march on Nanking. Before its arrival at that city, cadres within the walls were to assassinate the major officials in the hope that the government would fall without a battle.

This rather ambitious plan was never tested because after June 1905 Ao Chia-hsiung was plagued by family and business diffculties. He could not continue to support the guildhall, and he did not again play a really important role in the revolutionary movement. Without a source of funds the revolutionaries could no longer continue their activities in Kashing and soon turned elsewhere. About this time the guildhall also came under official suspicion because the head of the Ancestral Sect was arrested in Huchow and his testimony implicated Ao. The officials decided to take no additional action, but it was probably less possible for the revolutionaries to come and go freely in the Kashing area.

The Ta-t'ung School

About the time the Wen-T'ai-Ch'u Guildhall ran into difficulties Hsü Hsi-lin independently laid the groundwork for establishing the Ta-t'ung School, which was to become the new center of the revolutionary movement in Chekiang. Like other Chekiangese revolutionaries, Hsü preferred to establish his organization in his home town. Therefore, revolutionary headquarters shifted to the otherwise unlikely town of Shaohsing. Located on the fertile Chekiang plains, Shaohsing was in a rich agricultural area and famous winegrowing district. It was also a marketing center and a transfer point for silk and other goods en route from the interior of Chekiang to Shanghai. Many wealthy merchants and gentry lived there and this affluence had contributed to making the town a traditional scholarly center as well. By 1905 Shaohsing also had been subjected to some Western influence. There were a number of modern schools in and near the city. There was a foreign missionary community of about twenty Englishmen and American Protestants as well as Catholic missionaries. Some merchants in the area were involved in foreign trade and before 1906 a Chinese company had established a cotton mill in Shaohsing which was doing well enough to encourage another group of gentry and merchants to establish a second mill in the nearby district city of Yü-yao. Several bookstores sold "new books" and interest in current affairs was demonstrated by some agitation in favor of the anti-American boycott during the autumn of 1905. However, Shaohsing was still fairly isolated from the forces of modernity. Mail took three or four days from Shanghai—a trip of at least thirty-six hours of actual travel by boat and overland. There was a strong conservative strain in the gentry community. The government-sponsored modern schools in the city were inferior academically and had difficulty attracting students partly because of gentry opposition and official indifference.[49] If Hsü Hsi-lin had not happened to grow up in the vicinity, the town would probably never have figured prominently in revolutionary history.

The immediate background for the establishment of the Ta-t'ung School was the arrival in April of Ts'ai Yüan-p'ei's younger brother, who suggested robbing the local banks to raise funds for the Restoration Society. Hsü readily fell in with this scheme. He borrowed money from a merchant sympathizer, Hsü Chung-ch'ing, and went to Shanghai, where he bought 50 nine-caliber breach-loading guns and 20,000 rounds of ammunition. Hsü Hsi-lin was an old acquaintance of the Shaohsing prefect, under whom he had once served, and so he was able to obtain a permit to bring the arms back to Shaohsing by saying that they were to be used for drill in various schools. The guns were transported without incident and temporarily stored in the Shaohsing Middle School. Hsü and his associates then decided to establish a school where they could keep the weapons and hide stolen funds. Strong opposition from Hsü's father prevented their using Tung-p'u as a base. The younger Ts'ai and Hsü also found that none of their group could drive a getaway vehicle and so gave up the bank-robbery scheme.[50] Unlike the Bolsheviks in Russia, the Restoration Society members lacked the discipline and toughness to make a success of revolutionary crime.

After this initial failure T'ao Ch'eng-chang and Kung Pao-ch'üan visited Hsü and told him of the decline of the Wen-T'ai-Ch'u Guildhall. Hsü suggested that they establish a school in Shaohsing to replace it, and others agreed.[51] To circumvent his father's opposition, Hsü obtained permission from the expectant taotai in charge of the Shaohsing granaries to use an empty storehouse in Ta-t'ung just outside the west gate of Shaohsing city. Among those who helped Hsü, T'ao, and Kung run the school were the merchant and secret society leader Lü Hsiung-hsiang, the secret society leaders Chu Shao-k'ang and Wang Chin-fa, Chao Hung-fu[52] and the student Ch'en Po-p'ing. On September 23, 1905, it was formally opened under the full name of the Ta-t'ung Normal School (*Ta-t'ung shih-fan hsüeh-t'ang*).

Although Hsü Hsi-lin founded the school and had the necessary connections with local officials and gentry, T'ao Ch'eng-chang seems to have done the most to shape its organization and activities. Hsü, with characteristic ardor, wanted to celebrate the opening day by killing all the officials invited to the ceremonies and starting a rising—an interesting anticipation of his eventual assassination of En-ming. T'ao, who was firmly convinced that a revolution in Chekiang could not succeed without support from Anhwei and Nanking, dissuaded him. Instead, T'ao suggested that the school be used to build up a revolutionary force in the province in a way similar to Ao's guildhall. To further this aim, T'ao sent a petition to the provincial Commission for Educational Affairs in Hangchow arguing in favor of a national conscription army on a Western model. T'ao urged that Chinese students receive military training to prepare them for army service and that militia also be established to teach military drill to the townspeople and villagers. Thus a firm basis would be laid for a national army. To this end T'ao proposed establishing a special six-month military course at the Ta-t'ung School, open to all who wished to take it. Upon graduation the students would return home to their villages and organize militia as a foundation for a conscription army.[53] This petition was approved, somewhat surprisingly in view of official suspicion of student agitation for military training at the time of the Russo-Japanese War. The revolutionaries thus had a green light to go ahead with a plan which had obvious advantages for the creation of a revolutionary army.

Hsü stayed in Shaohsing and managed the school while T'ao, Kung, and Lü started on a tour of Chekiang urging secret society leaders to send their followers for training and offering travel expenses to any who came. They covered Kinhwa and Chuchow prefectures and then returned to Shaohsing to develop new plans. Consequently most of the secret society members who came to the Ta-t'ung School were either from those two prefectures or from Shaohsing, and it was these areas which were mainly involved in the plans for a rising in 1907.[54]

Once the revolutionaries had decided to use the school to build up the revolutionary forces in the province, every effort was made to gain the good will of the local power structure. The school was established with official consent. Leading officials and gentry were invited to opening and closing exercises. Diplomas were awarded to graduates by the prefect and bore the prefectural seal. Therefore, although there was some murmuring against the school, initially it was relatively immune to attack.[55]

The heart of the revolutionaries' program was the special six-month military course. However, a considerable range of other subjects, typical to modern schools of the time, were also studied by the regular students. These included Chinese literature, English, Japanese, geography, history, education, physics, ethics, mathematics, natural science, music, and art. The predominant atmosphere was nonetheless military. Each day began with army drill. Reveille, taps, and the opening and closing of classes were all announced by army bugle calls.[56]

Some of those who studied there were secret society members, others were local radical youngsters, and still others were friends or relatives of the revolutionaries. According to the recollections of one student who was there in 1907, there were not many outward signs of revolutionary spirit at the school. However, before summer vacations the head of the school met individually with each student to ascertain his views and to urge him to engage in revolutionary work during the holidays. It was also the fashion for students to form groups of five sworn brothers who took oaths to die together on the same day,[57] indicating the influence of the type of popular novel from which many young radicals drew inspiration.

Some financial support for the Ta-t'ung School came from the friend who had once helped Hsü Hsi-lin found the Je-ch'eng Primary School,[58] but the main source of funds throughout the duration of the school was the wealthy merchant Hsü Chung-ch'ing. He was a revolutionary sympathizer, although he seems not to have taken an active part in revolutionary work. Throughout the school's existence, he provided money for operating expenses and buying weapons.[59]

The founding of the Ta-t'ung School marked a significant advance in the relations between the revolutionaries and the secret societies. Certain of the well-educated secret society leaders shared closely in managing the school. Most of those who studied there joined the Restoration Society.[60] Since many of the students were secret society members, they were in this way bound more closely to the revolutionary movement than they would have been by simple alliances arranged between the Restoration Society and secret society leaders.

By the end of 1905, therefore, a promising beginning had been made. The revolutionaries had substantial contacts among the secret societies. They had established a front organization which had the good will of at least some of the local officials and gentry. They also had a plan of procedure which, if followed discreetly for a period of time, would gradually build up a sizable revolutionary-controlled force in the countryside. All these steps toward penetration of the local power structure quite closely followed methods traditionally used by dissatisfied gentry and scholars. When, however, they were used by the revolutionary intellectuals, new problems were created which eventually were to lead to the collapse of the entire effort.

The foundations laid by the revolutionaries in Chekiang during 1904 and 1905 did not culminate in an attempt to overthrow the government until the middle of 1907. The result then was a disastrous failure which gravely weakened the movement in the province. Behind this failure were a number of weaknesses which had been present almost from the beginning and were never overcome. The top leaders were not content to stay long in Shaohsing and soon began to search for new areas of activity. Revolutionary fronts outside the treaty ports were in a very exposed position, which increased the difficulty of balancing legal activities necessary to prevent discovery against genuine subversive purposes. Despite their many contacts with the revolutionaries, the secret societies remained a scattered, poorly armed, and weakly indoctrinated force. Finally, the leaders who ultimately planned the risings in 1907 were of a temper to risk their party organizations in desperate and almost hopeless gambles. After 1907 the activities of the student revolutionaries in Chekiang were greatly curtailed and began to be overshadowed by those of other groups. Remaining front organizations did not attempt any spectacular rising and must have been practically indistinguishable from moderate groups. The Restoration Society was no longer an organizational force in the province. Revolutionary Alliance activists relied more upon periodic trips, particularly to maintain contact with student and army radicals in the Hangchow area, than on continuing activity in the province. The new army replaced schools and secret societies as the most important potential revolutionary force. Equally important, the constitutionalist movement matured and eventually became a major source of opposition to the Ch'ing government. In 1907 agitation against a British railway loan began to drive a serious wedge between local modernizers and Peking. The radical intellectuals were peripherally involved in these developments, but they had slight influence upon them. When the Revolution did come student revolutionaries again played a significant role in immediate events, but they did not have the power to control the new governments.

The Chekiang and Anking Cases: Weaknesses and Defeat

Ephemeral Leadership

Many of the student radicals were too impatient to spend several years building a revolutionary organization which might have replaced the secret societies as a force in the countryside. They were too oriented toward the cities and too far removed from the peasants to spend a long time in provincial areas. Either they looked for a quick solution through an immediate rising or they were drawn away by the attractions of further travel or study abroad.

T'ao Ch'eng-chang initiated the plan that robbed the Ta-t'ung School of some of its most important organizers. He believed that because of the growth of the new army, training militia was not enough to ensure success of the revolution. Therefore, he proposed that several revolutionaries purchase titles and go to Japan for military study. Upon graduation he hoped that they would receive officers' commissions and thus gain command of troops which could be swung over to the revolution at the appropriate point. This plan was approved by the others and it was agreed that T'ao, Hsü, Kung Pao-ch'üan, and two others should purchase titles. They apportioned their ranks according to age. Hsü, the eldest, purchased that of a taotai, T'ao obtained a prefect's title, and the other three purchased the title of first-class subprefect (*t'ung-chih*).[1]

The revolutionaries turned again to traditional methods to facilitate this plan. They purchased titles, bribed officials, and relied on influential family connections. Hsü Chung-ch'ing supplied the large sum of fifty thousand gold yuan to purchase titles and meet other expenses. Hsü Hsi-lin then went to Hupeh to see his cousin Yü Lien-san, a former governor of Hunan with a wide acquaintance among high Ch'ing officials. His cousin gave him an introduction to the commander-in-chief of the Manchu forces in Chekiang, Shou-shan, who was then acting-governor. Hsü went to see Shou-shan and, realizing that he was corrupt, bribed him with three thousand gold yuan, whereupon Shou-shan granted permission for the five to study in Japan and also wrote a letter on their behalf to the Chinese minister in Tokyo.[2]

The group went to Japan about the end of 1905 or the beginning of 1906. When they arrived they found that their private funds would be insufficient and also that the superintendent of Chinese students in Japan was suspicious of them because they did not hold government scholarships. Hsü again asked his cousin to exert his influence on their behalf. Yü Lien-san telegraphed the new governor of Chekiang, Chang Tseng-yang. Hsü and the others were then awarded provincial scholarships. However, the super-intendent remained dubious and delayed the start of their studies. When the five were allowed to take the physical examinations to enter the military Preparatory School, they all failed. Hsü Hsi-lin was too near-sighted to fulfill the requirements. I do not know on what grounds the others were refused, but probably they were rejected as suspicious characters rather than for purely physical reasons. A second try at the Army Commissariat School (*Rikugun keiri gakkō*) brought similar results.[3]

With their plans thus stymied, Hsü and T'ao quarrelled over what their next step should be. The two men had basically very different natures; the one ardent and eager and the other cautious and thorough. When their intentions in Tokyo were frustrated, Hsü favored returning to China and infiltrating the police as well as trying to obtain positions in military schools or military administration. T'ao believed that it was necessary to directly control the army.[4] Certain other issues complicated the argument. T'ao believed that after the first class had been graduated by the Ta-t'ung School, the school should be abandoned to prevent possible discovery of its real purpose. Emphasis should instead be placed on forming and train-ing of militia by those who had studied at the school. Hsü and those left in charge in Shaohsing believed that the school should continue and produce as many graduates as possible. T'ao also joined the Revolutionary Alliance at this time. Because of their disagreement he joined without Hsü and Hsü decided not to join at all. The final result was that Hsü and T'ao went different ways and neither returned to Shaohsing. When Hsü began to plan a rising in Anking in 1907, T'ao believed that he was motivated by a desire for personal glory and refused to cooperate with him.[5]

After breaking with T'ao, Hsü tried once more to enter a police academy in Tokyo and then persistently sought a government post. He made another visit to his cousin Yü Lien-san, who arranged for Chang Chih-tung to give him an introduction to Yüan Shih-k'ai. Next, Hsü saw Shou-shan, who came forth with a letter to his father-in-law, Prince Ch'ing, I-kuang. Armed with these introductions, Hsü went to Peking. There he hoped to assassinate the powerful Manchu Minister of War T'ieh-liang, but after this idea came to nothing, he attempted to further his career through influential con-nections. However, Yüan Shih-k'ai refused to see him and, although the prince received Hsü, he did not give him any recommendation. Hsü next went to Manchuria to make the acquaintance of a bandit chieftain there. Then he returned to Chekiang, but Governor Chang Tseng-yang also refused to see him. Finally, he tried Anking and met with some success. The Anhwei governor, En-ming, had been a prefect in Shansi when Yü

Lien-san was governor there. Out of respect for his old superior, he gave Hsü a minor post as a low-ranking aide to the assistant director of the Military Primary School in Anking at the end of 1906.[6]

During this time T'ao Ch'eng-chang had been much less active. He remained in Tokyo until the summer of 1906, when he became ill. After being released from the hospital he returned to West Lake at Hangchow to convalesce. In October or November, while he was staying at the *Vernacular Journal*'s offices, rumors started that he and Kung Pao-ch'üan had assembled a force to seize Hangchow. The Manchu lieutenant-governor issued orders for T'ao's arrest, but Governor Chang hesitated to take precipitate action that would provoke resentment if the allegations could not be proven. T'ao was warned by a member of the governor's secretariat (presumably this was Chang Jang-san, the governor's private secretary, who was sympathetic to the revolutionary movement) and fled. For about ten days the city gates were closed part of the day and transients were watched carefully. It was at this time that Hsü Hsi-lin tried to see the governor and was refused. This minor incident indicated that the government was becoming increasingly suspicious of the group that had started the Ta-t'ung School. It also showed that Governor Chang, despite his later severity in the Ch'iu Chin case, was not the witch hunter depicted in revolutionary literature.

After fleeing Hangchow, T'ao Ch'eng-chang kept in touch with some members of the original Chekiang group, such as Ao Chia-hsiung. A few associates, particularly Kung Pao-ch'üan, chose to continue to work closely with him. However, he remained aloof from the Ta-t'ung School, which he still thought should be closed. The price was the comparative isolation and ineffectiveness of T'ao's own efforts. Evidently he traveled up and down the Yangtze River. After the Anking and Chekiang cases broke, a reward was offered for his capture and he fled to Japan.[7] The next year he again tried to organize revolutionary forces in cooperation with party members from other provinces. This group chose T'ao as grand commander for the five Lower Yangtze provinces. Ten hypothetical armies were established—two each in Chekiang, Kiangsu, Kiangsi, Anhwei, and Fukien.[8] After failure of plans for a rising following the deaths of the empress-dowager and emperor, T'ao again went to Japan and most of his subsequent revolutionary activities were abroad.

Problems of the Ta-t'ung School

The departure of the top leaders left a void at the Ta-t'ung School and slightly weakened its contacts with the Restoration Society. The man whom

Hsü had appointed to head the school before leaving for Japan was an old associate who had been director at the Je-ch'eng School. He had also taught Hsü Chung-ch'ing and evidently was responsible for the latter's introduction to Hsü Hsi-lin and willingness to finance the revolutionaries' projects.[9] The new director was a reputable scholar, but he was not familiar with the secret societies. Lü Hsiung-hsiang, Chu Shao-k'ang, and Chao Hung-fu, all of whom had much to do with running the school, had the secret society connections he lacked, but they were not originally from Shaohsing and had no close ties with the scholars and students from that area.

Potential conflict did not break out until after the graduation of the first class. Then Lü, Chu, and Chao invited a new group of secret society members to study at the school. A cleavage developed between students from Shaohsing and those from other parts of Chekiang. The director resigned to try to keep peace and was replaced by an outsider unacceptable to the party members, who forced his resignation. The man who took his place was also unfamiliar with the secret societies and the students became divided into two groups, for and against him. The quarrel degenerated into actual fighting within the school which overflowed into the streets. Naturally the school acquired a bad name with the local officials and gentry. In mid-autumn still another director was found in a sympathetic local landowner, Sun Te-ch'ing, who was soon succeeded by someone else.[10] However, in February 1907 Ch'iu Chin came to Shaohsing and became the real leader of the school.[11]

With the arrival of Ch'iu Chin the problem of leadership was solved, but that of relations with the community exacerbated. Ch'iu's revolutionary enthusiasm and militant feminism were just the right combination to provoke hostility among the gentry and officials. Her first mistake was to order girl students (possibly at the Ming-tao Girls' School rather than at the Ta-t'ung School, although none of the sources I have seen specify who the girls were) to practice military drill, for one of Ch'iu's favorite schemes was a national women's army. Many of the local elite were annoyed by such impropriety. Ch'iu attracted even more unfavorable attention by riding horseback astride and dressing in Western male clothing for military drill. One day some conservatives incited a small riot when she rode into town dressed in man's clothes. Ch'iu was rescued by students from the school, but bad feeling remained.[12]

About the end of March anonymous placards appeared in Shaohsing denouncing the Ta-t'ung School as a "den of rebels" (fei-k'o), a term which probably referred to the school's mores rather than to its revolutionary activities.[13] Whether because of gentry suspicion or for other reasons, the school was searched in April or early May on the pretext of looking for weapons. The revolutionaries had been warned in time and all incriminating documents were hidden and guns removed, so nothing was found. However, this was a strong indication that they did not have much more time.[14] The most damaging result of local hostility occurred early in July when the head of the prefectural education bureau, a relatively conservative returned student whose views Ch'iu Chin had criticized in Japan, reported to Prefect Kuei-fu that she was planning a rising.[15]

Behind the conflicts within the school and worsening relations with the local elite lay problems that also were evident in a number of other front organizations established by revolutionaries. Like the Patriotic School, Patriotic Girls' School, and Chinese Public Institute, the Ta-t'ung School was caught between its conflicting roles as an educational institution and as a revolutionary instrument. Eventually a critical point might be reached where the school would have to split, disband, or decide between a revolutionary or nonrevolutionary course. At the Ta-t'ung School the issue was resolved in favor of revolution by the arrival of Ch'iu Chin before the problem had developed very far. However, resolving this matter merely sharpened other problems. In Shaohsing the school's safety depended considerably more on acceptance by traditional local elites than did that of similar institutions in Shanghai. The radicals were constantly under public scrutiny, and though progressive merchants and gentry might give useful support, they were not generally ready to back the overthrow of the government. In the absence of a general abandonment of faith in the existing government such as occurred in 1911, revolutionary fervor had to be kept in check to maintain the secrecy necessary for survival.

Such secrecy ran the risk of encouraging safe inaction which might allow the organization to come under the control of moderates favoring a reformist approach. More immediately, many of the more radical members of the party felt that it conflicted with the psychological need to affirm their dedication. Like the *Su-pao* group, those at the Ta-t'ung School recall the style of the Tung-lin partisans. The school itself might be thought of as part revolutionary front, part modern school, and part Tung-lin Academy. Someone like Ch'iu Chin could not resist the opportunity to flaunt her views even though they provoked hostility which might be harmful to her main aims.

Secret Society Independence

Equally dangerous to the revolutionaries at the Ta-t'ung School was premature activity by secret society allies. The immediate problem was insufficient discipline—of local leaders over their followers and of Ta-t'ung leaders over the local leaders. Ch'iu Chin's reorganization of the Restoration Society and regulations for the Restoration Army were very elaborate, but in practice they mainly confirmed the existing situation. Since the Chekiangese secret societies were still highly fragmented, a hierarchial organization did not necessarily result in effective lines of command. These were problems which T'ao Ch'eng-chang, at least, had recognized. In discussing the differences between the sects (*chiao*) which were most prominent in North China and the Triad Societies (*hui*) which predominated in the south, he said that the societies were much more approachable and also could expand their membership most easily. However, despite the fraternal loyalties of members of Triad Societies, bonds were weaker than those that held together the more superstitious sects. Each Triad branch was a separate unity which was difficult to direct from the outside, so the actual number of troops available for a rising might be fairly small. Moreover, society members were generally less willing to fight to the death than were those of the sects.[16] Although T'ao may exaggerate the differences between sects and societies,[17] his thoughts on the shortcomings of the societies as political allies were the result of personal experience and to the point. When revolutionaries sought to unite with the societies, their initial successes might prove hollow at the crucial moment.

Revolutionary propaganda had influenced but not remolded the secret societies, which became involved in local economic and political grievances divorced from the main aims of the Restoration Society. The winter and spring of 1906–07 was a time of disastrous famine. The death toll was very high and that unfortunate year provided an alarming preview of the series of poor and bad harvests which were to occur through the end of the dynasty.[18] The hardest-hit areas were northern Anhwei and Kiangsu and adjacent portions of Shantung and Honan, where long neglect of the Huai River channel had resulted in uncontrollable flooding within its basin. Almost all the central provinces, including Chekiang, suffered flooding to some extent, however.[19] Rice prices were high and, in Chekiang, refugees moving south from the worst areas probably contributed to problems of maintaining order. There was much unrest throughout the countryside and frequent rice riots. This sort of dissatisfaction was a major cause behind the secret society rising encouraged by the Revolutionary Alliance in P'ing-hsiang, Liu-yang, and Li-ling in December 1906.[20] In Chekiang at least ten rice riots or related risings of some importance occurred between the beginning of March and the end of June.[21]

One is struck by the general aloofness of the Restoration Society revolutionaries from the economic discontent sweeping the lower classes at this time. I have seen no evidence of connections between them and any of these riots, even though two took place in Shaohsing. Possibly some fringe relations did exist, but the failure of revolutionary sources to mention them indicates that they were not considered important. The Restoration Society leaders based themselves in Shaohsing and made excursions through the interior for their own purposes or brought secret society members to their school. The middle-grade secret society leaders or the Ta-t'ung graduates who returned home were, however, closer to the unrest then prevalent. They were more likely to become involved in riots or get into extraneous fights with officials.

One graduate who returned home to Chuchow prefecture clashed with the local magistrate, who tried to prevent him from organizing militia. When the magistrate beat a student attending the school the Ta-t'ung graduate had founded, other students in the town were so aroused that the provincial authorities dismissed the magistrate to avoid serious riots.[22] Also in Chuchow the leader of a local branch of the Dragon Flower Society ordered his followers to beat a clerk who had been overly severe in collecting taxes. The new magistrate tried to avoid trouble by sending his son to visit Lü Hsiung-hsiang, a relative of the branch leader involved. This effort at official secret society cooperation backfired, for Lü realized that the government forces must be weak and called on another branch of the society to move across prefectural boundaries to harass grain collectors in neighboring districts. Local soldiers had to be reinforced from Hangchow, but the provincial officials were inclined to be conciliatory. They did not know that revolutionaries were involved in any way and believed that the only motive was protest against excessive exactions. One of the magistrates was dismissed and the secret society leaders in their turn demobilized their followers to await a better opportunity.[23]

As the date set for the rising approached, the secret societies became more difficult to control and periodic postponements added to the problem. Wang Chin-fa and other P'ing-yang Society members had been successfully organizing militia in the villages of Chenghsien and in April reached agreement with a discharged soldier who had assembled a bandit band of about a thousand men in the mountainous area along the southern border of Shaohsing prefecture. This man attacked government troops on June 26 without waiting for orders from the Restoration Society. When more soldiers arrived he withdrew across the prefectural border, but by then rewards had been posted for the P'ing-yang Society leaders. However, the Ta-t'ung School was not yet implicated.[24]

Within a few days more incriminating developments had occurred in

Kinhwa prefecture. In Wu-i district rumors had been prevalent for about two months. During June people began to pawn their valuables and hoard rice and salt. Moreover, the man who had been appointed "general" of the Restoration Society forces in the district was indiscreet, particularly after a few drinks, and some of his followers were also boastful. The magistrate could not help but become alarmed and requested troops from Hangchow. These caught the revolutionaries off guard on July 2 and the "general" was captured and executed. Another one of those captured implicated the Ta-t'ung School under torture.[25] Nearby in Kinhwa district a Dragon Flower Society member had already attracted attention by openly buying black cloth for revolutionary uniforms. In addition two society members who were to lead the revolutionary forces there were jailed because of a private dispute over property rights. On July 3 their followers attacked the jail to try and free them. They failed, however, and merely alerted officials.[26]

Romantic Individualism and Heroic Sacrifice

Despite the other problems, the attempted risings of 1907 would not have so greatly damaged the revolutionary movement if it had not been for the particular nature of the leadership of Ch'iu Chin and Hsü Hsi-lin. By early 1907 Hsü had succeeded in obtaining an official position in Anking and Ch'iu had come to the Ta-t'ung School from Shanghai. The two then collaborated closely in planning the abortive joint risings of July. Both were revolutionary romantics whose exceedingly impractical plans led to failure and death. Ch'iu and Hsü were the exact opposite of the Leninist type of revolutionary and their efforts ended in personal testimonies of faith in revolution with little thought of the futures of their organizations. The result was dramatic publicity for radical aims. Despite this propaganda success, however, the Restoration Society received a blow from which it never really recovered, and the revolutionary movement in Chekiang was badly shattered.

Before moving to Shaohsing, Ch'iu Chin had already established connections with the Ta-t'ung School and the Chekiang secret societies which helped her when she came to direct the school. In 1906 she spoke at the closing exercises before summer vacation and had received congratulations from the new prefect, Kuei-fu.[27] Later that year she conferred with secret society leaders at the school and also traveled about Shaohsing and Kinhwa prefectures meeting secret society members.[28] When she returned to Shaohsing in February 1907 she became directress of the Ming-tao Girls' School and was also invited to take charge of the Ta-t'ung's School's affairs.[29] Ch'iu's revolutionary contacts were broader than those of most of the others then active at the school. Once there, however, she associated herself with the local Restoration Society organization and does not seem to have brought many associates from Shanghai or Japan. She and Hsü used Shanghai as a contact point, but there was no tendency to return the center of Restoration Society activities to that city. Both the Chekiang and Anking cases were direct and rather narrow outgrowths of the previous activity at the Ta-t'ung School.

Ch'iu Chin did, however, initiate closer relations between the Ta-t'ung group and the new army in Hangchow, which was just becoming strong enough to provide worthwhile assistance. In 1906 Ch'iu had recruited Chu Jui and other army members to the revolutionary movement. The next spring she went to Hangchow to enlist support for her projected rising. Some of her original recruits were among those who helped her establish the physical-education association she appended to the Ta-t'ung School in order to give military training to more secret society members. A couple of army members taught there. In addition, one of the revolutionary officers contacted the Dragon Flower Society leader Chang Kung on a recruiting mission to Kinhwa in the spring of 1907 and enlisted some of his followers in the army.[30] The Revolutionary Alliance organizers in Hangchow, Huang Fu and others, played a minor role in helping to bring together a force that would rise in the capital once a successful strike had been launched in the interior. They were, however, limited in their ability to move about the interior of Chekiang because they had cut off their queues and thus easily attracted the suspicions of officials.[31] Because the Ta-t'ung group was discovered before the rising began, the army in Hangchow played no active role, although revolutionaries there tried to help those in Shaohsing by warnings and by providing funds to escape. After Ch'iu Chin's arrest, some of the army officers were suspected of complicity and the second infantry regiment, the unit most infiltrated by revolutionaries, was closely watched. However, the government had no proof and the revolutionists had at least one highly placed friend in the governor's secretary, Chang Jang-san. The officers, therefore, escaped dismissal or arrest.[32]

Despite the introduction of this new element, Ch'iu Chin followed the lines already established at the Ta-t'ung School and mainly concentrated on the secret societies. She made one trip in March and another in April or May to arrange agreements for a rising. In Shaohsing itself the secret society leaders Chu Shao-k'ang and Wang Chin-fa continued to be closely involved in running the Ta-t'ung School. Extensive contacts were also maintained in Chuchow and Kinhwa and these three prefectures formed the backbone of the revolutionary movement.

During the spring Ch'iu reorganized the Restoration Society and established the Restoration Army. Part of her blueprint was actually given effect.[33] Some secret society members were appointed army commanders and uniforms and banners were manufactured. However, the forces consisted only of those secret society and militia members who could be mustered in places where Restoration Society connections were strong. It seems unlikely that the paper ranks and organization were closely followed.

In May, Ch'iu called secret society leaders and revolutionaries to a meeting at the Ta-t'ung School. Ch'en Po-p'ing attended as a representative of Hsü Hsi-lin in Anking. The strategy decided upon was to begin with risings first in Kinhwa and then in Chuchow. When troops had been sent from Hangchow to suppress the secret societies in these prefectures, a force from Shaohsing would attack the capital with the aid of students and military within the city. If Hangchow did not fall, they would return to Shaohsing and, supported by forces in Kinhwa and Chuchow, advance on Anking through Kiangsi province.[34] Hsü Hsi-lin in Anking was to coordinate his rising with the one in Chekiang. The rising was first planned for early June. This date was postponed several times to later in June, July 6, and finally July 19.[35]

Ch'iu Chin's last major innovation was to establish the physical-education association connected with the Ta-t'ung School. At first it was located at the Chu-chi district records office (*ts'e-chü*),[36] which would seem to indicate that the school still enjoyed a substantial measure of official support in the first half of 1907. After the regular students left for summer vacation, the physical-education students moved to the Ta-t'ung School buildings. Representatives had been sent to areas where secret societies were numerous to invite participation. Somewhere between fifty and a hundred enrolled, and the Dragon Flower leader Chou Hua-ch'ang personally brought a group of his followers to attend.[37]

All these changes were aimed toward a rising in the near future. Because failure followed so shortly it is difficult to evaluate what effect the reorganization had. Ch'iu's plans for a rising were premature. The organizational changes which she made failed to solve the problems which were to bring about the movement's collapse: immature leadership, lack of secrecy, and the difficulties of coordinating and controlling the activities of the scattered secret societies.

While Ch'iu Chin was reorganizing the Restoration Society and the secret societies in Chekiang, Hsü Hsi-lin finally obtained an official post, from which he believed he could lead a rising. Hsü's first position at the military school turned out to be a disappointment. His salary was so low that he barely had enough money to live on. Other officials scorned him because of his relative ignorance of proper procedure, and he had difficulty in making contacts with the military students because he did not know the local dialect. He was ready to return to Chekiang but was dissuaded by Ch'iu with the argument that the Chekiang governor was already suspicious of him. Therefore, Hsü again appealed to his obliging cousin, who wrote En-ming once more urging that Hsü's talents be given recognition.[38]

At this time a police force was just being established in Anhwei. A police academy to give instruction in Japanese methods had been established as early as 1904,[39] although it evidently had not made much progress. En-ming gave special attention to developing the police when he became governor in the spring of 1906. He himself took the title of superintendent and, on the strength of Yü Lien-san's recommendations, appointed Hsü his assistant and placed him in charge of the police academy.[40]

In his new position Hsü soon won the confidence of the governor and had access to his private apartments. En-ming (1846–1907) was then sixty-one years old and nearing the end of a reasonably successful official career. He had obtained the *chü-jen* degree and then held a series of posts as a magistrate and taotai. In 1903 he was salt commissioner of the Liang-huai circuit and after serving in that position for over two years was appointed Anhwei governor.[41] He was regarded by Westerners as "antiforeign and reactionary" and the diplomatic corps had been displeased by his appointment.[42] More probably, he was a perhaps reluctant convert to the need of accepting foreign innovations while preserving the traditional customs which he preferred in his private life. In his own estimation he sincerely tried to promote education and industry, train troops and police, provide famine relief and suppress banditry during his tenure as governor. In the military sphere he evidently met with some success, for his troops had the reputation of being well trained and well paid.[43] As a Manchu, he was naturally regarded as an adversary by the revolutionaries, but he had not done anything to win their particular enmity. If En-ming had not had the misfortune of being the first official willing to employ Hsü, he would probably have lived on to die of old age.

By early 1907, therefore, Hsü had reached a very favorable position. The way in which he used his opportunity, however, almost ensured the failure of any rising he might plan. It is likely that the revolutionary movement in Anhwei was still too weak and general dissatisfaction with the government not yet strongly enough developed to permit revolution at that time. Furthermore, Hsü's hand was forced by events beyond his control. Nonetheless, up to that point he had done very little to build a reliable force or to consult other revolutionaries in Anhwei. Hsü had considered assassination before and was drawn to the idea of a dramatic individual act which would publicize the revolutionary cause. Probably he believed that this was the best way in which he could serve the Revolution and was not simply seeking personal glory. Whatever the explanation, Hsü played a fairly lone hand in Anking, except for maintaining contact with Ch'iu Chin, and he seems to have had no particular plan to follow after the initial stages of his rebellion.

His associates in Anking were Ch'en Po-p'ing and Ma Tsung-han. Both were Chekiangese student revolutionaries who had been to Japan. Ma had first met Hsü in Shanghai and Ch'en had been a student at the Ta-t'ung School and had accompanied Hsü to Japan in 1906 and then followed him to Anking.[44] Aside from these two, Hsü had no other close allies in the province. Through Ch'en Po-p'ing he made some acquaintance with secret societies in Anhwei and Kiangsi,[45] but they do not seem to have been enlisted for his rising. A Revolutionary Alliance front organization under the guise of a Norwegian Lutheran Mission (*Hsin-i hui*) had been eatablished in northern Anhwei. However, there is no evidence that Hsü tried to contact this group. Closer at hand, the Wuhu Middle School (*Wuhu chung-hsüeh*) had succeeded the Anhwei Public Institute (*An-hui kung-hsüeh*), which had also been located in Wuhu, as a center of student revolutionary activity in the southern part of the province.[46] In Anking the schools were reportedly "full of revolutionary propaganda" and an attempt to start a revolutionary newspaper was suppressed in 1906.[47] Again, Hsü does not seem to have made much use of these revolutionary beginnings, although he did make friends with a Hunanese living in Anking who allowed Hsü to use his house for meetings.[48]

Hsü had somewhat greater contacts with the new army. The center of revolutionary activity in the army was the 31st Mixed Brigade, then still being organized, and the Military Preparatory School, at which Hsü had briefly served. A group of radicals at the school had already organized a society called the *Yüeh-wang hui* (Yüeh Fei Society), which ran an inn on the side to raise money for revolutionary work.[49] A little over a year after the assassination of En-ming, revolutionary sentiment had spread through the army to such an extent that the major attack on Anking led by Hsiung Ch'eng-chi was possible. A number of revolutionaries in the army as well as members of one of the military staff organizations knew of Hsü's plotting.[50] However, they were not notified by him before he actually attempted his coup and so were in no position to give help.[51]

Failure to develop other contacts in Anking meant that Hsü had to rely entirely on the relatively small group of students at the police school to provide at least the initial force for a rising. He held regular Sunday meetings, attended by members of the police academy, at which patriotic speeches were given. However, Hsü only tried to introduce modern Western ideas and to excite the students' interest in free discussion. The principle of race was introduced unobtrusively, but revolutionary aims were not spelled out and many students were not at all clear about where Hsü's ideas were leading.[52] When the time for action came, most of the students were taken by surprise and wanted no part in the affair.

Very possibly Hsü chose this oblique approach because the police students simply were not very good revolutionary material. Provincial governments were first ordered to establish police forces on the Western model at the end of 1902. At the same time they were trying to establish modern armies and to disband the old, useless remnants of the Green Army. One way to alleviate the problems in returning disbanded soldiers to agriculture was to select the more promising of the younger men in the Green Army and other outmoded forces and retrain them as police.[53] The procedure was followed in police academies in Chekiang and Kiangsi[54] and probably was also pursued in Anhwei, although I do not have any direct information about this province.[55] If the police academy did draw many of its students from the Green Army it might be assumed that these men were relatively tradition-bound. Therefore, it is quite possible that Hsü had a rather unperceptive audience and felt that he had to prepare the students before they would accept unadulterated revolutionary ideas.

Even without openly lecturing on revolution, Hsü was in an exposed position and was able to continue only because of En-ming's trust in him. During the spring another official had already accused Hsü of being a revolutionary, but En-ming had refused to believe the charge and told Hsü of it.[56] In early June a Restoration Society member was captured in Shanghai while carrying a list of party members which included Hsü's pseudonym, Kuang Han-tzu.[57] Liang-Kiang Governor-General Tuan-fang notified En-ming, who gave the list to Hsü as the head of police with orders to find and arrest the revolutionaries. Hsü now feared that he was in immediate danger of discovery. Toward the end of June, Ch'en Po-p'ing and Ma Tsung-han met with Ch'iu Chin in Shanghai and decided that the rising in Chekiang would begin on July 6. At this time or on a subsequent trip, Ch'en acquired automatic pistols and had revolutionary leaflets printed in Shanghai.[58]

Hsü originally wanted to time his rising for two days after the Revolution had begun in Chekiang. His plan, such as it was, was to invite En-ming and all other top officials to graduation exercises at the police academy.

He would assassinate En-ming and any official who would not surrender. The academy gates would be closed to prevent students from running away and they would be organized into a force which would seize the armory, telegraph bureau, and other important government buildings. After gaining control of Anking, the revolutionaries would march on Nanking.[59] The first difficulty arose when En-ming insisted that the graduation be held on July 6 instead of July 8 because he wished to attend the celebration of his secretary's mother's eightieth birthday on the later date. Hsü had no choice but to revise his plans. Meanwhile, Ch'iu Chin had postponed the rising in Chekiang until July 19 and it is not clear whether or not she notified Hsü of this change.

When the Anking rising occurred it had all the attributes of comic opera, but it is worth describing as an extreme illustration of the dramatic, self-defeating style of many student revolutionaries. On the morning of July 6, before En-ming arrived, Hsü made a speech to the students saying that he had come to Anking only to save China, with no thought of personal ambition, and that they themselves should never lose sight of this aim. He then asked them to believe that what he was going to do was in the best interests of the country and that they should help him. Many of the students did not yet realize that anything unusual was afoot.

Hsü was able to persuade En-ming to examine the students indoors before reviewing their drill on the parade ground. After everyone had been seated Hsü announced that the Revolution had begun. He and Ch'en Po-p'ing, who had been waiting outside the door, shot at En-ming. Hsü was not wearing his eyeglasses, and under the stress of the moment Ch'en also shot wildly. En-ming was hit seven or eight times and one of the officials who tried to protect him was wounded, but nobody was killed outright. After using all the bullets in their four pistols, Hsü and Ch'en had to leave the hall to obtain more ammunition. During this respite En-ming was carried out and the rest of the officials took advantage of the confusion to escape. En-ming died within a day despite the efforts of an English missionary doctor. The lieutenant governor, Feng Hsü, took charge of suppressing the rebellion and succeeded En-ming when he died.[60]

Meanwhile, Hsü Hsi-lin had no choice but to carry on his plan. He ran outside the police academy brandishing a sword and tried to incite people in the street to join him. He frightened some, but obtained no recruits. Inside the academy Ch'en Po-p'ing and Ma Tsung-han attempted to mobilize the students. Despite threats that they would be killed if they tried to escape, only 30 or 40 of the 280 students followed them.[61] Hsü at first wanted to march on the governor's yamen, but he heard that it was prepared for an attack so he headed for the armory. En route some of the students dropped out so only about 20 or 30 reached their destination. The official in charge of the armory fled when he saw them coming and the few soldiers guarding it were killed.[62]

Although in possession of the armory, the revolutionaries still suffered from a shortage of ammunition. They were unable to open some of the storerooms, and presumably not all the ammunition they did find fitted their guns. Moreover, the police students had not been trained to use the modern large-caliber guns they found there.[63] The first government troops to arrive were from the new army and were led by an acquaintance of Hsü's, who did not seriously try to defeat him.[64] However, the more loyal Defense Forces (*hsün-fang tui*) soon came up and attacked the armory in earnest. Hsü attempted to enlist the aid of the new army stationed outside the city, but the city gates were closed and it was impossible to carry a message through. The group in the armory held out for four hours during the afternoon, inflicting fairly heavy casualties on the government troops. Then the attackers succeeded in breaking down the wall of the armory. Ch'en Po-p'ing had already been killed in the fighting. Nearly all the rest of the revolutionaries fled, but Hsü, Ma, and nineteen others were captured. When Hsü's office and lodging were searched, the provincial officials found swords, guns and ammunition, a seal for the general of the revolutionary army, copies of the declaration of the Restoration Society Military Government and numerous letters, especially from Hsü's younger brother and from another student in Peking.[65]

Hsü's interrogation was only a formality, for all concerned knew he would be executed shortly. Hsü used the opportunity to state his revolutionary principles. When he learned that En-ming had died, he felt that he had achieved his purpose, even though the rising had failed, and it did not matter that he would be executed. He confessed that he had come to Anking with the intent of assassination and revolution. En-ming had been killed to save Chinese from continued enslavement by the Manchus and it was, therefore, irrelevant that he was a good official or had shown Hsü favor. Originally he had hoped to follow up this assassination by killing Tuan-fang, Minister of War T'ieh-liang, and Assistant Minister of War Liang-pi. Hsü gave the names of Ma Tsung-han and Ch'en Po-p'ing, for they were implicated anyway, but he refused to identify other revolutionaries. He claimed, with considerable truth, that although there were many revolutionaries, his had essentially been an individual act. He specifically absolved the students of any blame for the rising—they had been coerced into taking part, had been of little use, and should not be punished. Upon being asked if he was a member of Sun Yat-sen's party, Hsü emphatically denied it and said that Sun was "not fit to order me to commit the assassination."[66]

Hsü was executed the next day and, on the insistence of En-ming's family, his heart was cut out as a sacrifice to the dead governor. Ma Tsung-han gave very little information in his testimony in which he represented Hsü and Ch'en as the main planners of the incident, while he himself had only imperfect knowledge of what was intended.[67] He remained in jail for a month and a half and then was executed on August 24.

Officials took immediate action to prevent any rising in support of Hsü Hsi-lin. Governor-General Tuan-fang quickly dispatched to Anking one battalion and four companies of infantry and two batteries of artillery from the new army at Nanking. A thousand troops from Hupeh and two cruisers were also sent.[68] The Anking city gates remained closed and, to prevent revolutionaries from communicating with one another, telegraph offices along the Yangtze and the coast were ordered not to send any coded messages.[69] Because there was no strength behind Hsü's revolt, the situation in Anking cooled down quickly. To prevent rumors spreading about the country, Tuan-fang ordered that the major newspapers in Shanghai and other cities be immediately informed so that the official version of the story would receive publicity.[70]

Tuan-fang took a very serious view of the case and had wanted to arrest all members of Hsü's family.[71] He was dissuaded from this course, but Hsü's brother, Hsü Wei, was arrested on July 10. Hsü Wei had been on his way to Anking when the assassination occurred. He was not a revolutionary, but the evidence he gave was of some use to the government because it linked Hsü Hsi-lin to Ch'iu Chin and the Ta-t'ung School.[72] This testimony on top of the evidence which had been accumulating in Chekiang helped seal the fate of the Shaohsing revolutionaries. On July 11 the governor ordered the arrest of those at the Ta-t'ung School and two companies from the first new army infantry regiment, which revolutionaries had not infiltrated, were sent to Shaohsing.[73]

Meanwhile, Ch'iu Chin had continued with plans for a rising on July 19, at which time Chinese students in Japan would have returned home for their summer vacation.[74] The news of Hsü Hsi-lin's failure, which Ch'iu read in the Shanghai papers, was a severe blow; she also realized that it would no longer be possible to rely on the secret societies in Kinhwa because of the premature incidents there. However, at a meeting at the Ta-t'ung School it was decided to rise and kill Prefect Kuei-fu on the appointed date with the support of the P'ing-yang Society in Chenghsien. The following day a rising would occur in Hangchow, spearheaded by a dare-to-die corps of secret society and new army members.[75]

The soldiers sent from Hangchow arrived in the vicinity of Shaohsing on the evening of July 12 and camped while their commander went to consult the prefect. The Ta-t'ung School had already received a warning from the students at the Military Primary School in Hangchow. By this time there was no hope that the school could survive an attack. The regular students had gone home for summer vacation and some of the physical-education students fled when they heard the news. Much of the ammunition supply had been exhausted because Ch'iu had permitted those attending the physical education association to practice with live ammunition.[76] Still, Ch'iu notified the P'ing-yang Society to prepare for action. Wang Chin-fa arrived at the school for brief consultations the next morning, July 13. Shortly after he left, Restoration Society spies reported that the government troops were on their way. Ch'iu refused to listen to students urging her to flee. When the troops arrived, she and the remnant of the student body resisted briefly. During the fighting two students were killed and several wounded. Ch'iu and seventeen others were captured.[77]

Upon searching the Ta-t'ung School, the soldiers eventually discovered 45 nine-caliber Mausers with five thousand rounds of ammunition and assorted other guns, with some ammunition, a few swords and pistols.[78] They also found a diary belonging to Ch'iu Chin, a few of her short revolutionary essays and poems, and the regulations that she had drawn up for the revolutionary army.[79] Ch'iu and those captured with her were questioned by Kuei-fu, the Shang-yin Magistrate, and the Kuei-chi Magistrate. Although examined three times and tortured, Ch'iu refused to admit anything of her revolutionary plans, and the written statement which she signed was brief and noncommittal. The testimonies of some of the others captured with Ch'iu indicated, however, that she was plotting revolution.[80]

The local officials knew that many of the leaders of the plot were still uncaptured and feared that if they did not act quickly a major rising might still occur.[81] Therefore, they memorialized Governor Chang for permission to execute Ch'iu. Permission was granted and she was beheaded on July 15.[82] The others captured with Ch'iu were treated much more leniently. One received a three-year jail sentence and two were imprisoned for one year. The rest were acquitted.[83]

The Results of the Chekiang Case

The arrival of troops at the Ta-t'ung School shattered the revolutionary movement in Chekiang, for it was not strong enough nor sufficiently unified to weather the loss of its main headquarters. However, officials were quite correct in fearing disorders would follow. Several secret society risings occurred during the rest of the year. These kept the province in turmoil for a few months, but in the end were more damaging to the societies than to the government. With the collapse of the Ta-t'ung School, the societies almost immediately began to slough off the influence of the revolutionaries. The risings of the second half of 1907 were uncoordinated and largely in the pattern of traditional risings or rebellions, with few modern aspects.

Some of the Restoration Society's closest secret-society allies were forced to flee the province immediately or to go into hiding. In Chuchow, Lü Hsiung-hsiang led a brief rising to avenge Ch'iu Chin, but he soon abandoned the attempt as hopeless.[84] The P'ing-yang Society leaders organized a rising in Shaohsing that had some success during October and November. Some of the rebels carried banners that read "The Revolutionary Army," but those leaders who still remained close to the Restoration Society depended upon the aid of a bandit with whom an agreement had been reached the previous spring. His men alienated the populace by plundering, and when local government troops were reinforced from Hangchow he withdrew and disbanded his force.[85]

Remaining Dragon Flower Society adherents in Kinhwa staged a somewhat more impressive effort in conjunction with the bandit brothers Kao Ta and Kao K'uei. During August a graduate of the Ta-t'ung School raised a force which capitalized on local resentment against government troops that had plundered and executed indiscriminately when sent to suppress those secret society allies of the revolutionaries who had been exposed early in July. Initial successes brought more soldiers from Hangchow. Part of the rebel force then defected while the remainder withdrew to the Kao brothers' stronghold. There the leaders tried to revive the idea of a Restoration Army. The bandits were instructed in modern military drill and dressed in uniforms bearing the characters "Sons of Han." This group reached agreement with other old Restoration Society allies in the White Cloth and Chung-nan societies and planned a major rising. Before all was ready, government officials learned of their preparations and sent troops to attack the rebels. After three months of determined resistance, the rebel force was destroyed and its leaders killed in a last battle.[86]

The most troublesome rising was that of the salt smugglers under Yü Meng-t'ing and Hsia Chu-lin, mainly in the area between Hangchow Bay and T'ai Lake.[87] They first rose at the end of 1907 and repeatedly defeated government troops, killing many soldiers and officers. Eventually the government sent at least twelve battalions of regular troops and put a million taels at the disposal of their commander.[88] Peking brought heavy pressure on Tuan-fang and the Kiangsu and Chekiang governors to suppress the smugglers and they were finally brought under control in May

1908.[89] The timing of the rising was influenced by the Chekiang and Anking cases because Yü and Hsia feared that troops shifted south to protect Nanking against revolutionaries presaged a move against them. However, the smugglers actually had little effective contact with the Restoration Society and their rising can scarcely be attributed to its influence. The closest they came to cooperation was an attempt to ally with the P'ing-yang Society in January which came to nothing when government spies intercepted the messenger.

These risings left the Dragon Flower Society much broken down and the P'ing-yang Society considerably weakened. The Crouching Tiger, White Cloth, and Double Dragon societies continued to flourish, with the last one remaining particularly strong.[90] The societies with the closest contacts with the revolutionaries had been the ones to suffer most because they were the ones that had resisted the Ch'ing most strongly. This circumstance probably contributed to a decline in effective secret society participation in the revolutionary movement after 1907. The societies took part in the events of 1911, but they were never again the main force of revolution in Chekiang.

Although the Ch'iu Chin case was a serious setback for the revolutionaries and their secret society allies, it paradoxically made a tangible contribution to weakening the government. The publicity that the case received was a direct consequence of Ch'iu's decision to sacrifice herself for the revolutionary cause. As a martyr she was an almost instantaneous success. Her sex, her deportment in front of the officials, her hasty execution, and doubts about whether she was really guilty in face of her denial of knowledge of revolutionary plans all disposed public opinion in her favor. Right after her execution, the story spread that in jail before she died she asked for paper and wrote "The autumn rain and the autumn wind will make me die of sorrow" (*Ch'iu-yü ch'iu-feng, ch'ou-sha jen*), the poem which has since practically been made into her trademark, inseparable from her revolutionary image. Probably the poem was actually coined by a sympathizer shortly after Ch'iu's death,[91] but that hardly matters because its real importance was its propaganda effect.

The press was generally sympathetic to Ch'iu. The Hangchow *Vernacular Journal,* which had revolutionary connections, published a cartoon of a ship under full sail floundering in heavy seas with the caption "The autumn wind and the autumn rain presage the coming storm. Chang's sail will be sent to obscurity in the tides of Chekiang."[92] (Governor Chang's *hao* was Hsiao-fan, the *fan* of which was the word for sail.) In Shanghai, *The Universal Gazette* (*Chung-wai jih-pao*) and *The Eastern Times* were both strongly critical of the hasty execution and the behavior of troops sent to Shaohsing. Even the conservative *Shen-pao* suggested that although there may have been justification for executing Ch'iu, officials had blundered in alienating public opinion at a time when the government was preparing for constitutionalism.[93] The *North China Herald* also took Ch'iu's side, believed her to be innocent, and criticized official handling of the case.[94] By the end of 1907 the first edition of Ch'iu's poems had probably been published,[95] and the Ch'iu Chin myth was well under way.

The favorable feelings toward Ch'iu were greatly encouraged by the maladroit handling of the case by provincial and local officials. Officials were profoundly upset by the assassination of En-ming, which seemed to show that they were all unsafe and which quickly followed the unsuccessful attempt to assassinate the Kwangtung naval commander-in-chief, Li Chun in June.[96] In addition the Revolutionary Alliance had inspired risings in Kwangtung in late May and early June and throughout the spring there had been countless nonrevolutionary riots resulting from the famine. No one knew whether the secret societies might still mount a serious rising in Chekiang. There was every reason, therefore, for officials to be worried. Kuei-fu, a humbugged Manchu and a near assassination victim, had particular reason to react strongly. He and Governor Chang thought to serve warning on the revolutionaries still at large in the province and thereby prevent later troubles.[97] With Ch'iu Chin out of the way, they hoped to be able to lay hold of other leaders and to win back the secret society rank and file by lenient treatment.[98]

This was a standard course of action and does not really justify the harsh treatment the governor has received from revolutionary writers.[99] The mistake was to alienate much of elite public opinion by unnecessary searches, arrests, and extortions. Officials had been impressed by the number of revolutionary and secret society members who were from the scholar class[100] and also had a vague idea that more than the Ta-t'ung School was involved in the revolutionary movement. This knowledge led to general suspicion of all modern schools and searches of some. A certain amount of cupidity was also involved. Troops plundered under the guise of hunting for revolutionary material and some of those arrested were not released until they had paid heavy fines.

Within a week after Ch'iu's execution troops had searched two other local schools and arrested some students, although no damaging evidence had been found. There were cases of textbook burning. Girl students with unbound feet were being required to bind them. Alarmed parents were withdrawing their children from school. Prominent individuals arrested included the former director of the Ta-t'ung School, Sun Te-ch'ing, and the school's financial supporter, Hsü Chung-ch'ing. Both were alleged to have had to pay large sums before being released. Hsü Hsi-lin's thoroughly conservative father had voluntarily surrendered himself on July 12. Soldiers then searched his house and shops, arrested his servants and employees, and sealed up the shops.[101]

There was considerable basis for at least some of the seizures, but the officials presented no evidence to support their actions. Some other arrests were obviously made without evidence and helped discredit all others. Under the circumstances it evidently appeared to many that a general purge of the new schools and of all those at all connected with Ch'iu or Hsü was under way. Since many moderate reformers in Shaohsing and other parts of Chekiang fell into these categories, the alarm was widespread and rumors prevalent. Guarantors came forward to aid those arrested.[102] Protest petitions were sent to the governor. Gentry complaints received support from the Shang-yin Magistrate, who resigned because of the way the case was being handled, and from a deputy sent from Hangchow to investigate. When word reached Peking, major officials there, including Yüan Shih-k'ai and Princes Ch'ing and Su, opposed what they considered excessive harshness of the provincial authorities.[103]

Under pressure from both above and below, the authorities had to moderate their approach. Even on the day after Ch'iu was executed, Kuei-fu had to deny rumors that all schools would be closed and that the prefectural government was suspicious of education in general or had any motive in sending troops to the Ta-t'ung School other than preventing the rebellion planned by Ch'iu Chin.[104] Ten days later Kuei-fu repeated his assurances,[105] but by then it was too late to eradicate the hostility that had been aroused. The evidence of Ch'iu Chin's treason, which was quite strong if the government had presented it properly, was overlooked by much of the literate public in their animosity toward Kuei-fu and Governor Chang. Since Kuei-fu was a Manchu, it was easy for criticism to take an anti-Manchu turn. Because widespread arrests had also occurred in Anking, affecting members of relatively influential families in the Lower Yangtze provinces, the Chekiangese opponents of the governor had support from opinion outside the province.[106]

Kuei-fu tried to throw blame on the ex-Shang-yin Magistrate who had resigned because of the case, with the result that the magistrate finally committed suicide in October. This false accusation did nothing to increase Kuei-fu's popularity. In the end he was transferred to Anhwei, where he was also unpopular because of the Ch'iu Chin case. Chang Tseng-yang, at his own request, was transferred to the post of Kiangsu governor at the beginning of September. Because of public opposition he held this office only a month. He then was appointed governor of Shansi, but soon retired from official life.[107]

A residue of distrust remained, however, and ultimately the Chekiang and Anking cases contributed to the success of the Revolution by under-ming public faith in the government. At the same time the results worked against control of the Revolution by the radical intellectuals. Their party was weakened while the spectrum of revolutionary support tended to widen beyond the point where the Restoration Society could assume leadership over all the diverse elements. While the radicals and the secret societies depleted their own ranks, more conservative gentry, scholars, and merchants increasingly found themselves in opposition to the government.

Eclipse of the Radical Intellectuals

After 1907 revolutionary work in Chekiang dropped to a lower key. As in Shanghai, earlier tendencies persisted, but much of the initial élan was lost. Until the Wuchang rising interjected sudden new hope, revolutionary activities were ineffectual and routine. Much more important was the progressive alienation of moderate reformers, who by 1911 were willing to abandon the government when a favorable opportunity arose. Understanding this crucial process requires analysis of the constitutional movement and railway politics, which are beyond the scope of this work. Here I will continue to concentrate on the activities of the revolutionary intellectuals and try to summarize how they operated in the new circumstances created by the shattering defeat at the Ta-t'ung School and what their relations were with the new modernizing elements who were becoming increasingly politically important.

Fragmentation of the Revolutionary Movement

After Ch'iu Chin was executed, many of the revolutionaries connected with the Ta-t'ung School left the province. Wang Chin-fa, Chao Hung-fu, and the Yin sisters were among those who fled to Shanghai. Others went to Tokyo. This debacle clearly demonstrated the weakness of the Restoration Society organization. When the leaders at Shaohsing withdrew, they left no organizational network behind them. For the next few years most revolutionary initiative in Chekiang came from Chekiangese in Shanghai and Tokyo. The remaining local groups were never welded together into a party capable of operating on a province-wide scale.

Revolutionary Alliance organizers from Tokyo seem to have concentrated particularly on Hangchow, where there was a local party branch and where the new army units were located. A favorite spot was West Lake, where Huang Fu[108] and others from the central party met with local radicals during summer vacations. Huang held meetings attended by promisingly radical students and others as well as party members. At these he talked about the Japanese national spirit and the Far Eastern international situation. He also passed out books translated from Japanese, including a secret volume on warfare which some students found useful in 1911. Quite a few people were recruited into the Revolutionary Alliance in this way.[109] Huang generally advised party members to concentrate primarily on the army and secondly on the schools.[110] During 1909 a few old Restoration Society members among new army officers also somewhat revived that party and brought in some new recruits.[111]

Other revolutionaries sporadically tried to reactivate the old Restoration Society alliances and organize a new rising. Most of this initiative came either from T'ao Ch'eng-chang on occasional trips back to China or from Ch'en Ch'i-mei. Ch'en mainly operated from Shanghai[112] and T'ao seems to have seldom entered Chekiang, where he was definitely wanted by the provincial authorities. After the deaths of the emperor and empress-dowager, T'ao met with revolutionaries from several Chekiangese prefectures to discuss the possibility of a rising. He sent a representative to Chekiang in the spring and another man during the summer to contact secret societies. This second man was arrested. T'ao himself spent most of these months in Shanghai, Shantung, and Tokyo. That fall he went to Southeast Asia to raise funds and nothing more was heard of these plans.[113] An overlapping, or perhaps complimentary effort, was begun by Ch'en Ch'i-mei in Shanghai. The meeting which he called in the summer of 1909 was to have been attended by revolutionaries or secret society members from all the prefectures of Chekiang. Many of these were part of the old Restoration Society group.[114] Before the meeting was held, however, Liu Shih-p'ei[115] informed Governor-General Tuan-fang, and Ch'en Ch'i-mei's headquarters in the International Settlement was raided. Chang Kung was arrested and the revolutionaries abandoned this effort. The last major attempt to start a rising before November 1911 was equally abortive. Revolutionaries in Kwangtung and Kwangsi contacted those in Chekiang before the Canton rising in April 1911. A meeting was held at West Lake to discuss how the Chekiangese could give support. T'ao Ch'eng-chang returned from Southeast Asia to help lead the revolt. However, by the time he reached Shanghai the Canton attempt had already failed.[116]

None of these efforts were very successful in rallying the remaining revolutionary groups in Chekiang. They bore even less relationship to the continuing peasant risings and riots which were almost always completely divorced from the revolutionary movement. This dichotomy again illustrates the gap which existed between student radicals and the lower classes when secret society leaders did not act as intermediaries. I know of only one connection between earlier activities of student radicals and what appeared to be a straightforward secret society and bandit rebellion. Then the person who provided the link had only been on the fringes of student circles. The Buddhist monk Huang Fei-lung had been a partner of Ch'en Meng-hsiung in founding the Monks' and People's School in Lotsing in 1906. Officials ordered his arrest at the time of the "Song of New Mountain" case and Huang fled to the mountainous interior of the district. He remained there for several years and received some money from Ch'en Meng-hsiung in Southeast Asia before Ch'en died. In the mountains Huang collected a band of about four hundred men. Some were former students at the Monks' and People's School. Others were probably secret society members, for Huang was a member of the Brothers and Elders Society. In January 1910 Huang and his followers rose. Government troops surrounded his force, but could not take its impregnable hill stronghold. After twenty days the outnumbered rebels successfully withdrew under the cover of a night storm and disbanded to wait another opportunity. The next year Huang and some followers took part in the revolutionary capture of Hangchow and the attack on Nanking. In 1913 he joined the "Second Revolution." When it failed he returned to being a monk, but a year later he was arrested and executed.[117]

In addition to the professional revolutionaries who only periodically returned to Chekiang, there were a number of largely independent groups of intellectuals who operated local revolutionary fronts or more loosely radical organizations in their home towns. Some of these groups began at the time of the Ta-t'ung School and had once had contact with the Restoration Society. Others developed new connections with revolutionaries in Shanghai. Even in smaller provincial towns there was a thin scattering of radical intellectuals who shared many of the attitudes of radicals in Shanghai and Tokyo. Many were returned students who came home to be teachers in the new schools or hold positions in modernizing associations. They welcomed and joined the Revolution when it came, but up to that point they had been only mildly subversive. Probably in many cases their contacts with local reformers were stronger than those with the revolutionary parties. Had they not been extremely circumspect, their groups would have been closed by officials, but just because they were cautious they tended to live unrevolutionary lives until November 1911.

In the prefectural cities of Kinhwa, Ch'ü-chou, Yenchow, and Chuchow, revolutionaries opened special surveying schools which were attached to local public institutes and served as revolutionary headquarters.[118] In Taichow the Yao-tzu Physical Education Association founded during the period of the Ta-t'ung School was succeeded by a normal school of the same name.[119] A particularly long-lived front was the utilitarian Cotton Cloth Mills (*Li-yung chih-pu kung-ssu*), established in 1904 by two returned students and some local scholars.[120] They had close relations with a number of returned students teaching at the prefectural school and at two elementary schools in the city. Together they operated the Cotton Cloth Mills as a revolutionary front and were approached by Wei Lan and Lü Hsiung-hsiang of the Ta-t'ung School. In 1906 a physical-education association was established to give military training and indoctrinate recruits. Wang Chin-fa and Lü Hsiung-hsiang helped them obtain arms via Shaohsing. Officials closed the physical-education association after Ch'iu Chin's arrest, but the mills continued to operate. In 1911 this group contacted Lü Hsiung-hsiang, took part in the Revolution in Chuchow, and several held positions in the local military government. Besides their revolutionary connections, however, they were on good terms with a number of progressive scholars and gentry in the town, some of whom were blood relatives. Some of these modernizers played a role in the Revolution and one held a major post in the military government. It seems very likely, therefore, that at least between 1907 and 1911 this revolutionary front was not a militantly subversive organization.

In Ningpo in 1904 a wealthy merchant established an agricultural and industrial school for *to-min,* a disadvantaged caste whose members were limited to a few lowly, menial jobs and forbidden to marry outside their group.[121] The director of the school, Ch'en Hsün-cheng, a number of the teachers at the school, and the son of the founder eventually helped organize the Revolution in Ningpo, and Ch'en and the founder's son held positions in the revolutionary military government. Ch'en was one of the more important revolutionaries in Ningpo, and his contacts in Shanghai eventually included Ch'en Ch'i-mei. Officials were suspicious of the school for *to-min* from time to time during the eight years from 1904 to 1911, but the radicals there were cautious and the school was never closed.

From its beginnings the school had undoubtedly been a radical or revolutionary organization. However, it was not until mid-1911, after revolutionary activity had begun to increase throughout Central China, that its members formed organizations which seriously threatened the government. The Ningpo branch of the Revolutionary Alliance, with Ch'en Hsün-cheng as second in command, was not established until late in the summer of 1911. It largely overlapped the branch of the Citizens' Martial Society (*Kuo-min shang-wu fen-hui*) which had been established shortly before to teach military drill, publish a radical journal, gain revolutionary recruits, and make alliances with gentry and others. Ch'en and at least two teachers at the school for *to-min* were members of this society.

The treaty port of Ningpo was more accessible to the radical center of Shanghai and had more Western contacts than did interior towns. It may also have had a stronger radical movement than any Chekiangese city other than Hangchow. Even so, the history of the *to-min* school again seems consistent with a picture of local radical groups remaining fairly quiescent until the political environment changed to favor the overthrow of the government.

Revolutionaries and the New Army

The intellectual revolutionaries by themselves were not a potent force in Chekiang. They needed allies and eventually found essential support from the new army stationed about Hangchow. After 1907, when the revolutionaries' secret society allies were badly shattered, they increasingly relied on the army for new recruits. Within the new army were a fair number of men, particularly among the lower- and middle-grade officers, who had joined for patriotic reasons. Their experience and attitudes were very similar to those of the radical intellectuals, among whom they had many acquaintances. One such man was Chiang Tsun-kuei, the commander of the second new infantry regiment to be established in Chekiang. Chiang had been a student at the Ch'iu-shih Academy and then had studied at military school in Japan. In Japan he had helped publish *Tides of Chekiang* and had joined first the Restoration Society and then the Revolutionary Alliance when these parties were founded. When he returned to Hangchow to become an officer in the embryonic Chekiangese new army, Chiang recruited revolutionaries and protected party members within the army ranks.[122]

Although the army played an important part in the Revolution in 1911, Chekiang was not among the leading centers of military reform. In the second half of 1906 the new army was still in the early stages of organization and just beginning to receive attention from revolutionary agitators. Before this time the Military Preparatory School in Hangchow had been, along with the Ch'iu-shih Academy, an early center of radical ideas. For several years it was headed by Wu Yüan-chih, a *chin-shih* from Kiangsu, who tolerated, or perhaps even encouraged, radicalism among the students.[123] This school was renamed the Military Primary School when Chekiang began seriously to organize a modern army. The province did not provide any middle- or higher-military education so graduates had to go to Nanking and Hankow or to Japan for further training. Most of the first officers were graduates of the Army Officers Academy in Tokyo or of the Nanking Military School. In 1906 one infantry regiment was already in existence, but it was commanded by a conservative, old-style officer. In the summer of 1906 the second regiment began to be established under the command of Chiang Tsun-kuei, assisted by Chu Jui, who was to succeed Chiang as military governor of Chekiang after the Revolution. As soon as the organization of the regiment had been outlined, Chiang Tsun-kuei established a School for Noncommissioned Officers (*pien-mu hsüeh-t'ang*), at which all the officers taught. Graduates provided noncommissioned officers for the expanding army after completing the six-month course. Chiang also established an artillery school and a training corps for new rank-and-file recruits. During the next five years the nucleus of the first two infantry regiments was gradually expanded to division strength. The original regiments around Hangchow were combined into the 41st Brigade under the command of Yang Shan-te, who was less politically suspect than Chiang Tsun-kuei. The 42nd Brigade, stationed at Ningpo, was added under the command of Hsiao Tzu-t'ing, a Hunanese who had graduated from the first class of the Chekiang Military Preparatory School. Hsiao then became commander of the 21st Division, which included cavalry, artillery, transport, and engineering units as well as the two infantry brigades.[124]

Revolutionary efforts to win converts among the troops began about the time of the establishment of the second infantry regiment which, under Chiang Tsun-kuei's leadership, was more amenable than the first to radical propaganda. In 1906 Ch'iu Chin visited Hangchow and contacted the army there as part of the groundwork for the rising planned for the end of that year. She recruited a considerable number from the second infantry regiment, the Military Primary School, and the School for Noncommissioned Officers. Yü Wei, Chu Jui, and Yeh Sung-ch'ing were the most important of this group. A few members, including Hsia Ch'ao, were also found in the Provincial Staff of New Troops (*tu-lien kung-so*), which was in charge of organizing the new army. Yü Wei also succeeded in winning over a couple of members of the governor's yamen guards.[125]

About this time, Huang Fu and other Revolutionary Alliance members were sent by Sun Yat-sen from Tokyo to establish contacts in Chekiang. They also recruited a number of officers, the most important of whom was Ku Nai-pin, who was to play a major role in 1911. Ch'iu Chin had evidently enrolled her contacts in the Restoration Society. However, the two groups formed a joint headquarters which was headed by Hsia Ch'ao, assisted by Ku Nai-pin.[126]

Cooperation between the new army and the Restoration Society at the Ta-t'ung School during 1907 has already been described. Afterwards, the general lull in revolutionary activity after Ch'iu Chin's death affected the new army as well as student circles. Chiang Tsun-kuei was hard pressed to protect some of his subordinates who had been closely connected with the Ta-t'ung School physical-education association and Chiang himself was suspect. From 1908 through 1910 the number of Revolutionary Alliance members in the new army continued to grow. Students and some of the faculty at the various military schools furnished many of the recruits. Party members in the army retained connections with student organizers. Some of the recruiting in the army was prompted from the outside, but most seems to have been done internally. Yü Wei and some other officers also found a number of recruits among police, railway employees, and other nonmilitary groups.[127]

Partially offsetting this progress, some of the original revolutionary leaders in the army moved away during these years. Chu Jui was transferred to Anhwei. In 1909 Chiang Tsun-kuei was transferred to Kwangsi and later to Kwangtung. In Kwangtung he briefly headed the revolutionary government in 1911 until a military governor was elected, and he did not return to Hangchow until mid-December. Yeh Sung-ch'ing temporarily retired because of personal problems.[128] These changes resulted in some loss of effective leadership. However, Chu Jui and Yeh Sung-ch'ing had already returned by the time the Revolution had taken place. Some early party members who had gone elsewhere for military study were also back. Among these was Lü Kung-wang, who was employed on the Provincial Staff of New Troops. After the Revolution, Lü served as Chu Jui's chief of staff and in 1916 succeeded him as military governor when Chu was ousted by the "Third Revolution."[129]

The revolutionary leaders in the new army played a large role in the planning of the 1911 Revolution in Hangchow, for they commanded the main forces which overthrew the government. Until the Revolution actually occurred there is little evidence of schism between student revolutionaries and those in the new army. In the long run, however, the army rejected the sweeping changes favored by the most radical intellectuals. Officers who had first joined the army as patriotic students eventually acquired the real power which intellectuals lacked. With troops at their command they were easily tempted to put personal aggrandizement ahead of loyalty to party aims. Moreover, there may never have been as much enthusiasm for sweeping changes in new army circles as there was among some of the students. New army officers were part of the modernization movement in China and were ready to endorse certain innovations, particularly in military and industrial spheres. However, they were also a professional group and had more to lose than the radical intellectuals. The discipline required by army life contrasted with the disordered freedom of student circles. Much of the army's job involved maintaining internal order, which may have dimmed their sympathy for popular risings, and even revolutionary party members in the army may have been influenced by professional and elitist concepts which left them suspicious of mass movements. Whatever the reasons, there was a difference between army and student circles which became evident shortly after the government was overthrown. The army supplied the revolutionaries with an effective fighting force, something the secret societies could not do. However, the radical intellectuals were no more able to control the former than the latter, and just because the army was more effective it was the more dangerous ally.

Diffusion of Antigovernment Sentiment

The most important events in developing antigovernment feeling in Chekiang after mid-1907 were the railway agitation of 1907 and 1908 and the sessions of the provincial assembly, whose members were elected in 1909. Both these subjects are largely outside the history of the intellectual revolutionary movement per se, although they had considerable significance in preparing the way for the 1911 Revolution in Chekiang by further alienating moderates from the government. Revolutionaries were marginally involved with railway investors and assembly members. Events again demonstrated that contacts existed between radicals and moderates and also showed that radicals did not have the political or financial resources to impose their solutions in matters of particular interest to modernizing merchants and gentry.

The Chekiang railway question dated back to 1898, when a British syndicate secured permission to build a line from Soochow to Ningpo via Hangchow. It never exercised its rights because of the Boxer Rebellion and a following stringency of the London money market. In 1905, under pressure from local gentry and merchants, the Chinese government announced that if work was not begun in six months the agreement was void. A merchant-gentry corporation, headed by the Chekiangese gentry T'ang Shou-ch'ien,[130] was then given permission to build the line. A similar Kiangsu Railway Company was to construct the section in Kiangsu, starting at Shanghai rather than Soochow. Some progress was made in constructing the railroad and a few miles of track were opened north of Hangchow. The Chekiang Railway Company was hampered, however, by lack of funds and probably by technical incompetence. In 1907 the British reopened the question by insisting that the original contract was still valid. The Chinese government, caught between external pressures and local interests, could not withstand British demands. Sheng Hsüan-huai and Wang Ta-hsieh, vice-president of the Wai-wu pu, negotiated a new contract with the British. They were able to argue that local opposition precluded the original terms. The new agreement called for a British loan of £1,500,000 to the Chinese corporations, which would be responsible for the actual construction with the advice of a British engineer. These terms were later modified to make the Ministry of Communications and Posts the recipient of the loan so that the local companies did not have to be directly involved.[131]

The news of the negotiations led to vigorous protests from Kiangsu and Chekiang merchants and gentry who were motivated both by patriotic reasons and fear that stockholders would lose their investment. Protest meetings were held in Hangchow and Shanghai and pledges of new funds were collected to prove that money could be raised without foreign loans.[132] The stockholders repeatedly telegraphed officials in Peking protesting the British loan. T'ang Shou-ch'ien led the opposition, which dragged on for many months. Finally T'ang overplayed his hand in the summer of 1910 in a memorial blaming Sheng Hsüan-huai for all the Chekiang and Kiangsu railway troubles and demanding he be relieved of his railway responsibilities. Sheng turned out to be the more powerful, and instead T'ang was dismissed for making wild accusations and was forbidden to intervene in railway affairs.[133] The government hoped both to discipline the troublesome T'ang and to open the way for national control of the line. The result, however, was that T'ang became a hero of antigovernment forces in Chekiang while Sheng was confirmed in his role as a reactionary villain. Protests against his dismissal continued throughout the year and merged into the opposition to railway nationalization.

Student revolutionaries were not in a position to influence the course of this dispute, but they were nonetheless agitated by the prospect of additional loss of Chinese rights. As early as 1903 radicals had shown that they were very sensitive to any instances of economic encroachment in Chekiang.[134] Now they took part in the protest against the British loan.

The Chekiang Provincial Club in Tokyo held an opposition meeting, students took part in the general meeting in Hangchow, a number of schools including the Chinese Public Institute pledged funds to the railway company, and at least one student committed suicide.[135] Articles in radical publications repeated the same nationalistic phrases that had been found in student journals since 1903.[136] There was not much difference between the nationalism of the radicals and that of the gentry and merchants, but they were far apart on methods which they proposed to use to avoid the loan. The stockholders relied on meetings, telegrams, fund raising, and political influence. Radicals called for more direct and drastic steps. At the meeting of the Chekiang Provincial Club in Tokyo, Chang Ping-lin called for a three-stage program beginning with a general strike of shopkeepers in the cities, proceeding to refusal to pay taxes, and ending with a declaration of independence. Foreign loans could only be avoided by overthrowing the government because the government, not the merchants or students, had the power to request or abrogate them.[137] These suggestions went far beyond what the merchants were seriously willing to do. At the Hangchow protest meeting Ku Nai-pin proposed that Chekiang refuse to pay taxes and declare its independence, but he received no support from the moderates.[138] The railway agitation resulted in increased contacts between revolutionaries and moderates, but the revolutionaries definitely were in a subsidiary role.

The establishment of the provincial assembly was a particularly significant preliminary to the Revolution in 1911. Several of its members played an important part in the political arrangements that preceded the 1911 Revolution. More generally, the existence of the assembly led to bickering between its members and administrative officials, demands for greater political power, and calls for rapid convening of a national assembly. As in other provinces these problems drove a greater wedge between constitutionalists and the government. The effect of the provincial assembly on the revolutionary movement was twofold. First, the self-government movement attracted some student radicals away from the revolutionary parties by providing new opportunities for legal political activity. Secondly, a number of the assembly members had friends who were revolutionaries and were reasonably sympathetic to revolutionary views. Cooperation was thus relatively easy in 1911. At the same time, because of their greater prestige and higher public position, assembly members who were willing to take part in the Revolution were often able to make their views prevail over those of the radicals.

Since the Boxer Rebellion there had been a steady growth in associations promoting local educational, agricultural, industrial, and other affairs. By 1908 numerous self-government associations (*tzu-chih hui*) and welfare societies (*kung-i she*) were being established to lay the basis for self-government, sometimes in conjunction with other modernization efforts. A local constitutionalist press also developed.[139] Elections for the provincial assembly were held early in 1909.

Many of those elected to the provincial assembly were degree holders who may be classified as gentry. They no longer held traditional gentry attitudes, however, and many were also constitutionalists who had studied in Japan.[140] At least a few of these already had connections among revolutionaries. Chao Ching-nien, a representative from Shaohsing, was a member of the gentry who was sympathetic to the radical movement.[141] The president of the assembly, the *chin-shih* Ch'en Fu-ch'en, was an old friend of Chang Ping-lin.[142] Shen Chün-ju, one of the vice-presidents, was a *chin-shih* who had gone to study in Japan in 1908. There he met revolutionaries, particularly members of the Restoration Society. He was close to Chang Ping-lin but didn't join any revolutionary party. After returning to Chekiang he was director at the Second Normal School, where there were many radical students. While he was vice-president of the provincial assembly, Shen attended the meeting of assembly representatives called by Chang Chien in Shanghai at the end of 1909 and was one of the delegates sent to Peking in January 1910 to request that a parliament be convened in 1911. In late October and early November 1911 he helped arrange the membership of the revolutionary government.[143]

The assembly member with the strongest revolutionary ties was the other vice-president, Ch'u Fu-ch'eng, a native of Kashing.[144] Ch'u held the title of Student of the Imperial Academy (*chien-sheng*) and was a graduate of the higher police course given at Toyo University. As a student, or shortly after graduation, he had been a revolutionary. In 1904 he helped T'ao Ch'eng-chang organize a headquarters in Shanghai. Later he met Ch'iu Chin and introduced her into the Hsün-ch'i School in Huchow prefecture in 1906. At some point Ch'u joined the Revolutionary Alliance; he was also a delegate to the abortive meeting of Chekiang revolutionaries called by Ch'en Ch'i-mei in Shanghai in 1909. Despite his involvement in revolutionary work, Ch'u does not seem to have shared the social alienation of many of the radical intellectuals. On the contrary, he also took part in reformist modernizing activities in his home town and province. He was president of the Kashing prefectural chamber of commerce. In September 1909 he presided as temporary chairman at a meeting of the Chekiang Educational Association. He was elected to the provincial assembly the same year. Certainly after mid-1909 his legal political activities over-shadowed his subversive ones and he was more a constitutionalist than a revolutionary. He still had friends in both camps, however. In 1911 he played a critical role as a liaison between the provincial assembly and the revolutionaries, influenced the composition of the new government, and held important posts himself.

Ch'u's history seems to provide an example of how the opportunities provided by the modernization and constitutionalist movements could attract intellectuals who otherwise would have committed themselves to revolutionary work. This progression was roughly symbolic of the general political evolution in Chekiang before 1911. In Shanghai there was a lull in radical politics between 1907 and 1911, but it is still possible to follow a major thread of activity by the intellectual revolutionaries. The city remained a center of the new intelligentsia from whom the revolutionaries derived their basic support. The revolutionary movement was compara-tively well-protected and was not really overshadowed by other events. In Chekiang there was not the same geographic coherence, concentration of student groups, and political immunity. The revolutionary movement suffered more severely from lack of a strong organization. It tended to fragment into small groups of intellectuals who could not hope to challenge the local power structure unaided. Other less radical modernizers in the new army and constitutional movement occupied intermediate positions between student radicals and conventional society. They played an impor-tant part in 1911 because the Revolution of that year marked a fundamental political and psychological break with the past without bringing immediate significant social change. Moderate modernizers and the new professionals were willing to accept change, but they did not uncompromisingly demand too much. They had more power than the intellectual revolutionaries and more influence on the events of 1911 even though they, too, in many places were not able to break the hold of still more conservative elements of society.

The Revolution of 1911 brought first great hope and then disappointment to the radical intellectuals. Events which seemed to promise a new era in Chinese history soon proved much more modest. The overthrow of the dynasty was an important break in the Chinese tradition. It did not, however, seriously undermine the power of existing provincial and local elites. Nor did it lead to a new national consensus. The results of the Revolution differed sharply from the aims of the radical intellectuals in the revolutionary movement. Symbolically, place after place in southern and central China declared its independence (*tu-li*) from the central government and not its adherence to revolution (*ko-ming*). The new governments were headed by military governors (*tu-tu*), not by revolutionary committees. The first military governors were a varied group which included professional revolutionaries, army officers, constitutionalists, and cooperative Ch'ing officials. Within a year or so, those who won out in the political struggles more literally embodied their titles and soon earned the popular name of warlord. The "Second Revolution" of 1913 completed the submergence of the 1911 radical intellectuals. Nationally, Sun Yat-sen and his followers failed to overthrow Yüan Shih-k'ai. Locally, the remaining old revolutionaries were suppressed by militarists and relatively conservative landlords and merchants. Many radicals were killed or forced to flee. Others came to terms with the new environment and either joined the new governments or concentrated on private professions. The radical foment of the New Culture and May Fourth movements, which began not long thereafter, was mainly created by a new generation of students and intellectuals who were both inspired and disillusioned by the 1911 Revolution, but who had not been deeply involved in the pre-1911 revolutionary movement.

The different histories of the revolutionary movements in Shanghai and Chekiang were at first reflected in different courses of the Revolution. In Shanghai the revolutionaries were stronger, more ably led, and played an important part in the Revolution and in the new government. In Chekiang radical intellectuals and secret society members played a secondary role to constitutionalists, members of the provincial assembly, and revolutionaries in the new army. In both places, however, radicals were not strong enough to act without moderate support and in the end were replaced by militarists and their conservative or moderate allies.

The Shanghai Revolution

The revolutionary movement in the Yangtze Valley was bolstered by the establishment of the Revolutionary Alliance Central China Bureau on July 13, 1911, with headquarters in Shanghai. Although theoretically subordinate to Sun Yat-sen and the Tokyo Revolutionary Alliance, this organization actually reflected disillusionment of some party members, notably Sung Chiao-jen and T'an Jen-feng, with Sun's leadership and southern border strategy after the failure of the Canton rising that spring. The Central China Bureau contacted existing local groups in the Yangtze provinces, and many of its activities were concentrated in Shanghai and Hupei and Hunan where the revolutionary movement was already relatively strong. There was also a Nanking branch, an Anhwei branch headed by Fan Kuang-ch'i, who had been on the staff of several of Yü Yu-jen's newspapers in Shanghai, and men were sent to Szechwan and Shensi as well. The bureau may have promoted a general quickening of revolutionary work and greater coordination between revolutionaries in different provinces. However, the Revolution began so soon after the bureau was established that there was little time for it to have much influence. In Shanghai it brought in a number of able revolutionaries who had not been in that area for some years. It may also have strengthened Ch'en Ch'i-mei's position. He was one of the five members of the bureau's executive committee and in charge of its Shanghai activities.[1] There was considerable overlap between the membership of the Central China Bureau and the group of revolutionaries which had already grown up around Ch'en and *The People's Stand*.[2] Ch'en now had another tool to enhance his revolutionary leadership, but it seems unlikely that his position was fundamentally altered.

The real story of the Revolution in Shanghai lay in the successful cooperation between the professional Revolutionary Alliance revolutionaries and other groups in the city. The revolutionaries were in the minority, but at first they were not overshadowed. Ch'en Ch'i-mei skillfully held the good will of student, gang, and certain merchant-gentry leaders. The armed forces were neither a formidable threat to the Revolution nor initially serious rivals to the radical intellectuals within the revolutionary ranks.

There were no new army units stationed near the city. The local Defense Forces and police had been sufficiently infiltrated to ensure their neutrality if not their cooperation, and neither was so strong a force that it inevitably dominated the political situation.

After over a decade of demonstrations, meetings, and boycotts, the Shanghai populace was generally more nationalistic and politically oriented than were people in the rest of China. Once the Revolution had begun in Wuchang, crowds hung about newspaper offices seeking the latest information. Revolutionaries deliberately used their organ, *The People's Stand,* to stir the populace with news of victories.[3] The constitutionalist *Eastern Times* also carried full accounts of revolutionary progress and hesitated to publish bad news for fear that a mob would attack its offices if the paper showed anything approaching "partiality" to the Manchus.[4] Individual students and others made their way up the Yangtze to join the revolutionary forces in the Wuhan area. After Han-yang had been retaken by Ch'ing troops, however, it became increasingly clear that unless revolutionaries gained control of another major center they would fail in Central China. Preparations for a rising in Shanghai were speeded and revolutionary leaders encouraged those who wished to aid the Revolution to remain in Shanghai.

During the three and a half weeks between the Wuchang and Shanghai risings, revolutionaries effectively mobilized their allies. Important and unexpected additions were Liu Fu-piao, T'ien Hsin-shan, and a number of other leaders of the local Red and Green gangs. These gangs were underworld organizations roughly comparable to the secret societies, but more frankly criminal than many societies. They were involved in extortion, gambling, prostitution, opium dealing, and numerous similar enterprises. Leaders might control gang activities in a certain part of the city or dominate a particular field of activity. Gang membership was often profitable and the protection it afforded was sometimes essential to merchants. Members ranged from unemployed riffraff, through workers and petty traders, to wealthy merchants and other men of substance. A few of the top leaders were powerful men by virtue of their control over crime in the city.[5]

Liu and T'ien approached the revolutionary leaders indirectly through Chang Ch'eng-yu, a one-time student at the Chinese Public Institute who was just back from Hankow and was working as a reporter for *The People's Stand.*[6] After some initial misunderstandings and hesitation, Chang found that he was the leader of a Dare-to-die corps of about three thousand gang members who wished to join in the fighting at Hankow. Chang then consulted *The People's Stand* publisher Yü Yu-jen, his former teacher at the

Chinese Public Institute, who brought him to see Ch'en Ch'i-mei. At their urging he persuaded the gang members to stay in Shanghai. This Dare-to-die group, augmented by students from the Chinese Public Institute and other schools, was one of the chief revolutionary forces in Shanghai, and T'ien and Liu supported Ch'en Ch'i-mei for military governor. Ch'en's political style was probably closer to that of the gangs than was that of many of the radical intellectuals, but even so there was not complete rapport between the two groups. Intellectuals such as Chang Ch'eng-yu had some difficulty believing that the lower-class gang members were seriously interested in the Revolution.[7] Chang was elected to head the Dare-to-die corps because gang members accepted his prestige as a scholar and the value of his connections in revolutionary circles. However, T'ien and Liu really controlled the men. They remained independent and devoted to their own interests, which at that point coincided with those of the revolutionaries. Chang was the front man of a temporary coalition.

The Merchant Volunteers, which altogether numbered five or six thousand, provided another organized force for the Revolution. Despite their name, the Volunteers included workers and students as well as shopkeepers, traders, and other businessmen. Most were young, nationalistic, and very sensitive to China's humiliation by Westerners. Many members believed that the Ch'ing dynasty would have to be overthrown before the country's weakness could be remedied and were determined to take part in the Revolution when it came. The Volunteers were partly comparable to old-style militia and self-help organizations, but were too influenced by new ideas to be strictly in the traditional mode. They also demonstrated that some young men of the professional and trading classes closely shared the ideas of student groups and that these ideas had probably reached some workers in the upper levels of the lower classes.

The Volunteers originated in physical-education associations established in 1906 to practice military drill. These were inspired by the nationalism generated by the anti-American boycott of the previous year. Later in 1906 Shanghai officials asked the five associations in southern and western Shanghai to be ready to help the police if plans for opium suppression led to serious rioting by addicts and dealers. A temporary corps was established under Li P'ing-shu and Tseng Shao-ch'ing, the head of the Fukien Guild in Shanghai who had led the anti-American boycott of 1905. The expected trouble never developed, but the five associations soon united into a permanent Merchant Volunteers' Association (*Shang-t'uan kung-hui*) led by another Shanghai merchant, Yeh Hui-chün. It helped patrol streets and maintain order. Arms and ammunition were supplied by the Shanghai

Taotai and the organization acquired a semiofficial character. In 1910 when Japan annexed Korea, the Merchant Volunteers added a reserve corps of over a thousand men.[8]

About this time various trades and communities in Shanghai organized their own groups. Among these were jewelers, cloth merchants, grocers, bookmakers, druggists, papermakers, and Moslems. Actors and entertainers had a fire brigade which served a similar function and joined the Merchant Volunteers in fighting during the Revolution.[9] An example of the activities of the various Volunteers is provided by the Moslem group. Moslem communities had existed in ports along the Lower Yangtze and South China coast since the T'ang and Sung dynasties, when Persian and Arab traders controlled much of China's sea trade with Islamic Asia. The Moslem settlers had dwindled and become Sinicized over the centuries. Therefore, although the Moslem Volunteers were not entirely typical of the other, nonreligious groups, their general activities were probably much the same. Their group was founded by a teacher in the spring of 1911. His assistant was a newspaperman and one other member was also a member of the Revolutionary Alliance. The young Moslems were enthusiastic, competitive, and influenced by Western ideas. They drilled regularly under a graduate of the Hupeh Military School and a former soldier in the new army, who was to head Ch'en Ch'i-mei's guard after the Revolution. In the evenings leaders often gave radical speeches on current topics.[10]

When they realized the Revolution was imminent, representatives of the various Volunteers elected Li P'ing-shu their temporary commander-in-chief on November 1. Li consulted Ch'en Ch'i-mei and the next day called a meeting of the corps heads to inform them that a rising was scheduled for November 3. The main body of the Volunteers took part in the attack on the Kiangnan Arsenal and other groups maintained order and guarded strategic spots in their own areas.[11]

Students participated in both the Dare-to-die corps and the Merchant Volunteers. The China Volunteers (*Chung-kuo kan-ssu-t'uan*), organized in the spring of 1911, was a similar group composed mainly of student radicals.[12] Some students went to Hankow after the Wuchang rising, but relatively few seem to have played a large part in the planning and brief fighting in Shanghai. However, the large number of students in the city contributed to the general support of the revolutionary intellectuals. Immediately after the Shanghai Revolution sizable numbers of students joined the revolutionary armed forces or formed their own special groups to join the fighting at Nanking or prepare for a northern expedition.[13]

The Dare-to-die corps and the Merchant Volunteers formed the basic revolutionary forces in Shanghai, but revolutionaries also had to take into account the police and the Defense Forces stationed at Shanghai and Woosung. The several thousand police at Nan-shih, Pootung, Chapei, and other parts of Shanghai had been fairly heavily infiltrated by revolutionaries. A number of officers were members of the China Volunteers.[14] Others were revolutionaries who had deliberately joined the police to further the radical cause. Chief among these was Ch'en Han-ch'in, the company commander of the Chapei police station, who headed a group of radicals at the station who had fled to Shanghai when their revolutionary activities elsewhere in China had been discovered.[15] Ch'en knew fellow Hunanese radicals in the army and police as well as the Hunanese Restoration Society leader Li Hsieh-ho. When the Revolution began he assumed command of the Chapei police station after the police chief fled. Some police took part in the assault in the Kiangnan Arsenal while others patrolled the streets to maintain order and prevent plundering.[16]

The main army troops were five battalions of the Defense Forces at Woosung and Shanghai under the command of Liang Tun-cho, a cousin of the Chinese ambassador to Britain. There were also about six hundred Cantonese troops at the mouth of the Woosung River. A guard of a few hundred men was stationed at the naval headquarters and another guard of three hundred Anhwei men protected the Kiangnan Arsenal.[17] Revolutionaries failed to subvert this last group, who were not interested in the arguments of men not from their own province and who were, moreover, strictly supervised by the arsenal director Chang Ch'u-pao, a nephew of Li Hung-chang who was thoroughly loyal to the dynasty.[18] The Defense Forces were more easily influenced. Ch'en Ch'i-mei finally extracted a promise of neutrality from Liang Tun-cho, using the head of the Dare-to-die corps, Chang Ch'eng-yu, as an intermediary.[19] Li Hsieh-ho was mainly responsible for winning over the troops at Woosung. Li was a Hunanese who had spent several years in Southeast Asia working first for the Revolutionary Alliance and then for the revived Restoration Society.[20] In 1911 he returned to China to help Huang Hsing organize the Canton rising of April 27. When it failed he fled to Shanghai, where he soon made friends with Hunanese in the army, particularly the radical Huang Han-hsiang. Huang introduced Li to other officers at Woosung, with the result that the troops there were more positively committed to the Revolution than was the army in the rest of the Shanghai area.[21] Through a mixture of persuasion and bribery, Li Hsieh-ho and Huang also obtained the neutrality of the commander of the Cantonese forces, Li T'ien-ts'ai.[22]

The political and strategic planning of the Revolution was largely the work of Ch'en Ch'i-mei, some other Revolutionary Alliance members, and their longstanding merchant and gentry acquaintances such as Li P'ing-shu, Shen Man-yün, and Yeh Hui-chün.[23] Li P'ing-shu was a particularly important figure. He was proctor of the Kiangnan Arsenal, head of the Shanghai City Council and of the self-government association, and a member of a politically oriented news association at *The Eastern Times* offices which included many active constitutionalists. He used his influence with other members of the self-government organizations to win their support for the Revolution.[24] His presence among the revolutionary leaders also helped convince the foreign consuls in the International Settlement that the revolutionary government would at least be fairly responsible.[25] Shen Man-yün provided funds for the rising from the resources of his Hsin-ch'eng Bank. Another merchant ally, who remained largely in the background but allowed revolutionaries to use his private park for meetings, was Silas A. Hardoon, whose connections with the radicals dated back to the time of the Patriotic School.[26] These intermediate figures who had connections with both revolutionaries and constitutionalists were extremely important in bolstering the position of the revolutionary forces. Ch'en Ch'i-mei's association with Li P'ing-shu contributed to his election as military governor of Shanghai. It is also possible that such connections facilitated the early discussions about organizing a national republican government between Ch'en and such moderates as the military governors of Kiangsu and Chekiang, Ch'eng Te-ch'üan and T'ang Shou-ch'ien, Chang Chien and Chao Feng-ch'ang.[27]

Support for the Revolution was sufficiently widespread in Shanghai that the city fell with little fighting. The rising began on the afternoon of November 3. The top officials in the city fled to the International Settlement, and the guards at the Kiangnan Arsenal put up the only serious resistance. Members of the Merchant Volunteers and the Dare-to-die corps unsuccessfully assaulted the arsenal during the evening of November 3. Li P'ing-shu and Ch'en Ch'i-mei went into the arsenal to urge the director to surrender. He not only refused but detained and almost executed Ch'en Ch'i-mei. On November 4 the revolutionary forces, augmented by some of the police and army, resumed the attack under Li Hsieh-ho's command. The director fled. Ch'en Ch'i-mei was rescued unharmed and became the chief hero of the Shanghai Revolution.[28]

Woosung fell to the Revolution on the same day. Army and police officers established the new government in consultation with the head of the chamber of commerce and the president of the self-government association. The army officer Huang Han-hsiang, the commander of the anti-smuggling naval force, and the head of the police at first held the most important government posts.[29] By the end of November 4 all the major parts of the Shanghai area, except the foreign concessions, were controlled by the revolutionaries.

The first few days after the Revolution were devoted to organizing the military government and restoring order to the city. The major immediate controversy was over the election of a military governor.[30] Ch'en Ch'i-mei was the chief candidate. He was supported by Revolutionary Alliance members, many newspapermen and other intellectuals, a sizable group of Huchow natives in Shanghai, gang leaders and other members of the Dare-to-die corps, and returned students from Japan, especially those from the Army Officers Academy, which Ch'en had once attended. Ch'en's role in the attack on the Kiangnan Arsenal won him considerable short-term admiration and support. He was also acceptable to Li P'ing-shu and other merchant and gentry adherents of the Revolution, although there was always a certain distance between these men and the professional revolutionaries no matter how closely they worked together.

Ch'en's chief rival was Li Hsieh-ho, who was favored by the police and army and by the Restoration Society revolutionaries. Niu Yung-chien, who had been a revolutionary since 1903 and would soon head the prefectural government as Sungkiang, had some support because he was a native of Shanghai. Neither Li nor Niu could match Ch'en's influence, however, and he was formally installed as military governor on November 7. Li and his supporters felt they had been betrayed and for a day or two there was danger of fighting. Li P'ing-shu and the monk Huang Tsung-yang, one-time member of the Educational Association, helped persuade Li Hsieh-ho to step aside. Li called a meeting of army and police officers at the Kiangnan Arsenal, urged them to support Ch'en Ch'i-mei, and then withdrew to Woosung.

Other major government positions were filled either by revolutionaries or by merchant and gentry allies who had prestige in the community, technical abilities, and financial connections useful in some of the most important offices. Returned students, newspaper men, and other intellectuals filled many of the second-level posts.[31] Li P'ing-shu headed the civil government, and Shen Man-yün was chosen finance minister because he could use the funds of his Hsin-ch'eng Bank to aid the new government.[32] Wang Chen, a merchant with longstanding Revolutionary Alliance connections, became minister of agriculture, industry, and commerce. Before he became minister of foreign affairs for the Nanking provisional government in January, Wu T'ing-fang was in charge of foreign relations at Shanghai, an important job because of the International Settlement. Members of the Revolutionary Alliance's Central China Bureau or of *The People's Stand* held a number of positions just below the top level. Ching Yao-yüeh was vice-minister of education; Lü Chih-i, vice-minister of justice; Yü Yu-jen, vice-minister of communications. Sung Chiao-jen headed the legislative bureau and Yang Po-sheng headed the commissariat bureau under the military governor.

Ch'en Ch'i-mei's second-in-command was the Chekiangese Revolutionary Alliance member and new army officer Huang Fu. Huang had been sent to Shanghai in October by his superiors to spy on revolutionary activity and report to Peking. Instead he aided the Revolution. Ch'en appointed him chief-of-staff and commander of the 23rd Army, one of the two divisions into which the various Shanghai forces were organized in the first few days after the Revolution. Huang chose many of his subordinates from among students who had attended the Army Officers Academy in Japan. One of these was Chiang K'ai-shek. Other members of his staff included the head of the Dare-to-die corps, Chang Ch'eng-yu, and Yao Yung-ch'en, an old Restoration Society member who had once been part of the Ta-t'ung School and had subsequently joined the Revolutionary Alliance.

Revolutionary intellectuals were numerous enough in Shanghai so that not only did they hold many positions in the new government, but they were able to afford the luxury of factional rivalries among themselves. These mainly took the form of competition between the Revolutionary Alliance and Restoration Society. These parties had been rivals abroad for the past two years, but the immediate issue was local. Ch'en Ch'i-mei resented any challenge to his position in Shanghai. Many Restoration Society members were Chekiangese and the control of the Chekiangese government was also involved. The issue, however, was decided in Shanghai. In Chekiang such rivalries were more irrelevant to the total political picture because the intellectual revolutionaries were in a weaker position vis-à-vis other elements in the government.

The Restoration Society and Revolutionary Alliance had loosely cooperated before and during the Revolution, but there was no real trust between the groups. Ch'en Ch'i-mei had tried to undermine the weaker Restoration Society headquarters at an earlier date[33] and shortly before the Shanghai rising had tried to make his own contacts with at least one army officer at Woosung who had already been won over by Li Hsieh-ho.[34] Ch'en was probably responsible for an attempt to assassinate Li when he left Shanghai for Woosung on November 9.[35] Li was elected military governor of Woosung by the local revolutionaries who were opposed to Ch'en Ch'i-mei and Ch'en continued to try to subvert him while Li remained in the Shanghai area.[36] This was a somewhat one-sided quarrel because Li seems to have tried to avoid political bickering and concentrated on building up his Restoration Army (*Kuang-fu chün*) to contribute to the capture of Nanking and a northern expedition against Peking.[37] He intended to use his force to further the Revolution as a whole and not to triumph over Ch'en Ch'i-mei.

T'ao Ch'eng-chang, who returned shortly after the Revolution, was a more serious rival who sought to revive the Restoration Society both in Chekiang, where he had support from a few of the new prefectural governments, and in Kiangsu, using the Restoration Army and the Chinkiang military government headed by Restoration Society member Lin Shu-ch'ing as bases. T'ao hoped to succeed T'ang Shou-ch'ien when T'ang resigned as military governor to become minister of communications in Sun Yat-sen's cabinet. However, T'ao had been away from China too much during the previous five years. Most of his support came from the few prefectures where the Ta-t'ung School group had been active before 1908. This backing was no match for the new-army officers and constitutionalists who had really engineered the Chekiang Revolution. Moreover Ch'en was determined to prevent T'ao from reaching a position where he could build up an effective rival organization. Some Chekiangese revolutionary intellectuals who believed T'ao and the Restoration Society were too narrowly oriented toward Shaohsing to the neglect of Ningpo, Hangchow, and northern Chekiang looked to Ch'en for leadership. Chekiangese groups in Shanghai, also under Ch'en's influence, supported the army officer Chiang Tsun-kuei, who was unanimously elected.[38] Shortly thereafter, early on the morning of January 14, T'ao was assassinated in a hospital in the French Concession of Shanghai where he was convalescing. It was widely believed that the murder had been arranged by Chiang K'ai-shek at Ch'en Ch'i-mei's orders. Although the charges have never been definitely proven, this act fitted Ch'en's methods and the suspicions are probably correct.[39] Lin Shu-ch'ing was reputedly poisoned by Yüan Shih-k'ai not many months thereafter.[40] Neither Chang Ping-lin nor Li Hsieh-ho were willing to become aggressive leaders of the Restoration Society and the party soon died out.[41]

Even in Shanghai these struggles between revolutionaries were less important than the question of whether revolutionary intellectuals could hold their own against prominent gentry and merchants and finally against the backers of Yüan Shih-k'ai. The revolutionaries' moderate allies enjoyed advantages because of their professional abilities and social connections and also because they were an important source of funds for the new government. The Shanghai military government remitted most taxes for a year.[42] This gesture, which was also made in many other places, left it dependent on loans and contributions. Wealthy merchant supporters were the most convenient immediate source. The Revolutionary Alliance businessman and anarchist Chang Jen-chieh contributed. Li P'ing-shu and Shen Man-yün both donated 300,000 taels.[43] Such services gave these men considerable influence without permanently solving the government's financial problems.[44]

Initially Ch'en Ch'i-mei was quite successful in cooperating with the moderates, both in operating the government in Shanghai and in discussions leading to the establishment of a temporary national government.[45] However, Ch'en spent much energy in organizing armies for the attack on the imperial forces at Nanking and, after that city was taken, for a northern expedition against Peking.[46] Like radicals elsewhere, the radicals in Shanghai were more concerned with extending the Revolution throughout the country than in deepening it by fostering greater political and social democracy in the areas which they controlled. Preoccupation with military problems and with the day-to-day problems of maintaining order, finding money to keep the government going, and personal and political rivalries left little time for fundamental reforms. It is very unlikely that radicals had the power to enforce striking changes, but their schedule of priorities precluded their trying. Meanwhile such constitutionalists in Shanghai as Chang Chien and Chao Feng-ch'ang played a leading role first in organizing the Nanking provisional government and then in facilitating the negotiations between representatives of Yüan Shih-k'ai and Nanking that led to the abdication of the emperor and selection of Yüan as president of the Republic.[47] When Shanghai became the center of these latter negotiations the political prestige of moderates with connections on both sides increased. Radicals who were suspicious of a compromise were pushed toward the sidelines.

Ch'en Ch'i-mei was against the accord, but he was powerless to prevent it. His position in Shanghai gradually weakened. He made enemies by his direct and sometimes ruthless methods of running the military government and dealing with political rivals. Since Ch'en was not a native of Shanghai he lacked long-term support in that city. Many Kiangsu natives, including Shanghai gentry, believed that the province should not have two major military governors.[48] When local military governorships were abolished throughout the province in mid-1912, Shanghai was included and Ch'en resigned. Yüan Shih-k'ai had already marked him as a potentially dangerous enemy and used various methods including bribery to undermine Ch'en's position.[49] Ch'en had intended to go abroad after resigning, but was diverted by the assassination of Sung Chiao-jen and the subsequent "Second Revolution" against Yüan Shih-k'ai. During the "Second Revolution," Ch'en again attacked the Kiangnan Arsenal, but this time he was not assisted by the Merchant Volunteers, the chamber of commerce, or the people living in the vicinity of the fighting. The Shanghai populace had little enthusiasm for the revolutionaries' quarrel with Yüan and knew Ch'en would fail.[50] After the "Second Revolution," Cheng Ju-ch'eng, whom Yüan had sent to put down the revolt, was the real power in the city.

For over a decade before 1911 Shanghai had been a center of radicalism in Central China and, in contrast to the situation in much of the rest of the country, professional revolutionaries played a decisive role in the Shanghai Revolution. Their early success was made possible by the relatively large numbers of students and intellectuals in Shanghai, the greater diffusion of modern and Western ideas among many segments of the population, the existence of an embryonic urban working class with the beginnings of a social and political consciousness, and the relative unimportance of the government armies and traditional bureaucracy in a city that was a commercial rather than an administrative center. Even in Shanghai, however, the radicals never fully controlled the government. Merchant-gentry allies such as Li P'ing-shu and Shen Man-yün had associated with the radical intellectuals for a number of years, but they were not wholly identified with that group and had equally strong or stronger ties with moderate constitutionalists and with the Shanghai business community. The revolutionaries in Shanghai needed the support, the expertise, and the financial resources of moderates in Shanghai just as revolutionaries elsewhere needed the cooperation of gentry, merchants, and ex-Ch'ing officials. Merchants and constitutionalists were the radicals' most important allies.

Revolutionaries' contacts with the lower classes were largely through the gangs as those of revolutionaries elsewhere were through secret societies. Shanghai workers were presumably more susceptible to Western-derived political and social ideology than were the rural lower classes, but gang leaders were uncertain allies. Their relations with their followers were traditional and paternalistic and, moreover, they were political opportunists. They were open to bribery and unlikely either to support any changes which would threaten their hold over their own gangs or to back a probable loser in outside power struggles.

Even though the Shanghai environment was more favorable to the radical intellectuals than was that of most of the rest of China, they were not able to remain in power long. After 1911 the city remained a center of radical ideas and politics, but in much the same way as it had been before 1911. The latest Western ideas were still readily available, nationalism remained strong, there were always many students and intellectuals, and the International Settlement was a limited political refuge. The beginnings of a labor movement eventually gave more substance to intellectuals' ideas of social reform. The city environment did not extend far beyond its boundaries, however, nor did it provide a secure base for a radical political group. Radicalism in Shanghai remained intellectual, disorganized, and vulnerable.

The Revolution in Chekiang

The Revolution occurred under different circumstances in Chekiang. A much larger area was involved than was involved in Shanghai. There was no one revolutionary organization or plan for the entire province. Neither was there one dominant radical leader. The Revolution was planned by revolutionaries in the new army in consultation with the Revolutionary Alliance in Shanghai and by members of the provincial assembly. Radical intellectuals and secret society members played a secondary role. The first military governor, T'ang Shou-ch'ien, was one of the modernizing gentry and his successors were chosen from the new army.

The primary aim of the men who planned the Revolution was to gain control of the provincial capital of Hangchow. Local groups, usually acting independently, then seized control in prefectural and district seats. The countryside in between was left to follow along as it would. Some of the new local governments were headed by revolutionary party members or secret society leaders, but they could not maintain their position for long against gentry, merchants, and army officers.

The Shanghai revolutionaries were interested in events in Chekiang, partly because Ch'en Ch'i-mei and a number of other important figures in Shanghai were Chekiangese natives. They also wanted to be sure of outside support in case the Kiangnan Arsenal proved difficult to take and, therefore, urged that the Hangchow rising immediately follow the insurrection in Shanghai.[51] Ch'en Ch'i-mei made one trip to Hangchow on October 12. Thereafter Huang Fu, Yao Yung-ch'en, and Chiang K'ai-shek represented him at various meetings.[52] Shanghai revolutionaries sent 3,600 yuan to Hangchow as well as a limited amount of arms and ammunition.

Most of the revolutionary party members with whom the Shanghai representatives met were army officers. Among the most active were Chu Jui, Yü Wei, and Ch'en Kuo-chieh of the 81st regiment; Ku Nai-pin, Wu Ssu-yü, and Fu Meng of the 82nd regiment; Huang Feng-chih and Lü Kung-wang of the provincial new army staff; and T'ung Pao-hsüan of the military police (*hsien-ping*). These men had been members of the Revolutionary Alliance or Restoration Society for several years. The commander of the 82nd regiment, Chou Ch'eng-t'an, was persuaded to join the revolutionaries by Wu Ssu-yü, and division commander Hsiao Tzu-t'ing agreed to remain neutral, although he refused to take part in the rising.[53]

New-army revolutionaries faced the problem that all their units were stationed outside the city and, because the governor suspected their loyalties, available ammunition was limited to a few bullets per man.[54] Within the city were banner troops, several battalions of Defense Forces, the guards at the governor's yamen, and the police. Many of these units were not very formidable and, moreover, the police and about half of the Defense Forces had been won over before the fighting began. But the combined strength of the loyal forces was sufficient to make the new-army revolutionaries send emissaries to request help from radicals and secret societies elsewhere in Chekiang.[55] Other men enlisted the sympathies of stationmasters along the Shanghai-Hangchow Railway so there would be no difficulty in transporting arms and troops. Because the new army was in the embarrassing position of being short of ammunition it imported what arms it could from Shanghai, and Yü Wei also obtained guns and ammunition from the head of one of the companies of Merchant Volunteers in Hangchow.[56]

While new-army revolutionaries took care of the military planning, most of the political arrangements were made by members of the provincial assembly. Ch'u Fu-ch'eng, who was also a Revolutionary Alliance member, was the key figure of this group and attended most of the meetings of new-army revolutionaries. The two assembly vice-presidents, Ch'en Shih-hsia and Shen Chün-ju, president Ch'en Fu-ch'en and a few other assembly members were also active.[57] Shen and Ch'en Shih-hsia were among those who drafted a proclamation of independence, telegrams, and other documents. Shen also approached Governor Tseng-yün on November 3 and urged him to tear down the walls around the Manchu garrison barracks and declare independence, but Tseng-yün refused.[58]

Revolutionary sympathizers in the assembly were more successful in winning over some members of the local elite. After the Wuchang rising Ch'en Fu-ch'en and some other assembly delegates established a bureau to organize militia headed by merchants and gentry. Ostensibly this force was to strengthen Hangchow's defenses, but its founders actually intended it to supply troops for a rising. However, the governor suspiciously deprived the group of the guns which it had obtained from the new army chief-of-staff, and the militia evidently did not play much part in the Revolution.

The major contribution the provincial assembly members made was to choose T'ang Shou-ch'ien as military governor. Revolutionaries in the new army, who controlled the real power in the city, believed they lacked political experience and were reluctant to assume this post. Both Ku Nai-pin and Chu Jui declined it at a meeting a few days before the Revolution.[59] Ch'u Fu-ch'eng then proposed T'ang, who had made his reputation as an opponent of the government during the Chekiang Railway dispute and who would be acceptable to gentry, merchants, and the assembly. This suggestion was accepted and T'ung Pao-hsüan of the military police was chosen temporary military governor until T'ang arrived. On November 3 Ch'en Shih-hsia left for Shanghai to offer T'ang the post. T'ang arrived on the afternoon train the day after the Revolution was completed and went directly to the provincial assembly, where he was elected by its members.

The radical intellectuals and secret society members made up the third element in the Hangchow Revolution. Students and teachers in the Hang-chow schools favored revolution, but did not take part in the planning which preceded it. Some students were members of hastily organized forces which helped the new army capture objectives within the city.[60] More significant were the five companies of Dare-to-die corps, composed mainly of revolutionaries from Shanghai or revolutionaries and secret society members from other parts of Chekiang. Somewhere between one hundred and a few hundred radicals arrived in small groups during the days before the scheduled rising and were lodged in several places about the city. A considerable number were Restoration Society members, some of whom had been active in the province before 1907. Among the Restora-tion Society members who returned from Shanghai were the old P'ing-yang Society leader Wang Chin-fa, the girl revolutionary Yin Wei-chün, Wang Wen-ch'ing, who had previously been active in Southeast Asia and had fled to Shanghai after taking part in the April 27 Canton rising, and Chang Po-ch'i, who commanded two companies of the Dare-to-die corps. Chiang K'ai-shek was also among those who came from Shanghai. Hsieh Fei-lin and Hu Shih-chün, who had headed radical schools in Shaohsing during the period of the Ta-t'ung School and Ch'en Ch'eng, who had been at the Ta-t'ung School itself, raised funds to send a force to Hangchow which included at least one other old member of the Ta-t'ung group. An-other familiar name was that of the monk Huang Fei-lung, one-time associate of Ch'en Meng-hsiung, who was part of the contingent from Wen-chow.[61] Revolutionaries in the Dare-to-die corps had some opportunities to show their individual bravery, but they were only of secondary importance in the total picture.

Hangchow, like Shanghai, fell quickly to the Revolution. During the night of November 4 revolutionaries within the city opened the main gates and let in the new army. The 82nd regiment and part of the Dare-to-die corps attacked and burned the governor's residence and captured the fleeing governor. The 81st regiment and the rest of the Dare-to-die corps led by Wang Chin-fa occupied the armory with little or no fighting.[62] The only serious resistance was put up by the Manchu garrison (banner troops) on November 5. The regimental colonel of the garrison, Kuei-lin, was a friend of T'ang Shou-ch'ien, Ch'en Fu-ch'en, and various Hangchow gentry. After revolutionary artillery bombarded his camp, he agreed to accept T'ang's guarantee of his troops' safety and formally surrendered November 6.[63] The city was then entirely in revolutionary hands.

During the day or two immediately after the Revolution the provincial assembly was essentially the government of Chekiang. Only after T'ang Shou-ch'ien was confirmed in his post by this body was his name submitted to army officers and local revolutionary leaders who had taken part in the Hangchow fighting. At this meeting opposition to T'ang was led by Wang Chin-fa, who bitterly resented the choice because T'ang was suspected of having advised in favor of executing Ch'iu Chin in 1907. However, Ch'u Fu-ch'eng strongly defended T'ang, and the majority of the meeting ratified this choice. The same meeting selected Chou Ch'eng-t'an, the commander of the 82nd infantry regiment, as commander-in-chief of the Chekiang army and appointed Ch'u Fu-ch'eng to head political affairs. After these basic decisions had been made, a larger meeting of representatives of major groups in the city was called to endorse the arrangements further. Evidently at this point the old government organs were replaced by an initially somewhat amorphous revolutionary government.[64]

The top levels of this new government were distinctly moderate. T'ang was not a revolutionary, Chou had not joined the revolutionary forces until shortly before the rising, and Ch'u Fu-ch'eng, who was at home in both revolutionary and constitutionalist circles, was fundamentally a moderate. The head of the Finance Department, Kao Erh-teng, was an army officer who was evidently not a party member.[65] The major spokesman for the radicals, Wang Chin-fa, lost to this faction and soon left Hangchow to head the military government in Shaohsing—a move encouraged by T'ang Shou-ch'ien, for the irreconciled Wang had just enough support to be an embarrassment.[66] Some department heads below the very top level were members of the revolutionary parties. Shen Chün-yeh, who headed the Education Department, had recruited for the Restoration Society in Southeast Asia, and the head of the Industrial Department, Sun Shih-wei, was also a member of the Restoration Society.[67] These men were not necessarily very radical, however. Both remained in office at the time of the "Second Revolution," when the more conservative orientation of the Hangchow government became explicit. Still further down the line much of the work was carried on by existing officials. A few top Ch'ing bureaucrats were forbidden to hold office, but the others were ordered to conduct business as usual.

The Senate (ts'an-i hui), which was organized as a temporary deliberative body to bridge the gap between the old provincial assembly and the new assembly elected early in 1912, was more representative of the revolutionary intellectuals and revolutionaries in the new army. It was headed by T'ao Ch'eng-chang and included the old Dragon Flower Society leader Chang Kung, who had been freed from jail by the Revolution. It also included a number of Ningpo revolutionaries who had been active party members for some years. Among the new-army revolutionaries were Ku Nai-pin, Wu Ssu-yü, and Huang Yüan-hsiu.[68] However, this Senate seems to have been mainly a bow in the direction of the legislative principle. It was not an influential body that could do much to shape government policy.

Other revolutionary party members in the new army concentrated solely on military affairs. Chu Jui commanded the Chekiangese forces in the attack on Nanking and Lü Kung-wang was his chief-of-staff. The control that these two men gained over troops enabled them to become the third and fourth military governors of the province.

Revolutionaries seem to have believed that once the capital was secured the rest of the province would fall to the Revolution, and in practice this was very close to what happened. Within a day or two most of the prefectural cities had declared their independence from the Ch'ing government. Practically no fighting was necessary. In some cases the Hangchow military government sent troops or sent a man to head the prefectural government where there was no strong local leader. However, almost everywhere the Revolution was the work of local groups. The provincial government was preoccupied with organizing an army to attack the imperial forces at Nanking rather than with consolidating its control in Chekiang.[69] It did not really control the province outside of Hangchow. Similarly, the new governments in the prefectural capitals did not always control the district cities and usually had little influence over the surrounding countryside. This situation partly reflected the decentralization of the traditional government, in which the bureaucracy did not reach below the district city. More immediately, it indicated the incompleteness of the Revolution and the diversity of the elements involved in it. Some heads of the prefectural governments were opposed or at least lukewarm to the government in Hangchow. Conservative landlords and gentry in the smaller towns and villages continued to run local affairs much as before. Bandits took advantage of the confusion to engage in widespread lawlessness. Other disorders represented popular discontent and desire for social reforms which were not forthcoming. In mid-1912 prefectures were abolished and some district lines redrawn.[70] Hangchow then acquired somewhat firmer control over the province, but the basic problem of fragmentation remained.

Many of the new governments were established by local intellectuals, often teachers at new schools, in cooperation with certain modernizing gentry. Defense Forces were seldom strong enough to be much of a factor and their commanders often fled. The top civil officials usually also disappeared, although a few joined the Revolution. Probably many minor officials continued in their old jobs. In three prefectures Restoration Society and secret society members who had been associated with the Ta-t'ung School were among the leaders. In three others, new governments were headed by local gentry.[71] Cutting of the queue, or "pigtail," the hair style imposed upon the Chinese by the Manchu conquerors, was the order of the day. This act symbolized adherence to the Revolution, but there was little violence aimed at Manchus.[72] The new governments were often disorganized and always short of funds. Possibly those controlled by intellectuals, who had little administrative experience, had the most difficulty maintaining order and were most rapidly replaced.

I cannot here describe the Revolution in all parts of the province and will instead summarize events in those places that seem particularly typical or interesting and about which information is available. The Revolution in Ningpo, a treaty port and major city, bore the greatest resemblance to that in Shanghai and Hangchow.[73] It was the work of a broad coalition of Revolutionary Alliance revolutionary intellectuals, new-army members,[74] merchants, gentry, and officials. Some of the intellectuals had been active radicals in Ningpo for years; others had spent much time in Shanghai. Although there was strong Shanghai influence, the Ningpo Revolution was still primarily a local affair. On November 1 the Society to Protect the Peace (*Pao-an hui*) was established. This was an embryonic coalition government headed by the old magistrate, who was assisted by Ch'en

Hsün-cheng, a long-time revolutionary. It included other Revolutionary Alliance members, the heads of the chamber of commerce and self-government association, and representatives of the new army, Defense Forces, and police. This body elected the military government which took office peacefully on November 6. The military governor was the new-army officer Liu Hsün and the magistrate headed the civil government. Revolutionary intellectuals filled many major posts, but gentry and merchant collaborators probably retained their influence behind the scenes.

Teachers and administrators in the new schools supplied the initiative in Huchow, Kashing, and Wenchow. In Huchow the first military governor was the head of the middle school, a student army was the main revolutionary force, and many teachers and educators were included in the new administration.[75] This government was plagued by financial and banditry problems and had difficulty controlling the old Ch'ing naval forces which remained in the area. Huchow was the home prefecture of Ch'en Ch'i-mei, Yao Yung-ch'en, and Chang Jen-chieh. The Shanghai revolutionary government, therefore, took a strong interest in the local affairs and after three months replaced the government. The new military governor, a *chü-jen*, brought a contingent of Kwangtungese troops which ended the disorders. The student army was disbanded at this time and the political situation became more settled.

The Revolution in Kashing was led by Fang Yü-ssu, the head of the Hsiu-shui district elementary school, who was chosen to lead the military government by representatives of the local schools and the anti-opium bureau.[76] As in Huchow, teachers filled many positions in the new departments. The Ch'ing prefect and the military commander fled, but the magistrate had already reached agreement with revolutionaries in his district. The self-government association and chamber of commerce supported the Revolution and helped to maintain order and to reopen shops for business. Some long-time revolutionary party members, notably Kung Pao-ch'üan, also took part. Ch'u Fu-ch'eng was a native of Kashing and through him the local government had relatively strong ties with Hangchow. Troops came from the capital to deal with Ch'ing forces threatening Kashing from a nearby town.

After the Wuchang Revolution a group of about twelve teachers at two schools in Wenchow asked local officials to join in organizing a revolutionary government.[77] The liberal taotai refused to head the government because he feared reprisals against his father, who was an official in Peking, and the prefect declined out of loyalty to the dynasty. The military commander joined the Revolution for purely opportunistic reasons and soon was at odds with some of the teachers running the interim government. Most of the lower level prerevolutionary officials remained in office.

The original group of teachers evidently never intended to retain control. When the old provincial assembly president Ch'en Fu-ch'en returned home to Jui-an after the Revolution, he indicated that he would like to head the Wenchow government. The teachers agreed, but the Hangchow authorities refused to accept Ch'en[78] and sent Hsü Pan-hou instead. Hsü was a *chin-shih* from Wenchow prefecture who had been a taotai in Shantung and then had headed the Chekiang Normal School in Hangchow. He had been sympathetic to the radicals before the Revolution,[79] but his appointment stabilized the philosophy of the Wenchow government as no more than moderately progressive. This choice evidently was acceptable to the intellectuals who had begun the Wenchow Revolution, however, for they had never shown any disposition to overturn the social structure nor even much enthusiasm for a thorough political reorganization.

The Taichow prefect joined the Revolution and headed the new government for two weeks until a new military governor arrived. This man was not popular and was eventually replaced by a member of the local gentry.[80] An interesting aspect in that prefecture was the bandit band led by Tsui She-ping.[81] Tsui's group threatened to attack the city of Taichow, but then moved into Shaohsing prefecture, where it was received into Sinchang district city as a revolutionary force. Once inside Tsui plundered the town and burned the magistrate's yamen before withdrawing. He left behind a proclamation calling for the extermination of foreigners, officials, and scholars and the destruction of new schools. Tsui continued to operate for at least six months in mountainous and border areas where he presumably had some popular support. Besides being a bandit, Tsui evidently represented the unrest of peasants who looked for a different sort of upheaval than that envisaged by the intellectuals, gentry, and others heading the new governments.[82]

In the old centers of Restoration Society activity, Shaohsing, Kinhwa, and Chuchow, secret society leaders and party members were among the leaders of the Revolution. When Chang Kung was freed from jail he returned to Kinhwa and helped organize the military government and establish a militia. He did not head the government himself, however, preferring to organize some of his old followers for a northern expedition, and he was not long an influence in the prefecture.[83]

The political situation in Shaohsing was one of the most confused in the province.[84] Shaohsing declared independence immediately after hearing the news of the Revolution in Hangchow. The old prefect became head of the civil government. Merchants and gentry took part in organizing the new government, as did some returned students and at least one of the Shaohsing delegates to the provincial assembly. Among the returned students were a younger brother and a cousin of Hsü Hsi-lin and Ch'en Hsieh-shu, who became a delegate to the new provincial assembly which convened at the beginning of 1912. Hsieh Fei-lin, who had headed a radical school contemporaneous with the Ta-t'ung School, and Sun Te-ch'ing, a former director of the Ta-t'ung School, were also involved in postrevolutionary politics. From the beginning the city suffered from not having enough troops to keep order. Consequently Wang Chin-fa was invited to become military governor and bring his Dare-to-die corps with him. Wang had a stormy tenure until prefectures were abolished in the summer of 1912. He was at odds with the provincial government and also had enemies within the city. Some opponents were even more radical students and teachers—members of a new political generation who believed Wang was selling out to conservative gentry. Other opposition was personal and factional. Wang was often away in Shanghai, and the Shaohsing disorders continued. The guards and militia were short of weapons and used what they had to fight each other.[85] In view of the confusion and bickering it is unlikely that the government had much popular support. Wang was in Shanghai when the prefectural government was abolished and he never returned to Shaohsing. Not long afterwards he was assassinated in Hangchow on Chu Jui's orders.

Radicals were more successful in establishing a government in Chuchow.[86] Lü Hsiung-hsiang, a member of the Dragon Flower Society and Restoration Society who had been one of the most important administrators of the Ta-t'ung School, assembled a force of secret society members at Huchen, to the north of the prefectural city. Among his chief assistants were Chao Shu, a gentry sympathizer of the revolutionary movement,[87] and several of the Lü clan, which evidently furnished many secret society members. The bulk of this little army marched south toward the city of Chuchow. Inside the city the group of teachers and other returned students connected with the old revolutionary front at the Utilitarian Cotton Cloth Mills contacted Lü. They and certain scholars and gentry persuaded the commander of the Defense Forces to withdraw. The prefect and magistrate fled and Lü peacefully approached the city in a sedan chair flanked by four horsemen. He became military governor. The civil governor was a member of the gentry and three of the bureau chiefs were local radical intellectuals. This government evidently was fairly viable. It organized a northern expeditionary force under Chao Shu. Some money to run the administration was raised from the surrounding districts and some more from heavy fines extracted from a few conservative landlords for offenses such as failure to cut their queues.

The initial political arrangements, both in Hangchow and the prefectures, did not last long. Changes which began early in 1912 led toward greater military control on the provincial level and reassertion of conservatism in the smaller cities and towns after the initial wave of queue cutting had passed. This trend culminated in the summer of 1913 with the failure of the "Second Revolution." Running counter to this development was a continuing and deepening radicalism in schools throughout the province which was to pave the way for the May Fourth Movement a few years later. The students and intellectuals who provided the new radical impetus were largely different from those who had been involved in the 1911 revolutionary movement. Like their predecessors they, too, were removed from the sources of political power and were frustrated in their desire to revitalize China. They were, therefore, driven to look for still more thorough solutions than the overthrow of the dynasty. Thus the radical trend continued, but the intellectuals of the 1911 period no longer remained an identifiable group. Some joined militarist governments. Some such as Chang Ping-lin and Chang Shih-chao became culturally and politically much more conservative after the immediate issues of Manchu rule and imperial "tyranny" were removed. Others opposed the current political trends and were killed in the "Second" or "Third" Revolutions. A few, generally men like Ts'ai Yüan-p'ei who had not been deeply involved politically in the events of 1911, became part of the May Fourth radicalism. Those in the last category were important in the intellectual evolution of Republican China, but had little effect on Chekiangese politics.

Some of the initial leaders of the Revolution were drawn away from Chekiang by political opportunities on the national level. T'ang Shou-ch'ien devoted much of his attention to organizing a provisional government in Nanking and at the beginning of January 1912 resigned as military governor to become minister of communications in Sun Yat-sen's cabinet. Ch'en Shih-hsia also aided in organizing the Nanking government.[88] Early in 1913 a number of others were elected to the national parliament in Peking. These included Ch'u Fu-ch'eng, the army officer Yü Wei, the Ningpo revolutionary Chiang Chu-ch'ing, and the Restoration Society and Revolutionary Alliance member Yao Yung-ch'en.[89]

T'ang Shou-ch'ien was succeeded by the army officer Chiang Tsun-kuei, who had friends in both the revolutionary and constitutionalist camps. Chiang had joined both the Restoration Society and Revolutionary Alliance and had done much to foster radicalism in the Chekiangese new army. He also developed contacts with Liang Ch'i-ch'ao and, before returning to Chekiang from Kwangtung in December, had conferred with Liang's representative in Shanghai about establishing a pro-Liang government.[90] Furthermore, Chiang's father was a friend of T'ang Shou-ch'ien and also of one of the provincial assembly members who had cooperated with the revolutionaries. These connections helped smooth the way for his election, and, moreover, Chiang was popular both in student circles and with gentry and merchants in Hangchow.[91] He was openly opposed by T'ao Ch'eng-chang, who represented the original Restoration Society intellectuals in the province. However T'ao simply did not have either a strong enough political base in the province or sufficient general popularity. Chiang was elected unanimously and T'ao was assassinated in Shanghai three days later. Another opponent, not declared at the time of Chiang's election, was Chu Jui.[92] Also a new-army officer and a member of the Restoration Society, Chu had made his reputation as commander of the Chekiangese forces in the capture of Nanking and was enthusiastically welcomed when he returned to Hangchow. Chiang was something of an intermediate figure between the old party intellectuals and the new militarists. Chu was more narrowly oriented toward the army, which he effectively used as a power base. In July 1912 he replaced Chiang as military governor, marking the ascendancy of militarist politics in the province.

After mid-1912 many of the alignments in the Hangchow government reflected factionalism and struggles for personal aggrandizement, with few ideological overtones. One such split within the army was between officers who had studied in Japan and those, including Chu Jui, who had not. It was a factor in Chu's ouster by his lieutenant, Lü Kung-wang, in 1916 and in Lü's replacement by Yang Shan-te, a Tuan Ch'i-jui supporter, at the beginning of 1917.[93] Chu had allied himself with Yüan Shih-k'ai and helped suppress the "Second Revolution" in mid-1913. After that he had Yüan's limited confidence, but Yüan did not fully trust southerners and the partnership was never complete.[94] By mid-1913 the immediate political issue dividing radicals from other groups was opposition to Yüan Shih-k'ai. Many long-time radicals and secret society members, therefore, were aligned against Chu Jui in the "Second Revolution." Nonetheless some old Restoration Society members found it more advantageous to associate themselves with Chu, notably Ch'ü Ying-kuang, who became head of the civil government in 1912 and remained until Chu was ousted.[95]

Although primarily nonideological, militarist rule favored the position of conservatives, who would cooperate with the government as long as their privileges remained intact. Without having thoroughly studied the post-1911 period, I would suggest that conservatives in the towns and villages decisively regained political authority at the time of the "Second Revolution." Some confirmation of this view is found in events in the former Chuchow prefecture. There Lü Hsiung-hsiang led a force against the government. When the Second Revolution failed he had to flee, and he died soon after. In Li-shui (the former Chuchow city) the manager, and one of the original founders, of the Utilitarian Cotton Cloth Mills was arrested and died in jail. Other members of the one-time revolutionary front dispersed. Some were arrested, some gave up all political activities, and others accepted the new situation and became officials.[96] In the town of Sung-yang the conservative landlord who had been heavily fined in 1911 for failure to cut his queue had adjusted so well to the new political environment that he now had much influence in the local government office. Those who had headed the revolutionary government in 1911 had to flee to avoid arrest.[97]

The final submergence of the 1911 revolutionary intellectuals in Chekiang was not surprising because in most places they had been overshadowed from the beginning by moderates and by the new army. In Hangchow the initial political influence of the provincial assembly was particularly striking. There were many connections between liberal assembly members, new-army revolutionaries, and radical intellectuals. For a brief period distinctions between moderates and revolutionaries were obscured by common nationalism and opposition to the dynasty. Assembly members, who occupied a ready-made political position midway between radicals and more conservative groups, were in a key position and their leadership was acceptable to many who did not fully share their views. Divergences did soon occur, however. Then many moderates, who usually had some professional experience and were accustomed to promoting modernization within the existing social framework, returned to private life. Professional revolutionaries who had been at variance with traditional society for up to eight or ten years remained unsatisfied in the not-very-new Republican China and resumed their oppositional role. Because no effective substitute replaced the collapsed traditional political order, army officers, with their command over troops, emerged as the holders of real power. They then cooperated with whoever would bolster their personal positions.

Outside the capital the political situation was quite varied, with strong overtones of localism. In a considerable number of towns teachers in the modern schools and other intellectuals were among the leaders of the Revolution. Many of these men had studied in Japan, where they had been exposed to Western ideas and radical ideology. Nonetheless, their personal radicalism often was not great. They were at least as ready to cooperate with modernizing merchants and gentry as with revolutionaries.

Teachers and other intellectuals who followed an open career contrasted with the professional revolutionaries, who were particularly prominent in the treaty port of Ningpo, and with the old secret society leaders and revolutionaries in Shaohsing and Chuchow. Except for the major cities of Hangchow and Ningpo, the radicals made their major contribution to the Revolution in prefectures where the Restoration Society had been most active before 1908. The work of T'ao Ch'eng-chang, Hsü Hsi-lin, and Ch'iu Chin had not been altogether ephemeral, but neither was it deep-rooted enough to triumph over more conservative influences. Most remnants of the 1911 revolutionaries were driven from their positions by mid-1913 and their contribution to radical politics in twentieth-century Chekiang largely ended.

Because the revolutionary intellectuals failed to dominate the Revolution of 1911 their chief historical significance is as prototypes of twentieth-century Chinese radicals. The political style of the late Ch'ing radicals and the issues which excited them characterized left-wing politics throughout the succeeding Republican period. Even after the Communist victory, vestiges of earlier attitudes have continued to influence policy. Therefore, it is worthwhile to summarize some of the main attributes of the 1911 revolutionaries, for many of these general characteristics remained politically important after the first revolutionaries had disappeared.

The 1911 revolutionary movement was primarily a movement of students and scholars. Secret society members, merchants, overseas Chinese, and others all played parts, but the main thrust came from "student circles." From these groups there emerged a radical strata, roughly similar to the nineteenth-century Russian intelligentsia, from which most revolutionary leaders continued to be drawn throughout the Republic. The nature of radical politics was also influenced by its close association with the schools. Much of it was student politics. Like their counterparts the world over, Chinese students were idealistic, impatient, emotional, and volatile.[1] Their opinions were more likely to be sweeping and intolerant than carefully reasoned. Their organizations were often ephemeral. Relations with older generations were frequently strained and students were extremely sensitive to any efforts to control their activities.

The dominant theme in radical politics was nationalism. A nationalistic explosion in 1903 precipitated the divorce of the revolutionary and reform movements. Thereafter, nationalism played an important part in all major radical surges—the May Fourth Movement of 1919, the early stages of the Northern Expedition in the mid-1920's, the anti-Japanese agitation of the 1930's, and the triumph of the Communists, who had resolutely opposed the Japanese during the war and inspired hopes of a strong, united China. The nationalism of the early revolutionaries was complicated on the one hand by anti-Manchuism and on the other by their often sincere admiration for the West. During the Republic, nationalism was more simply identifiable with anti-imperialism.[2]

A secondary theme was individualism. The radical intellectuals sought new freedom and new opportunities for self-realization. Student radicals tended to interpret freedom largely in terms of their personal needs to escape from the restraints of family and tradition. Later, after the Chinese became more familiar with Western socialist theories during the Republic, there was a greater disposition to associate freedom with social and economic equality which would ensure a genuine similarity of opportunities for all. However, many radicals always bore the stamp of youthful revolts against the old ways, which perhaps eventually encouraged them to believe that traditional society was a greater menace to the individual than were totalitarian attempts to eradicate tradition.

A third basic orientation, which embraced the first two, was to modernization and change. The ultimate demand of the 1911 revolutionaries was for modernization, not social upheaval. A modernizing revolution makes two partly contradictory requirements. One is for a united effort to overcome grave national difficulties. The other is for the elimination of traditional groups that would impede change. In 1911 the radical minority embraced the former approach and hoped the nation would accept their analysis of the needs of the time. Only the Manchu court and those most closely identified with it had to go. Therefore, the 1911 Revolution was inclusive and surprisingly mild. When the radical minority discovered their allies were not going to follow their lead, they had no way to maintain control. During the Republican period, the Communists successfully united the aims of national modernization and social revolution to produce a much more fundamental upheaval in 1949. Destruction of class enemies also served to remove traditional barriers. Yet the Communists, too, were influenced by the idea of modernization achieved by the united efforts of all society. At least during the first decade of Communist rule, Maoist theory defined the existence of progressive elements, even among the bourgeoisie, who could accompany the peasants and workers all the way to socialism.

Although the aim of modernization was less radical per se than a commitment to class struggle, the attendant emphasis on newness made it extremely difficult for any government to satisfy the 1911 radicals. They had irretrievably abandoned tradition as a whole, and they demanded that the government also be revolutionary—that it pursue the new as ardently as they did. The Ch'ing dynasty, the warlords, and the Kuomintang successively failed to meet this demand and were abandoned. By the end of the Japanese War, only the Communists offered a sweeping program and a radical image. It is also possible that intellectuals were predisposed to accept total solutions as they sought a new order and set of values to replace those they had forsaken.[3]

Once they had turned from traditional ways, radicals sought security in their own groups: schools, associations, and parties. These played an essential role in replacing old ties of family and occupation while Western theories were used to justify the break with the past. Radicals also took from the West new concepts of morality and discipline and new ways to order their lives. At first they were attracted by vague axioms from Western liberal democratic philosophy. However, individualism, which was perhaps the essential element which Chinese intellectuals extracted from liberalism, was mainly useful for attacking traditional ways. It did not offer a coherent program for reconstruction and, if anything, intensified the loneliness of the radical who had rejected his past. The revolutionary intelligentsia in China, as in other traditional societies in the early stages of modernization, were subject to great psychological strains. They suffered the pain of personally rejecting family and society. Thereafter, they were frustrated by being unable to bring about the changes for which they had sacrificed so much. Consequently they led an emotionally charged and rather isolated existence. Early revolutionaries found a sustaining example in the popular hero—a traditional, nonreligious, individualistic figure who exemplified the devotion to duty and sacrifice which was demanded of those who sought to create the new order.[4] Emulation of the hero's tragic end also provided one form of escape for individuals for whom the strains had become overwhelming. After 1920 Communism attracted a gradually increasing number of intellectuals by offering both programs to solve China's problems and a safer, more total psychological haven.[5]

Whatever their personal insecurity, radicals were nonetheless confident that they possessed special insight into the problems of how to save the nation and reform society. They pictured themselves as foreknowers and dared to act on this conviction. Along with their self-assurance went an evangelical zeal to spread their ideas among the populace. The 1911 radicals were the first group that sought to awaken and activate the Chinese masses. They vehemently condemned the superstition, ignorance, and political passivity which characterized the Chinese people, and they aspired to guide them toward modernity. Their concrete attempts to contact the masses were actually very limited and mainly took place through the intermediary of traditional secret societies. The concern to reach and enlighten the people was, however, carried on by the new generation of radicals after 1911 and led to more positive evangelical efforts at mass movements during the 1920's and 1930's. Communists after 1949 converted this impulse into the practice of totalitarian mass politics.

Despite their espousal of Western and radical ideas, there was a certain traditional-modern ambiguity in the revolutionaries' attitudes. In part this was the result of the inclusion in the 1911 revolutionary movement of men such as Chang Ping-lin whose views were largely traditional. However, the iconoclasm of even the most radical was tempered by their love for China and determination to remake it into a strong nation of which they could be proud. They identified "modern" with "Western" and "traditional" with the Chinese heritage, and it was psychologically painful for the revolutionaries to totally reject their history.[6] It was also impossible because most of the early radicals had been raised in traditional homes and only broke with their past when exposed to Western ideas in school or sometimes even later. No matter how vehement their iconoclasm they inevitably retained a good deal of their upbringing. Moreover, their knowledge of the West was far from complete. It could not provide a total alternative pattern of behavior. Therefore, they sought out parts of their own history which they could use. The 1911 revolutionaries' admiration for popular heros and the Communists' identification of progressive elements in various stages of Chinese history served to rescue aspects of China's tradition.

There were numerous ways in which nationalism and even modernization could be made emotionally compatible with at least part of tradition.[7] Moreover, many of the new concepts overlapped and redirected the old rather than completely negating them. Nationalism was not altogether different from culturism. Nor was individualism that aimed at both self-fulfillment and good citizenship entirely divorced from the self-cultivation of the Confucian "gentleman."

A second, external influence of tradition on the 1911 revolutionaries can be seen in the way their radicalism was undermined in the lesser towns and the countryside. Several factors were involved in this dilution. Because they still retained links with their past, even the most intensely dedicated radicals tended to behave more conventionally when they returned from the major cities to the midst of a still largely traditional society. When faced with problems not covered by their new Western-inspired theories, they might revert to traditional practices, such as bribery, which in theory they would condemn. Their radicalism was partly submerged during day-to-day life, but would periodically rise to the surface, often in self-defeating explosions.

Traditional society frustrated the radicals on two levels. They were overwhelmed by the local elite groups, whose complexion had begun to change[8] but whose general structure still remained much the same and was too stable for the revolutionaries to overthrow. They could not seriously challenge elite power. Moreover, since many of the radical intellectuals came from backgrounds that entitled them to elite status if they chose to fit into traditional society, less intense radicals were likely to become moderates after returning home. Throughout the Republican period, radicals continued to be frustrated by the power of the traditional local establishment, which was not broken until after the Communist victory.

On a lower social level the revolutionaries were also stymied by the conservatism, superstition, and ignorance of the peasantry. Peasant discontent was expressed in immediate and local opposition to such abuses as high rents and taxes and there was no effective bridge between their grievances and the nationalistic and modernizing aims of the revolutionaries. Although in theory the revolutionaries wished to convert and mobilize the masses, in practice they usually approached them through the traditional secret societies and treated them more like troops than disciples. During the Republic student radicals made more direct efforts to reach the peasants and the Maoist Communists maintained their Kiangsi base for several years, relying on support from the villages. It has been argued that there was still no strong rapport between revolutionaries and peasantry until the Japanese invasion awakened peasant nationalism.[9] Rural localism and political indifference broke down under the experience of the occupation and the Communists, who were the most effective organizers of anti-Japanese resistance, were the beneficiaries. After coming to power with mass support, Communists could bring force to bear to back up their ultimate aim of collectivization. However, they, too, have found it difficult to mobilize and control the peasantry permanently and have had to modify their ideal program to make some concessions to opposing rural viewpoints.

Another factor which contributed to the 1911 revolutionaries' failure was organizational weakness. The revolutionaries were politically inexperienced and the groups they were trying to create were foreign to Chinese traditions. They, therefore, suffered all the difficulties of pioneers. Radical bands had many characteristics of traditional sworn brotherhoods except that new recruits pledged their faith to an ideology rather than to other individuals. Dedication to the cause then took precedence over old loyalties and virtues. This sort of voluntary political commitment and the basic egalitarianism of radical groups were innovations in themselves.[10] However, these changes did not produce sufficiently strong bonds to compensate for lack of leadership and discipline. Leaders could not claim the kingship or other traditional sanctions and new justifications had not fully developed. The problem was compounded since many revolutionaries were highly individualistic intellectuals who were suspicious of all authority. Parties also had to compete with the modern schools for the intellectuals' loyalties. From shortly after 1900 until the Communist victory, schools were the bases of Chinese radicalism. They simultaneously introduced students to new ideas and insulated them from the forces of family and tradition. In this way they met some of the needs for identification which otherwise might have been supplied by the parties. Volatile students were more likely to participate in dramatic demonstrations over immediate issues than to undertake continuous party work. The radicals' organizational difficulties were again illustrated during the Republic when the two viable parties of the period, the Kuomintang and the Communist Party, were only effectively organized with Russian aid. When the political situation altered to favor the Communists they had the advantage over their 1911 predecessors in organization, political experience, and the possession of a party army. They were thus able to control political events and dominate their allies.

Even though the 1911 radicals were unsuccessful, they nonetheless introduced new concepts of politics to the Chinese scene. They aimed to reconstruct society rather than to seize power for personal ends, and revolution continued to be the serious aim of a segment of educated Chinese after 1900. Oppositional politics was made respectable if combined with sincere devotion to a cause. The radicals' activities were purposive and progressive. Politics was also seen as the concern of all members of society. In place of their old passivity, members of the lower classes were to become active, disciplined citizens participating in efforts to change government and society.

The 1911 revolutionary movement began during a period when dynastic decline coincided with decay of tradition. Its timing, therefore, was analogous to that of other modern political upheavals which came after enough change had occurred to inspire certain groups to demand more than the existing enfeebled and fundamentally conservative government could produce. However, only a small segment of the population—mainly intellectuals—called for genuine revolution in 1911 as opposed to the overthrow of the dynasty. The revolutionaries could not prevail after their most immediate objective was achieved. Aside from their own small numbers they were hampered by the variety and diffusiveness of Chinese society. Local society and politics were characterized by many informal and flexible relationships which could be adapted relatively easily to new conditions and could accommodate individual ambitions and needs for social mobility. The power of the local elites was likewise flexible[11] and difficult to eliminate short of brutal and uncompromising measures such as those taken by the Communists after 1949. Decay of tradition had not proceeded far enough to shake the local structures and it was possible to eliminate the more rigidly defined elements of the Chinese polity—the monarchy and parts of the bureaucracy—without greatly affecting the towns and villages, where the direct activities of the traditional governmental apparatus had been minimal. The historical role of the 1911 revolutionaries was to begin the Chinese revolution, not to complete it.

The very failure of the 1911 revolutionaries ensured their relevance as forerunners of later twentieth-century radicals. Their successors were concerned with the same unsolved problems of national strength, individual liberty, restructuring the family system, energizing the masses, and combatting all aspects of tradition that interfered with modernization. Radicals during the Republic suffered the same kinds of frustration and went through the same crises of identity as did those of the late Ch'ing. The solutions they chose might be different or at least more detailed as knowledge of the range of Western thought increased. However, differences were of degree not of kind. This is particularly true of the New Culture and May Fourth movements of 1915 to 1920, which are often characterized as the beginnings of Chinese radicalism. The scale of these movements was larger, but almost all the issues raised had already been discussed, and similar conclusions reached, by radicals before 1911. They were the ones who had taken the fundamental step of wedding nationalism to the beginnings of social radicalism and cultural iconoclasm.

One indication of how basic the attitudes and psychology of the 1911 radicals are to the entire history of radicalism in twentieth-century China is the extent to which parallel motivation can be seen behind Maoist policies of the late 1950's through the mid-1960's—from the time of the Great Leap Forward to the Cultural Revolution. There are also differences. Mao Tse-tung obviously is not merely a more effective frustrated liberal nationalist, but the similarities suggest a continuity in the Chinese revolutionary impulse independent of party and ideology. The 1911 Revolution was the first political event to profoundly influence Mao Tse-tung, and even in his old age he has retained some of his early concerns and some of the style of student radicals of the late Ch'ing and early Republic.[12] He also, even now, is subject to some of the same frustrations in trying to transform a traditionalistic, underdeveloped nation into a modern world power. Like the 1911 radicals he is intensely nationalistic. China must be recognized as the foremost power in Asia and the leader of world revolution. He himself must be acknowledged as the world's leading Communist theoretician as a matter of national honor as well as personal pride. Also, like many of the early revolutionaries, Mao has been influenced by Western ideology without having had much direct acquaintance with the West. Despite being a Communist he remains in many ways a traditional figure who writes poetry and is versed in Chinese history. In his younger days he was influenced by the Chinese bandit-hero tradition[13] and in his old age has taken on some of the characteristics of a paternalistic sage-emperor. Like such early revolutionaries as Ch'iu Chin, Mao believes in the power of the individual will to overcome great obstacles—whether these be difficulties in industrializing China or the bureaucratization of the revolution. He is a romanticist who places much importance on the revolutionary spirit—the comradeship and élan of the dedicated band—and who believes that it is possible to recapture the original enthusiasm many years after the party came to power.

As a final example, running through many aspects of Communist policy is the conviction, first expressed by the reformer Liang Ch'i-ch'ao and later by the 1911 radicals, that the Chinese character must be reformed to pave the way for national resurgence. This belief is manifested in many ways from intensive ideological remolding of intellectuals through combined intellectual work as well as work in the villages for students, teachers, and professionals, to mass calisthenics and sports programs that encourage respect for physical exercise. The determination to turn the populace into good Communists has been grafted onto efforts to combat the traditionalism and superstition that had aroused the early radicals to anger and despair.

There is every reason to argue that the radical intellectuals of the last decade of the Ch'ing began the revolutionary modernization of China. It was their unfortunate lot to make little progress toward their goals. Traditional forces were too strong to be overthrown by small bands of students and scholars. However, they did spark the overthrow of the monarchy and the ensuing chaos did much to undermine the old order and encourage the spread of radical ideas. Just as important, the student radicals were in themselves a revolutionary social phenomenon. They had broken away from traditional society to form a restless, dissatisfied strata of nationalistic, iconoclastic intelligentsia. Their emancipation, though never complete, paved the way for growing numbers of intellectuals dedicated to the principle of sweeping change. The 1911 revolutionaries' romantic, dramatic gestures of defiance were followed by more effective opposition from more numerous and politically sophisticated successors. As they had predicted, history did ultimately honor the late Ch'ing radicals' sacrifices, although the eventual results of revolution no longer corresponded to their early dreams.

I have translated the names of most of the associations, periodicals, and books that appear in the text. The romanization is given in parentheses the first time the name appears, and thereafter only the English translation is used. I have not generally translated the names of schools because many of these are place names and many others sound particularly awkward in English. Some other names have been left untranslated for lack of a suitable English equivalent, and a few because, idiosyncratically, I found them overwhelmingly more convenient to render in the Chinese romanization. After years of reading about *Su-pao an*, I could not adjust to writing about *The Kiangsu Journal* case. Most of the translations appearing in the text are listed here for the benefit of specialists accustomed to thinking only of the Chinese name. The 1911 Revolution is relevant enough to contemporary Chinese events so that translation to make names intelligible to non-specialists seems a worthwhile effort. I hope others will be encouraged to follow this course and improve upon those given here.

About Face!   *Meng hui-t'ou*
The Alarm Bell   *Ching-chung jih-pao*
Ancestral Sect   Tsu-tsung chiao
Anecdotes of the End of the Ming   *Ming-chi p'i-shih*
Army Commissariat School   Rikugun keiri gakkō
(Japanese) Army Officers' Academy   Rikugun Shikan gakkō
Association for the Education of a   Chün-kuo-min chiao-yü hui
   Militant People
Association of Chekiangese Students   Che-chiang lü-Hu hsüeh-hui
   in Shanghai
Association of Comrades to Resist Russia   Tui-O t'ung-chih hui
Bamboo Forest Primary School   Chu-lin hsiao-hsüeh-hsiao
A Bell to Warn the World   *Ching-shih chung*
A Bitter History   *T'ung-shih*
Bookshop for the Diffusion of Knowledge   Kuang-chih shu-chü
Chekiang Public Institute   Liang-Che kung-hsüeh
Chekiang Society   Che-hui
Chihli Speaks   *Chih-shuo*
The China National Gazette   *Kuo-min jih-jih-pao*
China Volunteers   Chung-kuo kan-ssu-t'uan
Chinese and Western School   Chung-Hsi hsüeh-t'ang

The Chinese Daily   *Chung-kuo jih-pao*
Chinese Educational Association   Chung-kuo chiao-yü hui
The Chinese National   *Kuo-min pao*
The Chinese Progress   *Shih-wu pao*
Chinese Public Institute   Chung-kuo kung-hsüeh
Chinese Student Union   Chung-kuo liu-hsüeh-sheng hui-kuan
Chinese Students' Military Preparatory School   Seijo gakkō
The Chinese Vernacular Journal   *Chung-kuo pai-hua pao*
The Chinese Women's Journal   *Chung-kuo nü-pao*
Citizens' Committee   Kuo-min kung-hui
Collected Statutes of Ch'ing Dynasty   *Ta-Ch'ing hui-tien*
Collections of the New   *Ts'ui-hsin pao*
Commercial Press   Shang-wu yin-shu kuan
Committee of the Four Social Classes   Ssu-min tsung-hui
Crouching Tiger Society   Fu-hu hui
Determination Society   Li-chih hui
Double Dragon Society   Shuang-lung hui
Dragon Flower Society   Lung-hua hui
Earthly Lord Religion   Ti-chu chiao
The Eastern Miscellany   *Tung-fang tsa-chih*
Eastern Continent Bookshop   Tung-ta-lu t'u-shu-chü
The Eastern Times   *Shih-pao*
Educational Association   see Chinese Educational Association
Encompassing Love Society   Kung-ai hui
The Essence of Confucius   *Kung-fu-tzu chih hsin-kan*
The Gaiety Journal   *Fan-hua pao*
Gold Coin Society   Chin-ch'ien hui
The Globe Magazine   *Wan-kuo kung-pao*
(Tokyo) Higher Normal School   Kōtō shihan gakkō
A History of the Ebb and Flow of the Power   *Chung-kuo min-tsu ch'üan-*
    the Chinese Race   *li hsiao-ch'ang shih*
A History of the Imperial Military   *Sheng-wu chi*
Hundred Sons Society   Pai-tzu hui
A Journal for Setting the Age in Order   *Ching-shih pao*
Journal of Natural Law   *T'ien-i pao*
The Lion's Roar   *Shih-tzu hou*
Merchant Volunteers (Association)   Shang-t'uan kung-hui
Military preparatory school   Wu-pei hsüeh-t'ang
(Tokyo) Military Preparatory School   Shimbu gakkō
Military primary school   Lu-chün hsiao-hsüeh-t'ang

Mirror of Today Bookshop   Ching-chin shu-chü
The Monks' and People's School   Seng-min hsüeh-t'ang
Mutual Assistance Primary School   Li-tse hsiao-hsüeh-hsiao
Nanking Military Academy   Nan-ching lu-shih hsüeh-t'ang
National Association   Kuo-hui
National Studies Association   Kuo-hsüeh hui
New Century   *Hsin shih-chi*
New Hunan   *Hsin Hu-nan*
New People's School   Hsin-min shu
The News   *Hsin-wen pao*
Norwegian Lutheran Mission   Hsin-i hui
Patriotic Girls' School   Ai-kuo nü-hsüeh-hsiao
Patriotic School   Ai-kuo hsüeh-she
The People's Cry   *Min-hu jih-pao*
The People's Journal   *Min-pao*
The People's Sigh   *Min-hsü jih-pao*
The People's Stand   *Min-li pao*
Preparatory School for Chinese Students   Seika gakkō
Pure Criticism Journal   *Ch'ing-i pao*
A Record of Ten Days at Yangchow   *Yang-chou shih-jih chi*
"A Record of the *Su-pao* Case"   "*Su-pao* an chi-shih"
The Renovation of the People   *Hsin-min ts'ung-pao*
The Republican Miscellany   *Min-kuo tsa-chih*
Restoration Army   Kuang-fu chün
Restoration Society   Kuang-fu hui
The Revival Journal   *Fu-pao*
Revival Society   Fu-she
Revolutionary Alliance   T'ung-meng hui
The Revolutionary Army   *Ko-ming chün*
School for Noncommissioned Officers   Pien-mu hsüeh-t'ang
Revolutionary Party   Ko-ming tang
Society for China's Revival   Hua-hsing hui
Society for Diffusion of Knowledge   Kuang-hsüeh hui
Society for Self-Strengthening   Ch'iang-hsüeh hui
Society of Friends of the School   Hsiao-yu hui
Society to Protect the Emperor   Pao-huang hui
Society to Protect the Peace   Pao-an hui
Society to Restore China's Prosperity   Hsing-Chung hui
"The Song of New Mountain"   "Hsin-shan ko"
The Soul of Huang-ti   *Huang-ti hun*

Southern Society   Nan-she
Steadfast Conduct Public Institute   Chien-hsing kung-hsüeh
Straight Talk   *Ch'ang-yen pao*
The Struggle   *Ching-yeh hsün-pao*
Student World   *Hsüeh-sheng shih-chieh*
Ten Men Corps   Shih-jen t'uan
Thousand Men Society   Ch'ien-jen hui
Tides of Chekiang   *Che-chiang ch'ao*
Translations by Chinese Students Abroad   *Yu-hsüeh i-pien*
The Twentieth Century Stage   *Erh-shih shih-chi ta-wu-t'ai tsa-chih*
The Universal Gazette   *Chung-wai jih-pao*
Utilitarian Cotton Mills   Li-yung chih-pu kung-ssu
Vernacular Journal   *Pai-hua pao*
Volunteer Corps to Oppose Russia   Chü-O i-yung tui
Warnings on Russian Affairs   *O-shih ching-wen*
The Women's Journal   *Nü-pao*
World Association   Shih-chieh she
Youth Association   Ch'ing-nien hui
Youth Study Association   Ch'ing-nien hsüeh-she

CCC	*Che-chiang ch'ao*
CNL	*Hsin-hai ko-ming wu-shih chou-nien chi-nien lun-wen chi*
CSL-KH	*Ta-Ch'ing li-ch'ao shih-lu*
HCH	*Hsing-Chung hui*
HHKM	*Hsin-hai ko-ming*
KMCC	*Ko-ming hsien-lieh chuan-chi*
KML	*Hsin-hai ko-ming hui-i lu*
KMWH	*Ko-ming wen-hsien*
KSKF	*Ko-sheng kuang-fu*
NCH	*North China Herald and Supreme Court and Consular Gazette*
SLHC	*Hsin-hai ko-ming ch'ien shih-nien chien shih-lun hsüan-chi*
TMH	*Chung-kuo T'ung-meng hui*

1. Introduction

1. "Chih Hsü Hsiao-shu chüeh-ming tzü" (Poem to Hsü Hsiao-shu in contemplation of death); in Hsiao Ping, *Hsin-hai ko-ming lieh-shih shih-wen hsüan* (A selection of writings by martyrs of the 1911 Revolution; Peking, 1962), p. 156.

2. The concept of a progressive Chinese reaction to the challenge of Western imperialism during the nineteenth and twentieth centuries is set forth in Teng Ssu-yü and John K. Fairbank, *China's Response to the West* (Cambridge, Mass., 1954), *passim*.

3. The terms modern and modernization are used here in light of the discussion in Marius Jansen, ed., *Changing Japanese Attitudes towards Modernization* (Princeton, 1965), pp. 17–35. Particularly applicable is the suggested definition by Benjamin Schwartz (*Ibid.*, pp. 23–24). "Modernization involves the systematic, sustained and purposeful application to the 'rational' [in the Weberian sense] control of man's physical and social environment . . ." Certain characteristics of political, social and intellectual modernization listed in *Ibid.*, pp. 20–23, are directly relevant to the 1911 revolutionary movement. It should be noted that although modernization should not be equated with Westernization, modernization efforts in China were strongly influenced by Western examples; the stimulus and the pattern were external. It is also important to remember that the new and the modern (often conceived rather vaguely) had strong emotional appeal to the student radicals, particularly when linked with concepts of national strength and individual liberty.

4. In this book I make frequent use of such terms as radicals, revolutionaries, radical intellectuals or student radicals, revolutionary intellectuals, and professional revolutionaries. The first five terms are often used interchangeably, although, strictly speaking, radical might be used to describe those who desired sweeping change without necessarily trying to overthrow the government, whereas revolutionaries sought to replace the dynasty with a republic. Many students classified themselves as radicals during their school years without clearly defining the consequences of their views. By 1911, however, radicals were generally revolutionaries and the distinction had become fairly meaningless. Most of the radicals or revolutionaries with whom I deal were students or scholars—hence radical intellectuals, and so on. Revolutionaries were not necessarily intellectuals (although in this particular book they usually are). Professional revolutionaries were members of a revolutionary party who were seriously devoting much of their time to party work and/or trying to overthrow the government. They were a considerably smaller and more politically involved group than were the radicals as a whole.

5. In the Society for China's Revival, and to a lesser extent in the Society to Restore China's Prosperity, the central leadership virtually was the party. The Restoration Society really had no central leadership before 1910. A theoretically closer approximation to a central-subordinate party organization was achieved by the Revolutionary Alliance. However, connections between the Tokyo party and local branches were actually informal, depending on sporadic visits, personal friendships, and the accidental interests of individual members.

2. Ideology and Morality: The Regeneration of China

1. Tsou Jung was born in 1885, the second son of a well-off merchant of Chengtu, Szechwan. He began the traditional classical education, but rebelled against studying

the eight-legged essay. However, his father insisted he continue his lessons and sent him to study under Lü I-wen, a well-known scholar in Chungking. In Chungking, Tsou was influenced by the 1898 Reform Movement, particularly the philosophy of the reformer T'an Ssu-t'ung and by T'an's sacrifice when the Reform Movement collapsed. Next Tsou read translations of Rousseau and other political philosophers and became acquainted with certain progressive Japanese at the consulate in Chungking. He studied English and Japanese with two of these men. In 1901 Tsou applied for, but failed to receive, a government scholarship to study in Japan. However, his father agreed to give him some funds and in the fall of 1901 Tsou left for Shanghai. There he studied Japanese and taught English at the language school attached to the Kiangnan Arsenal. After two months he went to Tokyo, where he continued to study Japanese and also read translations of such Western works as Thomas Carlyle's *History of the French Revolution* and books by John Stuart Mill and Herbert Spencer. He took part in the anti-Russian agitation at the beginning of 1903 and joined the Volunteer Corps to Oppose Russia. Shortly after the corps was dissolved Tsou, Chang Chi, and three other students cut off the queue of Yao Wen-fu, the unpopular superintendent of Chinese military students in Japan, and hung it in the Chinese Student Union. Because of this prank Tsou and Chang Chi had to flee Japan. They returned to Shanghai where they became sworn brothers of Chang Ping-lin and Chang Shih-chao. Tsou lived with Chang Ping-lin at the Patriotic School and wrote *The Revolutionary Army*. He voluntarily surrendered to the police on July 1 and was a codefendant at the *Su-pao* trial. He was sentenced to two years' imprisonment and died in the spring of 1905 shortly before the end of his term. This information comes from Tu Ch'eng-hsiang, *Tsou Jung* (Nanking, 1946); Ch'en Hsü-lu, *Tsou Jung yü Ch'en T'ien-hua ti ssu-hsiang* (The Thought of Tsou Jung and Ch'en T'ien-hua; Shanghai, 1957); Mixed Court, "Verbatim Report," *NCH*, 71:1302 (12/18/03).

2. Tsou Jung, *Ko-ming chün* (The revolutionary army), in *HHKM*, 1:333. *Ko-ming chün* has been reprinted in numerous editions and collections. Others include *HCH*, 2:542–572; Tu Ch'eng-hsiang, pp. 56–96; and a separate volume published in Shanghai, 1958.

3. The revolutionaries thus contrast with the characterization by Schwartz of Yen Fu as a Westernizer and a conservative. Benjamin Schwartz, *In Search of Wealth and Power: Yen Fu and the West* (Cambridge, Mass., 1964), p. 84.

4. *Ibid.,* p. 79; chap. 4, *passim.*

5. Joseph Levenson, *Liang Ch'i-ch'ao and the Mind of Modern China* (Cambridge, Mass., 1959), pp. 68–69.

6. Tsou Jung, p. 334.

7. On the shift away from anti-imperialism in revolutionary literature see Michael Gasster, *Chinese Intellectuals and the Revolution of 1911* (Seattle, 1969), pp. 68–69. From 1909 through 1911 *Min-hu jih-pao, Min-hsü jih-pao,* and *Min-li pao* all published numerous attacks on Western imperialism and the danger of the destruction of China. The immediate issues had changed somewhat since 1903–1905. Railway and mining concessions, foreign loans, and Japanese expansionism were now the chief targets. However, the attitudes and terminology that characterized articles in earlier radical journals were all still there. I suggest that because *The People's Journal* was the vehicle for the debate between the revolutionaries and the constitutionalists, represented by Liang Ch'i-ch'ao, an inordinate amount of space was devoted to combatting the constitutionalist movement at the expense of discussing nationalist questions. My general impression is that *Min-li pao* devoted more space to constitutionalism than did its two predecessors. By 1910–11 provincial assemblies had been established and the struggle for a national parliament was in full swing, so constitutionalism was a timely topic. Ch'ing constitutionalism was attacked, but one does not find the same

strong criticism of nonofficial constitutionalists as appeared in *The People's Journal*. Constitutionalists and revolutionaries were moving together in opposition to the government. Examples of anti-imperialist articles are *Min-hu jih-pao* (The people's cry; photolithograph, Taipei, 1969), no. 1, p. 1 (May 15, 1909); no. 12, p. 1 (May 26, 1909); *Min-hsü jih-pao* (The people's sigh; photolithograph, Taipei, 1969), no. 17, p. 1 (October 19, 1909); no. 36, p. 1 (November 7, 1909); *Min-li pao* (The people's stand), no. 7, p. 1 (October 16, 1910); series on two hundred years of Russian troubles, beginning in no. 127, p. 1 (February 20, 1911).

8. A Yokohama branch of the Society to Restore China's Prosperity was established by Sun Yat-sen after the failure of the 1895 Canton rising. Sun soon left to travel to Hawaii, the United States, and Europe and the Yokohama branch was directed by Feng Ching-ju, a Chinese merchant who operated a foreign-language printing shop in that city. It was the effective headquarters of the Society to Restore China's Prosperity whenever Sun Yat-sen was in Japan. The Kwangtung Independence Association (*Kuang-tung tu-li hsüeh-hui*) was established in the spring of 1901 by Feng Ching-ju's young son, Feng Tzu-yu, and other Kwangtungese students in response to inaccurate newspaper reports that the Ch'ing government was about to yield Kwangtung to Japan. This group urged that the province declare its independence. It received encouragement from Sun and was a means of furthering cooperation between the Society to Restore China's Prosperity and Kwangtungese students in Japan Feng Tzu-yu, *Chung-hua min-kuo k'ai-kuo ch'ien ko-ming shih* (A history of the revolution prior to the founding of the Republic of China, 3 vols.; Shanghai, 1928, 1930; Chungking, 1944), 1:30; Feng Tzu-yu, *Ko-ming i-shih* (Fragments of revolutionary history; 5 vols., Shanghai, 1945–1947), 1:98.

9. Those active on *The Chinese National* included Ch'in Li-shan, Ch'i I-hui, Shen Hsiang-yün, Chang Chi, Feng Tzu-yu, and at least one other member of the Kwangtung Independence Association, and several members of the staff of *Translations by Students Abroad (Yu-hsüeh i-pien)*. The paper listed Feng Ching-ju's English name, Kingsell, as publisher for additional safety. Feng, *I-shih*, 1:96.

10. The estimate of less than 100 students in 1900 is by Feng Tzu-yu, *Chung-hua*, 1:54; according to a study based on the *Japanese Weekly Mail* there were still only 500 students in 1902 and 1,500 in 1904. In 1905 and 1906 the figures jumped to 8,000 and 13,000 respectively. Roger F. Hackett, "Chinese Students in Japan, 1900–1910," *Papers on China*, 3:142 (Harvard University, East Asian Research Center, 1949). Feng Tzu-yu gives somewhat higher figures, e.g., 1,500 in 1902.

11. Li Chien-nung, *The Political History of China*, tr. by Teng Ssu-yü and Jeremy Ingalls (New York, 1956), p. 193; Feng, *I-shih*, 2:104.

12. This meeting was prohibited by the Japanese police at the request of the Chinese minister, Ts'ai Chün. It is worth noting that its main organizers were men who already had political records. Chang Ping-lin, Feng Tzu-yu, Ch'in Li-shan, and other survivors of T'ang Ts'ai-ch'ang's rising. They were more experienced radicals than the students who were to lead the anti-Russian demonstrations in 1903. Both Sun Yat-sen and Liang Ch'i-ch'ao signed the declaration, but Liang asked that his name not be made public. Feng, *I-shih*, 1:57–61.

13. The decision to allow only officially sponsored students to enter military schools in Japan was aimed at keeping radicals from gaining knowledge useful in a rebellion. The demonstrations led by Wu lasted a week. Minister Ts'ai Chün then asked the Japanese police to expel the demonstrators from the legation grounds and to deport Wu and one other student. Wu attempted to drown himself in protest, but he was rescued by the police and left Japan on August 7. Kuo T'ing-i, *Chin-tai Chung-kuo shih-shih jih-chih* (A chronology of modern Chinese history; Taipei, 1963), 2:1165; Chang Wen-po, *Chih-lao hsien-hua* (Chats about Wu Chih-hui; Taipei, 1952), pp. 13–14; Chang Wen-po,

Wu Ching-heng hsien-sheng chuan-chi (A biography of Wu Ching-heng; Taipei, 1964), p. 7. A memorial from Ts'ai Chün explaining his refusal to grant students permission to enter the Chinese Students' Military Preparatory School (*Seijō gakkō*) appears in Shu Hsin-ch'eng, *Chin-tai Chung-kuo liu-hsüeh-shih* (A history of modern Chinese students abroad; Shanghai, 1929), p. 151.

14. *The Chinese National* group had been revolutionary, but it died without any direct successors. The Youth Association was also short-lived, but the line of developments it started continued. Among its founders were Yeh Lan, Tung Hung-wei, Ch'in Yü-liu, Chang Chi, and Feng Tzu-yu. Feng Tzu-yu mentions membership in the Youth Association in nineteen biographies. Six men were attending Waseda University. Four were later active in Shanghai. These figures are very fragmentary, but perhaps they give some idea of the society's membership. Feng, *I-shih*, 3:67–70.

15. The anti-Manchu speeches were made by Ma Chün-wu of Kwangsi and Liu Cheng-yü of Hupeh. Their message was enthusiastically received by most of the audience and a Manchu student who tried to protest was shouted down. Liu was expelled from the Chinese Students' Military Preparatory School. Feng, *Chung-hua*, 1:56.

16. The schedule of Russian troop withdrawal was in the Russo-Chinese Treaty of March 21, 1902. The new demands, presented April 18, 1903, were designed to prevent further opening of ports in Manchuria, to keep foreigners (other than Russians) out of the local Manchurian administration, to reserve certain telegraph and banking privileges and administrative posts for Russia, and to allow Russians to keep all rights they had acquired during the occupation after troops withdrew. B. A. Romanov, *Russia in Manchuria, 1892–1906*, tr. by Susan Wilbur Jones (Ann Arbor, 1952), p. 458.

17. *HCH*, 2:122. The main meeting was followed by highly emotional meetings at many of the provincial clubs. About 130 students volunteered for fighting in the Volunteer Corps and another 50 promised to work in a noncombatant headquarters in Tokyo. Twelve women students voted to join the Red Cross and study first aid so they could serve as nurses. Two days later, on May 2, a second meeting changed the name of the corps to The Student Army (*Hsüeh-sheng chün*). Lan T'ien-wei, a military student, was chosen commander. Below him the corps was divided into three branches, each with commanders. Every day one hour each was to be devoted to drill and to lectures. Ordinary expenses were to be met mainly through student contributions. Niu Yung-chien and T'ang Erh-ho were the representatives sent to see Yüan Shih-k'ai. Feng, *I-shih*, 1:105; 2:104; 5:34–36; *HCH*, 2:116–118, 123.

18. The Volunteer Corps to Oppose Russia's charter stated that its aim was to oppose Russia and that it would be organized under the government. Feng, *I-shih*, 1:105; 5:35.

19. Romanov, p. 293; *Hsin-min ts'ung-pao*, 31:50–51.

20. "Telegram from Grand Council to Governors and Governors-General," *Su-pao* (The Kiangsu journal), June 6, 1903, p. 1; reprinted in *HCH*, 2:134. It warns that the Boxer Rebellion was not long past and that this development might upset the peaceful course of international relations.

21. According to one report, a student told Minister Ts'ai Chün that the real aim of the Volunteer Corps to Oppose Russia was revolution. Ts'ai Chün telegraphed the warning to Governor-General Tuan-fang, adding that local officials should be on the alert for student agitators who had already left Japan for the interior of China. Feng, *I-shih*, 1:106. A clear statement of the government's misgivings appears in "Telegram from Grand Council to Governors and Governors-General," *Su-pao*, June 6, 1903, p. 1. On June 1 the paper had previously published a similar telegram from Tuan-fang to the governors of the Yangtze provinces. He warned that the present student radicals were better armed and more numerous than the 1900 rebels and sug-

gested that they must have the support of K'ang Yu-wei and Liang Ch'i-ch'ao. *HCH*, 2:133–134. The government denied the authenticity of the Grand Council edict after it appeared in *Su-pao*. The attitudes and phraseology in the telegram are consistent with those in other undoubtedly genuine official documents, however, and the telegram is probably also authentic.

22. Some support for this view is found in Chi-tzu, "Ko-ming chi k'o-mien hu" (Can revolution be avoided?), *Chiang-su*, no. 4 (July 1903), in *SLHC*, 1.2:560. The author states that the Manchus might have avoided revolution and cites the rebuff of the Volunteer Corps as one of the factors driving the students to revolt. The Manchus hate the students. Therefore, the students will return the sentiment. This statement is at variance with the secret declaration of the Association for the Education of a Militant People which alleges that the Volunteer Corps, too, was anti-Manchu and only sought to cooperate with the government as a tactic to further its aim of independence. However, this may not have been a really accurate description of the students' attitudes ten days earlier, but instead betrayed the effect of disappointment and anger caused by the government's rejection. Whether or not the members of the Volunteer Corps sincerely believed the government could be persuaded to go to war with Russia, they at least thought they should try to persuade it to do so. In the excitement of the moment they may not have given much thought to the likelihood of the government adopting their aims. What seems significant is that initially their nationalism was directed against a Western power, not the Manchu court. Once rebuffed they could link the two together as enemies. The text of the declaration of the Association for the Education of a Militant People is reprinted in Feng, *I-shih*, 1:109–112. Most of it is translated in Chün-tu Hsüeh, *Huang Hsing and the Chinese Revolution* (Stanford, 1961), pp. 10–11.

23. The Association for the Education of a Militant People published a public set of regulations in *Hupeh Student Circles* that defined its aims as fostering a martial spirit and patriotism. Rights and duties of members, the number of officers and procedures for meetings were set forth in considerable detail. See *HCH*, 2:104–108. An appeal for support, particularly for donations from gentry and merchants, was published in *Su-pao* on June 4, 1903. See reprint in *HCH*, 2:108–109. Actually the organization was highly secret, had few members, held no regular meetings, and had no fixed headquarters. Feng, *I-shih*, 1:109, 112. Most members returned to China or went to Southeast Asia to promote revolution. They were united by a common belief in assassinations and armed revolt, not by organizational bonds.

24. Government policy toward radical magazines was inconsistent. Officials disapproved of their circulation, but only suppressed those which had specifically aroused government anger. Radical journals and papers such as *Tides of Chekiang, Kiangsu,* and *The China National Gazette* openly listed their outlets in various cities on the covers of each issue. At least a few issues of some radical publications were available in the sizable towns. See, e.g., lists in *CCC*, 3:195; *CCC*, 7:199-200; *Kuo-min jih-jih pao* (The China National Gazette; photolithograph, Taipei, 1965), 178 (Sept. 22, 1903); 259 (Sept. 30, 1903); 328 (Oct. 7, 1903). Some popular periodicals published several editions of their issues. *Tides of Chekiang*, for instance, published at least four. An example of sporadic suppression occurred in the fall of 1903 when *The Renovation of the People* was not permitted to pass Chinese customs and *The China National Gazette* was banned from the mails. *Chiang-su*, 6:145.

25. These clubs were distinctly fraternal in conception. The Kiangsu association was established in 1903 when there were a hundred to a hundred and fifty Kiangsu students in Japan. At least in principle it was open to merchants, gentry, and officials as well as students, and the first meeting was attended by ten or so merchants from Yokohama. Members were to aid fellow members who had suffered misfortune or

insult, help bring fellow provincials to Japan and aid them in entering school, chastize wayward members and supervise the conduct of youngest members. In contrast to these traditional aspects, the society's regulations contained detailed enumerations of rights and duties of members and officers, election procedures and rules governing meetings which were based on Western notions of political democracy and parliamentary procedure. Special club activities were under four departments: publishing; education; industry, which was to seek economic prosperity for China in the future; and investigations, which was to study and report on corruption and other such problems in China. *Chiang-su*, no. 1; reprinted in *HCH*, 2:89–95. Regulations of the Chekiang provincial club were roughly similar, but less detailed. They do not enumerate rights and duties of members, election procedures, and rules for meetings at great length. There were only two special club activities: publishing and investigations of Chekiangese affairs. Consequently the traditional, fraternal aspects of the regulations are more prominent. See *CCC*, no. 1, n.p.

26. Ko Kung-chen, *Chung-kuo pao-hsüeh shih* (A history of Chinese journalism; Peking, 1955), p. 163.

27. Shen Tieh-min, "Chi Kuang-fu hui erh-san shih" (Recollections of two or three things about the Restoration Society); in *KML,* 4:131; Feng, *I-shih,* 3:68, 70, 84.

28. Examples of politically neutral or reformist articles include P'i-chih, "Hsien-cheng fa-ta shih" (A history of the development of constitutional government), *CCC,* 8:47–52; Yüan Yün, "Ssu-k'o cheng-lun" (A political debate by four travelers), *CCC,* 7; in *SLHC*, 1.2:503–508; Kung Fa-tzu, "Ching-kao wo hsiang-jen" (Summoning our villagers), *CCC,* 2; in *SLHC*, 1.2:496–503; "Chiang-su jen chih tao-te wen-t'i" (The question of the morality of Kiangsu natives), *Chiang-su*, 9–10:1–10. *Kiangsu* was the more obviously radical of the two periodicals.

29. Examples of articles in *Tides of Chekiang* and *Kiangsu* in which revolutionary implications are obvious or openly stated include Fei-shih, "Chung-kuo ai-kuo-che Cheng Ch'eng-kung chuan" (A biography of the Chinese patriot Koxinga), *CCC,* 2:57–63 and following issues; Chi-tzu, pp. 560-564; Yüan Sun, "Lu-hsi-ya hsü-wu-tang" (The Russian nihilist party), *Chiang-su*, 4; in *SLHC*, 1.2:565–571; Han-erh, "Wei min-tsu liu-hsüeh Shih K'o-fa chuan" (A biography of Shih K'o-fa, a man who shed blood for the nation), *Chiang-su*, 6:71–81. Student authors tended to concentrate on a few themes so there is much repetition in radical literature. Although I have read more articles and pamphlets than those specifically cited in this chapter, *Kiangsu, Tides of Chekiang, The Revolutionary Army,* and the two major tracts by Ch'en T'ien-hua seemed fairly characteristic of contemporary radical writings. They furthermore have particular relevance to the area dealt with in this book (except for Ch'en T'ien-hua, who was relevant to student circles everywhere in China). Since this book is not solely an intellectual history, it is impossible to discuss all the radical literature, and it seems logical to concentrate on the above selection.

30. Wu-min, "Chiang-su yü Han-tsu chih kuan-hsi" (The relation between Kiangsu and the Chinese race), *Chiang-su*, 6:11; Fei-shih, "Che-feng p'ien" (On the customs of Chekiang), *CCC*, 5:2–3. William R. Johnson illuminates part of the problem of nationalism and provincialism in the revolutionary movement by pointing to connections revolutionaries saw between national survival, development of a politically aware and militant citizenry, and inauguration of local self-government. See William R. Johnson, "Revolution and Reconstruction in Yunnan: A Sketch," paper for Conference on the Revolution of 1911 in China, mimeo., 1965, p. 4.

31. Yü I, "Min-tsu chu-i lun" (On nationalism), *CCC*, nos. 1 and 2; in *SLHC*, 1.2:485.

32. Fei-sheng (Chiang Fang-chen), "Kuo-hun p'ien" (On the national spirit), *CCC*, 1: *she-shuo* 3–4, 6–11; 7:33.

33. Tsou Jung, pp. 357–358. Tsou may have taken this characterization of Tseng Kuo-fan and others from Chang Ping-lin.

34. Robert Scalapino stresses the high racial content of the radical's message in Robert A. Scalapino, "Prelude to Marxism: The Chinese Student Movement in Japan, 1900–1910"; in Albert Feuerwerker, et al., eds., *Approaches to Modern Chinese History* (Berkeley, 1967), pp. 196–197.

35. Yü I, pp. 487–488.

36. E.g. in Chi-tzu, p. 564.

37. E.g. Tsou Jung, chap. 4. Tsou is concerned only with the yellow race, which he divided into two main categories, Chinese and Siberian. The Manchus are a Tungusic people, a subdivision of the Mongol group under the Siberian heading.

38. Han Chü, "Hsin cheng-fu chih chien-she" (Construction of a new government), *Chiang-su,* nos. 5 and 6; in *SLHC,* 1.2:591.

39. Chi-tzu, p. 560.

40. Ching An, "Cheng-t'i chin-hua lun" (On the evolution of political systems), *Chiang-su,* nos. 1 and 3; in *SLHC,* 1.2:546. Another formulation of this idea appears in "Chih-na fen-ko chih wei-chi" (The danger of the partition of China), *Chiang-su,* 6:89–90. The author states that if the Manchus won't fight Russia and won't let others fight Russia, then Chinese must first fight the Manchus. Both fighting Manchus and fighting Russians would constitute saving the country. Ch'iu Chin gave a special twist to this line of thought by treating imperialism as an anti-Manchu portent. "Suddenly a warning comes from the West and together the Chinese weep for the land east of K'un-lun Mountains./Now we know that today's 'pig-tail' is not the custom of the great Han of yore." Ch'iu Chin, "Tiao Wu lieh-shih Yüeh" (In memory of Wu Yüeh); in Hsiao P'ing, ed., *Hsin-hai ko-ming lieh-shih shih-wen hsüan* (A selection of writings by martyrs of the 1911 Revolution; Peking, 1962), p. 137.

41. Ch'en T'ien-hua, *Ching-shih chung* (A bell to warn the world); in *HHKM,* 2:119–120, 124; Ch'en T'ien-hua, *Meng hui-t'ou* (About face!); in *HHKM,* 2:152, 157.

42. Ch'en T'ien-hua, *Meng hui-t'ou,* p. 168.

43. Ch'en T'ien-hua, *Ching-shih chung,* p. 126.

44. Ch'en T'ien-hua, *Meng hui-t'ou,* p. 147.

45. Ch'en T'ien-hua, *Ching-shih chung,* pp. 135–142.

46. Ch'en T'ien-hua, *Meng-hui t'ou,* pp. 167-168.

47. E.g., Tsou Jung, pp. 362-363.

48. Communist writers have recognized and criticized this lack of anti-Western imperialist bias. Ch'iu Chin, for instance, is said to have been blinded to the fact that liberty and equality did not actually exist in the West by her admiration for the slogans of Western "bourgeois" revolutionaries. She set out to save China from foreign aggression, but she blamed the country's difficulties on the government and the people instead of directly on the Western imperialists. "Introduction" to *Ch'iu Chin chi* (The collected works of Ch'iu Chin; Shanghai, 1960), p. 7.

49. Han Chü, p. 591.

50. *Ibid.,* p. 590; "Ko-ming chih-tsao-ch'ang" (The factory of revolution), *Chiang-su,* no. 5; in *SLHC,* 1.2:578.

51. "Kung-ssu p'ien" (An essay on the concepts of public and private), *CCC,* no. 1; in *SLHC,* 1.2:494.

52. Tsou Jung, p. 359.

53. The text of the declaration of the Society for the Education of a Militant People is reprinted in Feng, *I-shih,* 1:109–112. A translation of most of it appears in Chün-tu Hsüeh, *Huang Hsing and the Chinese Revolution* (Stanford, 1961), pp. 10–11. Stokely Carmichael's news conference was reported in *The Washington Post,* p. 8 (April 6, 1968).

54. Yün Wo, "Chiao-yü t'ung-lun" (A general essay on education), *Chiang-su,* no. 3; in *SLHC,* 1.2:552–554. Tsou Jung similarly argued that before their revolutions the Americans and French were slaves. They became citizens and the Chinese could too. Tsou Jung, p. 359. This interpretation of French and American history is not very convincing, but it was necessary for Tsou to claim that the Western peoples also went through a period similar to the one in which the Chinese still found themselves if the "slavish" Chinese character was not to appear unique and irredeemable.

55. *Su-pao,* p. 232 (April 8, 1903).

56. Ch'iu Chin, "T'ung-pao k'u" (Our brothers' sorrows); in Hsiao P'ing, p. 147.

57. Han Chü, p. 582.

58. "Ko-ming chih-tsao-ch'ang," p. 577.

59. Ya Lu (Liu Ch'i-chi), "Chung-kuo ko-ming chia ti-i jen Ch'en She chuan" (A biography of China's first revolutionary, Ch'en She), *Chiang-su,* 9–10:108.

60. Tsou Jung, p. 333.

61. Yüan Sun, pp. 569–571. Articles on Russian terrorism, anarchism, or nihilism (all treated as if they were nearly the same) or admiring biographies of terrorists were common in radical periodicals.

62. Ya Lu (Liu Ch'i-chi), "Chung-kuo li-hsien wen-t'i" (China's constitutional question), *Chiang-su,* no. 6; in *SLHC,* 1.2:594–596.

63. Yüan Yün, "Ju-chiao-kuo chih pien-fa" (Reform in a Confucian country), *CCC,* 10:19.

64. Fei-sheng (Chiang Fang-chen), "Chin-shih erh-ta-shuo chih p'ing-lun" (A critique of two current theories), *CCC,* nos. 8 and 9; in *SLHC,* 1.2:522–523,524.

65. Han Chü, p. 582.

66. Ching An, p. 543.

67. E.g., one article describes the Teutonic race as having achieved effective political organization after the fall of Rome. Its members established representative government, delineated the rights of government and of the individual, and distributed power between the central and local governments. The race was thus able to develop its particular characteristics and the nation grew stronger and victorious. The nation took the people's authority as its own, their will as its will, and their strength as its strength. Yü I, p. 487. This picture of the Teutons probably comes from Liang Ch'i-ch'ao. See *Hsin-min ts'ung-pao* (The Renovation of the People), 2:5–6.

68. *Ibid.,* p. 491.

69. E.g., Tsou Jung, pp. 361–362; Chih-na-tzu, "Fa-lü shang jen-min chih tzu-yu ch'üan" (The people's right of freedom under law), *CCC,* 10:36–38.

70. "Ang-ko-lu So-sun jen-chung chih chiao-yü ping Chung-kuo chiao-yü chih fang-chen" (The education of the Anglo-Saxon people is the prescription for Chinese education), *CCC,* 1: *chiao-yü* 4–5, 6.

71. Chia-t'ing li-hsien-che, "Chia-t'ing ko-ming shuo" (On the family revolution), *Chiang-su,* 7:15.

72. Yüan Sun, p. 565.

73. Tsou Jung, pp. 340–341.

74. Ching An, pp. 541–542.

75. Han Chü, p. 584.

76. *Ibid.,* p. 586.

77. Radical students were criticized for knowing only how to destroy and not how to reconstruct in moderate articles in so-called revolutionary publications. See, e.g., Chung K'an, "Tzu-chih p'ien" (On self-government), *CCC,* 6: *she-shuo* 2.

78. See "Chiang-su jen chih hsin-kuei" (Belief in ghosts by Kiangsu natives), *Chiang-su,* 9–10:29–32. The theme of this article is that belief in ghosts confuses the people's ideas and enfeebles their spirits until they have no hope of developing freedom of

thought and independence.

79. Shu Lou, "Chiao-yü hui wei min-t'uan chih chi-ch'u" (The Educational Association is the basis for a militia), *Chiang-su,* nos. 1 and 3; in *SLHC,* 1.2:548.

80. Yün Wo, 551; Pu-nan-tzu, "Chiao-yü hsüeh" (A study of education), *CCC,* 2:51. The latter article argues that the important struggle is to mold the character of citizens and that this is the business of education.

81. Shu Lou, p. 550.

82. Fei-sheng, "Chin-shih erh-ta-shuo chih p'ing-lun," p. 521. This article also quotes and criticizes Liang Ch'i-ch'ao's statement in the first of his series of editorials, "On the Renovation of the People" (*Hsin-min shuo*) that "if there is a renovated people, what matter if there is no renovated system, nor renovated government, nor renovated nation." (*Ibid.,* p. 519. The quote is from *Hsin-min ts'ung-pao,* 1:3.) If social change were to precede political change the process would be intolerably long according to the author. Moreover, in China change might never occur without leadership. This criticism was aimed specifically at Liang Ch'i-ch'ao, but points to a general difference between revolutionaries and reformers or constitutionalists. A relatively conservative Westernizer like Yen Fu believed that the need to educate the masses justified slow political evolution geared to the people's ability to participate in government. See Schwartz, pp. 146–147. Revolutionaries believed such an approach would negate the possibility of change.

83. Tsou Jung, p. 349.

84. E.g., *Su-pao,* pp. 180–181 (March 30, 1903); p. 315 (April 22, 1903); "Fa-lü kai-lun" (Summary of law), *CCC,* 3:34–36.

85. Tsou Jung, p. 357.

86. *Ibid.,* p. 356. Similarly, some people are barbaric and others civilized not because of inherent differences, but because of differences in education. Therefore, China must learn the ways that made the West civilized. *Su-pao,* p. 180 (March 30, 1903).

87. These points were made in numerous writings and lay behind the radicals' schemes for educating a "militant people" through military drill. See, e.g., "Chiang-su jen chih hsin-kuei," p. 33; Yüan Yün, "T'ieh-hsüeh chu-i chih chiao-yü" (Iron and blood education), *CCC,* 10:63; Fei-sheng, "Chen chün-jen" (Real military men), *CCC,* 3:65, 71–72.

88. Tsou Jung, p. 350.

89. *Ibid.,* p. 349. Pre-1911 radicals also used phrases that can be precisely translated as foreknowers—e.g., Ching An (p. 546) uses *hsien-chüeh.* Liang Ch'i-ch'ao, in a somewhat different context, also used this term when he said that those people with the greatest sense of self-respect and responsibility were like I Yin, the famous minister of the founder of the Shang dynasty, who was "*t'ien-min hsien-chüeh.*" *Hsin-min ts'ung-pao,* 14:5.

90. It is possible that Western heroes like Napoleon and George Washington were assimilated to the Chinese heroic concept. Ch'iu Chin regarded Mme. Roland and Sophia Perovskaya in that way.

91. Robert Ruhlman, "Traditional Heroes in Chinese Popular Fiction," in Arthur Wright, ed., *The Confucian Persuasion* (Stanford, 1960), pp. 151–152. Heroism is one of the traditional influences stressed in Mary B. Rankin, "The Tenacity of Tradition," in Mary C. Wright, ed., *China in Revolution: The First Phase, 1900–1913* (New Haven, 1968), p. 335.

92. Ch'en T'ien-hua (1875–1905) was a Hunanese who obtained a government scholarship to study in Japan in 1903. There he became a revolutionary, joining the Association for the Education of a Militant People after the 1903 anti-Russian demonstrations. He was an associate of Huang Hsing and returned with him to promote revolution in Hunan. Ch'en joined the Society for China's Revival in Changsha in December

1903. He helped plan the abortive Hunan rising in 1904. When the plot was discovered he fled to Japan. In 1905 he joined the Revolutionary Alliance and wrote for *Min-pao*. He committed suicide to protest the apathy of Chinese students in Tokyo and the Japanese Ministry of Education's new regulations governing Chinese students in Japan by drowning himself off Ōmori Beach, Tokyo, on December 8, 1905. Ch'en was an accomplished pamphleteer whose best known works were *About Face!* (*Meng hui-t'ou*) and *A Bell to Warn the World* (*Ching-shih chung*). He was never active in the Lower Yangtze provinces, but many radicals from that area knew him in Tokyo and his death had great impact on students in Shanghai. He was one of the most influential revolutionary writers and the manner of his death clearly placed him in the group under discussion. Feng, *I-shih*, 2:129–132. A good English-language analysis of Ch'en T'ien-hua appears in Ernest P. Young, "Ch'en T'ien-hua (1875–1905); A Chinese Nationalist," *Papers of China* (Harvard University, East Asian Research Center, 1959), 13:113-162, *passim*.

93. Ch'iu Chin's birthdate is variously given as 1875, 1877, and 1879. Her family home was just outside Shaohsing city in Shan-yin district, Chekiang, but she was born and grew up in Amoy, where her grandfather was a prefect. Her father's status is not entirely clear. Certain sources, e.g., Ch'iu Ts'an-chih, *Ch'iu Chin ko-ming chuan* (A revolutionary biography of Ch'iu Chin; Taipei, 1953), p. 2, claim he was a local official. Another source says he was a *chü-jen* and served in Taiwan as well as in Fukien and Hunan (*KMCC*, p. 209). More probably he had passed the lower examinations and was a legal secretary who served under local officials and held a few minor posts in his own right. Her mother was an educated woman. Arthur W. Hummel, ed., *Eminent Chinese of the Ch'ing Period* (Washington, D.C., 1943–1944), 1:169.

94. Chiu Ts'an-chih, pp. 3–4; Hsü Shuang-yün, "Chi Ch'iu Chin" (Recollections of Ch'iu Chin); in *KML*, 4:206.

95. Ch'iu Chin, "Man-chiang-hung tzu," *KMCC*, pp. 216–217.

96. T'ao Ch'eng-chang, "Che-an chi-lüeh" (A brief account of the revolts in Chekiang); in *HHKM*, 3:60–61; *KMCC*, p. 217. Some sources say she went to Japan during the summer, e.g., Ch'iu Ts'an-chih, p. 34. Hsü Shuang-yün (p. 208) says the autumn.

97. Wang Shih-tse, "Hui-i Ch'iu Chin" (Recollections of Ch'iu Chin); in *KML*, 4:224; Yü Chao-i, *Ch'iu Chin nü-hsia* (The heroine Ch'iu Chin; Hongkong, 1961), p. 51.

98. Yü Chao-i, p. 51.

99. P'eng Tzu-i, *Ch'iu Chin* (Shanghai, 1941), p. 9. The sources on Ch'iu's life indicate that she and Ch'en founded the Encompassing Love Society. However, a group by the same name had been established in the spring of 1903 to promote women's rights and education. The women students who had intended to become nurses for the Volunteer Corps to Oppose Russia were largely or entirely drawn from its members. An article in *Kiangsu*, no. 6, wishing well to the Encompassing Love Society and the regulations of the society are reprinted in *HCH*, vol. 2, pp. 95–98. The society had evidently almost died out and existed in name only when it was revived by Ch'en and Ch'iu.

100. Hsü Shuang-yün, p. 209. This *Vernacular Journal* was published for six issues by the Society for the Study of Oratory (*Yen-shuo lien-hsi hui*). It was founded in 1904 to combat reformist ideas among the Tokyo students.

101. Wang Shih-tse, pp. 225–226; Feng, *Chung-hua*, 2:60. Wang, who joined at the same time as Ch'iu, gives the following description of the initiation ceremony. After being briefed beforehand by Feng Tzu-yu, each was asked the following questions: "Why have you come?" To which the reply was, "To be a soldier." "Are you loyal?" "Loyal." "What will happen if you are disloyal?" "If I flee into the mountains, I will be eaten by tigers. If I flee elsewhere, I will be set upon by powerful men." After the

questioning, a cloth was unfurled on which was written "Overthrow the Ch'ing and restore the Ming." Each recruit had to demonstrate his loyalty to that sentiment by bowing down and passing under the banner. Next they jumped through a fire. After that a cock was killed and its blood drunk. Finally, the Triad rules and practices were described to them and they were given a book containing regulations and depicting the many banners and symbols. Each paid an initiation fee of ten yen.

102. Feng, *Chung-hua*, 2:60. The first Chekiangese to join the Revolutionary Alliance was Chiang Tsun-kuei. Ch'iu Chin was the second.

103. The new regulations governing Chinese students in Japan were a result of the rapid increase in their numbers after 1904. Estimates vary widely, but there were probably eight or ten thousand by late 1905. This increase put a severe strain on schools specializing in the education of Chinese students. The gap was filled by dubious institutions, some of which would sell diplomas. Moreover, many students were academically ill-qualified and were more interested in politics than study. Chinese officials were concerned over student radicalism and put pressure on Japanese authorities, who in turn were concerned over the prostitution of education standards. The new regulations, announced in late November 1905, required all students attending school in Japan to have a letter from the Chinese Minister. Only certain schools were approved and students had to live in quarters selected by the Japanese authorities. Marius B. Jansen, *The Japanese and Sun Yat-sen* (Cambridge, Mass., 1954), p. 112; Hu Han-min, *Tzu-chuan* (Autobiography); in *KMWH*, 3:18.

104. T'ao, "Che-an," p. 61; Feng, *I-shih*, 2:130; Ch'iu Ts'an-chih, pp. 34, 39; Hsü Shuang-yün, p. 210.

105. Hsü Shuang-yün, p. 212; T'ao, "Che-an," p. 61. Hsü says Ch'iu was very popular with the students who were angry at her dismissal. Virtually all other sources say that the students found her too radical and she found them too tradition-bound. Quite possibly there is some truth in both versions.

106. T'ao, "Che-an," p. 61; Feng, *I-shih*, 2:179. This is a standard story which appears in all accounts.

107. T'ao, "Che-an," p. 87. The Chinese Public Institute was a radical school founded in Woosung in 1906 to provide education for students who returned from Japan to protest the new education regulations.

108. The *Chinese Women's Journal* was directed particularly at women students with the idea of subsequently establishing a women's association. The paper was written in a simple style and avoided overly erudite subjects. The aim was to exhort women to study and be active outside the home. Ch'iu originally also planned to publish books for women and give aid to girls coming to study in Japan or passing through on the way abroad. She had hoped to raise 10,000 yuan by selling 500 shares of stock of 20 yuan each. Actually few shares were sold. Hsü Tzu-hua and her younger sister, Hsü Shuang-yün, contributed 1,500 yuan to start publication. Ch'iu was publisher and general manager. Ch'en Po-p'ing, who later helped Hsü Hsi-lin assassinate En-ming, was editor, and Hsü Shuang-yün corrected proofs. Draft regulations for the *Chinese Women's Journal* appear in *Ch'iu Chin shih-chi* (Manuscripts of Ch'iu Chin; Shanghai, 1958), pp. 11–12. Hsü Shuang-yün (p. 213) lists the articles in the second and last issue. Other sources of information are Hsü Shuang-yün, pp. 212–213; P'eng Tzu-i, p. 11.

109. Ch'iu Chin, "Tiao Wu lieh-shih Yüeh," in Hsiao P'ing, p. 137.

110. Ch'iu Chin, "A speech," in P'eng Tzu-i, p. 75. Here Ch'iu says that if Chinese women are determined, they can find ways to escape from their traditional position.

111. E.g., Ch'iu Chin, "Ch'un-t'ien ou-chan" (A sudden revelation on a spring day); "Wu-yeh" (Leaves of the Wu tree); "Tu-tui"; in Ch'iu Ts'an-chih, p. 10. This last poem begins:

I, alone, toward the spring cherish melancholy thoughts.
Sunset and fragrant blossoms—it is a time of heartbreak.
The hundred-foot walls of melancholy are strong and hard to breech;
I drink three cups of clear wine without stopping.

112. *NCH*, 84:205 (7/26/07); Ch'iu Chin, "Letter to brother Ch'iu Yü, dated September 12, 1905"; in *Ch'iu Chin chi,* pp. 35–38. This and some of the other letters contain passages defending her actions in reply to letters received from him.

113. Ch'iu Chin, "Letter to brother Ch'iu Yü, dated November 28, 1905"; in *Ch'iu Chin chi,* p. 42.

114. Ch'iu Chin, "Che-ku t'ien"; in Hsiao P'ing, p. 148.

115. Ch'iu Chin, "Introductory editorial to *Chung-kuo nü-pao*"; in Hsiao P'ing, p. 150. The concept of the bodhisattva is suggested by the line "I know you can not bring all the people in the world across [to Nirvana]."

116. Ch'iu Chin, "Chien-ko" (Song of the sword); in Ch'iu Ts'an-chih, p. 28; "Tseng Chiang Lu-shan hsien-sheng yen chih chieh wei t'a-jih ch'eng-kung chih hung-chao yeh" (Sending word to Chiang Lu-shan that his resolution bears the trace of successes of other days); in Hsiao P'ing, p. 145; "Tiao Wu lieh-shih Yüeh"; in Hsiao P'ing, p. 137.

117. Ch'iu Chin, "Chü" (Chrysanthemums); in Ch'iu Ts'an-chih, p. 6.

118. Ch'iu Chin, "Fan tung-hai ko" (Song while drifting on the eastern sea); in *HHKM*, 3:210.

119. *Ibid.,* p. 210; "Tseng Chiang Lu-shan . . ."; in Hsiao P'ing, p. 145; "Pao-tao ko" (Sword song); in Hsiao P'ing, p. 140. Ch'iu's poems are full of references to traditional Chinese poets and to mythical figures such as Jo Yeh and Nü Wa. Ch'iu was obviously thoroughly familiar with the *Romance of the Three Kingdoms,* to which she alludes in a number of poems. The ranks of heroes are not only filled with famous men, however; they also encompass those nameless people who accomplished a great deed. See "Mou kung-jen chuan" (Biography of a palace woman); in P'eng Tzu-i, pp. 66–70. The heroine insisted upon changing clothes with one of the princesses when the capital fell to the bandit Li Tzu-ch'eng at the end of the Ming. She planned to allow herself to be captured so that she might assassinate Li. However, she was given to one of his generals as a concubine. Fearing that she would never have an opportunity to carry out her original intention, she stabbed the general instead. When his cries summoned the servants, she stabbed herself as well. This story is of interest because its chief figure is a woman and because it dramatizes the self-sacrifice theme.

120. Ch'iu Chin, "Jih-pen Suzuki hsüeh-shih pao-tao ko" (Sword song of the Japanese scholar Suzuki); in Ch'iu Ts'an-chih, p. 41.

121. Ch'iu Chin, "Tseng Chiang Lu-shan . . ."; in Hsiao P'ing, p. 145.

122. Ch'iu Chin, "Pao-tao ko," in Hsiao P'ing, p. 140.

123. Ch'iu Chin, "Chi Hsü Chi-ch'en" (To Hsü Chi-ch'en); in Hsiao P'ing, p. 143.

124. Ch'iu Chin, "Tui-chiu" (To wine); in Hsiao P'ing, p. 142; "Che-ku t'ien"; in *Ibid.,* p. 148.

125. Ch'iu Chin, "Tseng Chiang Lu-shan . . ."; in Hsiao P'ing, p. 145. "Political moves after failure will be difficult to repeat;/ Time, time will not wait for us." The note on this poem suggests that it was written to a secret society leader whose aid was being enlisted for the planned rising. Although the poem was obviously written to flatter and encourage him, it also can be read as an example of Ch'iu's concept of the ideal hero. The sense of urgency it expresses may well be genuine, too. If Ch'iu had been disappointed when plans for a rising in December 1906 had to be abandoned, it is reasonable to believe that she was deeply committed to going through with the second try.

3. Beginnings of Revolutionary Activity in Shanghai I: Leadership and Institutions

1. Lu Tan-lin, *Ko-ming shih t'an* (Chats on revolutionary history; Chungking, 1946), pp. 163–167 gives a summary of missionary reformist publications.
2. A. M. Kotenev, *Shanghai, Its Mixed Court and Council* (Shanghai, 1925), p. 107.
3. Feng, *I-shih*, 2:77.
4. *Ibid.*, 2:75. Ts'ai Yüan-p'ei was one of the organizers of this meeting.
5. *NCH*, 66:539 (5/20/01). One of the speakers presented arguments strikingly similar to those used by radical students two years later. It was a mistake to believe that other powers would prevent Russia from annexing Manchuria. The others could not help China if she would not help herself. Instead, they would let Russia take Manchuria and demand territory in China proper to maintain the balance of power. The Western powers would all gain by agreeing to partition China, and would prefer this alternative to fighting among themselves over the fate of the Chinese empire.
6. Feng, *I-shih*, 1:115–116. The revised regulations of the Educational Association, which were provisionally adopted in late April 1903 and formally adopted three months later, stated that the aim of the society was to educate the Chinese people and elevate their character to lay the basis for restoration of China's rights. *HCH*, 2:346.
7. Chiang Wei-ch'iao, "Chung-kuo chiao-yü hui chih hui-i" (Recollections of the Chinese Educational Association); in *HHKM*, 1:485. The Educational Association held a meeting on April 26, 1903, to review its first year and elect officers. *Su-pao*, p. 350 (April 28, 1903). If this meeting was held on the anniversary of the founding of the association, it was established April 26, 1902.
8. Chiang Wei-ch'iao, p. 485.
9. Ts'ai Yüan-p'ei as told to Huang Shih-hui, "Ts'ai Chieh-min hsien-sheng ti ch'ing-nien shih-tai" (The youth of Ts'ai Chieh-min); in *HCH*, 2:362.
10. Choong Lee, "Chang Ping-lin and the *Su-pao* case" (Harvard East Asia Regional Studies, January 1963), p. 2.
11. Sources for Wu Chih-hui's early career, except otherwise cited, are Chang Wen-po, *Chih-lao hsien-hua* (Chats about Wu Chih-hui; Taipei, 1952), pp. 3–14; Chang Wen-po, *Wu Ching-heng hsien-sheng chuan-chi* (Biography of Wu Ching-heng; Taipei, 1964), pp. 1–8. These two books contain very similar accounts of Wu's early career.
12. Sources for Ts'ai Yüan-p'ei's early years, except otherwise cited, are Hsin-ch'ao she (The New Tide Society), ed., *Ts'ai Chieh-min hsien-sheng yen-hsing lu* (A record of the words and deeds of Ts'ai Chieh-min; Peking, 1920), pp. 1–3; Robert K. Sakai, "Ts'ai Yüan-p'ei as a Synthesizer of Western and Chinese Thought," *Papers on China*, 3:172–173 (1949), Harvard University, East Asian Research Center.
13. Biographical information on Huang Tsung-yang is from Feng, *I-shih*, 3:170–172; "Ko-ming hua-seng Wu-mu" (The revolutionary artist monk Wu-mu), *Chung-yang jih-pao* (June 1948); in *HCH*, 2:356–359.
14. Feng, *Chung-hua*, 1:112; for a biography of Yü Yüeh see Arthur W. Hummel, ed. *Eminent Chinese of the Ch'ing Period*, 2 vols. (Washington, D.C., 1943–1944), 2:944–945.
15. T'ao Ch'eng-chang, "Che-an chi-lüeh" (A brief account of the revolts in Chekiang); in *HHKM*, 3:11; Feng, *Chung-hua*, 1:114, 137; Feng, *I-shih*, 1:53–54.
16. Feng, *Chung-hua*, 1:112.
17. Feng, *I-shih*, 1:53.
18. Feng, *Chung-hua*, 1:113.
19. Chang Ping-lin, "K'o-ti lun" (On guest emperors); in *Ch'iu-shu* (Book of Grievances; 1905), pp. 2–5.
20. Chang Ping-lin, "K'o-ti k'uang-miu" (Correcting the error of 'guest emperors');

in *Ch'iu-shu* (Book of Grievances; Shanghai, 1958), pp. 2–5. I have only looked at these essays in very cursory fashion.

21. "Nan-yang kung-hsüeh ti i-chiu-ling-erh nien pa-k'o feng-ch'ao ho Ai-kuo hsüeh-she" (The student strike at the Nan-yang Public Institute in 1902 and the Patriotic School); in *KML*, 4:77.

22. *Ibid.*, p. 76.

23. E.g., references to the Hungarians, Italians, and Greeks rebelling against foreign rulers. In Chang Ping-lin, "Cheng-ch'ou Man-jen" (The principal enemies are the Manchus), *Kuo-min pao*, no. 4 (1901); in *SLHC*, 1.1:97. Also see the statement that the Western countries can ignore racial principles because they are ruled by those of the same race as the populace. Chang Ping-lin, "Po K'ang Yu-wei shu" (Letter disputing K'ang Yu-wei); in *HCH*, 2:592.

24. E.g., reference to such upright, honored officials as Hsiung Yang-lü, Wei Hsiang-shu, and Lu Lung-ch'i as examples of Chinese subservience to the Manchus. Chang Ping-lin, "Po K'ang Yu-wei shu," p. 601.

25. Chang Ping-lin, "Cheng-ch'ou Man-jen," p. 96.

26. Chiang Shen-wu, "Ai-kuo hsüeh-she shih-wai i-yeh" (A page out of the history of the Patriotic School), *Ta-feng pan-yeh-k'an* (The typhoon magazine), no. 67; in *HCH*, 2:372.

27. A good discussion of Chang Ping-lin's thought, especially during the *Min-pao* period, appears in Michael Gasster, *Chinese Intellectuals and the Revolution of 1911* (Seattle, 1969), chap. 7, *passim*.

28. Chang Ping-lin, "Po K'ang Yu-wei shu," p. 592.

29. *Ibid.*, pp. 594, 596.

30. *Ibid.*, p. 596.

31. *Ibid.*, pp. 601–602. Chang was often unfair in debate and this suggestion, of course, ignores the fact that the government would never accept K'ang Yu-wei. At the time Chang was writing, K'ang, Liang Ch'i-ch'ao, and Sun Yat-sen were considered equally dangerous, as were their oppositional views.

32. *Ibid.*, pp. 599–600.

33. Hu Sheng-wu and Chin Ch'ung-chi, "Hsin-hai ko-ming shih-ch'i Chang Ping-lin ti cheng-chih ssu-hsiang" (The political thought of Chang Ping-lin during the period of the Revolution of 1911); in *CNL*, p. 338.

34. Chang Ping-lin, "Po K'ang Yu-wei shu," p. 598. Chang believed Li Tzu-ch'eng had changed during his rebellion from a mere bandit to a hero concerned with alleviating popular misery. Recent rebellions had likewise broadened the understanding of the masses. They now knew that they could not wipe out the Westerners as the Boxers had tried to do, and that they could not place exaggerated faith in Western promises of support as had T'ang Ts'ai-ch'ang.

35. Sun Te-chung, *Ts'ai Yüan-p'ei hsien-sheng i-wen lei-ch'ao* (A topical selection of Ts'ai Yüan-p'ei's writings; Taipei, 1960), p. 153.

36. Ts'ai Yüan-p'ei, "Shih ch'ou-Man" (Explaining enmity to the Manchus), *Su-pao* (March 1903); in *SLHC*, 1.2:678–680.

37. Li Shu-hua, "Wu Chih-hui hsien-sheng ts'ung wei-hsin p'ai ch'eng wei ko-ming tang ti ching-kuo (Wu Chih-hui's change from the reform to the revolutionary movements), *Chuan-chi wen-hsüeh* (Biographical literature), 4.3:35 (April 1964).

38. Chiang Wei-ch'iao, p. 486.

39. Chang Wen-po, *Chih-lao,* p. 14; Chang Wen-po, *Wu Ching-heng,* p. 8.

40. *HCH*, 2:611.

41. Chang Wen-po, *Chih-lao,* p. 24. A discussion of *The New Century* appears in Robert A. Scalapino and George T. Yu, *The Chinese Anarchist Movement* (Berkeley, 1961), pp. 5–28.

42. *Hsin-min ts'ung-pao* (The renovation of the people), 25:165. Lo Chia-ling's father was a former chief of French police in Shanghai and her mother was from Fukien. Her father died when she was six. Three years later her mother also died. Lo lived in poverty with her maternal grandmother until she was discovered and aided by old friends of her father.

43. Holmes Welch, *The Practice of Chinese Buddhism, 1900–1950* (Cambridge, Mass., 1967), pp. 159–160, 228.

44. *Su-pao*, p. 388 (May 4, 1903).

45. Other examples of revolutionaries associated with Buddhism were Chang Ping-lin and Su Man-shu. Ch'iu Chin used Buddhist imagery in some of her writings. (See chap. 2). The Chekiangese revolutionary Ch'en Meng-hsiung and a Buddhist monk founded the radical Monks' and People's School in Lotsing, Chekiang, in 1906 and this same monk took part in the 1911 Revolution (see chaps. 7 and 9). A monk in one of the temples on West Lake, Hangchow, let revolutionaries meet there. Huang Yüan-hsiu, "Hsi-hu pai-yün an yü Hsin-hai ko-ming chih kuan-hsi" (The relation of the White Cloud Temple at West Lake to the 1911 Revolution); in *KML*, 4:150–151.

46. *Su-pao*, p. 388 (May 4, 1903).

47. Chiang Wei-ch'iao, p. 485.

48. Feng, *I-shih*, p. 115; Tso Shun-sheng, *Chung-kuo chin-tai shih ssu-chiang* (Four essays on modern Chinese history; Hong Kong, 1962), p. 87.

49. *NCH*, 69:433 (8/27/02).

50. Chiang Wei-ch'iao, p. 487; *NCH*, 69:433 (8/27/02).

51. Chiang Wei-ch'iao, p. 487, states that over a hundred students withdrew. *KML*, 4:72, says over two hundred. Not all who withdrew joined the Patriotic School. Presumably some went home. Sheng Hsüan-huai tried to persuade students to return and about 30 percent did so according to the estimate in *KML*, 4:73. The names of 145 students who withdrew were listed in *Su-pao* (November 29, 1902); in *HCH*, 2:353–354.

52. *KML*, 4:63, 66; Albert Feuerwerker, *China's Early Industrialization: Sheng Hsüan-huai and Mandarin Enterprise* (Cambridge, Mass., 1958), pp. 69–70. The school was supported by annual grants of 50,000 taels each from Sheng's shipping and telegraph companies. In 1905 it became a school of technology under the Ministry of Commerce and in 1907 a polytechnical institute under the Ministry of Posts and Communications. It eventually became Nan-yang College.

53. *KML,* 4:64.

54. Yü Chao-i, *Ch'iu Chin* (Hong Kong, 1956), p. 41.

55. Feuerwerker, p. 70.

56. *KML*, 4:63–65; *NCH*, 69:1122 (11/26/02); *Su-pao,* 350 (April 28, 1903).

57. *KML*, 4:67–68; *NCH*, 69:1183–1184 (12/03/02).

58. *KML*, 4:68.

59. *NCH*, 69:1122 (11/26/02); Yü Chao-i, p. 50.

60. *KML,* 4:69. A slightly different version relates that Kuo Chen-ying questioned a student who falsely accused another student of being responsible. Kuo had the student he named expelled and the other students in the Fifth Form given major demerits for trying to shield him. The demands of the striking students were for the dismissal of Kuo and of the student who made the accusation and for the reinstatement of the expelled student. *HCH*, 2:350–351.

61. *KML,* 4:70.

62. *NCH*, 69:1122 (11/26/02).

63. *KML,* 4:73.

64. "Nan-yang kung-hsüeh t'ui-hsüeh-sheng i-chien shu" (A letter expressing the views of the students who withdrew from the Nan-yang Public Institute), *Su-pao*

(November 25, 1902); in *HCH*, 2:352.

65. Chiang Wei-ch'iao, p. 487.

66. *KML,* 4:73.

67. Chiang Wei-ch'iao, p. 488.

68. *KML,* 4:76.

69. Tu Ch'eng-hsiang, *Tsou Jung* (Nanking, 1946), p. 70; Ch'en Hsiung, *Min-tsu ko-ming wen-hsien* (Documents on the nationalist revolution; Taipei, 1954), p. 4.

70. *KML,* 4:76–77.

71. Chiang Wei-ch'iao, p. 488. For instance, Ts'ai Yüan-p'ei was head of the Commercial Press translation bureau. Wu Chih-hui worked for the *Wen-ming shu-chü*. Chiang Wei-ch'iao translated Japanese newspapers for *Su-pao*. Science teachers were drawn from members of the *K'o-hsüeh i-ch'i kuan*.

72. Tu Ch'eng-hsiang, p. 72; Chang Huang-ch'i, "*Su-pao* an shih-lu" (A true account of the *Su-pao* case); in *HHKM*, 1:368.

73. Chiang Wei-ch'iao, p. 489.

74. Feng, *I-shih,* 1:116; Chiang Wei-ch'iao, pp. 489–490.

75. Chiang Wei-ch'iao, p. 488.

76. E.g., *Su-pao,* p. 184 (March 31, 1903); p. 380 (May 3, 1903).

77. Chiang Wei-ch'iao, p. 490, says that there were 96 faculty and student members of the student army organized at the Patriotic School in 1903. It is not clear whether any students from other schools were included. Feng, *I-shih,* 3:76, says there were 138 members of the school. *HCH*, 2:357, gives the figure 132 students.

78. Feng, *I-shih,* 1:123; Tu Ch'eng-hsiang, p. 71. After the *Su-pao* case, Hsü continued his customary book-selling and speech-making activities. Eventually he was reported to the Ch'ing officials, who found a way to entice him to Nanking and arrest him. There, so the story goes, some officials argued that because his name was so inelegant he could not really be a member of the revolutionary party and should be allowed another chance. He was released and returned to Shanghai. Revolutionaries feared that he had made a deal to turn informer. However, he did not aid the government. Neither did he resume his old propaganda activities, but dropped out of sight. At some point, I do not know whether before or after his arrest, his daughter died. This blow considerably reduced his effectiveness and may have contributed to his foresaking revolutionary work.

79. Chiang Wei-ch'iao, p. 488; *KML,* 4:75. The latter source says there was a senate which was responsible for disciplinary cases among other functions. There is no mention of a senate in the regulations of the Patriotic School (*HCH*, 2:361–362). The Educational Association did have a senate (*Su-pao*, p. 350; March 5, 1903), and so the *KML* source may have been confusing the two organizations.

80. "Regulations of the Patriotic School," in *HCH*, 2:361–362.

81. *Ibid.*

82. Chiang Wei-ch'iao, p. 488; *KML,* 4:76.

83. *KML,* 4:75.

84. Feng, *I-shih,* 1:118.

85. The first meeting using this name was held on February 15, 1903. A report on the second appears in *Su-pao,* pp. 100–101 (March 16, 1903).

86. *Ibid.,* p. 101 (March 16, 1903); p. 172 (March 28, 1903).

87. Chiang Wei-ch'iao, pp. 489–490.

88. Sun Te-chung, p. 153.

89. Ch'en Hsieh-fen was an accomplished essayist who helped her father with *Su-pao* in addition to her activities at the Patriotic Girls' School and managing *The Women's Journal*. When the *Su-pao* case broke, she fled with Ch'en Fan to Japan, where she studied and continued to play a part in radical student politics. After graduation

from a Christian girls' school in Yokohama, she went to study in the United States. Feng, *I-shih*, 3:86.

90. Chiang Wei-ch'iao, pp. 487–488.

91. Feng Tzu-yu, *Chung-kuo ko-ming yün-tung erh-shih-liu nien tsu-chih shih* (Twenty-six-years organizational history of the Chinese revolutionary movement; Shanghai, 1948), pp. 70–71.

92. *Su-pao*, p. 106 (March 17, 1903); p. 133 (March 21, 1903).

93. Lo Chia-ling donated five hundred yuan to the Chekiangese students. *Su-pao*, p. 324 (April 23, 1903). The school established by the Chekiangese students was called the New People's School (*Hsin-min shu*) in *Su-pao* (p. 293; April 18, 1903) and the Determination School (*Li-chih hsüeh-she*) in *Tides of Chekiang* (*CCC*, 4:116). Late in the summer the Determination School combined with another school to form the Chekiang Public Institute (*Liang-Che kung-hsüeh*). *CCC*, 8:174.

94. Feng, *I-shih*, 1:118–119.

95. *Su-pao*, p. 94 (March 15, 1903).

96. A fund-raising letter sent to overseas Chinese clearly shows how the Educational Association linked the Patriotic School to the regeneration of China. The letter asserted that the difference between strong and weak countries was a knowledgeable or ignorant population. However, Chinese education was poisoned by tyranny and the students' capacity destroyed by incessant drills and the accumulation of useless knowledge. Unlike government schools, the Patriotic School was not willing to turn out slaves. Students were very sincere in their studies and possessed a pioneering spirit similar to that of the English who settled North America. The text of the letter appears in Feng, *I-shih*, 1:116–118, and in Ch'en Hsiung, pp. 3–4.

97. The increasingly radical speeches at the Educational Association's meetings in Chang's Garden led to attacks on the association. There were critical articles in *Shen-pao* and *The News* (*Hsin-wen pao*). Wu Chih-hui suggested the association establish a paper to combat the unfavorable publicity.

98. Li Shu-hua, 1:38.

99. Chang Huang-ch'i, p. 367; Chang Hsing-yen, p. 388. Chang Hsing-yen says the paper was originally the organ of the Black Dragon Society. I do not know the basis for this allegation. Shang-hai yen-chiu tzu-liao hsü-chi (Shanghai Research Section), comp., "*Su-pao* an shih-mo" (An account of the *Su-pao* case), in *HCH*, 2:530, says Ch'en Fan bought the paper in 1898. Other sources are vague or give later dates.

100. Except where otherwise noted, the biographical information on Ch'en Fan is from Feng, *I-shih*, 1:120–121.

101. Some of the radicals whom Ch'en Fan met in Tokyo after the *Su-pao* case disapproved of his keeping concubines and Ch'iu Chin undertook to emancipate them. Radicals in Tokyo were also upset by reports that Ch'en tried to insist that his revolutionary daughter become the concubine of a Cantonese merchant. *Ibid.*, 2:178.

102. Chang Huang-ch'i, p. 367.

103. Chün-tu Hsüeh, *Huang Hsing and the Chinese Revolution* (Stanford, 1961), pp. 9, 13. In early 1903 *Su-pao* became the Shanghai outlet for the *Translations by Students Abroad*.

104. Chang Huang-ch'i, p. 367.

105. Ch'en Fan was not directly responsible for *Su-pao*'s revolutionary course, but he had to assume the blame. He fled to Japan at the beginning of July. There he called on Sun Yat-sen and associated with other revolutionaries. After a year or two in Japan he went to Hong Kong to visit the offices of the revolutionary *Chinese Daily*. He ran out of money to support himself abroad and had to return to Shanghai the next year. He was arrested, but friends procured his release. During the next few years Ch'en was commonly short of funds. He also drank a lot. His brother-in-law Wang

Wen-p'u had been appointed magistrate of Li-ling district in Hunan, but was dismissed because of the P'ing-Liu-Li rising in 1906, which was partly inspired by the revolutionaries. After that Wang went to Changsha, where he worked to overthrow the government, and Ch'en traveled about Hunan helping him. At some point Wang was arrested, but Ch'en and others managed to have him released. Evidently Ch'en remained in Hunan until the Revolution. In 1911 he and Wang joined the Hunan-Kwangsi revolutionary army after Han-yang fell to the revolutionary forces. However, they soon resigned and went to Shanghai because they felt that the commander was not using his forces to their full effect. After 1911 Ch'en tried to resume his newspaper career: first in Shanghai as editor of *The Pacific Ocean* (*T'ai-p'ing-yang pao*) and then in Peking as manager of *The Democrat* (*Min-chu pao*). Not long after going to Peking he fell ill and returned to Shanghai, where he died in January 1913 at the age of fifty-three. Feng, *I-shih*, 1:120–121.

106. Feng, *Chung-hua*, 1:134. It is difficult to estimate the number of copies published. One report says circulation reached a thousand by the end of June. J. Lust, "The *Su-pao* Case," *Bulletin of the School of Oriental and African Studies*, University of London, 27.2:413 (1964). Lust cites F. O. 228/1505, 19/03 from the British Foreign Office archives. The March issue of *Tides of Chekiang* lists fifty copies of *Su-pao* among the papers sold in Hangchow. *CCC*, 3:195. If this figure is correct and refers to daily sales, it might indicate that the total figure was above a thousand if as many as fifty were sold in Hangchow alone.

107. Accounts of student withdrawals or unrest appear in many issues of *Su-pao* during March, April, and May. I have not tabulated all of them. A check of complaints from twenty schools gives the following breakdown of issues:

Prohibition of free discussions and new books, conservative teachers	7
Unfair discipline or expulsion of students	7
General allegations of tyranny, conservatism, corruption	7
Refusal to expel a homosexual student	1
Strict school regulations	1
Bad food	1
Pressure to become Christian	1
Some students demanded that they only study physical education	1
Rivalry and fighting between schools	1

Most of the reports came from Chekiang and Kiangsu, but some came from a considerable number of other provinces. There is a definite concentration on Central China, either indicating that student unrest was greater in this area or that *Su-pao* had superior news sources there. The two major student incidents during the spring of 1903, the withdrawal of thirty-two students from Nanking Military Academy on April 3 and of most of the students in Chekiang College on April 17, were reported in detail.

108. E.g., *Su-pao*, p. 19 (March 2, 1903); p. 54 (March 8, 1903).

109. Examples of articles favoring revolution are found in *Su-pao*, p. 17 (March 12, 1903); p. 145 (March 23, 1903); p. 166 (March 27, 1903). An article appearing on March 14 criticized anti-Manchuism as irresponsible. *Su-pao*, p. 89 (March 14, 1903). The most frankly revolutionary article before Chang Shih-chao became editor appeared in mid-May. *Su-pao*, p. 454 (May 13, 1903). However, some later articles were still basically reformist. E.g., *Su-pao*, p. 470 (May 16, 1903).

110. Li Shu-hua, 2:10.

4. Beginnings of Revolutionary Activity in Shanghai II: The Clash with the Government

1. In May 1903 it was announced that Chang's Garden would soon be leased to a

Western company as an amusement park, thus curbing its use by Chinese. *NCH*, 70:885 (5/7/03).

2. *NCH*, 70:832 (4/30/03). The French ambassador to Peking and the Hanoi government strongly denied the rumors. J. Lust, "The *Su-pao* Case," *Bulletin of the School of Oriental and African Studies,* University of London, 27.2:416 (1964).

3. Lai Hsin-hsia, "Shih-lun Ch'ing Kuang-hsü mo-nien ti Kuang-hsi jen-min ta ch'i-i" (The great rising of the Kwangsi people in the last years of the Kuang-hsü period), *Li-shih yen-chiu* (Historical research), 11:65–70 (1957). This was a purely traditional rebellion. However, certain secret society leaders such as Wang Ho-shun joined the Revolutionary Alliance after defeat. See Feng, *I-shih,* 2:216–217.

4. Chiang Wei-ch'iao, "Chung-kuo chiao-yü hui chih hui-i" (Recollections of the Chinese Educational Association); in *HHKM,* 1:489–490.

5. *NCH, 70:834* (4/30/03); *Su-pao,* p. 332 (April 25, 1903).

6. Many of the students attending the meeting were from the Patriotic School, but some other Shanghai schools were also represented. Some students from the Nanyang Public Institute attended and signed the manifesto. They were disciplined by school authorities who took the view that students should not interfere in matters which the central government was handling. *Su-pao,* p. 365 (April 30, 1903).

7. Lung Tse-hou (Lung Chi-chih) was a native of Kueilin, Kwangsi. He was a member of the lower gentry who in 1887 had become a senior licentiate by recommendation (*yu-kung*). He received the rank of expectant district magistrate and in 1891 was appointed to a post in Szechwan. He served in that province until he returned home for mourning upon the death of his father. Lung participated in the National Association·(*Kuo-hui*) and in T'ang Ts'ai-ch'ang's rebellion. After its failure he returned to Shanghai, where he was active in reformist circles. *NCH*, 71:1246 (12/11/03); Feng, *I-shih,* 3:55.

8. *NCH, 70:834–835* (4/30/03).

9. *NCH*, 71:226 (7/31/03).

10. Speeches by Educational Association members are summarized in *Su-pao. Su-pao*, pp. 344–346 (April 27, 1903). The proposal for a nationwide militia was made by Ch'ien Yün-sheng, a somewhat dubious character who associated with the Patriotic School group and was one of the defendants at the *Su-pao* trial that summer.

11. *NCH,* 70:832 (4/30/03); Feng, *Chung-hua,* 1:130. The proposal for the telegram was made by Lung Tse-hou. *Su-pao,* p. 344 (April 27, 1903). Telegrams were also sent to students in Tokyo and gentry in Kwangtung and Kwangsi. *Hsin-min ts'ung-pao,* 30:115.

12. *NCH,* 70:835 (4/30/03); Feng, *Chung-hua,* 1:130; *Su-pao,* p. 350 (April 28, 1903); *Hsin-min ts'ung-pao,* 30:115. The *Hsin-min ts'ung-pao* account states that the proposals for boycotts and strikes were made at the April 28 meeting.

13. *NCH,* 71:398 (8/21/03); *Hsin-min ts'ung-pao,* 31:77. Protest meetings were held in Hangchow, Hong Kong, Canton, and other places in Kwantung and Kwangsi, and presumably in other major cities. According to the *North China Herald,* Ch'ü Hung-chi, a Hunanese member of the Grand Council, interceded for Wang Chih-ch'un and prevented his further punishment. Ch'ü argued that given the unrest in the country it would be unwise to arrest a high official whose only real fault was that he did not command enough troops. Wang's dismissal was perhaps not as great a triumph for public opinion as it seemed, for he was in danger of being dismissed anyway for failure to suppress the rebellion.

14. *Su-pao,* pp. 398–399 (May 6, 1903).

15. *Ibid.* The Educational Association was impressed by the rising merchant nationalism and welcomed it, but the radical scholars and merchants lacked real rapport. Reformers were almost as upset as radicals over the threat to Chinese sovereignty

in Manchuria, but favored strengthening the country by reforming, not overthrowing, the government. *Hsin-min ts'ung-pao*, 30:59–60.

16. *NCH*, 70:832 (4/30/03).

17. *Ibid.;* Feng, *Chung-hua*, 1:128–129.

18. The regulations of the Citizens' Committee, which were published in *Su-pao* on May 31, 1903, are reprinted in *HCH*, 2:377. The committee adopted an elaborate constitution of fifty-one articles. It dealt at length with rights and duties of members and officers, elections, meetings, and procedures at meetings. Since the group collapsed quickly, the regulations are not of great interest except as an example of the constitution-making complex which pervaded radical circles.

19. *Su-pao*, p. 363 (May 1, 1903). *Hsin-min ts'ung-pao*, 23:63–64. The Citizens' Committee also planned a middle school with a curriculum designed to renovate the people.

20. Feng, *I-shih*, 2:78–79; *Su-pao*, p. 299 (May 6, 1903). Feng Ching-ju was a Cantonese merchant in Yokohama who headed the Yokohama branch of the Hsing-Chung hui. In 1903 he was in Shanghai as manager of the Bookshop for Diffusion of Knowledge.

21. *NCH*, 70:885 (5/7/03); *Su-pao*, pp. 368–369 (May 1, 1903).

22. *Su-pao*, pp. 398–399 (May 6, 1903).

23. *Ibid.*, p. 399 (May 6, 1903).

24. Feng, *I-shih*, 2:79.

25. Wu Chih-hui, "Wu Chih-hui shu Shang-hai *Su-pao* an chi-shih" (Wu Chih-hui recounts the *Su-pao* case); in Feng, *I-shih*, 3:175.

26. Chang Hsing-yen (Chang Shih-chao), "*Su-pao* an shih-mo chi-hsü" (A complete narration of the *Su-pao* case); in *HHKM*, 1:390.

27. Chang Shih-chao was from Changsha, Hunan. After the *Su-pao* arrests he briefly fled to Japan, where he began to study English; he then returned to Shanghai to found the radical *China National Gazette* later in 1903. When it was closed, he again went to Japan, joined in founding the Society for China's Revival, and then helped Huang Hsing plan his abortive Changsha rising in the fall of 1904. He was one of those arrested after Wan Fu-hua's attempt to assassinate Wang Chih-ch'un, although he was not involved in the plot. In 1905 he refused to join the Revolutionary Alliance. Later he studied law and economics at the University of London and his revolutionary activities became secondary. He did, however, contribute to *The People's Stand* (*Min-li pao*) from London in 1911 and edited the paper from January to July 1912. Soon after the Revolution, Chang became much more conservative. He held aloof from the May Fourth Movement and particularly opposed the use of the written vernacular. In 1925 he was minister of justice and minister of education in Tuan Ch'i-jui's government in Peking. For some of Chang's activities during the May Fourth period see Chow Tse-tsung, *The May Fourth Movement* (Cambridge, Mass., 1960), pp. 216, 270–271, 272, 282–283.

28. Chang Chi (1882–1947) was a Chihli native who went to study at Waseda University in Tokyo in 1900. In 1901 he joined the staff of the revolutionary paper. *The Chinese National* and in 1902 was a co-founder of the Youth Association. He was one of the students who cut off the queue of the superintendent of Chinese military students in Tokyo, Yao Wen-fu, and he fled to Shanghai with Tsou Jung in May 1903. That summer and autumn he served on the staff of *The China National Gazette*. In December 1903 he joined the Society for China's Revival in Changsha and taught at the radical Ming-te School there. In 1905 he joined the Revolutionary Alliance. He spent much of 1906 traveling in Southeast Asia and then returned to Japan. During 1907 he edited *The People's Journal* (*Min-pao*). In 1908 he went to Paris. Chang had been interested in anarchism as early as 1903, and in Paris he joined the staff

of the anarchist journal *New Century*. He remained in Europe until the 1911 Wu-chang rising. After the Revolution he was a member of the Kuomintang and followed Sun Yat-sen through his vicissitudes. He held various party and government posts under the Nationalist government until his death. Kuomintang, Committee for the Compilation of Materials on the Party History of the Central Executive Committee, ed., *Ko-ming hsien-lieh hsien-chin chuan* (Biographies of martyrs and forebearers of the revolution; Taipei, 1965), pp. 754–769.

29. The story of Chang Shih-chao's appointment as editor is from Chang Hsing-yen, p. 388. Wu's suggestion that Ch'en was looking for a son-in-law appears in Feng, *I-shih*, 3:174. The editorial Chang drafted appeared in *Su-pao* on June 8.

30. Charles O. Hucker, "The Tung-lin Movement of the late Ming Period"; in John K. Fairbank, ed., *Chinese Thought and Institutions* (Chicago, 1957), pp. 132–162.

31. The definition and history of *Ch'ing-i* is discussed in Lloyd Eastman, "Ch'ing-i and Chinese Policy Formation During the Nineteenth Century," *Journal of Asian Studies*, 24.4:595–600.

32. Ai-tu-*Ko-ming chün*-che (Chang Shih-chao), "Tu *Ko-ming chün*" (Read *The revolutionary army*), *Su-pao* (June 9, 1903); in *SLHC*, 1.2:683–685. *Su-pao* also published Chang Ping-lin's preface to *The Revolutionary Army*.

33. Tzu-jan sheng (Chang Chi), "Tu Yen-na liu-hsüeh-sheng mi-yü yu-fen" (Anger at reading the secret edict ordering the arrest of the returned students), *Su-pao* (June 10–11, 1903); in *SLHC*, 1.2:685–686. The *Su-pao* articles during June were noteworthy for their extremely violent attacks on Manchus. It is not clear whether the students at the Patriotic School were genuinely more anti-Manchu and those in Japan more nationalistic. Chang Ping-lin's vehement anti-Manchuism may have influenced the tone of more articles than he actually wrote. Not all the articles which appeared during June were extraordinarily violent. Nationalism clearly played a part in crystallizing the revolutionary movement in Shanghai as well as in Japan. Possibly the *Su-pao* authors were simply carried away by their own propaganda. Exhortations to kill the Manchus may show the influence of Russian terrorism.

34. "K'ang Yu-wei," *Su-pao* (June 1, 1903); in *SLHC*, 1.2:681; Chang Ping-lin, "Po K'ang Yu-wei shu," in *HCH*, 2:601–602. High officials were also attacked. Yüan Shih-k'ai was accused of toadying to the empress-dowager for his own advantage. He desired to become Pei-yang Commissioner for the same reason Ts'ao Ts'ao became prime minister, i.e., he aspired to the throne himself. However, Yüan lacked the abilities of a Ming T'ai-tsu, so his ambitions were of no use to the Chinese race. He could not lead a restoration of Chinese rule. Je-erh-wei-hun-chu, "Tu Chün-kuo-min chiao-yü hui chi-chüan chi'i" (On reading An appeal for contributions by the Association for Universal Military Education), *Su-pao* (June 6, 1903); in *HCH*, 2:110. In light of Yüan's later attempt to become emperor, this is an interesting statement.

35. "K'ang Yu-wei," p. 682.

36. Han-chung-chih-chung-i-Han-chung, "Po ko-ming po-i" (Arguing against opposition to revolution), *Su-pao* (June 12–13, 1903); in *SLHC*, 1.2:688–692. The authorship of this article is attributed to Ts'ai Chih-min and Chang Ping-lin in Ch'en Hsiung, comp., *Min-tsu ko-ming wen-hsien* (Documents on the nationalist revolution; Taipei, 1954), p. 146.

37. "Fan-mien chih fan-mien shuo" (On the opposite of the opposite), *Su-pao* (June 23, 1903); in *SLHC*, 1.2:698–699.

38. "Hsü-wu tang" (The nihilist party), *Su-pao* (June 19, 1903); in *SLHC*, 1.2:696–698.

39. "Sha-jen chu-i" (The doctrine of killing men), *Su-pao* (June 22, 1903); excerpt in Mixed Court, "Verbatim Report," *NCH*, 71:144 (7/17/03).

40. "Ho Man-chou-jen" (Congratulations to the Manchus), *Su-pao* (June 18, 1903);

excerpt in *Ibid.,* p. 143.

41. In his letter to K'ang Yu-wei, for instance, Chang accused the Manchus of the usual abuses, but embellished them with such passages as this one: "Since 1895 the emperor in great anxiety has shrunk from looking about and sits on the throne without warming it, thinking only that the empress-dowager might set him aside. Since he despaired of the internal situation, he laid plans for foreign developments. He knew that without reform he could not communicate with foreigners on a satisfactory basis and, if he could not do so, he would not have their support to quash the empress-dowager's power. Tsai-t'ien, a little clown who cannot distinguish rice from wheat; a deer driven almost to death, he certainly does not give a thought to the whole of the Manchu territory." Chang Ping-lin, "Po K'ang Yu-wei shu" (Letter disputing K'ang Yu-wei); in *HCH,* 2:594. The use of the emperor's personal name was, of course, a deliberate insult which caused this passage to be cited as part of the charges against Chang at the trial. This is not the only place where Chang charges members of the court with personal incompetence as well as attacking Manchus in general.

42. Tzu-jan-sheng (Chang Chi), Mi-yü, p. 685.

43. Tzu-jan-sheng (Chang Chi), "Chu Pei-ching Ta-hsüeh-t'ang hsüeh-sheng" (Extolling the students at Peking University), *Su-pao* (June 6, 1903); in *SLHC,* 1.2:683.

44. Chiang Wei-ch'iao, p. 496. This was a reformist argument.

45. Chang Wen-po, *Chih-lao hsien-hua* (Chats about Wu Chih-hui; Taipei, 1952), p. 15.

46. Chiang Wei-ch'iao, pp. 490–491; Wu Chih-hui, in Feng, *I-shih,* 3:175.

47. Wu Chih-hui, in Feng, *I-shih,* 3:175.

48. The split between the Patriotic School and the Educational Association is commemorated in "Ching-hsieh Chiao-yü hui" (Respectful thanks to the Educational Association), *Su-pao* (June 19, 1903); in *HCH,* 2:359–361. This article affirmed the school's determination to chart its own course, even though the students did not disagree with the Educational Association on principles. The Educational Association reply was by Huang Tsung-yang, "Ho Ai-kuo hsüeh-she chih tu-li" (Congratulations on the independence of the Patriotic School), *Su-pao* (June 25, 1903); in *HCH,* 2:354–356.

49. E.g., see the telegram to the Liang-Kiang governor-general to ask if Sun Yat-sen was one of the Kwangsi secret society rebels. *Kuo-min jih-jih-pao* (The China National Gazette; photolithograph, Taipei, 1965), p. 434 (October 18, 1903).

50. "Telegram from Grand Council to Governors and Governors-General," *Su-pao,* June 6, 1903, p. 1; reprinted in *HCH,* 2:134.

51. *NCH,* 70:1046 (6/4/03); Feng, *Chung-hua,* 1:135.

52. For an example of the wide initiative Tuan-fang took with regard to the *Su-pao* case see "Telegram of Acting Hu-kuang Governor-General Tuan-fang to the Grand Council dated June 23, 1903," in *HHKM,* 1:443.

53. For a biography of Tuan-fang, see Arthur W. Hummel, ed., *Eminent Chinese of the Ch'ing Period,* 2 vols. (Washington, D.C., 1943–1944), 2:781–782.

54. Chang Huang-ch'i, "*Su-pao* an shih-lu" (A true account of the *Su-pao* case); in *HHKM,* 1:372.

55. Chang Wen-po, *Chih-lao,* p. 15.

56. Chang Wen-po, *Wu Ching-heng,* p. 9. The significance of the inquiry as to whether Wu Chih-hui and others possessed arms was that the Municipal Council considered the public meetings and the articles in *Su-pao* to be legitimate expressions of opinion, but using the Settlement as a base from which to prepare an armed rising would be grounds for arrest.

57. Wu Chih-hui, in Feng, *I-shih,* 3:175; *Hsin-min ts'ung-pao,* 31:114.

58. J. Lust, "The *Su-pao* Case," *Bulletin of the School of Oriental and African Studies,*

University of London, 27:2 (1964), p. 425. Wei Kuang-tao's subordinates such as Yü Ming-chen were also suspected as being overliberal, which further reflected on Wei. "Telegram of Tuan-fang to Wei Kuang-tao dated July 6, 1907," in *HHKM*, 1:453.

59. Chang Huang-ch'i, p. 372.

60. *NCH*, 71:69 (7/10/03); A. M. Kotenev, *Shanghai: Its Mixed Court and Council* (Shanghai, 1925), p. 108. The Chinese authorities had tried unsuccessfully to have a proclamation condemning the anti-Wang meetings posted in the International Settlement. Lü Hai-huan's requests evidently also stressed the subversiveness of the speeches.

61. Correspondence between W. G. Bayne, Chairman, Shanghai Municipal Council, and John Goodnow, U.S. Consul-General and Senior Consul, *NCH*, 71:69–70 (7/10/03).

62. Chang Huang-ch'i, pp. 372–373. The comment on the Patriotic School was taken from an "Edict transmitted by the Wai-wu pu to the Governors-General and Governors of the Coastal and Yangtze provinces dated June 21, 1903," in *HHKM*, 1:408. An English translation appears in *NCH*, 71:21 (7/3/03). The edict in turn quoted a telegram received from Governor-General Wei Kuang-tao for its information on the school. Ch'en Shu-ch'ou did not exist. The name was evidently an alias of Ch'en Fan.

63. It was believed at the time that Lung was arrested for his activities at Chang's Garden. See *NCH*, 71:75 (7/10/03).

64. Chang Hsing-yen, p. 390.

65. Chang Huang-ch'i, p. 373.

66. *Ibid.* Chang Huang-ch'i so suggests, and there seems no other good reason why Chang Shih-chao should not have been arrested. Recalling the incident, Chang Shih-chao did not deny that this was the case, but he also said that after leaving the Nanking Military Academy he had broken with Yü and had attacked him in *Su-pao*. He also claimed to have been out of town distributing revolutionary literature when the arrests occurred. Chang Hsing-yen, p. 390. Such a temporary absence, however, would not explain why his name was not on the warrant.

67. Wu Chih-hui, in Feng, *I-shih*, 3:176–178.

68. Chang Shih-chao's father-in-law was Wu Yen-fu, the son of General Wu Ch'ang-ch'ing. Wu Ch'ang-ch'ing was a protégé of Li Hung-chang, who in 1882 led Chinese troops to suppress rebellion in Korea. He entered Seoul and forced the Taiwonkun, father of the Korean king, to accompany him back to China. *HHKM*, 1:405; Hummel, 1:483; 2:950.

69. This is a blend of accounts in Feng, *I-shih*, 3:178–179; Chang Huang-ch'i, pp. 375–376; and Feng, *Chung-hua*, 1:135. There are discrepancies in these accounts as to the exact order and dates of the arrests. Wu Chih-hui claims that Ch'en Chi-fu was arrested and Ch'en Fan recognized but not arrested on the evening of June 28. Therefore, the first arrests had occurred before he went to see Chang Ping-lin and Chang was all the more obstinate in brushing off Wu's warning. Probably this is inaccurate. Other accounts place these arrests on the 29th. Some accounts place all arrests but that of Tsou Jung on the 29th and others on the 29th and 30th. All agree that Tsou gave himself up on July 1. For Chinese official confusion over Ch'en Fan's son see, for instance, "Telegram of Dr. J. C. Ferguson to Tuan-fang dated July 1, 1903," in *HHKM*, 1:409. The mistake was realized by July 3. See "Telegram of Shanghai Taotai Yüan Shu-hsün to Tuan-fang dated July 3, 1903," in *HHKM*, 1:410.

70. The Chinese accused the Municipal Council of obstructing the closing despite the agreement of the United States and British consuls and ordered the Chinese magistrate on the Mixed Court to refuse to try any cases in retaliation. "Telegram of Taotais Yü and Yüan to Tuan-fang dated July 7, 1903," in *HHKM*, 1:415; "Telegram of Dr. J. C. Ferguson to Tuan-fang dated July 7, 1903," in *HHKM*, 1:415–416.

71. After Tsou Jung's death a long controversy began between Chang Ping-lin and Wu Chih-hui. Chang accused Wu of making a deal with Yü Ming-chen whereby he escaped arrest by giving information against the *Su-pao* group. He also claimed that Wu failed to warn the others and contrasted his escape with the righteousness of Tsou Jung and Lung Tse-hou in surrendering themselves. Wu says he tried to warn Chang on the night of the 27th after his dinner with Yü Ming-chen, but Chang would not listen. The basis for Chang's charges is not at all clear, and they seem mainly to have been the product of the animosity between the two men. Certainly Wu had little sympathy with Chang Ping-lin's intention to accept arrest in order to make the *Su-pao* case a cause célèbre. Chang, on the other hand, considered Wu's escape cowardly and a betrayal in itself. Since all the evidence indicates that Chang deliberately courted arrest, it seems unnecessary to suggest any treachery on Wu's part. The basic facts about *Su-pao* and the Patriotic School were well known to officials, and the trial record gives no indication of any unusual information that might have come from Wu. Chang Ping-lin, "Yü Wu Chih-hui t'an *Su-pao* an shu" (Letters to Wu Chih-hui discussing the *Su-pao* case); in *HHKM*, 1:398–400; Wu Chih-hui; in Feng Tzu-yu, *I-shih*, 3:179. Besides the writings of Chang and Wu, some of the issues involved are discussed in Chang Shih-chao, "Su *Huang-ti hun*" (An explanation of *The soul of Huang-ti*); in *KML*, 1:275–278.

72. *NCH*, 71:341 (8/14/03).

73. Orders restricting "new books" in the schools were reportedly promulgated by Governor-General Wei Kuang-tao. *Kuo-min jih-jih-pao*, p. 96 (August 16, 1903). School authorities at the Chiang-pei Higher School read student letters for subversive material. *Kuo-min jih-jih-pao*, p. 190 (Sept. 23, 1903).

74. For examples of reports of other arrests see *NCH*, 71:421–422 (8/21/03); "Lun Shen Chin ts'an-ssu shih" (On the cruel death of Shen Chin), *CCC;* in *HHKM*, 1:309; *Kuo-min jih-jih-pao*, pp. 38–39 (Aug. 10, 1903). Large numbers were reported arrested in Yangchow and forty-seven in Shanghai. The Yangchow reports were rumors. *Kuo-min jih-jih-pao*, p. 200 (September 24, 1903). Four men were arrested in the Shanghai area and released on missionary intervention. *Kuo-min jih-jih-pao*, pp. 158–159 (August 22, 1903). Some other Shanghai reports were probably spurious.

75. Huang Chung-huang (Chang Shih-chao), "Shen Chin," in *HHKM*, 1:287–303. This author believes Shen was a revolutionary. *Kuo-min jih-jih-pao*, pp. 18–19 (August 8, 1903); *Hsin-min ts'ung-pao*, 35:114–115. For fears aroused by the palace negotiations see *Hsin-min ts'ung-pao*, 33:65; 34:56–57.

76. "*Su-pao* an" (The *Su-pao* case); in *SLHC*, 1.2:777.

77. *Ibid.*, pp. 284–307; "Lun Shen Chin ts'an-ssu shih," in *HHKM*, 1:308–311; *NCH*, 71:421 (8/21/03); 71:701 (10/2/03); *Hsin-min ts'ung-pao*, 35:78.

78. "Telegram of Tuan-fang to Chang Chih-tung dated August 27, 1903," in *HHKM*, 1:476; "Telegram of Yüan Shu-hsün to Tuan-fang and En-shou dated September 4, 1903," in *HHKM*, 1:435.

79. Feng, *I-shih*, 2:82.

80. *NCH*, 71:225 (7/24/03). *The Shanghai Times* was also opposed on similar grounds. See *HCH*, 2:655–657. *Hsin-min ts'ung-pao*, 23:64–65.

81. *Hsin-min ts'ung-pao*, 31:64; 33:64–65; 35:77.

82. E.g., the account in J. Lust, 422–429.

83. "Telegram of Grand Secretary Chang Chih-tung to Tuan-fang dated July 21, 1903," in *HHKM*, 1:427–428.

84. Ch'en Hsü-lu, p. 30. The French press was also less favorably inclined toward the prisoners than was the English-language press. See the *North China Daily News* article translated in *HCH*, 2:658–659. United States Consul-General Conger favored extradition because he feared revolutionary activity would lead to secret society risings

in which foreigners would be killed. The French favored extradition partly to embarrass the British.

85. "Telegram of Chang Chih-tung to Tuan-fang dated August 22, 1903," in *HHKM*, 1:432; "Telegram of Tuan-fang to Dr. J. C. Ferguson dated August 23, 1903," in *HHKM*, 1:472; "Telegram of Tuan-fang to Chang Chih-tung dated August 25, 1903," in *HHKM*, 1:475; "Telegram of Tuan-fang to Chang Chih-tung dated July 16, 1903," in *HHKM*, 1:465. The main concessions which the government offered were that the defendants would be imprisoned rather than executed and that the charges against Ch'ien Yün-sheng, Ch'en Chi-fu, and Ch'en Chung-i would be dropped. Chinese officials by then knew that they were not important. Ch'en Chi-fu was an accountant for *Su-pao*. Ch'ien Yün-sheng was a "*liu-min*" from Chinkiang. He attended meetings in Chang's Garden and often spoke there. Ch'en Fan trusted him and he was employed by the Women's Journal (*Nü-pao*). Both Wu Chih-hui and Chang Shih-chao disliked and distrusted him. They believed that he was trying to get money from Ch'en by posing as a follower of Sun Yat-sen trying to promote a rising in Kwangsi. Wu Chih-hui, in Feng, *I-shih*, 3:180; Chang Hsing-yen, p. 389. Chang Ping-lin adds that Lung Tse-hou had once hired Ch'ien when Lung was in Chinkiang. Later Ch'ien got into trouble for stealing. Eventually he fled to Shanghai, where he took part in meetings and said he was a member of the Triads. *HCH*, 2:631–632.

86. "Telegram of Yüan Shu-hsün to Tuan-fang dated December 7, 1903," in *HHKM*, 1:440–441; Mixed Court, "Verbatim Report," *NCH*, 71:1246 (12/11/03).

87. Chang Huang-ch'i, p. 384; *NCH*, 72:1121 (5/27/04); 72:1175 (6/2/04); "Communication from Shanghai Taotai to Senior Consul General," in *HCH*, 2:653–654.

88. Shen Yen-kuo, *Chi Chang T'ai-yen hsien-sheng* (Recollections of Chang T'ai-yen; Shanghai, 1946), p. 17.

89. Mixed Court, "Verbatim Report," *NCH*, 71:1250–1251 (12/11/03).

90. *Ibid.,* pp. 1251–1252.

91. *Ibid., NCH*, 71:1301–1302 (12/18/03). A portion of the transcript of Tsou Jung's examination by the prosecution is as follows:

Answer: I don't want to dethrone the dynasty, but I want to be a second Rousseau.
Question: Do you want to bring about another French revolution?
Answer: If Rousseau was a revolutionist why was a monument erected to him?
Question: Then you don't want to produce a revolution in China?
Answer: No; my idea is that there should be no rich and no poor, but everyone should be on the same footing.

92. Chang Ping-lin's reply from jail to *Hsin-wen pao* was published in *Su-pao* on July 6, 1903. It is reprinted in Chang Huang-ch'i, pp. 378–379. In it he recounted how he reached his revolutionary views and maintained that the *Su-pao* case was one of the Manchu government against the 400 million Chinese people represented by the prisoners. The case, therefore, should be tried by the English and Americans, who were neutral in the struggle. He concluded with an emotional appeal to end Chinese slavery and restore the ancient condition of Chinese rule. Until then no reform would be possible. Ch'en T'ien-hua discussed the trial in the seventh chapter of his *Lion's Roar (Shih-tzu hou)* (Ch'en T'ien-hua, *Ch'en T'ien-hua chi* [A collection of writings by Ch'en T'ien-hua; Shanghai, 1946], pp. 75–78). In August "Yü-hsüeh sheng" (pseud. meaning born bathed in blood) wrote *The Story of the Revolutionary Army (Ko-ming chün ch'uan-ch'i)*, see Ch'en Hsü-lu, p. 31; *Chiang-su*, 6:97–104. An article entitled *The Su-pao Case*, also written during the trial, was included in the miscellany of revolutionary writings, *The Soul of Huang-ti* ("*Su-pao an,*" in *SLHC*, 1.2:775–780).

93. Mark Elvin, "The Mixed Court of the International Settlement at Shanghai (until 1911)," *Papers on China*, 17:144–145 (1963), Harvard University, East Asian Research Center. Conditions in the Mixed Court jail were probably typical of Chinese

jails, but they were bad enough by Western standards to produce demands for reform. In 1904 the Municipal Council summarily took charge of all Chinese male prisoners, so an improvement probably occurred while Chang and Tsou were in jail.

94. *NCH*, 75:28 (4/7/05); *HHKM*, 1:394–397. This is an account of a visit to Chang Ping-lin in jail by Chang Huang-ch'i.

95. Revolutionaries in Japan sent Chang Chi to Shanghai to investigate the charge. See Tu Ch'eng-hsiang, *Tsou Jung* (Nanking, 1946), p. 84. Many students were aroused and upset. E.g., Wu Yüeh wrote Chang Ping-lin expressing his suspicions about Tsou's death (Feng, *I-shih*, 3:197).

96. Hsü Hsi-lin believed the reports firmly enough to make an unsuccessful trip to Shanghai to procure Chang Ping-lin's release. T'ao, "Che-an," p. 57.

97. Chang Huang-ch'i, pp. 384–385.

5. The Urban Revolutionary Environment: Continued Activity in Shanghai

1. Information about the Educational Association and the Patriotic Girls' School after the beginning of the *Su-pao* case comes mostly from Chiang Wei-ch'iao, "Chung-kuo chiao-yü hui chih hui-i" (Recollections of the Chinese Educational Association); in *HHKM*, 1:492–495, and also from Feng, *I-shih*, 2:84. Information on the revolutionary aspects of the curriculum is from Ts'ai Yüan-p'ei as told to Huang Shih-hui, "Ts'ai Chieh-min hsien-sheng ti ch'ing-nien shih-tai" (The youth of Ts'ai Chieh-min); in *HCH*, 2:368. The official funds received by the Patriotic Girls' School in 1907–08 were from the Shanghai Taotai and the Kiang-nan Financial Bureau. Aside from the Shanghai institutions, certain branches of the Educational Association, notably the Independence School (*Tzu-li hsüeh-she*) in T'ung-li, Wu-ching hsien, survived the *Su-pao* case. The Patriotic Girls' School was revived after the Revolution. Ts'ai Yüan-p'ei gave a speech there in 1916.

Ch'en Ch'i-mei was among those who attended the Educational Association's evening course.

2. Feng, *I-shih*, 1:125; 2:84; Feng, *Chung-hua*, 1:139; "Wu lieh-shih Yang-ku ko-ming shih" (A revolutionary history of the martyr Wu Yang-ku), in *HHKM*, 7:188.

3. Feng, *I-shih*, 2:85; Feng, *Chung-hua*, 1:141–142; Feng, *Tsu-chih*, p. 76; Chang Hsing-yen, "*Su-pao* an shih-mo chi-hsü" (A complete narration of the *Su-pao* case), in *HHKM*, 1:388–389; *HCH*, 2:539. Former Patriotic School students who worked for *The China National Gazette* included Ho Mei-shih and Liu Ch'i-chi. Ch'en Tu-hsiu was one of the newcomers to the group.

4. *Kuo-min jih-jih-pao* (The China National Gazette; photolithograph, Taipei, 1965), pp. 14–15 (August 8, 1903). This reprint is very incomplete, but it contains enough issues to give a good idea of the nature of the paper.

5. Yen Tu-hou, "Hsin-hai ko-ming shih-ch'i Shang-hai hsin-wen chieh tung-t'ai" (Shanghai newspaper circles during the period of the 1911 Revolution), in *KML*, 4:78.

6. See *Kuo-min jih-jih-pao*, pp. 430–431 (October 17, 1903); pp. 438–439 (October 18, 1903); pp. 450–451 (October 19, 1903). This complex scandal involved prostitutes, a French friend of Lu Ho-sheng's impersonating a policeman, deliberately false accusations, and a fight in the street. Lu ended by being quite unpopular around the newspaper's office. The full facts are a bit obscure.

7. Feng, *I-shih*, 2:85.

8. Feng, *Tsu-chih*, pp. 76, 83; *Chung-hua*, 1:142.

9. Chiang Wei-ch'iao, pp. 492–494; Feng, *I-shih*, 2:85; *NCH*, 74:667 (3/31/05);

75:52–53 (4/7/05). A clear example of linking anti-imperialist and antidynastic themes in *Warnings on Russian Affairs* appears in an article addressed to the revolutionary party, *O-shih ching-wen* (Warnings on Russian affairs; photolithograph, Taipei, 1968), no. 14, p. 2 (December 28, 1903). The warning about Japanese imperialism appears in *Ching-chung jih-pao* (The alarm bell; photolithograph, Taipei, 1968), no. 3, p. 1 (February 28, 1904).

10. The longest list of names of those connected with *Warnings on Russian Affairs* and *The Alarm Bell* appears in Feng, *I-shih*, 2:85. Besides Ts'ai Yüan-p'ei and Liu Shih-p'ei, Lin Hsieh, Yeh Han, Wang Te-yüan, and Liu Ch'i-chi had already been active during the *Su-pao* period. Lin also founded *The Vernacular Journal* and had been connected with *The China National Gazette*. Liu had worked for *The China National Gazette*, as had Ch'en Ch'ü-ping, who also established *The Twentieth Century Stage*. Sun Huan-ching wrote for *The Twentieth Century Stage*. Of these eight, four were from Kiangsu, two from Chekiang, one from Anhwei, and one from Fukien. Feng, *I-shih*, 3:82, 83, 87, 88, 116.

11. The radical pamphlets written in Shanghai must have been quite numerous. I have not seen copies of any but the best known works and many may now be lost. In addition to titles mentioned in the text a partial list follows.

Chang Shih-chao:	*Tang-lu ts'ung-shu*
Liu Shih-p'ei:	*Jang-shu, Chung-kuo min-tsu chih*
Ch'en Ch'ü-ping:	*Ch'ing pi-shih, Lu-ch'en ts'ung-shu*
Chin T'ien-ko:	*Nü-chieh chung*
Su Man-shu:	*Ts'an shih-chieh*

12. Mei Lan-fang, "Hsi-chü chieh ts'an-chia Hsin-hai ko-ming ti chi-chien shih" (A few items about actors participating in the 1911 Revolution); in *KML*, 1:355.

13. Hu Shih, *Ssu-shih tzu-shu* (Autobiography at forty; Hong Kong, 1957), p. 53.

14. *Ibid.*, p. 56.

15. *Ibid.*, pp. 57–59.

16. Pao T'ien-hsiao, "Hsin-hai ko-ming ch'ien-hou ti Shang-hai hsin-wen-chieh" (Shanghai newspaper circles before and after the Revolution of 1911); in *KML*, 4:87. Pao had worked for *The Eastern Times*.

17. Hu Shih, p. 53. Local Shanghai opposition to Russia was further inflamed in December when a drunken Russian sailor accidentally killed a Chinese passerby during an argument with a rickshaw coolie on the Whampoa waterfront. The victim's fellow townsmen from Ningpo believed the court-martial sentence of five years' imprisonment was ridiculously inadequate. Large-scale rioting was imminent for several days. Student feeling also ran high and the Shanghai Taotai was blamed for failing to have the sailor tried by a Chinese court. *NCH*, 73:1382 (12/16/04); 73:1401, 1422 (12/23/04); 73:1491–1492 (12/30/04); 74:117, 135, 141–142 (1/20/05); *Ching-chung jih-pao* (The alarm bell), p. 1 (January 21, 1903); Hu Shih, p. 53. Hu Shih and a number of his friends wrote a long letter to Shanghai Taotai Yüan Shu-hsün castigating his weakness. Hu also left school to avoid being examined by Yüan.

18. *HCH*, 2:382; Su P'eng, "Wan Fu-hua tz'u Wang Chih-ch'un an yü-chung chi-shih (An account in jail of Wan Fu-hua's attempt to assassinate Wang Chih-ch'un), in *HCH*, 2:397. An editorial on the alleged proposal for an agreement with Russia and Wang's role in the negotiations appears in *Ching-chung jih-pao* (The alarm bell), p. 1 (November 13, 1904). According to *NCH*, 73:1186 (11/25/04), Wang was in Shanghai to assist gentry agitation to prevent the American syndicate building the Hankow-Canton Railway from selling its interest to a Belgian, French, or Russian group.

19. *HCH*, 2:382. At his trial Wan testified he was thirty-nine years old. *Ibid.*, p. 384.

20. Feng, *Chung-hua*, 1:168.

21. *Ibid.*
22. Feng, *Chung-hua,* 1:168–169; *NCH,* 73:1186 (11/25/04); 73:1257 (12/2/04); 73:1374 (12/16/04).
23. Hu Shih, p. 53. For a time in November and December the Wan Fu-hua case overshadowed questions of imperialism in *The Alarm Bell.* A long article on the case appears in *Ching-chung jih-pao,* p. 1 (December 15, 1904).
24. Chün-tu Hsüeh, *Huang Hsing and the Chinese Revolution* (Stanford, 1961), pp. 23–25.
25. "Instructions of Yüan Shu-hsün to the Mixed Court dated January 14, 1905"; in *Ibid.,* p. 389. Summaries of the trial appear in *NCH,* 73:1257, 1374, 1431–1432 (12/2/04, 12/16/04, 12/23/04).
26. At the trial Wan testified he had tried to assassinate Wang because of Wang's plan to use French troops when he was governor. *HCH,* 2:384. Revolutionaries in Shanghai raised funds to hire two Chinese and two Western lawyers to defend Wan at the trial. In 1906 Wan attempted to escape from jail and received an additional ten-year sentence. After the Revolution, his son, supported by the Shanghai *tu-tu* Ch'en Ch'i-mei, petitioned for Wan's release on the grounds that the political situation had changed. The Mixed Court agreed and Wan was freed December 7, 1912. Correspondence on this subject appears in *Ibid.,* pp. 390–394. After his release Wan worked on land reclamation in Manchuria. He died in Peking in 1918 after having been in poor health for some time. *Ibid.,* p. 383.
27. Chün-tu Hsüeh, p. 20.
28. Other Shanghai radicals who joined the assassination corps included Chang Shih-chao, Ch'en Tu-hsiu, Ts'ai Yüan-p'ei's younger brother Ts'ai Yüan-k'ang, and Wang Hsiao-shu. Lu Man-yen, *Shih-hsien pieh-chi* (Another record of contemporary worthies), 2 vols. (Chungking, 1943), 1:2–3; Sun Te-chung, *Ts'ai Yüan-p'ei hsien-sheng i-wen lei-ch'ao* (A topical selection of Ts'ai Yüan-p'ei's writings; Taipei, 1960), p. 584.
29. Shen Tieh-min, "Chi Kuang-fu hui erh-san shih" (Recollections of two or three things about the Restoration Society); in *KML,* 4:131–134. This account contrasts with the standard account of Kung Pao-ch'üan and Ts'ai Yüan-p'ei forming the Restoration Society and inviting T'ao Ch'eng-chang to join afterwards, but is probably reconcilable with it. Shen says T'ao Ch'eng-chang credits Ts'ai Yüan-p'ei with the founding of the Restoration Society out of modesty (see T'ao, "Che-an," p. 17). Shen was one of the students who took part in the meetings he describes and who went to Changsha to make contact with Huang Hsing.
30. T'ao, "Che-an," p. 17.
31. Shen Tieh-min, pp. 133–134.
32. Ch'en Wei, "Kuang-fu hui ch'ien-ch'i ti huo-tung p'ien-tuan" (Miscellany about activities preceding the founding of the Restoration Society); in *KML,* 4:127.
33. E.g., Ts'ai Yüan-p'ei initially prevented T'ao Ch'eng-chang's close associate Wei Lan from joining. The Chekiangese revolutionary Ao Chia-hsiung refused to join, although he worked with members. T'ao, "Che-an," p. 17.
34. Feng, *I-shih,* 5:63; in *HHKM,* 1:516.
35. *Ibid.,* 5:63; Ch'en Wei, p. 127.
36. Ch'en Wei, p. 127.
37. Shen Tieh-min, p. 134.
38. Since the Restoration Society membership was supposedly secret, lists of party members are mainly limited to those who achieved some prominence. Carryover from the 1902–1904 included Ts'ai Yüan-p'ei and Liu Shih-p'ei. Chung Hsien-ch'ang of the Educational Association was a member, as was Wang Hsiao-hsü, who had written for *The Alarm Bell.* Ts'ai Yüan-p'ei as told to Huang Shih-hui; in *HCH,*

2:368. Members of the Association of Comrades to Resist Russia joined the Restoration Society with Ts'ai Yüan-p'ei. Sun Te-chung, p. 560.

39. See chap. 7

40. Shen Tieh-min, pp. 139–141.

41. E.g., Yüan Sun, "Lu-hsi-ya hsü-wu-tang" (The Russian Nihilist party), *Chiangsu*, no. 4; in *SLHC*, 1.2:565–571; "Hsü-wu tang" (The Nihilist party), *Su-pao* (June 19, 1903); in *SLHC*, 1.2:696–698; Yang Shou-jen (Yang Yü-lin), "Hsin Hu-nan" (New Hunan); in *SLHC*, 1.2:641; T'an Pi-an, "O-kuo min-ts'ui chu-i T'ung-meng hui ti ying-hsiang" (The influence of Russian populism on the Revolutionary Alliance), *Li-shih yen-chiu*, 1:35–44 (1959), deals mainly with a slightly later period.

42. Robert A. Scalapino and George T. Yu, *The Chinese Anarchist Movement* (Berkeley, 1961), pp. 29, 33.

43. E.g., T'ao suggests anarchism as one possible form of government after the revolution. T'ao Ch'eng-chang, "Lung-hua hui chang-ch'eng" (Regulations of the Dragon Flower Society); in *HHKM*, 1:534.

44. Biographical information about Wu Yüeh is from Feng, *I-shih*, 3:197–198; Feng, *Chung-hua*, 1:206; Wu Yüeh, "Tzu-hsü" (Personal introduction); in Feng, *I-shih*, 3:199–201; *HHKM*, 4:320–321.

45. Wu Yüeh, "Ching-kao wo t'ung-chih" (A warning to my comrades); in Ch'en Hsiung, comp., *Min-tsu ko-ming wen-hsien* (Documents on the nationalist revolution; Taipei, 1954), p. 289.

46. Wu Yüeh, "Tzu-hsü," in Feng, *Chung-hua*, 1:210.

47. Wu Yüeh, "Ching-kao wo t'ung-chih," in Ch'en Hsiung, p. 288.

48. Wu Yüeh, "Tzu-hsü," in Feng, *Chung-hua*, 1:209.

49. Wu Yüeh, "Ching-kao wo t'ung-chih," in Ch'en Hsiung, p. 289.

50. From a letter Wu Yüeh wrote to his wife before his assassination attempt. In Ch'en Hsiung, p. 291.

51. Shen Tieh-min, p. 133.

52. T'ao, "Che-an," p. 24.

53. Chün-tu Hsüeh, p. 46.

54. Feng, *I-shih*, 2:178–179. Feng Tzu-yu introduced Ch'iu Chin into the Revolutionary Alliance.

55. T'ao, "Che-an," p. 81; Feng, *Chung-hua*, 2:46; Tsou Lu, *Chung-kuo Kuo-min-tang shih-kao* (A draft history of the Kuomintang; Shanghai, 1938), p. 738. Feng Tzu-yu attributed Hsü Hsi-lin's failure to join the Revolutionary Alliance to his "independent spirit" (Feng, *I-shih*, 5:63). Such spirits were no novelty in the revolutionary movement and, although the reasons why Hsü did not join are unclear, this does not seem to be a very complete explanation.

56. Information on the Shanghai Revolutionary Alliance and Steadfast Conduct Public Institute appears in Feng, *I-shih*, 2:88–90.

57. Chiang Shen-wu, "T'ung-meng hui shih-tai Shang-hai ko-ming tang-jen ti huo-tung" (The activities of revolutionaries in Shanghai during the Revolutionary Alliance period), *I-ching* (Unorthodox classics), 26:103.

58. Feng, *I-shih*, 2:88–90.

59. T'ao, "Che-an", p. 17.

60. Tsou Lu, pp. 879–880; Chou Ya-wei, "Kuang-fu hui chien-wen tsa-i" (Miscellaneous recollections of the Restoration Society); in *KML*, 1:629.

61. T'ao, "Che-an," p. 32.

62. Liu K'uei-i, pp. 14–15. After Ch'iu's failure, Huang was convinced that the revolutionaries should abandon the Lower Yangtze region.

63. Feng, *I-shih*, 5:72; in *HHKM*, 1:517.

64. Shen Tieh-min, p. 136. Shen was a Restoration Society member and worked for

this association.

65. Chou Ya-wei, p. 635. The sisters were named Yin Jui-chih and Yin Wei-chün.

66. Pang Kung-chan, *Ch'en Ch'i-mei* (Taipei, 1954), p. 20.

67. Chou Ya-wei, p. 635. The Restoration Society-Revolutionary Alliance split in Shanghai did not precisely follow old lines. Yao Yung-ch'en and Hu Shih-chün, who had also fled from Shaohsing, worked at Ch'en Ch'i-mei's Revolutionary Alliance headquarters. Ch'u Fu-ch'eng, "Che-chiang Hsin-hai ko-ming chi-shih" (A record of the 1911 Revolution in Chekiang); in *HHKM*, 7:153.

68. Journals not discussed in the text include the *Kuo-ts'ui hsüeh-pao*, published by Chang Ping-lin and Liu Shih-p'ei; the *K'o-fu hsüeh-pao*, a revolutionary journal very similar to the *Kuo-ts'ui hsüeh-pao*; Ch'iu Chin's *Nü-pao*; its successor, the *Shen-chou nü-pao* and Ch'en Ch'i-mei's *Chung-kuo kung-pao* and *Min-sheng ts'ung-pao*. The Shanghai World Society served as an outlet for *New Century*, the anarchist publication of Wu Chih-hui and other revolutionary students in Paris. Feng, *Tsu-chih*, pp. 112, 117, 118, 149, 194, 211; *HCH*, 2:553–554; *TMH*, 2:549.

69. The main detailed source for the Chinese Public Institute is Hu Shih, pp. 63–65, 81–88. Brief accounts appear in Feng, *I-shih*, 2:88; *TMH*, 2:548; some biographies of Ch'iu Chin and various other standard sources.

70. Liu Ch'i-chi (Liu Ya-tzu), *Nan-she chi-lüeh* (An account of the Southern Society; Shanghai, 1940), p. 38.

71. Hu Shih, pp. 66–75.

72. Yü Yu-jen (1879–1964) came from a poor farming and merchant family. His father, nonetheless, had great respect for learning and Yü was educated in a series of local schools, culminating in the Shensi middle school in Sian. He became interested in modern subjects and international affairs and was influenced by reformist scholars and teachers. After he fled to Shanghai, Yü studied there for two years. He helped found the Chinese Public Institute early in 1906 and in the autumn went to Tokyo to investigate journalistic methods. He became a well-known revolutionary through his Shanghai publishing ventures from 1907 to 1911. From January to March 1912 he was vice-minister of communications in Sun Yat-sen's provisional government. During the Republic he was a loyal Kuomintang member. As a reward for long party service, Yü was appointed president of the Control Yüan in 1931. He held this post for thirty years despite occasional resignations to protest his lack of genuine authority. Feng, *I-shih*, 3:346–350; a series of articles on Yü Yu-jen appear in *Chuan-chi wen-hsüeh*, 5.6:4–22.

73. Feng, *I-shih*, 2:263.

74. *TMH*, 2:557–558.

75. Feng, *I-shih*, 2:321.

76. Reports of the Mixed Court hearings appear in *NCH*, 92:342–344, 357–358 (8/7/09); 92:406–409 (8/14/09); 92:462 (8/21/09); 92:521–522, 534 (8/28/09); 92:632 (9/11/09). An account of the trial, reprints of articles sympathetic to *The People's Cry* in *The Eastern Times* and *Shen-chou jih-pao*, and a few telegrams appear in *Tung-fang tsa-chih*, 6.8: chih-shih, 229–239. Sympathetic accounts appear in Feng, *I-shih*, 3:314–321 and Chiang Shen-wu, pp. 107–108. Statements of the mission of *The People's Cry* appear in *Min-hu jih-pao* (The people's cry; photolithograph, Taipei, 1969), no. 1, p. 1 (May 15, 1909); no. 2, p. 6 (May 16, 1909). A rebuttal of the case against Yü Yu-jen appears in *Ibid.*, no. 84, p. 1 (August 6, 1909).

77. An example of attacks on Japan appears in *Min-hsü jih-pao* (The people's sigh; photolithograph, Taipei, 1969), no. 46, p. 1 (November, 17, 1909). For the Mixed Court hearings see *NCH*, 93:793 (11/27/09); 93:622 (12/11/09); 93:791, 803–804 (12/31/09); *Tung-fang tsa-chih*, 6.12: chi-shih 410–414; Feng, *I-shih*, 3:322–330; Chiang Shen-wu, pp. 107–108.

78. *NCH*, 93:537 (12/4/09); 93:660 (12/11/09);94:26 (1/7/10).

79. Feng, *I-shih*, 3:321, 329–330; *NCH*, 93:793 (12/31/09); *Tung-fang tsa-chih*, 6.12: *chi-shih* 410–411.

80. Probably not all Chinese officials were happy about the way *The People's Sigh* case had been handled. There was a report that the minister of interior, Prince Su, was in the process of ordering the paper reopened and that the hasty verdict was designed to forestall this possibility. *NCH*, 94:26 (1/7/10).

81. Ch'en Ch'ü-ping is one of the few names from the earlier period which appears with that of Ch'en Ch'i-mei. He was on the staffs of *Chung-kuo kung-pao*, founded by Ch'en in 1909, and *Min-sheng ts'ung-pao*, founded in 1910. Yao Yung-ch'en, who had been a Restoration Society member in Chekiang before mid-1907, also worked for the latter paper. Feng, *Tsu-chih*, pp. 194, 211.

82. Fan Kuang-ch'i was from a poor but scholarly family of Ho-fei, Anhwei. When he was twenty-seven years old he went to Shanghai, where he worked for *The People's Cry*, *The People's Sigh*, and *The People's Stand*. He headed the Anhwei branch of the Revolutionary Alliance's Central China Bureau. During the Revolution he helped organize the Kiangsu-Chekiang army and took part in the attack on Nanking. Then he raised an "Iron Blood Army" in Kiangsu and Anhwei for a northern expedition against Peking. After the North-South Accord he returned to Shanghai to devote himself to literature. During the "Second Revolution" he led anti-Yüan Shih-k'ai forces that briefly held Anking. When the revolt failed he fled to Japan and joined Sun Yat-sen's Revolutionary Party. In 1915 he returned to Shanghai to plot another rising and was assassinated by orders of General Cheng Ju-ch'eng. Wang Chung-ch'i was also from Anhwei. He was an editor of *Shen-chou jih-pao* and on the staff of *The People's Sigh* and *The People's Cry*. He was noted as a writer of poetry and short stories. Ching Yao-yeh was vice-minister of education in the Nanking provisional government in 1912. Liu Ch'i-chi, *Nan-she*, pp. 15, 25; Kuomintang, Committee for the Compilation of Materials on the Party History of the Central Executive Committee, ed., *Ko-ming hsien-lieh hsien-chin chuan* (Biographies of martyrs and forebearers of the revolution; Taipei, 1965), pp. 364–365.

83. Ch'en Ch'i-mei is one of the Revolutionary Alliance heroes. There are a number of standardized biographies of his life. My information is mainly from Ho Chung-hsiao, *Ch'en Ying-shih hsien-sheng nien-pu* (A chronological biography of Ch'en Ying-shih; Shanghai, 1946).

84. Mei Lan-fang, "Hsi-chü chieh ts'an-chia Hsin-hai ko-ming ti chi-chien shih" (A few items about actors participating in the 1911 Revolution); in *KML*, 1:349; *HHKM*, 7:80.

85. *Who's Who in China*, 5th edition (Shanghai, 1936), p. 249.

86. Mei Lan-fan, p. 349.

87. An English-language biography of Chang Chien is Samuel Chu, *Reformer in Modern China, 1853–1926* (New York and London, 1965). Chu characterizes Chang in 1911 as neither directly involved in revolutionary activities nor having a vested interest in the survival of the Ch'ing. He switched from constitutionalism to republicanism after the Wuchang rising as the best way to save China (p. 69). This characterization is useful, but does not take account of Chang's prior contacts with radicals nor of the erosional effects which the constitutional struggles before October 1911 had on loyalty to the dynasty.

88. *Chuan-chi wen-hsüeh* (Biographical Literature), 6.2:32–33. Chang suffered ill health and gradually increasing paralysis during the last twenty years of his life. He left China for Europe in 1938, and then settled in New York, where he remained until his death in 1950, just before his seventy-third birthday.

89. Chiang Wei-ch'iao, p. 495; Ch'en Hsü-lu, *Tsou Jung yü Ch'en T'ien-hua ti ssu-*

hsiang (The thought of Tsou Jung and Ch'en T'ien-hua; Shanghai, 1957), p. 32. This meeting was held under the auspices of the Educational Association.

90. Chiang Wei-ch'iao, p. 495; Feng, *I-shih*, 2:55–56.

91. A brief history of the Revival Society appears in Arthur W. Hummel, ed., *Eminent Chinese of the Ch'ing Period*, 2 vols. (Washington, 1943–1944), 1:52–53.

92. Chiang Shen-wu, *I-ching*, 26:107. Lists and brief biographies of members attending meetings appear in Liu Ch'i-chi, *Nan-she, passim*.

93. E.g., Liu Ch'i-chi had returned home in the fall of 1906. He married and spent several years studying ancient texts. Hsin-lü wen-hsüeh she, ed., *Ming-chia chuan-chi* (Biographies of famous men; Shanghai, 1934), p. 91. Lin Hsieh was another Southern Society member no longer politically active in Shanghai.

94. Parallels may perhaps be drawn with the liberal movement of the 1920's and 1930's or with non-Communist leftists of the same period. Those who joined the Communist Party were subject to discipline which made it more difficult to leave the movement.

95. Except as otherwise noted, Su Man-shu's biography is from Liu Wu-chi, *Man-shu ta-shih chi-nien chi* (A commemorative collection of Su Man-shu's works; Hong Kong, 1953), pp. 1–17.

96. Feng Tzu-yu, "Su Man-shu chih chen mien-mu" (The true face of Su Man-shu), *I-ching*, 21:1185–1187.

6. Revolutionary Origins in Chekiang

1. T'ao, "Che-an," p. 104; Arthur W. Hummel, ed., *Eminent Chinese of the Ch'ing Period*, 2 vols. (U.S. Government Printing Office, Washington, D.C., 1943–1944), 1:552.

2. T'ao, "Che-an," p. 18; Feng, *Chung-hua*, 2:6.

3. Feng, *Chung-hua*, 2:11–12.

4. P'ing-ti Ho, *Studies on the Population of China, 1368–1953* (Cambridge, Mass., 1959), pp. 157, 240–244; T'ao, "Che-an," p. 52.

5. P'ing-ti Ho, pp. 243–244, 246.

6. T'ao, "Che-an," pp. 18–21, and various biographies, pp. 52–77. Besides the societies described in the text, T'ao lists the following as active in Chekiang, but says the revolutionaries failed to develop important contacts with them. *Kuan-ti hui* and *Yü-ch'üan hui; Ch'ien-jen hui* and *Ku-ch'eng hui* in Kinhwa prefecture; *Wu-tai hui, Hung-ch'i hui, Hei-ch'i hui* and *Pai-ch'i hui* in Shaohsing, Kinhwa, and Ningpo prefectures; *Shen-ch'üan*, who were most numerous in Wenchow; *Pai-lien*, who were most numerous in Kinhwa; *Chai-chiao* in Kinhwa. The *Hung-ch'i hui* and *Hei-ch'i hui* in Chang-chou and Ch'üan-chou had relations with the Dragon Flower Society. T'ao Ch'eng-chang is unquestionably the best informed writer on the Chekiangese secret societies. His reliability is somewhat difficult to ascertain because other authors have often taken their information from him. This is particularly true of the section on the Chekiang case in Feng, *Chung-hua*, vol. 2. Where accounts of secret society risings or missionary incidents can be found in the *North China Herald* they are generally roughly compatible with T'ao's account. Where I have found differing interpretations they will be indicated in the notes.

7. T'ao, "Che-an," pp. 18–21. T'ao states that the Ping-yang Society was said to have ten thousand members and that the Dragon Flower Society was reputed to have fifty thousand but actually had twenty thousand members. A "Telegram of Shaohsing prefect Kuei-fu to Chekiang Governor Chang Tseng-yang," reprinted in T'ao, "Che-an," p. 43, also gives the figure of ten thousand for the P'ing-yang Society.

8. *Ibid.*, p. 19.

9. *Ibid.*, pp. 50–51. T'ao claims that the Ch'ing government and the foreigners both believed that Liu Chia-fu's followers in the city were responsible and incorrectly assumed that his rising was antimissionary. T'ao, "Che-an," pp. 50–51. Reports in the *North China Herald,* however, indicate that at least the Westerners blamed the local officials and gentry rather than Liu. His society is referred to as "Vegetarians," showing that Westerners still remembered the massacre of missionaries in Ku-t'ien, Fukien, by the *Ts'ai-hui* in 1895. E.g., *NCH,* 45:885 (10/24/00). However, the fullest reports definitely blame the taotai and militia, not the rebels. E.g., *NCH,* 45:1107–1108 (11/21/00). At trials of suspects later that year, a Ch'ü-chou member of the gentry confessed inciting the mob to kill the magistrate. *NCH,* 45:1253 (12/12/03). The British government demanded punishment of a brigadier-general, the local taotai and prefect, a local captain, and two members of the gentry. It also demanded that the Chekiangese governor and provincial judge be permanently dismissed from office for distributing decrees from the court, written while the Boxer proponents had the upper hand, which ordered the killing of foreigners. *NCH,* 66:499–500 (3/13/01).

10. T'ao, "Che-an," pp. 18–19, 25; *NCH,* 71:882–883 (10/23/03). In March 1905 the *North China Herald* reported that in Ninghai a man named Wang, who called himself a leader of patriots, had issued a proclamation in a recent riot. This proclamation promised decapitation of followers who were guilty of a number of disorders, including killing of Protestants. The *North China Herald* interpreted this incident as the beginning of attacks on Roman Catholic converts. *NCH,* 74:541 (3/17/05). Later that spring and summer there were reports of attacks on Catholics. *NCH,* 75:13 (4/7/05); 76:267 (8/4/05). Reports on the burning of Catholic churches, killing of Catholics, and the reluctance of local officials to oppose Wang appear in *Kuo-min jih-jih-pao* (The China National Gazette; photolithograph, Taipei, 1965), p. 367 (October 11, 1903); p. 414 (October 16, 1903). A list of other anti-Christian societies in Chekiang which revolutionaries allegedly tried to influence toward anti-Manchuism appears in Hirayama Shū (P'ing Shan-chou), *Chung-kuo pi-mi she-hui shih* (A history of Chinese secret societies), Commercial Press Translation Department, tr. (Shanghai, 1912), p. 80.

11. Tao, "Che-an," pp. 19, 53–55.

12. *Ibid.,* p. 19. Sun I-yen was a *chin-shih* of 1850. He assisted Tseng Kuo-fan in campaigns against the Taipings and one of his sons was killed in the civil war. In 1858 his family returned home to Jui-an while Sun was busy with Tseng's campaigns. After the death of his parents in 1864 and 1865, Sun retired for the customary mourning period. He taught at the Tzu-yang Academy in Hangchow. Later he returned to official life until his retirement in 1879 (Hummel, 2:677–678). T'ao Ch'eng-chang says the founder of the society was Sun I-yen himself, that the real purpose of the society was antidynastic, and that it was dissolved because Sun realized the time for a rising had passed. If true, this would be an interesting example of a fairly highly placed official playing both sides of the game. Wei Chien-yu says the society was founded by Sun's younger brother and that its original purpose was to oppose the Gold Coin Society. Some disagreement between Tso Tsung-t'ang and the Sun family led to the impeachment of the Jui-an district magistrate and the decision to disband the society after Tso's troops occupied Hangchow. This account seems more probable. Wei Chien-yu, "Hsin-hai ko-ming ch'ien-yeh ti Che-chiang hui-tang huo-tung" (Activities of Chekiangese secret societies on the eve of the 1911 Revolution), in *CNL,* pp. 541–542.

13. T'ao, "Che-an," pp. 19, 51–53; *NCH,* 69:1111 (11/26/02); 69:1288 (12/24/02); 70:24 (1/7/03); 70:58 (1/14/03). The reports in the *North China Herald* say nothing of any warning to the Catholics at the beginning of the rising, whereas T'ao does not mention any instances of genuine rivalry between Catholics and members of the White Cloth Society. The *North China Herald* reported church burnings, but no

killings of missionaries and converts by P'u's followers, and it is possible that these two sources emphasize two different aspects of the rising. One of the newspaper articles states that in the opinion of local gentry the root of the rising was in quarrels between some of the people and Catholics who had been "overbearing." However, because of the behavior of government troops the original dispute was transformed into a fight between the people and the government. (*NCH*, 70:58). Wei Chien-yu characterizes the White Cloth Society rising as an example of shifting from an antiforeign to an antidynastic attitude. (Wei Chien-yu, p. 525). There may have been such an element involved.

14. T'ao, "Che-an," pp. 67–68.

15. *Ibid.*, pp. 20, 65–66; Feng, *Chung-hua*, 2:3, 11.

16. T'ao, "Che-an," pp. 12, 20; Feng, *Chung-hua*, 2:3; Feng, *I-shih*, 3:97–98. The revolutionaries who sent warning were T'ao Ch'eng-chang and Wei Lan. No dates are given for this case. The paper could have been started any time from the latter half of 1903 through 1904. The attempt to suppress it may have occurred in the first half of 1905.

17. After fleeing to Shanghai, Chang Kung went to Tokyo, where he wrote for and helped edit *The People's Journal* and its supplement, *T'ien-t'ao*. In 1909 he was back in Shanghai, where he planned to take part in a meeting of Chekiangese revolutionaries called by Ch'en Ch'i-mei. Chang was arrested when an informer told government officials of the meeting. He was imprisoned until released by the Revolution. Upon returning to Chekiang he held a position in the revolutionary government and briefly was head of the Chekiang Revolutionary Alliance. See biography by Ch'en Ch'ü-ping in Kuomintang, Committee for the Compilation of Materials on the Party History of the Central Executive Committee, ed., *Ko-ming hsien-lieh hsien-chin chuan* (Biographies of martyrs and forebearers of the Revolution; Taipei, 1965), pp. 1025–1026. Ch'en stresses Chang's role as a revolutionary, not as a secret society member.

18. Information on the salt smugglers comes from T'ao, "Che-an," pp. 21, 72–73; Feng, *Chung-hua*, 2:8–9; "Memorial of the Liang-kiang Governor-General and the Kiangsu Governor on the pacification of salt smugglers," in T'ao, "Che-an," pp. 97–98; Wei Chien-yu, p. 543; Hirayama Shū, p. 75; Hsiao I-shan, *Chin-tai pi-mi she-hui shih-liao* (Historical material on modern secret societies; Peking, 1935), *chuan* 2, *fu-lu*, p. 5a; Hsi-pei yen-chiu she (Northwest Research Society), ed., *Ko-lao hui yü ch'ing-pang kai-k'uang* (General account of the Ko-lao hui and the Green Gang; 1941), pp. 62–64; Ch'ien Sheng-k'o, *Ching-hung-pang chih hei-mu* (The black curtain of the Red and Green gangs; Shanghai, 1929), pp. 2–4.

19. T'ao, "Che-an," pp. 72–73.

20. An example of a merchant with high secret society connections was Lü Hsiung-hsiang, who was a relative of a Dragon Flower Society branch leader and an intimate of Chou Hua-chang and Shen Yung-ch'ing. He operated a general store. Through his secret society membership he was introduced to the revolutionaries and was active in the Wen-T'ai-Ch'u Guildhall, one of the revolutionary fronts in Chekiang. Feng, *I-shih*, 3:114; T'ao, "Che-an," p. 23. There were quite a few secret society members among the Lü clan.

21. Yuji Muramatsu, "Some Themes in Chinese Rebel Ideologies," in Arthur Wright, ed., *The Confucian Persuasion* (Stanford, 1960), pp. 255–256. Communist writers qualify their descriptions of secret societies as peasant organizations by pointing to the various social origins of both leaders and rank and file and to the societies' secret natures, which kept them from representing all the peasantry. Li Wen-hai, "Hsin-hai ko-ming yü hui-tang" (The 1911 Revolution and the secret societies), in *CNL*, pp. 170–172; Wang I-sun, "Hsin-hai ko-ming shih-ch'i tzu-ch'an chieh-chi yü nung-min ti kuan-hsi wen-t'i" (The question of the relationship between the bourgeois

and the peasantry during the period of the 1911 Revolution), in *CNL,* pp. 120–121.

22. Ko Kung-chen, *Chung-kuo pao-hsüeh shih* (A history of Chinese journalism; Peking, 1955), p. 125.

23. T'ao, "Che-an," pp. 10–11; Sheng Lang-hsi, *Chung-kuo shu-yüan chih-tu* (The system of Chinese academies; Shanghai, 1934), p. 239; Hummel, 2:678; *CCC,* 8:165–166; Ts'ai Yüan-p'ei as told to Huang Shih-hui, "Ts'ai Chieh-min hsien-sheng ti ch'ing-nien shih-tai" (The youth of Ts'ai Chieh-min); in *HCH,* 2:364. Ts'ai briefly directed this school in 1898 and 1899, but had to resign because of his support of two reformist faculty members.

24. Chekiang College later became Chekiang Higher School. *CCC,* 8:165–166, 168; *Su-pao,* p. 294 (April 23, 1903).

25. *NCH,* 70:160 (1/27/03); 70:926 (5/14/03).

26. *Su-pao,* p. 298 (April 19, 1903).

27. The founding and first meeting of the Shaohsing Educational Association is reported in *Su-pao,* p. 62 (March 9, 1903), p. 80 (March 12, 1903), p. 85 (March 13, 1903), p. 139 (March 22, 1903). Shaohsing Educational Association members were dissatisfied with the prefectural school in Shaohsing which had originally been founded in 1897. There were conflicts between liberals and conservatives on the faculty. In 1902, when it became a government school, it merged with an academy in the city and the conservatives became dominant. Moreover, the prefect was misappropriating some of the funds due the school. Because of the corruption of the official school, association members wished to establish a *kung-hsüeh. Su-pao,* p. 192 (April 1, 1903).

28. T'ao, "Che-an," p. 68; Feng, *Tsu-chih,* p. 53.

29. Hummel, 1:312, 2:945.

30. T'ao, "Che-an," p. 20; Yü Chao-i, *Ch'iu Chin* (Hong Kong, 1956), p. 118.

31. Ma Hsü-lun, "Wo tsai hsin-hai che-i-nien" (My experiences during the year 1911), in *KML,* 1:176. The Ch'iu-shih Academy was heavily influenced by the ideas of the 1898 Reform Movement. Sung P'ing-tzu, for instance, was a close friend of three of the executed "six gentlemen" of 1898. Students there also read works of early Ch'ing nationalists such as Wang Fu-chih and Huang Tsung-hsi. Ma Hsü-lun, "Kuan-yü Hsin-hai ko-ming Che-chiang sheng-ch'eng kuang-fu chi-shih ti pu-ch'ung tzu-liao" (Supplementary material on the 1911 Revolution in the provincial capital of Chekiang); in *Chin-tai shih tzu-liao* (Materials on modern Chinese history), 1:48–49 1957).

32. T'ao, "Che-an," p. 11.

33. Ma Hsü-lun, p. 170.

34. Chou Ya-wei, "Kuang-fu hui chien-wen tsa-i" (Miscellaneous recollections of the Restoration Society); in *KML,* 1:624. Contact between students at the Ch'iu-shih Academy and the Military Preparatory School is indicated by the presence of military students teaching military drill at the school established by students who withdrew in 1903 from Chekiang College (the old Ch'iu-shih Academy). *CCC,* 8:174.

35. Ma Hsü-lun, pp. 176–177; T'ao, "Che-an," pp. 10–11; Feng, *Chung-hua,* 2:3. Ma Hsü-lun says Chin-liang told his brother who was commander of the Manchu garrison in Hangchow. The brother told the commander-in-chief of the Manchu forces, who told the governor. The literary society involved in the "On Abolishing the Queue" case aimed to establish a cooperative library to which students would donate their copies of "new books," to encourage progressive members of the upper grades to give lectures and write articles on modern subjects, and to invite a progressive teacher to take charge of a school where students would be taught from new books instead of traditional texts. Ch'ien Chün-fu says the society was established in 1900 and the essay "On Abolishing the Queue" was written for a course it gave the following summer. Ch'ien Chün-fu, "Hang-chou Ch'iu-shih shu-yüan 'Tsui-pien wen' an shih-

mo chi-lüeh" (A complete account of the "On abolishing the queue" case at the Hang-chow Ch'iu-shih Academy); in *Chin-tai shih tzu-liao*, 1:58–59 (1957).

36. T'ao, "Che-an," pp. 10–11.

37. These included Wang Chia-chü, Sun I-chung, Chiang Chih-yu, Chiang Tsun-kuei, and Chiang Fang-chen. Feng, *Chung-hua*, 2:1–2; Shen Tieh-min, "Chi Kuang-fu hui erh-san shih" (Recollections of two or three things about the Restoration Society); in *KML*, 4:131–132.

38. *NCH*, 66:665.

39. The group of radical students from the Ch'iu-shih Academy went to Tokyo in 1902. According to one source twenty students had gone to Japan from Shaohsing by mid-March 1903. This figure may or may not be accurate and I do not know whether it refers to the entire prefecture or just the prefectural city. *Su-pao*, p. 85 (March 13, 1903).

40. Information on available literature is very sketchy. *Su-pao* lists sales outlets in Hangchow, Kashing, Ningpo, Taichow, and Wenchow. *Tides of Chekiang* occasionally published surveys of papers and periodicals sold in various cities. One of these listed fifty copies of *Su-pao* and two hundred copies of *The Renovation of the People* sold in Hangchow. (*CCC*, 3:195). Another listed thirty copies of *The Renovation of the People*, eight of *Tides of Chekiang*, two of *Translations by Chinese Students Abroad*, and one of *Hupeh Student Circles* sold in Haining bookstores and schools. (*CCC*, 7:199–200). Two new bookstores specializing in "new books" had been established in Shaohsing late in 1902 and early in 1903 (*CCC*, 8:181). There is no indication of how complete or accurate this information is or how it was obtained.

41. *CCC*, 8:118. It is not clear whether the attitude expressed in this article reflects only that of the author, very possibly a graduate of the Ch'iu-shih Academy who was sorry to see it become an official school, or whether it was a factor among students there in 1903.

42. *NCH*, 70:576 (3/26/03); 70:983 (5/21/03); 70:1254 (6/26/03). The incident was reported in several articles in *Su-pao*. See *Su-pao*, pp. 61–62 (February 9, 1903), p. 288 (April 17, 1903), p. 293 (April 19, 1903), p. 309 (April 21, 1903), pp. 375–376 (May 2, 1903), p. 381 (May 3, 1903).

43. *Su-pao*, p. 293 (April 18, 1903).

44. *Ibid.*, p. 324 (April 23, 1903).

45. *CCC*, 8:174.

46. *Su-pao*, p. 328 (April 24, 1903).

47. *CCC*, 4:111–114; *Su-pao*, p. 405 (May 7, 1903); pp. 416–417 (May 8, 1903).

48. *Su-pao*, p. 282 (April 16, 1903).

49. E.g., in Jui-an during the summer of 1903 students from six schools founded a society to study physical drill and scholarly subjects. There was also a debating society in Jui-an which was criticized by local conservatives and other opponents. *Kuo-min jih-jih-pao*, p. 230 (September 27, 1903).

50. *Su-pao*, p. 324 (April 23, 1903).

51. Eric J. Hobsbawm, *Primitive Rebels: Studies in Archaic Forms of Social Movements in the 19th and 20th Centuries* (New York, 1965), p. 24.

7. Development of the Revolutionary Movement in Chekiang I: Foundations

1. Sources for the early life of Hsü Hsi-lin are T'ao, "Che-an," pp. 56–58; *KMCC*, pp. 183–186; Yü Chao-i, *Ch'iu Chin* (Hong Kong, 1956), pp. 68–69; *TMH*, 3:188.

2. *Su-pao*, pp. 528–529 (May 24, 1903). This article pictures Hsü Hsi-lin as a self-seeking opportunist and derogates his mathematical knowledge. It is an interesting contrast to Hsü the idol of radical youths.

3. T'ao, "Che-an" pp. 56–57. This anti-Catholic agitation is reported briefly in *NCH*, 75:609 (6/16/05).

4. I have seen two poems in Hsiao P'ing, *Hsin-hai ko-ming lieh-shih shih-wen hsüan* (A selection of writings by martyrs of the 1911 Revolution; Peking, 1962), pp. 128–129. Hsü's testimony after assassinating En-ming appears, among other sources, in Tsou Lu, *Chung-kuo Kuo-min-tang shih-kao* (Draft history of the Kuomintang, Shanghai, 1938), pp. 737–738. A collection of essays, some of which were written for school examinations when Hsü was teaching at the Shaohsing Middle School, appears in Kuomintang, Committee for the Compilation of Materials on the Party History of the Central Executive Committee, *Ko-ming hsien-lieh hsien-chin shih-wen hsüan-chi* (Selected writings of martyrs and forebearers of the revolution), 6 vols. (Taipei, 1965), 1:163–175. These essays are sometimes radical in tone, but conventional in subject and style. Probably Hsü Hsi-lin accepted most of the Western political ideals current among radical students. He was nationalistic and aimed to establish a republic. However, like Ch'iu Chin he continued to be influenced by his early education and probably was also influenced by the traditional image of the hero.

5. Sources on T'ao Ch'eng-chang's life are Chang Huang-ch'i, "Kuang-fu hui ling-hsiu T'ao Ch'eng-chang ko-ming shih" (The revolutionary activities of Restoration Society leader T'ao Ch'eng-chang), in *HHKM*, 1:521–529; Ma Hsü-lun, "T'ao Ch'eng-chang chih ssu" (The death of T'ao Ch'eng-chang), in *HHKM*, 1:520.

6. T'ao, "Che-an," pp. 22–25, 54–55; Feng, *Chung-hua*, 2:9–10; Chang Huang-ch'i, "T'ao Ch'eng-chang," pp. 522–523.

7. T'ao Ch'eng-chang, "Lung-hua hui chang-ch'eng" (Regulations of the Dragon Flower Society); in *HHKM*, 1:534–544.

8. The immediate assumption is that these regulations were written during the 1904–1906 period, when T'ao was most active in organizing the secret societies. E.g., the date 1904 is given in Wang I-sun, "Hsin-hai ko-ming shih-ch'i tzu-ch'an chieh-chi vü nung-min ti kuan-hsi wen-t'i" (The question of relations between the bourgeoisie and the peasantry during the period of the 1911 Revolution); in *CNL*, 1:128.

However, the date 1908 is given in Hirayama Shū (P'ing Shan-chou), *Chung-kuo pi-mi she-hui shih* (A history of Chinese secret societies), Commercial Press Translation Department, tr. (Shanghai, 1912), p. 80. Wei Chien-yu argues that the regulations were written in 1908, mainly on the grounds that the association was obviously distinct from the original Dragon Flower Society and that the second article of its regulations uses both the names Revolutionary Association and Dragon Flower Society. Revolutionary Association (*ko-ming hsieh-hui*) was the name generally given to the group in which T'ao tried to unite secret societies from Kiangsu, Chekiang, Fukien, Anhwei, and Kiangsi in 1908. Wei Chien-yu, "Hsin-hai ko-ming ch'ien-yeh ti Che-chiang hui-tang huo-tung" (Activities of Chekiangese secret societies on the eve of the 1911 Revolution); in *CNL*, pp. 538–539. T'ao was also appointed *ta-tu-tu*, the term used to indicate the rank of army commanders in his regulations, in 1908 and the five armies in the regulations conveniently correspond to five provinces. These points are still not conclusive, especially since T'ao might have made use of earlier ideas in 1908, but they do seem to indicate the later date.

9. T'ao Ch'eng-chang's terms and the corresponding Triad terms are listed in T'ao, "Lung-hua hui," p. 541.

10. *Ibid.,* pp. 540–544.

11. See Joseph R. Levenson, "The Suggestiveness of Vestiges: Confucianism and Monarchy at the Last," in David S. Nivison and Arthur Wright, eds., *Confucianism in Action* (Stanford, 1959), pp. 248–249.

12. T'ao, "Lung-hua hui," pp. 534–535. The term *ko-ming* is, of course, ambiguous since it can either mean breaking the emperor's mandate in the traditional Chinese

sense or revolution in the modern Western sense. I have translated it here as breaking the mandate because in these passages T'ao seems to be trying to revise tradition while staying as much as possible within the traditional framework.

13. E.g., T'ao quotes the *I-ching* statement that "T'ang's and Wu's breaking the mandate was in accord with the wishes of heaven and favorable to the people" (*Ibid.*, p. 534). Other examples are Confucius's exclamation that "Yung might occupy the place of a prince" and his defense of Kuan Chung because of Kuan's beneficial role and civilizing influence even though he served as minister to the man who murdered his first lord. (*Ibid.*, p. 535; for full texts of quotes see James Legge, *The Chinese Classics*, vol. 1, *Confucian Analects, The Great Learning and The Doctrine of the Mean* [Oxford, 1893], pp. 184, 282). T'ao found more pertinent quotes in Mencius, citing the statement that the people are the most and the sovereign the least important elements in the state, and the justification of the overthrow of the last rulers of the Hsia and Shang dynasties because they had degenerated to the level of "robbers and ruffians." (T'ao, "Lung-hua hui," p. 535; Legge, vol. 2, *The Works of Mencius* [Oxford, 1895], pp. 483, 167).

14. *Ibid.*, pp. 535–537.

15. *Ibid.*, p. 538.

16. *Ibid.*

17. *Ibid.*, pp. 538–539.

18. *Ibid.*, p. 539.

19. Chang Huang-ch'i, "T'ao Ch'eng-chang," p. 523. T'ao was willing to consider many methods to further the revolutionary cause. At one point, impressed by the superstitiousness of most Chinese, he even studied hypnotism as a way to attract and influence a crowd. However, the main method was distribution of literature.

20. T'ao, "Che-an," p. 25. The tracts written by Wei Lan and Ao Chia-hsiung were *The Essence of Confucius* (*Kung-fu-tzu chih hsin-kan*) and Song of New Mountain (*Hsin-shan ko*).

21. The "*Meng hui-t'ou* (About Face!) case" of mid-1906 indicated some recruits were gained this way. A boxer from Kinhwa became acquainted with revolutionary ideas and sought to enter the Dragon Flower Society. Chang Kung gave him a copy of *About Face!* which he carried about and read repeatedly. He lost the book in a fight with some local bullies who had stolen his father-in-law's cattle. The robbers denounced him to the authorities. At the insistence of the Manchu prefect he was interrogated and executed. The "rebellious book" was banned, thereby increasing its circulation in the villages. *Ibid.*, pp. 12–13; Feng, *Chung-hua*, 2:5.

22. T'ao, "Che-an," p. 62.

23. *Ibid.*, pp. 77–79; also in the Grand Council archives on the Ch'iu Chin case in *HHKM*, 3:206–210; *KMWH*, 1:136–139; Ch'iu Ts'an-chih (Wang Ts'an-chih), *Ch'iu Chin ko-ming chuan* (A revolutionary biography of Ch'iu Chin; Taipei, 1953), pp. 82–85; P'eng Tzu-i, *Ch'iu Chin* (Shanghai, 1941), pp. 64–66.

24. Japanese titles with their Chinese pronunciation appear in H. S. Brunnett and V. V. Hagelstrom, *Present Day Political Organization of China*, A. Beltchenko, tr. (Shanghai, 1912), pp. 293–294. Ch'iu's titles are given in T'ao, "Che-an," p. 78.

25. Shao Hsün-cheng, "Hsin-hai ko-ming shih-ch'i tzu-ch'an chieh-chi ko-ming p'ai ho nung ti kuan-hsi wen-t'i" (The question of the relations between the revolutionary strata of the bourgeoisie and the peasantry during the period of the 1911 Revolution), in *CNL*, p. 100.

26. This verse tells of the ties that bind society brothers after the oath-taking ceremony and states that anyone may join, no matter from what class of society he comes— officials, scholars, yamen runners, servants, and soldiers are all welcome. Hsiao Kung-chuan, *Rural China: Imperial Control in the Nineteenth Century* (Seattle, 1960), p. 472.

The verse was translated by Hsiao from *T'ung-ch'uan fu-chih,* 1897 ed., 30 chuan, 17/42b.

27. Hung failed the examinations for the *hsiu-ts'ai* degree several times. Wei Ch'ang-hui was a landlord and a pawnshop owner, an educated man who had experience in dealing with local officials. Shih Ta-k'ai had studied for some time, but had no examination degree and had turned to farming because of his lack of success. Among Wei Ch'ang-hui's adherents were merchants, a few rich farmers, and well-educated people. Some other scholars such as Wang T'ao, Yung Wing, and possibly Ch'ien Chang approached the Taipings after their initial successes and when rebuffed aided the government instead. Ssu-yü Teng, *New Light on the Taiping Rebellion* (Cambridge, Mass., 1950), pp. 29–34, 51–52, 58–59, 73.

28. Some members of the gentry who joined the Nien enhanced their influence by bringing with them their own armed force which had originated as local militia raised at the behest of imperial orders. Other gentry became independent leaders of bandit bands also based on militia. Usually in the end they joined the Nien because both were in defiance of the government. Chiang Siang-tse, *The Nien Rebellion* (Seattle, 1954), pp. 14, 45–54. These pages contain much interesting information on members of the local elite joining the Nien.

29. John Israel, *Student Nationalism in China, 1927–1937* (Stanford, 1966), pp. 134–137.

30. Communist writers also recognize this gap between peasants and the 1911 revolutionary intellectuals. E.g., Shao Hsün-cheng says that the revolutionaries relied upon alliances with the secret societies because they could not approach the peasant class directly. Their revolutionary aims and those of the peasants remained somewhat different. The revolutionaries did not give the peasants a free hand, but insisted that they follow the bourgeois revolutionaries' plans. Although aware of peasant problems, the intellectuals failed to produce the leadership necessary to realize the basic peasant demands for land. Shao Hsün-cheng, p. 101.

31. In 92 riots and rebellions in Central and South China recorded in *HHKM,* vol. 3, schools or the houses of teachers and education officials were attacked in twenty-two instances, education associations in three, self-government offices in one, new police stations in ten, chambers of commerce in two, anti-opium officials or bureaus in four, and members of municipal councils in seven. Sometimes more than one of these modern institutions was attacked in one riot. *HHKM,* 3:367–536.

32. *NCH,* 73:686 (9/23/04).

33. In addition to the main revolutionary organizations, revolutionary influence was important in a number of other schools in Chekiang. These included:

The Tung-hu Middle School, established by Hsieh Fei-lin in Shaohsing

The Shaohsing Prefectural Middle School

The Patriotic Girls' School (Ai-hua nü-hsüeh) in Chenghsien, founded by Hsieh Fei-lin and Hu Shih-chün

The Ming-ch'iang Girls School, founded in Lotsing by Ch'en Meng-hsiung, and The Monk's and People's School (Seng-min hsüeh-t'ang), founded in Lotsing by Ch'en Meng-hsiung and Huang Fei-lung

The Ming-tao Girls School in Shaohsing, directed by Ch'iu Chin in 1907

The Buddhist Educational Association (Seng chiao-yü hui) in Chenghsien

Militia and night schools organized by revolutionaries and secret societies in Chenghsien

Physical-education associations (*T'i-yü hui*) in Chuchow, Chin-yün, and Hu-chen

The Li-yung Cotton Mills in Chuchow

The Yao-tzu Physical Education School in Taichow

An agricultural and industrial school for *to-min* in Ningpo

Some of these institutions were genuine revolutionary fronts. Others just had some revolutionary teachers and made use of revolutionary literature. Most of these names are from Ch'u Fu-ch'eng, "Che-chiang Hsin-hai ko-ming chi-shih" (A record of the 1911 Revolution in Chekiang); in *HHKM*, 7:150–152. Others are from T'ao, "Che-an," p. 14, and Arthur W. Hummel, ed., *Eminent Chinese of the Ch'ing Period*, 2 vols. (Washington, D.C., 1943–1944), 1:170; Mao Hu-hou, "Hsin-hai ko-ming tsai Li-shui" (The 1911 Revolution in Li-shui), in *KML*, 4:200–202; Chou Ch'i-wei, "Lo-ch'ing Hsin-hai ko-ming shih liao" (Historical materials on the 1911 Revolution in Lotsing), in *KML*, 4:188–189; Lü Yüeh-p'ing, "Hui-i Hsin-hai ko-ming shih-ch'i ti chi-chien shih ho Ch'u-chou kuang-fu ching-kuo" (Recollections of a few things of the period of the 1911 Revolution and experiences during the Revolution in Chuchow), in *KML*, 4:196; Lin Tuan-fu, "Ning-po kuang-fu chin li-chi" (A personal chronicle of the 1911 Revolution in Ningpo), in *KML*, 4:174–175.

34. Tsou Lu, *Chung-kuo Kuo-min-tang shih-kao* (A draft history of the Kuomintang; Shanghai, 1938), p. 892.

35. For instance, during 1904 see edicts rewarding Chekiangese gentry or officials dated September 18, 1904, and November 28, 1904, and two edicts dated December 25, 1904, in *CSL-KH* 534/4b, 536/12b and 538/7a.

36. *NCH*, 72:1040 (5/20/04).

37. Hummel, 2:678.

38. Information in this case is from T'ao, "Che-an," pp. 13–14; Chou Ch'i-wei, p. 188; Feng, *Chung-hua*, 2:41 mainly paraphrases T'ao.

39. Ch'en Meng-hsiung was a native of Lotsing district, Chekiang. Some of his ancestors had cooperated with the Taiping's in the mid-nineteenth century, so he was heir to a certain rebellious tradition. Before 1905 he had studied in Hangchow, Shanghai, and Tokyo. In 1905 he was active in Ao Chia-hsiung's Wen-T'ai-Ch'u Guildhall in Kashing. After the conclusion of the Song of New Mountain case he taught overseas Chinese in Java. He died there in 1908. Chou Ch'i-wei, pp. 188–191.

40. Chang Ch'i-yün, "Sun I-jang chih cheng-chih ssu-hsiang" (The political thought of Sun I-jang), *Che-chiang hsüeh-pao* (Chekiang studies), 1.1:2.

41. *Ibid.*, pp. 1–2.

42. This man was T'ao Pao-lien, another reformist gentry who knew some radicals such as Ao Chia-hsiung and Wu Chih-hui. Wu had briefly worked with him in Canton during the winter of 1901–02 before joining the revolutionary movement. T'ao, "Che-an," p. 14; Chang Wen-po, *Chih-lao hsien-hua* (Chats about Wu Chih-hui; Taipei, 1952), p. 13.

43. T'ao, "Che-an," pp. 68–71 is the basic source for Ao Chia-hsiung's life. The *NCH* report of the disappearance of a young man from "a prominent moneyed family" probably refers to Ao and is consistent with T'ao's story of his death. *NCH*, 86:774 (3/27/08).

44. *Su-pao*, p. 350 (April 28, 1903).

45. *CCC*, 6:*shih-p'ing*, 2–3.

46. Shen Tieh-min, "Chi Kuang-fu hui erh-san shih" (Recollections of two or three things about the Restoration Society); in *KML*, 4:133.

47. Ao Chia-hsiung also planned to found branches of the guildhall in Huchow, Sungkiang, and Hangchow to develop secret society contacts in those areas. It is not clear whether or not they were established. Information on the guildhall is from T'ao, "Che-an," pp. 25, 69–72; Chang Huang-ch'i, "T'ao Ch'eng-chang," p. 523; Feng, *Chung-hua*, 2:11–13. The latter two accounts mainly follow T'ao, with some additional information. Wei Chien-yu is a secondary, Communist source. Feng, *I-shih*, 3:113–115, gives brief biographical information.

48. On illegality see Ch'ü T'ung-tsu, *Local Government in China under the Ch'ing*

(Cambridge, Mass., 1962), pp. 187, 333.

49. Chang P'eng-yuan, oral communication. *NCH*, 75:608 (6/16/05); 77:395 (11/17/05); 78:497 (3/2/06); 79:298 (5/11/06); 82:201 (1/25/07); Ch'iu Chin, "Letter dated June 3, 1907," in *Ch'iu Chin chi* (The collected works of Ch'iu Chin; Shanghai, 1960), p. 49; *CCC*, 2:179–180; 8:181–182.

50. T'ao, "Che-an," pp. 26–27.

51. *Ibid.*

52. Ch'iu Ts'an-chih, pp. 64–66; Feng, *I-shih*, 3:115. Chao Hung-fu was a good boxer and also allegedly a scholar who had passed the district examinations. Since he was too poor to continue his studies he turned to trade for a livelihood. He was a secret society member and also was active in the Wen-T'ai-Ch'u Guildhall. Then he helped found the Ta-t'ung School and was the school's accountant. His daughter married Chu Shao-k'ang's eldest son and took part in the revolutionary armies' attack on Nanking in 1911.

53. T'ao, "Che-an," p. 27; Feng, *Chung-hua*, 2:23.

54. T'ao, "Che-an," pp. 27–28, Chu Tsan-ch'ing, "Ta-tung shih-fan hsüeh-t'ang" (The Ta-t'ung Normal School), in *KML*, 4:145, 149; Ch'u Fu-ch'eng, pp. 149–150.

55. T'ao, "Che-an," p. 28; Feng, *Chung-hua*, 2:24.

56. Chu Tsan-ch'ing, pp. 144–145; *Ch'iu Chin chi*, p. 49.

57. Chu Tsan-ch'ing, p. 147.

58. Testimony of Hsü Wei, in T'ao, "Che-an," p. 84 and Feng, *Chung-hua*, 2:51; "Telegram of Liang-Kiang Governor-General Tuan-fang to the Grand Council dated August 21, 1907"; in *HHKM*, 3:175.

59. Hsü Chung-ch'ing's contributions are summarized in Ch'en Wei, "Kuang-fu hui ch'ien-ch'i ti huo-tung pien-tuan" (Miscellany about activities preceding the founding of the Restoration Society); in *KML*, 4:128.

60. T'ao, "Che-an," p. 28.

8. Development of the Revolutionary Movement in Chekiang II: Limitations

1. T'ao, "Che-an," p. 28; Chang Huang-ch'i, "Kuang-fu hui ling-hsiu T'ao Ch'eng-chang ko-ming shih" (The revolutionary activities of Restoration Society leader T'ao Ch'eng-chang); in *HHKM*, 1:524. Each of the five planned to specialize in different aspects of military training. T'ao and Hsü were going to enter the infantry, Kung was to study engineering, and the other two were going to seek artillery or cavalry training. Ch'en Wei, "Kuang-fu hui ch'ien-ch'i ti hou-tung p'ien-tuan" (Miscellany about activities preceding the founding of the Restoration Society); in *KML*, 4:129.

2. T'ao, "Che-an," p. 28. In recording the bribe money T'ao uses only the character *chin* (gold), but does not specify whether the unit of account is ounces (*liang*) or yuan.

3. *Ibid.*, p. 29; Ch'en Wei, p. 130. Ch'en intimates that they were refused because of official suspicions.

4. T'ao, "Che-an," p. 29.

5. *KMCC*, pp. 192–194.

6. T'ao, "Che-an," pp. 29–30.

7. Chang Huang-ch'i, p. 524.

8. *Ibid.*, p. 524.

9. T'ao, "Che-an," p. 58.

10. *Ibid.*, pp. 29–31, 34; Lu Hsün, *Selected Works*, 4 vols. (Peking, 1956), 1:416. Sun Te-ch'ing is here described in a footnote as an enlightened landlord who joined the anti-Manchu revolution.

11. Ch'iu Chin was head of the physical-education association which she established

and also taught at the Ta-t'ung School, but evidently she did not formally head the school. Chu Tsan-ch'ing, a one-time student there, lists Huang I as head of the school in 1907. Chu Tsan-ch'ing, "Ta-t'ung shih-fan hsüeh-t'ang" (The Ta-t'ung Normal School); in *KML,* 4:144.

12. T'ao, "Che-an," p. 31.

13. Chu Tsan-ch'ing, pp. 145–146.

14. T'ao, "Che-an," p. 32.

15. "Telegram of Kuei-fu to Governor Chang Tseng-yang," in T'ao, "Che-an," p. 43; T'ao, "Che-an," p. 41; Wang Shih-tse, "Hui-i Ch'iu Chin" (Recollections of Ch'iu Chin); in *KML,* 4:227.

16. T'ao, "Che-an," pp. 109–111.

17. Jerome Ch'en, "Secret Societies," *Ch'ing-shih wen-t'i,* 1.3:14.

18. The international relief effort was organized by a famine relief committee of prominent Shanghai citizens, both Chinese and Western. Most of the contributions from abroad came from the United States, and the American consul-general in Shanghai acted as sort of a manager and an intermediary between his country's donors and the relief committee in China. Considerable information about the famine may be found in reports of the Shanghai and other American consuls. See U.S. Department of State, Record Group 59, Numerical File, 1906–07, *passim.* The nature and effect of rural famine and unrest at the end of the Ch'ing is beyond the scope of the book and still awaits study. Yamashita Yoneko has studied popular movements, particularly peasant risings, in Kiangsu and Chekiang. Her thesis is that the 1911 Revolution was fundamentally caused by popular revolts against imperialism. She believes the series of peasant risings and riots, largely caused by food shortages and by the local impact of the Ch'ing modernization effort, were a basic factor in the collapse of the dynasty. Her interpretation seems to overestimate the degree of anti-imperialism in the countryside, the effectiveness of the Restoration Society–secret society relationship, and the importance of the peasantry in the Revolution. It does have the merit of calling attention to the serious rural demoralization and the inability of the dynasty to remedy these disorders that sapped its vitality. Yamashita Yoneko, "Shingai kakumei no jiki no minshu undo" (The mass movement at the time of the 1911 Revolution), *Toyo bunka kenkyujo kiyo* (Memoirs of the Institute of Oriental Culture), 37:111–164, *passim.*

19. "Edict to the Grand Council dated November 18, 1906," *CSL-KH,* 565/3b.

20. "Edict dated July 5, 1906," *CSL-KH* 560/7b–8a; Li Shih-yüeh, *Hsin-hai ko-ming shih-ch'i Liang-Hu ti-ch'ü ti ko-ming yün-tung* (The revolutionary movement in the Hunan and Hupei areas during the period of the 1911 Revolution; Peking, 1957), p. 95. When Liu Tao-i and his associates went to Hunan they had no particular plans for a rising, but wished to distribute revolutionary materials and make alliances with the secret societies. The rising, when it did occur, grew out of the local situation and was not directed by the Revolutionary Alliance headquarters in Tokyo. (Feng, *Chunghua,* 2:56). The Revolutionary Alliance agitators in Hunan took advantage of certain favorable factors, the chief of which were the 1906 floods and famine and the desire of secret society members to revenge the execution of the Brothers and Elders Society leader Ma Fu-i in 1904. Kuomintang, Committee for the Compilation of Materials on the Party History of the Central Executive Committee, ed., *Kuo-fu nien-p'u ch'u-kao* (A preliminary draft of the chronological biography of Sun Yat-sen; Taipei, 1958), p. 166. The famine was probably the most important factor behind the timing of the rising. It was behind numerous unrelated robberies and riots and was responsible for unrest among coal miners and secret society members which might well have led to a rising without any direction from the revolutionaries. What the Revolutionary Alliance representatives did was to try to unite the various elements and enlarge the

scale.

21. Kuo T'ing-i, *Chin-tai Chung-kuo shih-shih jih-chih* (A chronology of modern Chinese history), 2 vols. (Taipei, 1963), 2: 1271–1279.

22. T'ao, "Che-an," p. 32–33.

23. *Ibid.,* p. 33. Lü Chia-i had about three thousand followers and two leaders in Taichow prefecture each led six to seven thousand. (*Ibid.,* p. 20). Ch'iu Chin was not ready to revolt at this point, and Lü, who was closely involved with the Ta-t'ung School, was not justified in terms of party objectives in risking a premature rising of such a purely local nature.

24. T'ao, "Che-an," pp. 34–35, 74–75; Kuo T'ing-i, 2:1279. Wang Chin-fa and Chu Shao-k'ang had already come under suspicion when a former associate had gone to Ningpo and had unsuccessfully attempted to start a rising there at the end of 1906.

25. T'ao, "Che-an," pp. 35, 64–65.

26. *Ibid.,* pp. 35–36, 66.

27. *NCH,* 84:205 (July 26, 1907).

28. *KMCC,* p. 225; T'ao, "Che-an," p. 32. Ch'iu Chin was in Chekiang during the fall of 1906 to help plan a rising in conjunction with the "P'ing-Liu-Li" rising in Hunan and Kiangsi. This revolt never occurred in Chekiang.

29. Arthur W. Hummel, ed., *Eminent Chinese of the Ch'ing Period,* 2 vols. (Washington, D.C., 1943–1944), 1:170.

30. Che-chiang chün ssu-i-chiu lü ssu-ling-pu (Headquarters of the 419th brigade of the Chekiang army), "Che-chün Hang-chou kuang-fu chi" (An account of the Chekiang army in the Revolution at Hangchow); in *KSKF,* 2:132. Chu Tsan-ch'ing (p. 48) states that Chiang Tsun-kuei made this trip and also says that many of the noncommissioned officers under Chiang (or possibly students at the School for Noncommissioned Officers, which Chiang then headed) attended the Ta-t'ung School. Another source claims that in the spring of 1907 the first class of the School for Noncommissioned Officers held maneuvers from Hangchow to Shaohsing. At the end they visited the Ta-t'ung School and many joined the Restoration Society. Ko Ching-en, "Hsin-hai ko-ming tsai Che-chiang" (The 1911 Revolution in Chekiang); in *KML,* 4:93–94. The author taught at the school, so this report may be accurate, but I have not seen mention of it in other sources.

31. Headquarters of the 419th brigade of the Chekiang army, p. 133.

32. *Ibid.,* p. 132.

33. Ch'iu appointed at least three army commanders. Liu Yao-hsün commanded in Wu-i district. In Kinhwa district the commander was a relative of Chang Kung's personal lieutenant, and Shen Yung-ch'ing's lieutenant was in charge in Yung-k'ang district. Quite possibly there were more who are not mentioned in the literature. Liu Yao-hsün was a *lin-kung* who was generous and popular but addicted to opium. He was influenced by the revolutionary propaganda which was spread in the interior of Chekiang. He met one of the revolutionaries, who introduced him to Ch'iu Chin. Liu then joined the Restoration Society and, so the story goes, pursued his duties so earnestly that he gave up opium. T'ao, "Che-an," pp. 35, 64, 66; Yü Chao-i, *Ch'iu Chin* (Hong Kong, 1956), p. 132.

34. Yü Chao-i, p. 133.

35. T'ao, "Che-an," pp. 62–63.

36. *Ibid.,* p. 88.

37. Yü Chao-i, p. 118; Chu Tsan-ch'ing, pp. 146–147, estimates that eighty or ninety came to the physical-education association. Many of these were skilled in boxing. Chiang Chi-yün, in his testimony after being captured with Ch'iu Chin, said sixty attended the physical-education association. T'ao, "Che-an," p. 88.

38. T'ao, "Che-an," p. 37.

39. *Tung-fang tsa-chih,* 1:6: *chiao-yü,* p. 144.

40. Tsou Lu, *Chung-kuo Kuo-min-tang shih-kao* (A draft history of the Kuomintang; Shanghai, 1938), p. 736; T'ao, "Che-an," p. 37. Hsü was also appointed director of the military school, but he does not seem to have actively assumed this position.

41. "Telegram of Liang-Kiang Governor-General Tuan-fang to the Grand Council dated July 8, 1907"; in *HHKM,* 3:123.

42. *NCH,* 84:70 (7/12/07).

43. *NCH,* 84:210 (7/26/07); "Telegram of Governor En-ming to the Grand Council," in T'ao, "Che-an," p. 92; Tsou Lu, p. 739; Feng, *Chung-hua,* 2:12, 58–59. This telegram was composed after En-ming was shot and just before his death.

44. Ch'en Po-p'ing's family originally came from Chekiang. He grew up in Foochow but returned to Chekiang and eventually entered the Ta-t'ung School, where Hsü Hsi-lin singled him out as a particularly apt pupil. He accompanied Hsü and the others to Japan in 1906 and studied at a police academy there after failing to be admitted to military school. He then returned to Shanghai, where he continued to associate with other revolutionaries and experimented with explosives. One day he and Ch'iu Chin were slightly injured by an explosion in his room. He returned briefly to Japan to learn more about bomb-making. Upon returning to China he wanted to go to Peking to kill T'ieh-liang, but Hsü Hsi-lin urged him to come to Anking instead. During the spring of 1907 he was the main link between Hsü in Anking and the Ta-t'ung School. He was killed in July 1907 during Hsü's rising at the age of twenty-five. T'ao, "Che-an," pp. 58–59.

Ma Tsung-han was from a Chekiangese scholar-gentry family. His uncle was a *chin-shih* and held office in Kwangtung. His father was a scholar, but he held no office and evidently did not take, or failed to pass, any examination. As a youth Ma was impressed by the poetry of Yüeh Fei, and when older he became converted to anti-Manchuism through the study of history. He attended the Chekiang Higher School. After graduation he established an elementary school where he taught anti-Manchu ideas. He also distributed revolutionary literature and wrote a book attacking the Manchu constitutional movement. In 1906 he went to Japan, but had to return home because of a death in his family before receiving the military training which he sought. He then went to Shanghai, where he was introduced to Hsü Hsi-lin by Ch'en Po-p'ing. After Hsü persuaded Ch'en to join him in Anking, Ch'en wrote Ma urging him to come to Anhwei. Ma did so with the avowed intention of overthrowing the dynasty. In Anking he worked particularly closely with Ch'en, with whom he was more intimate than he was with Hsü. He took part in Hsü's rising, was arrested, and was executed on August 24, 1907. He was then twenty-three years old. T'ao, "Che-an," pp. 31, 59–60, 81.

T'ao gives a brief biography of Ma and also reprints his testimony at the trial. This testimony was evidently intended to cover up his revolutionary intentions and, therefore, is not accurate.

45. Tsou Lu, p. 892.

46. Feng, *Chung-hua,* 2:27.

47. H. B. Taylor to Wm. Martin, 7/26/07, encl. in Report of Hankow Consul Wm. Martin, 1/29/07, U.S. Department of State, General Records, Record Group 59, Numerical File, no. 8019/2–3.

48. Feng, *Chung-hua,* 2:28.

49. Tsou Lu, p. 764.

50. Feng, *Chung-hua,* 2:28.

51. Tsou Lu, p. 765.

52. Feng, *Chung-hua,* 2:21.

53. E.g., "Memorial of Ching-chou Tartar-General dated November 19, 1907,"

CSL-KH, 581/10b; "Memorial of Police Bureau dated February 17, 1906," *CSL-KH*, 581/13b. The problem of resettling ex-soldiers was particularly difficult at the end of the Ch'ing because large areas of the country were suffering from a series of natural disasters.

54. "Memorial of Min-Che Governor-General dated July 2, 1904," *CSL-KH*, 531/2b; "Memorial of acting Kiang-pei Ti-tu dated December 22, 1907," *CSL-KH*, 583/2a.

55. One piece of evidence indicating such policies were pursued is an announcement that Anhwei was going to convert militia into police. *Tung-fang tsa-chih*, 2.1: *nei-wu* 10.

56. T'ao, "Che-an," p. 37.

57. *KMCC*, p. 197.

58. T'ao, "Che-an," p. 37. Ch'en Po-p'ing was the author of the revolutionary declaration that Hsü planned to distribute. It was fairly typical revolutionary fare which described the tyranny and humiliation of two hundred years of Manchu rule and attacked the dynasty's plans for a constitution. Foreign aggression as well as lack of freedom and other internal troubles were blamed on the Manchu government's oppression of the Chinese race. Through revolution, the Chinese would avenge themselves on their old enemies, restore China's primacy, and construct a new republican nation. It assured the populace of the revolutionary army's good intentions and asked people to report violations by troops. However, all Chinese traitors and all those who followed the Manchus, resisted the army, plundered, or spread disturbing rumors would be shot.

59. Ma Tsung-han's testimony in *Ibid.*, p. 82. The testimonies of Hsü Hsi-lin, Ma, and Hsü Wei are found in a number of other sources including Feng, *Chung-hua*, and Tsou Lu.

60. *Ibid.*, pp. 38–39; "Telegram of Tuan-fang and Feng Hsü to the Grand Council dated July 10, 1907," in *HHKM*, 3:133; *KMCC*, pp. 198–199.

61. "Telegram of Kiang-nan Salt Taotai Chu En-fu to Liang-Kiang Governor-General Tuan-fang dated July 12, 1907," in *HHKM*, 3:145; "Telegram of Tuan-fang to the Grand Council dated July 10, 1907," in *HHKM*, 3:175; Testimony of Ma Tsung-han, in T'ao, "Che-an," p. 83.

62. T'ao, "Che-an," p. 39.

63. Feng, *Chung-hua*, 2:42; Ts'ao Ya-po, *Wu-ch'ang ko-ming chen-shih* (A true history of the Wuchang revolution), 3 vols. (Shanghai, 1930), 1:220.

64. Feng, *Chung-hua*, 2:42.

65. T'ao, "Che-an," p. 40; "Memorial of Liang-Kiang Governor-General and Anhwei Governor," in T'ao, "Che-an," p. 92; Tsou Lu, p. 739; or Feng, *Chung-hua*, 2:38–39. Seven of those arrested were subsequently released because they had been "captured by mistake."

66. Hsü testified orally and also wrote out a confession. See T'ao, "Che-an," pp. 80–81; Feng, *Chung-hua*, 2:44–46; Tsou Lu, pp. 737–738; Ts'ao Ya-po, 1:221–222.

67. T'ao, "Che-an," pp. 81–83; Feng, *Chung-hua*, 2:46–49.

68. "Telegram of Tuan-fang to the Grand Council dated July 8, 1907"; "Telegram of Tuan-fang to the Grand Council dated July 8, 1907," in *HHKM*, 3:124, 128.

69. "Telegram of Tuan-fang to the Director of the Shanghai Telegraph Office Yang I-ch'ing dated July 11, 1907"; in *HHKM*, 3:117.

70. "Telegram of Tuan-fang to T'ai-ts'ang Military Taotai Jui Cheng dated July 8, 1907"; in *HHKM*, 3:120.

71. "Telegram of Tuan-fang to Chekiang Governor Chang Tseng-yang dated July 11, 1907"; in *HHKM*, 3:140.

72. Testimony of Hsü Wei in T'ao, pp. 84–86. Probably it was Hsü Wei who made

it clear to Tuan-fang and Anhwei officials that the Ta-t'ung School involved was in Shaohsing and not in the town of Ta-t'ung on the Yangtze River as they had first thought. "Telegram of Tuan-fang to Wuhu Taotai dated July 11, 1907"; in *HHKM*, 3:143.

73. "Order to Shaohsing Prefect," in *HHKM*, 3:188; *KMWH*, 1:98; "Tuan-fang to Chang Tseng-yang dated July 10, 1907," in *HHKM*, 3:135; "Telegram of Chekiang Governor to Shaohsing Prefect," in *KMWH*, 1:99.

74. "Testimony of Chiang Chi-yün," in Ch'iu Ts'an-chih, p. 122; and *KMWH*, 1:129.

75. T'ao, "Che-an," pp. 41–42; P'eng Tzu-i, *Ch'iu Chin* (Shanghai, 1941), p. 13. *KMCC*, p. 228. Chou Hua-ch'ang was to be one of the leaders of the Dare-to-die corps.

76. Thus reducing the ammunition available from twenty thousand to six to seven thousand rounds. T'ao, "Che-an," p. 31.

77. *Ibid.*, p. 41–42, 63–64; "Communication of Battalion Commander Hsü of the Chekiang new army to the Shaohsing Prefect on the subject of capturing the revolutionaries dated July 18, 1907," in *KMWH*, 1:104; and in Ch'iu Ts'an-chih, p. 138.

78. "Rescript of the Chekiang Governor, probably dated October 29, 1907"; in *KMWH*, 1:119–120.

79. "Memorial of Shaohsing Prefect Kuei-fu, Shan-yin Magistrate Li Chung-yo, and Kuei-chi Magistrate Li Jui-nien to Chekiang Governor dated July 30, 1907," in *KMWH*, 1:112; and in Ch'iu Ts'an-chih, pp. 131–132. None of the sources go into detail about the contents of the documents seized at the Ta-t'ung School, but they are presumably among those included in the collection of documents on the Ch'iu Chin case in the Grand Council archives. These are very clearly subversive. See *HHKM*, 3:205–211; *KMWH*, 1:135–140.

80. The written testimonies of Ch'iu and seven others captured with her are given in *HHKM*, 3:194–199; *KMWH*, 1:125–132; Ch'iu Ts'an-chih, pp. 121–123, 125–126. The statements of two of those captured, Chang Chi-yün and Ch'eng I, appear in very different versions in *HHKM* and Ch'iu Ts'an-chih and there are very minor differences in the versions of some of the other statements. *KMWH* contains both versions and according to the editors different versions are found in the Grand Council and Shaohsing prefectural archives. The *HHKM* versions are from the Grand Council archives whereas Ch'iu Ts'an-chih took hers from the Shaohsing collection.

81. "Memorial of Kuei-fu, Li Chung-yo and Li Jui-nien dated July 30, 1907"; in *KMWH*, 1:112.

82. "Telegram of Shaohsing prefect," in *HHKM*, 3:190; "Telegram of Chang Tseng-yang to Kuei-fu dated July 14, 1907," in Ch'iu Ts'an-chih, p. 126.

83. T'ao, "Che-an," p. 97. None of those who were captured with Ch'iu were important figures and only two, Chiang Chi-yün and Ch'eng I, had more than brief connections with the revolutionaries.

Chiang Chi-yün was originally from Kinhwa. He had gone to Shanghai to meet Ch'iu Chin in 1906 with an introduction from Lü Hsiung-hsiang. Ch'iu tried to persuade him to help her extort contributions from wealthy merchants and gentry by threatening to expose them after "discovering" planted revolutionary literature. He refused to become involved, however. Ch'iu evidently did not consider him entirely trustworthy. *HHKM*, 3:197–198.

Ch'eng I was a *hsiu-ts'ai* from Honan. After graduating from the Honan Higher School he went to Shanghai in 1905. There he attended the Chinese Public Institute and the Shanghai Normal School and became a friend and confidant of Ch'iu Chin. He refused, however, to join the Restoration Society because he was a constitutionalist, not a revolutionary. Ch'eng was tortured, but he did not reveal any new information about the Restoration Society. He died in jail in 1909. T'ao, "Che-an," p. 64; "Testimony of Ch'eng I," in *HHKM*, 3:195; Chou Ya-wei, p. 628.

84. T'ao, "Che-an," p. 47.

85. *Ibid.*, pp. 46, 74–75; *Chung-hsing jih-pao* (November 11, 1907); in *TMH*, 3:272–273; *Tung-fang tsa-chih*, 5.1: *chün-shih*, p. 23. *NCH* has occasional reports of this rising, November-December 1907, *passim*.

86. T'ao, "Che-an," pp. 47, 66–67.

87. *Ibid.*, pp. 72–74; *Chung-hsing jih-pao* (February 6, 1908); in *TMH*, 3:273–274. Scattered reports appear in *NCH*, November 1907–April 1908, *passim*.

88. "Edict dated January 13, 1908," *CSL-KH*, 584/8b; Chao Chin-yü, "Su-Hang-Yung t'ieh-lu chieh-k'uan ho Chiang-Che jen-min ti chü-k'uan yün-tung" (The Shang-hai-Hangchow-Ningpo Railway loan and the opposition to the loan by the people of Kiangsu and Chekiang); in *Li-shih yen-chiu*, 9:58 (1959). Chao states that the real reason that at least some of the troops were sent to the T'ai Lake area was to intimidate the gentry-merchant opponents of the British railway loan. I do not know whether this was a factor or not. The smugglers' revolt was certainly troublesome enough to justify the importation of troops to suppress it and Chao may be seeing dark imperialist influence behind too many decisions.

89. "Edict to the Grand Council dated January 29, 1908," in *CSL-KH*, 584–8a-b; "Memorial of Liang-Kiang Governor-General Tuan-fang dated May 26, 1908," in *CSL-KH*, 590/9b.

90. T'ao, "Che-an," p. 21.

91. *Ibid.*, p. 42. It should be noted that the plays on words involved, the double meaning of the character *ch'iu*, meaning both autumn and Ch'iu Chin's surname, the appearance of that character as an element in the character *ch'ou*, meaning melancholy or sorrow, and the easy analogy of wind and rain with tears and sighs all had been used by Ch'iu in her earlier poetry. E.g., "Ch'iu-feng ch'ü" (Song of the autumn wind), in P'eng Tzu-i, p. 25; "Ch'iu yen" (Wild geese in autumn) and "Ch'iu-jih tu-tso" (Sitting alone on an autumn day), in Ch'iu Ts'an-chih, p. 6.

That the poem was widely publicized right after the execution is shown by a telegram from Chang Tseng-yang to Kuei-fu asking if Ch'iu had really written it. "Telegram of Chekiang Governor to Shaohsing Prefect dated July 30, 1907"; in *KMWH*, 1:112.

92. Chou Ya-wei, p. 629. A similar cartoon was published in *Shih-pao*. Yen Tu-ho, "Hsin-hai ko-ming shih-ch'i Shang-hai hsin-wen chieh tung-t'ai" (Shanghai newspaper circles during the period of the 1911 Revolution); in *KML*, 4:81.

93. See articles from these papers in Ch'iu Ts'an-chih, appendix, pp. 1–4, 16.

94. E.g., *NCH*, 84:205 (7/26/07).

95. Under the title of *Ch'iu Chin shih-tz'u* (Poems of Ch'iu Chin), Hummel, p. 170. Pamphlets about Hsü Hsi-lin also appeared. See an English summary of one in *NCH*, 87:371–373 (5/11/08).

96. The revolutionary Liu Shih-fu had attempted to assassinate Li Chun. See Feng, *I-shih*, 2:207–211. After En-ming's assassination high officials such as Yüan Shih-k'ai, Chang Chih-tung, and Tuan-fang received threats on their lives. There were evidently false reports that Tuan-fang had sent his family back to Peking from Nanking. *NCH*, 84:494 (8/30/07); "Rockhill to Root, 8/9/07," U.S. Department of State, General Records, Record Group 59, Numerical File, no. 215/66–67.

97. "Telegram of Tuan-fang to Feng Hsü dated July 15, 1907"; in *HHKM*, 3:153.

98. "Memorial of the Chekiang Governor reporting on the Chekiang case dated September 24, 1907," in T'ao, "Che-an," p. 96; *KMWH*, 1:117; *TMH*, 3:289; and *HHKM*, 3:213.

99. The Ch'iu Chin case essentially ended Chang Tseng-yang's official career. Chang was a *han-lin* and a distant relative of Chang Chih-tung. Before becoming governor of Chekiang he had been governor of Shensi and had held various lesser posts. He

was a proponent of reform and probably a more upright official than most. Fei Ching-chung (pseud. Wu-ch'iu chung-tzu), *Tang-tai ming-jen hsiao-chuan* (Brief biographies of contemporary famous men), 2 vols. (Shanghai, 1921), 2:128–129; Li Chiang-ch'iu, "Ch'iu Chin hsün-nan chi" (The death of Ch'iu Chin), in *TMH*, 3:241.

100. "Memorial of the Chekiang Governor reporting on the Chekiang case dated September 24, 1907," in T'ao, "Che-an," p. 95; *HHKM*, 3:211; *KMWH*, 1:115; and *TMH*, 3:282–283.

101. Feng, *Chung-hua*, 2:65; *TMH*, 3:188, 282–283.

102. Among the six who guaranteed Hsü Hsi-lin's father was Hu Tao-nan, who had informed on Ch'iu Chin. *TMH*, 3:189. The *North China Herald* reported that a large meeting in Hangchow to protest the behavior of officials was dispersed by police. *NCH*, 84:554 (9/6/07).

103. *NCH*, 84:203 (7/26/07). Prince Su, Shan-ch'i had some dealings with revolutionaries either out of sympathy or as a hedge against the future. Feng Tzu-yu credits him with helping to save Hsü Hsi-lin's family from extermination by arguing that the government should not alienate public opinion by meting out severe punishment at a time when preparations for a constitution were in progress. Feng, *I-shih*, 5:251.

104. "Proclamation of the Shaohsing Prefect dated July 16, 1907," in *KMWH*, 1:103; and Ch'iu Ts'an-chih, p. 131.

105. "Proclamation of the Shaohsing Prefect dated July 26, 1907," in *KMWH*, 1:108–109; and Ch'iu Ts'an-chih, pp. 146–147. In this second proclamation Kuei-fu also denied that Hsü Hsi-lin's father's property had been seized and that other members and friends of the family had been arrested.

106. The *North China Herald* reported that 196 arrests were alleged to have occurred on the day of En-ming's assassination. I do not know whether there is any truth in that figure or not, but it is significant that such stories were circulating. The *North China Herald* also reported that a son of the comprador of one of the (Shanghai?) foreign banks had been arrested in Anking because he was suspected of connections with Hsü Hsi-lin. Again I do not know whether there was any basis for this suspicion, but a significant point is that the newspaper article assumed that the real reason for his arrest was to extort money from his father. *NCH*, 84:203, 228 (7/26/07).

107. Feng, *Chung-hua*, 2:65; Hummel, p. 170. A highly sympathetic account of the Shan-yin Magistrate's role which was written by his son is, Li Chiang-ch'iu, in *TMH*, 3:238–242.

108. Huang Fu studied at the military preparatory schools in Hangchow and Tokyo. In Tokyo he joined the Revolutionary Alliance and spent vacations recruiting for the party in Chekiang. From 1908 to 1911 he was employed in the Fourth Section of the General Staff Council in Peking. In 1911 he was sent to Shanghai to spy on revolutionaries, but actually he helped plan both the Shanghai and Hangchow revolutions. He was Ch'en Ch'i-mei's chief-of-staff and helped organize the revolutionary attack on Nanking. Huang took part in the Second Revolution and fled to Tokyo when it failed. Soon thereafter he broke with Ch'en Ch'i-mei and Sun Yat-sen over revolutionary strategy. In 1916 he was military commissioner of the anti-Yüan Shih-k'ai forces during the Third Revolution. In 1917 he went to Tientsin and remained in the north for nine years. During this time he held ministerial and other posts under President Li Yüan-hung in 1923–24 and in the government organized by Feng Yü-hsiang in 1924–25. In November 1926 he joined Chiang Kai-shek, whom he helped outmaneuver the Communists and left-wing Kuomintang. After briefly serving as Mayor of Shanghai in 1927 and minister of foreign affairs in 1928, he retired from politics until after the 1931 Mukden incident. From 1932 to 1935 he was chairman of the Peiping Political Affairs Council, which was in charge of five north Chinese provinces, and was bitterly criticized for making concessions to Japan. He died at age fifty-six in 1936. Tsou Lu,

p. 880; Ko Ching-en, pp. 96–97; *KSKF,* 2:32; Howard L. Boorman, ed., *Biographical Dictionary of Republican China* (New York, 1967), 2:187–190. *KSKF,* 2:32.

109. *Chuan-chi wen-hsüeh* (Biographical Literature), 7.1:8.

110. Huang Yüan-hsiu, "Hsi-hu pai-yün an yü Hsin-hai ko-ming chih kuan-hsi" (The relation of the White Cloud Temple at West Lake to the 1911 Revolution); in *KML,* 4:150–151.

111. Lü Kung-wang, "Hsin-hai ko-ming Che-chiang kuang-fu chi-shih" (An account of the 1911 Revolution in Chekiang), *Chin-tai shih tzu-liao,* 1:109 (1954). Chu Jui, Lü Kung-wang, and Ku Nai-pin were among the leaders of this group. It seems to have been narrowly confined to the new army and quite different in character than the student-secret society Restoration Society before 1908.

112. Ch'en did make at least one trip to Hangchow. Huang Yüan-hsiu, p. 151.

113. Feng, *Chung-hua,* 2:17; Chang Huang-ch'i, 1:524, 526.

114. A list of those scheduled to attend the meetings appears in Ch'u Fu-ch'eng, "Che-chiang Hsin-hai ko-ming chi-shih" (A record of the 1911 Revolution in Chekiang); in *HHKM,* 7:152.

115. Liu Shih-p'ei was a personal casualty of the revolutionary movement. He was from a scholarly Kiangsu family noted for its study of the *Tso-chuan* through several generations. Liu became a *chü-jen* and continued the family studies. In Shanghai from mid-1903 to the spring of 1905, he wrote for the revolutionary *China National Gazette, Warnings on Russian Affairs,* and *The Alarm Bell.* He then joined the Wen-T'ai-Ch'u Guildhall in Kashing and after that taught at radical schools in Anhwei. In Tokyo in 1907 he was on the staff of *The People's Journal.* He also was a founder of the anarchist *Society for the Study of Socialism* and the anarchist *Journal of Natural Law* (*T'ien-i pao*). His wife was also an anarchist and he may have been coerced into spying for the government to protect her when her part in an unsuccessful assassination plot was discovered. After he turned informer Liu was ostracized by the radicals. He then served as a private secretary to Tuan-fang and taught. After the Revolution he continued to teach and write. He supported Yüan Shih-k'ai's attempt to become emperor in 1915. When Yüan failed Liu lived in retirement and poverty in Tientsin until Ts'ai Yüan-p'ei invited him to teach at Peking University. He taught there from 1917 until his death in 1919 at the age of thirty-five. Feng, *I-shih,* 3:190–192; Hummel, 1:534–536.

116. Chang Huang-ch'i, p. 527; Tsou Lu, p. 881.

117. Chou Ch'i-wei, "Lo-ch'ing Hsin-hai ko-ming shih-liao" (Historical materials on the 1911 Revolution in Lotsing); in *KML,* 4:188–193. Huang's Buddhist name was Yüeh-kung.

118. Tsou Lu, p. 880; Che-chiang chün ssu-i-chiu lü ssu-ling-pu (Headquarters of the 419th brigade of the Chekiang army) "Che-chün Hang-chou kuang-fu chi" (An account of the Chekiang army in the Revolution at Hangchow); in *KSKF,* 2:134.

119. Ch'u Fu-ch'eng, p. 152.

120. Information on the Utilitarian Cotton Cloth Mills is from Mao Hu-hou, "Hsin-hai ko-ming tsai Li-shui" (The 1911 Revolution in Li-shui); in *KML,* 4:200–202.

121. Information on the Ningpo group is from Lin Tuan-fu, "Ning-po kuang-fu ch'in li-chi" (A personal chronicle of the 1911 Revolution in Ningpo), in *KML,* 4:174–180; *Hsin-hai ko-ming tzu-liao* (Materials on the 1911 Revolution), *Chin-tai shih tzu-liao,* 1:545 (1961).

122. Shen Tieh-min, "Chi Kuang-fu hui erh-san shih" (Recollections of two or three things about the Restoration Society), in *KML,* 4:131; Chou Ya-wei, "Kuang-fu hui chien-wen tsa-i" (Miscellaneous recollections of the Restoration Society), in *KML,* 1:625, 633.

123. Ko Ching-en, p. 91. The Military Preparatory School was established in 1900. It offered a three-year course with Japanese military instructors and Chinese teachers

for general subjects. For the first three years there were not many applicants and most of those who did apply were low-grade officers from the old army. In 1903 the numbers increased, however, and a number of applicants were degree holders. That year a one-year supplementary course was added. In 1904 and 1905 the number of students greatly increased. The school was converted into the Military Primary School in 1905. Ssu Tao-ch'ing, "Che-chün shih-pa nien ti hui-i lu" (Recollections of eighteen years in the Chekiangese army), *Chin-tai shih tzu-liao,* 2:76–77 (1957).

124. Chou Ya-wei, pp. 625–626; Ko Ching-en, pp. 93, 103; *Kuo-feng pao* (The national spirit), 1.21:72; Wen Kung-chih, *Tsui-chin san-shih nien Chung-kuo chün-shih shih* (A military history of China during the past thirty years; Shanghai, n.d.), 1:189. At the time of the Revolution, Ts'ai Ch'eng-hsün was commander of the 41st Brigade and Liu Hsün commanded the 42nd Brigade. Ting Mu-han commanded the 81st infantry regiment and Chou Ch'eng-t'an the 82nd infantry regiment, both stationed outside of Hangchow. Lü Kung-wang, p. 110.

125. Chou Ya-wei, pp. 626–627; Headquarters of the 49th Brigade of the Chekiang Army, p. 132. Tsou Lu (pp. 879–880) closely follows the latter source.

126. Headquarters of the 419th Brigade of the Chekiang Army, p. 132.

127. *Ibid.,* pp. 133–134; Chou Ya-wei, p. 631.

128. Chou Ya-wei, p. 630.

129. *Ibid.,* pp. 630, 633; U.S. Department of State, Record Group 59, Decimal File, 893.02/73a.

130. T'ang Shou-ch'ien was a *chin-shih* and had been a member of the Han-lin Academy. He had served as a magistrate in Anhwei and as commissioner of education in Kiangsi. T'ang was a reformer and a constitutionalist who was one of the organizers of the Association to Prepare for the Establishment of Constitutional Government in 1906. He made a name for himself as an opponent of the government by leading the protest against a British loan to build the Shanghai-Hangchow-Ningpo Railway. In November 1911 he was chosen military governor of Chekiang and in January 1912 became minister of communications in Sun Yat-sen's cabinet. Early in 1912 he joined Chang Chien, Chao Feng-ch'ang, Chang Ping-lin, Ch'eng Te-ch'üan, and others to form the United Party (*T'ung-i tang*). Ma Hsü-lun, "Wo tsai hsin-hai che-i-nien" (My experience during the year 1911), in *KML,* 1:171; Samuel C. Chu, *Reformer in Modern China, Chang Chien, 1853–1926* (New York, 1965), pp. 64, 77, 79.

131. U.S. Department of State, General Records (Record Group 59), Numerical File, 5315/15–16; "Tuan-fang to the Shanghai Taotai, the Kiangsu-Chekiang Railway Company and the Shanghai Chamber of Commerce," enclosure in 1518/105–106; *North China Daily News* (February 6, 1907), enclosure in 5315/1; "Edict dated August 26, 1905," *CSL-KH,* 547/13b; "Edict dated June 25, 1908," *CSL-KH,* 592/8b.

132. Headquarters of the 419th Brigade of the Chekiang Army, p. 134; *TMH,* 6:668–669; *Tung-fang tsa-chih,* 6.9: *chi-shih* 277.

133. "Edict dated August 23, 1910"; *Tung-fang tsa-chih,* 7.8: first *chi-tsai* 109–110. The government had tried to get rid of T'ang Shou-ch'ien the previous year by appointing him to a post in Kiangsi, but the railway stockholders refused to elect another president and early in 1910 reelected T'ang. *Tung-fang tsa-chih,* 6.9: *chi-shih* 277; 7.1: third *chi-tsai* 7.

134. E.g., students protested Italian loans to a company in Chekiang to develop mines in several prefectures. *Su-pao,* p. 204 (April 3, 1903); *CCC,* 8:117–118, 125–129; *Kuo-min jih-jih-pao* (*The China National Gazette;* photolithograph, Taipei, 1965), p. 414 (October 16, 1903).

135. Headquarters of the 419th Brigade of the Chekiang Army, p. 134; *TMH,* 6:669–670. The chief protest meeting in Hangchow, which followed a similar one in Shanghai, is reported in *Tung-fang tsa-chih,* 7.9: first *chi-tsai* 67–70.

136. E.g., *TMH*, 6:673–675.

137. *Ibid.*, 6:671–673.

138. Headquarters of the 419th Brigade of the Chekiang Army, p. 134. Ch'u Fu-ch'eng developed contacts with revolutionaries in the army during the railway agitation.

139. *Tung-fang tsa-chih*, 5.3: *nei-wu* 212;5.6: *nei-wu* 264;5.1: *chiao-yü* 44.

140. Liu Hou-sheng, *Chang Chien chuan-chi* (Biography of Chang Chien; Hong Kong, 1956), p. 177.

141. Ch'u Fu-ch'eng, p. 152.

142. Ma Hsü-lun, p. 176.

143. Shen Chün-ju, "Hsin-hai ko-ming tsa-i" (Miscellaneous recollections of the 1911 Revolution), in *KML*, 1:138–139; Fan Yin-nan, comp., *Tang-tai Chung-kuo ming-jen lu* (Who's Who in Contemporary China; Shanghai, 1931), p. 123.

144. Information on Ch'u Fu-ch'eng is from Ch'u Fu-ch'eng, pp. 151–158; *Tung-fang tsa-chih*, 6.11: *chi-shih* 356; Lu Yüeh-p'ing, "Hui-i Hsin-hai ko-ming shih-ch'i ti chi-chien shih ho Ch'u-chou kuang-fu ching-kuo" (Recollections of a few things of the period of the 1911 Revolution and experiences during the Revolution in Chu-chow), in *KML*, 4:197; Fan Yin-nan, comp., *Tang-tai Chung-kuo ming-jen lu* (Who's Who in Contemporary China; Shanghai, 1931), p. 406.

9. Revolutionaries and Revolution

1. *KMCC*, pp. 45–46; K'ung Fan-lin, *Ch'en Ying-shih* (Nanking, 1946), pp. 25–27, 31.

2. See the abbreviated lists of *The People's Stand* staff and the Central China Bureau members. Feng, *Tsu-chih*, pp. 212, 235.

3. *KML*, 4:48.

4. Huang Yen-p'ei, "Wo ch'in-shen ching-li ti Hsin-hai ko-ming shih-shih" (Facts of the 1911 Revolution that I personally experienced), in *KML*, 1:65; the *Shen-pao* offices were attacked once because the paper was unsympathetic to the Revolution. Ma Hsü-lun, "Wo tsai hsin-hai che-i-nien" (My experiences during the year 1911); in *KML*, 1:178.

5. The biography of a prominent gang leader during the Republic appears in Y.C. Wang, "Tu Yüeh-sheng (1888–1951): A Tentative Political Biography," *Journal of Asian Studies*, 26.3:433–455.

6. Chang Ch'eng-yu's account in Feng, *I-shih*, 5:271–277. A similar account appears in *KSKF*, 1:373–385. T'ien Hsin-shan and Chang Ch'eng-yu were both from Hupeh and Chang was living above the tailor shop where T'ien worked. Chang was approached because he was easily available and seemed to know about the Revolution.

7. Feng, *I-shih*, 5:271.

8. Information on the Merchant Volunteers is from "Shang-hai shang-t'uan hsiao-shih" (A short history of the Shanghai Merchant Volunteers); in *HHKM*, 7:86.

9. Mei Lan-fang, "Hsi-chü chieh ts'an-chia Hsin-hai ko-ming ti chi-chien shih" (A few items about actors participating in the 1911 Revolution); in *KML*, 1:346.

10. Ch'ing-chen shang-t'uan (The Ch'ing-chen Merchant Volunteers), "Ch'ing-chen shang-t'uan chi-lüeh" (A summary of the Ch'ing-chen Merchant Volunteers); in *HHKM*, 7:90–91.

11. "Shang-hai shang-tuan hsiao-shih," p. 87.

12. See three short articles in *KSKF*, 1:365–373.

13. *KSKF*, 1:368. Among the Shanghai student armed forces were the *hsüeh-sheng chün*, *nü-tzu pei-fa tui*, and the *shao-nien she*.

14. *KSKF*, 1:366.

15. Kuo Han-chang, "Lüeh-t'an Shang-hai kuang-fu chih i" (A short talk about the

police in the Shanghai Revolution); in *KML*, 4:38. The author was one of this group of radical police. He had been a low-grade officer in the army in Kiangsi and Soochow and fled to Shanghai when his superiors discovered he was a member of the Revolutionary Alliance. All thirteen of this group had changed their given names to begin with the character *Han*.

16. Ch'ien Chi-po, "Hsin-hai Chiang-nan kuang-fu shih-lu (A true account of the 1911 Revolution in southern Kiangsu); in *HHKM*, 7:41, 43–44.

17. *Ibid.*, p. 42; Feng, *I-shih*, 5:275–277.

18. *KSKF*, 1:377.

19. Feng, *I-shih*, 5:282–284.

20. Li Hsieh-ho had been a revolutionary in Hunan before going to Shanghai, where he met T'ao Ch'eng-chang and joined the Restoration Society. He then went to Japan and joined the Revolutionary Alliance in 1905. He hoped to assassinate Governor-General Tuan-fang during the 1906 P'ing-Liu-Li rising. When his plans failed he fled from Nanking to Hong Kong. In 1907 Li went to Singapore and was sent to Java by the Singapore branch of the Revolutionary Alliance. He taught and organized overseas Chinese for the Revolutionary Alliance until the Restoration Society was revived in 1910. Li then switched allegiance, bringing the Revolutionary Alliance branches he had organized with him. He still was on good terms with some Revolutionary Alliance leaders, however, and went to Canton in March 1911 at Huang Hsing's request. Li persuaded overseas Chinese to contribute heavily to finance the Canton rising and was in their bad graces when it failed. He, therefore, went to Shanghai instead of returning to Southeast Asia. After the Revolution, Li supported Yüan Shih-kai and in 1915 was a member of the *Ch'ou-an hui*, which promoted the revival of the monarchy. Ch'ien Chih-po, pp. 38–40; *KML*, 4:27.

21. *KSKF*, 1:423; Han Shih-shih, "Wu-sung Kuang-fu chün chi-lüeh" (A summary of the Restoration Army of Woosung), in *HHKM*, 7:33–34.

22. Ch'ien Chih-po, pp. 42, 45. Han Shih-shih, p. 34. The gang leader T'ien Hsin-shan also contacted some soldiers in Li T'ien-ts'ai's force.

23. *KML*, 4:48.

24. *Ibid.*, 4:3.

25. U.S. Department of State, General Records (Record Group 59), Decimal File, 893.00/924.

26. *KML*, 4:2. The meeting of representatives of thirteen provinces called by Ch'en Ch'i-mei, Kiangsu Military Governor Ch'eng Te-ch'üan, and Chekiang Military Governor T'ang Shou-ch'ien in December to discuss the formation of a national government also met at Ho-t'ung's Ai-li Gardens.

27. Chao Feng-ch'ang was an expectant prefect and a protégé of Chang Chih-tung. He was a constitutionalist, but also knew some Revolutionary Alliance members. He served as a messenger and go-between during negotiations between the revolutionaries and Yüan Shih-k'ai in the early months of 1912. *KML*, 4:3.

28. Kuo Hsiao-ch'eng, "Chiang-su kuang-fu chi-shih" (An account of the Revolution in Kiangsu), in *HHKM*, 7:1–2; Ch'ien Chih-po, p. 45; Feng, *I-shih*, 5:286–291.

29. Kuo Hsiao-ch'eng, "Kiangsu," pp. 4–5; Han Shih-shih, pp. 33–34; Ch'ien Chih-po, p. 45.

30. On the question of the Shanghai military governor, see *KML*, 4:7; Ch'ien Chih-po, p. 48; Feng, *I-shih*, 3:172. The earliest composition of the military government is given in *Min-li pao* (The people's stand), no. 386, p. 1 (November 7, 1911). Ch'en Ch'i-mei's two chief rivals for military governor, Li Hsieh-ho and Niu Yung-chien, were originally included in his general staff.

31. Names of the officials in the Shanghai government are from *KML*, 4:7, 9; *KSKF*, 1:368–369; "Shang-hai shang-t'uan hsiao-shih," p. 89.

32. *KML*, 4:11. Wang Chen, the first finance minister, was replaced by Shen Man-yün because he did not have Shen's access to private funds.

33. Chou Ya-wei, "Kuang-fu hui chien-wen tsa-i" (Miscellaneous recollections of the Restoration Society); in *KML*, 1:635.

34. Chou Nan-kai, "Shang-hai kuang-fu shih ti hsün-fang ying ho Wu-sung pao-t'ai" (The Defense Forces and the Woosung forts at the time of the Shanghai Revolution); in *KML*, 4:42.

35. Ch'ien Chih-po, p. 49.

36. Chou Nan-kai, p. 47.

37. The Restoration Army was composed of soldiers from the army regiments at Woosung and the mouth of the Woosung River, students in the Woosung area, and volunteers recruited in Shaohsing and Kashing, Chekiang. *KSKF*, 1:423–426.

38. Chou Nan-kai, p. 45; for positions of Chekiangese in Shanghai, see telegrams reprinted in *KSKF*, 2:171–172.

39. Ma Hsü-lun, "T'ao Ch'eng-chang chih ssu" (The death of T'ao Ch'eng-chang), in *HHKM*, 1:520; Chang Huang-ch'i, "Kuang-fu hui ling-hsiu T'ao Ch'eng-chang ko-ming shih" (The revolutionary activities of Restoration Society leader T'ao Ch'eng-chang), in *HHKM*, 1:528. Because Chiang Kai-shek was responsible for his death, T'ao is officially ignored on Taiwan. His name, or at least part of the name, has been deleted wherever it appears in the *Chung-hua min-kuo k'ai-kuo wu-shih-nien wen-hsien* (Documents on the fiftieth anniversary of the founding of the Republic of China).

40. Yang-chou shih-fan hsüeh-yüan li-shih hsi (History department of the Yangchow Normal School), *Hsin-hai ko-ming Chiang-su ti-ch'ü shih-liao* (Historical materials on the 1911 Revolution in localities of Kiangsu; Nanking, 1961), p. 239.

41. Chang Ping-lin was too oriented toward scholarship and literature to be an effective party organizer. Moreover, his basic conservatism became evident right after the Revolution. He had more in common with Chang Chien, T'ang Shou-ch'ien, and Ch'eng Te-ch'üan, with whom he organized the United Party, than he did with the revolutionary intellectuals.

42. "Proclamation of the Shanghai Military Government," in *HHKM*, 7:72.

43. *KML*, 4:13, 48.

44. The revolutionary government generally solicited contributions to provision the armies and for other purposes. The names of contributors, however small, were regularly published in *The People's Stand*. Ch'en Ch'i-mei also resorted to kidnapping and extortion to raise funds. At one point he had the head of the Imperial Bank of China kidnapped and held for ransom. Because this incident occurred in the International Settlement, foreign consuls protested to Nanking, and Wu T'ing-fang persuaded Ch'en to release his victim (*KML*, 4:13; U.S. Department of State, Record Group 59, Decimal File, 893.00/1342). In the fall of 1912 the Bank of China was established in Shanghai with Sun Yat-sen as nominal president. Directors included Ch'en Ch'i-mai, Hsü Shao-chen (the army officer who led the Kiangsu army against imperial forces at Nanking), Wang Chen, and other merchants in Shanghai. By then, revolutionaries were about to lose control of the government. Lu Tan-lin, *Ko-ming shih t'an* (Chats on revolutionary history; Chungking, 1946), pp. 84–88.

45. Ch'en Ch'i-mei and the moderate military governors of Chekiang and Kiangsu, T'ang Shou-ch'ien and Ch'eng Te-ch'üan, were leaders of a group based in Shanghai which challenged Li Yüan-hung and others in Wuchang over who was going to shape the provisional republican government. Telegrams relating to the meeting of provincial representatives held in Shanghai in mid-November appear in *KMWH*, 1:2–4.

46. See, for instance, telegram of Ch'en Ch'i-mei urging the organization of a united northern expedition army shortly after the fall of Nanking, in *KSKF*, 2:395. The joint Kiangsu-Chekiang army was the main force in the capture of Nanking. Hsü

Shao-cheng commanded the Kiangsu troops, but Ch'en was involved in the general organization and supply.

47. Huang Yen-p'ei, p. 62; Liu Hou-sheng, *Chang Chien chuan-chi* (Biography of Chang Chien; Hong Kong, 1956), pp. 192–197.

48. *KML*, 4:18.

49. *Ibid.*

50. *Ibid.*, 4:18–19.

51. *KSKF*, 2:128; *Chuan-chi wen-hsüeh* (Biographical Literature), 7.1:7.

52. Ch'u Fu-ch'eng, "Che-chiang Hsin-hai ko-ming chi-shih" (A record of the 1911 Revolution in Chekiang), in *HHKM*, 7:153; Che-chiang chün ssu-i-chiu lu ssu-ling-pu (Headquarters of the 419th brigade of the Chekiang army), "Che-chün Hang-chou kuang-fu chi" (An account of the Chekiang army in the Revolution at Hangchow), in *KSKF*, 2:128–129, 136.

53. Ch'u Fu-ch'eng, p. 153; Headquarters of the 419th Brigade of the Chekiang Army, pp. 135–136.

54. Ch'u Fu-ch'eng, p. 153; Chao Te-san, "Chi kung-fen Che-chiang fu-shu chih i" (An account of attacking and burning the Chekiang governor's yamen); in *KML*, 4:161.

55. Headquarters of the 419th Brigade of the Chekiang Army, p. 138; Ch'u Fu-ch'eng, p. 154; Chou Ya-wei, p. 632.

56. Headquarters of the 419th Brigade of the Chekiang Army, pp. 130, 137; Chung Li-yü, "Kuang-fu Hang-chou hui-i lu" (Recollections of the Revolution in Hangchow), *chin-tai shih tzu-liao*, 1:95.

57. Information about the provincial assembly's role, unless otherwise noted, is from Ch'u Fu-ch'eng, pp. 155–156; Shen Chün-ju, "Hsin-hai ko-ming tsa-i" (Miscellaneous recollections of the 1911 Revolution), in *KML*, 1:139–140; Ko Ching-en, "Hsin-hai ko-ming tsai Che-chiang" (The 1911 Revolution in Chekiang), in *KML*, 4:98–100; Kuo Hsiao-ch'eng, "Che-chiang kuang-fu chi" (An account of the Revolution in Chekiang), in *HHKM*, 7:135; Ma Hsü-lun, "Wo tsai hsin-hai che-i-nien" (My experiences during the year 1911), in *KML*, pp. 172–173. Ch'u Fu-ch'eng had replaced Ch'en Shih-hsia as a vice-president of the assembly. Other assembly members who promoted the Revolution included Chang Ch'uan-pao from Ningpo and Lou Shou-kuang of Shaohsing.

58. Late the next day, November 4, Governor Tseng-yün evidently changed his mind and prepared a draft declaration of independence. However, the Revolution began before it could be posted and the revolutionaries never knew of the governor's half-hearted conversion. Hsü Ping-k'un, "Hang-chou kuang-fu chih yeh ti i-t'zu kuan-shen chin-chi hui-i" (An urgent meeting of officials and gentry on the eve of the Hangchow revolution); in *KML*, 4:165–166. Kuo Hsiao-ch'eng says that the governor never agreed. Kuo Hsiao-ch'eng, "Che-chiang," in *HHKM*, 7:135. However, Hsü was present at the meeting on November 4 where the question of independence was discussed and his account would seem to supercede Kuo.

59. This meeting was attended by new-army officers, Ch'u Fu-ch'eng and Hsü Hsing-pin from the provincial assembly, and Huang Fu, Ch'en Ch'üan-ch'ing, and Chiang Kai-shek from Shanghai. Headquarters of the 419th Brigade of the Chekiang Army, pp. 128–129; Ko Ching-en, pp. 98–99.

60. E.g., students from the Military Primary School formed a separate force which occupied the railway station and fire station and opened one of the city gates to let in new army cavalry. Ko Ching-en, pp. 101–102.

61. Information on the Dare-to-die corps is from Headquarters of the 419th Brigade of the Chekiang Army, pp. 130–131; Ch'u Fu-ch'eng, pp. 154–155; Chou Ya-wei, p. 632; Chou Ch'i-wei, "Lo-ch'ing Hsin-hai ko-ming shih-liao" (Historical materials

on the 1911 Revolution in Lotsing), in *KML,* 4:193. Chiang Kai-shek's name is excluded from mainland accounts.

62. Chou Ya-wei, *KML,* p. 632; Ko Ching-en, p. 101; Kuo Hsiao-ch'eng, "Che-chiang," p. 135; Headquarters of the 419th Brigade of the Chekiang Army, pp. 142–143. The governor was held briefly by the revolutionaries and then allowed to go to Shanghai. The lieutenant-governor and provincial judge had already fled there.

63. About a week after the Manchu garrison surrendered, it was discovered that Kuei-lin had hidden over two thousand rifles in case there should be a chance to over-throw the revolutionary government. He and his son were sentenced to death by a tribunal presided over by ex-assembly vice-president Shen Chün-ju. They were executed while T'ang Shou-ch'ien was away in Shanghai. T'ang and some of the Hangchow gentry were displeased. Kuo Hsiao-ch'eng, "Che-chiang," p. 135; Shen Chün-ju, pp. 139–141; *NCH,* 101:441 (11/18/11).

64. Ch'u Fu-ch'eng, pp. 156–157; Shen Chün-ju, p. 141. The department headed by Ch'u Fu-ch'eng initially had broad responsibility for almost all aspects of civil govern-ment, but soon various functions such as finance were separated into distinct depart-ments.

65. Chung Li-yü, pp. 96–97, 101. Kao Erh-teng was a graduate of the Army Officers Academy in Tokyo, where he had been a fellow student of the commander of the 82nd infantry regiment, Chou Ch'eng-t'an. He replaced the first finance minister, an agricultural specialist who didn't know much about military affairs. Kao didn't know much about finance, but most of the money available to the government at that time was being used for the army.

66. Regional, party, and personal issues as well as political radicalism possibly also influenced Wang Chin-fa's attitude. He also opposed Chiang Tsun-kuei, the second military governor, presumably because Chiang had been chosen over T'ao Ch'eng-chang. U.S. Department of State, General Records (Record Group 59), Decimal File, 893.00/1325.

67. Chang Huang-chi, p. 526; Chang Kuo-kan, *Hsin-hai ko-ming shih-liao* (Historical materials on the 1911 Revolution), Shanghai, 1958, p. 239.

68. For a list of members of the Senate, see Ch'u Fu-ch'eng, p. 157.

69. Preparations for an attack on Nanking were begun almost immediately after the Hangchow Revolution. Han Shih-shih, p. 37.

70. Prefectures were abolished on May 18. Actual liquidation of the prefectural governments took place somewhat later. Wu Hsin-mu, "Hsin-hai ko-ming shih-ch'i ti Hsia-shih shang-t'uan ho kung-ping t'ieh-tao ta-tui (The Hsia-shih Merchant Vol-unteers and the laborers' railway brigade of the period of the 1911 Revolution); in *KML,* 4:173.

71. Lü Kung-wang, "Hsin-hai ko-ming Che-chiang kuang-fu chi-shih" (An account of the 1911 Revolution in Chekiang), *Chin-tai shih tzu-liao,* 1:115–116.

72. An interesting illustration of the shallowness of the anti-Manchuism of at least one group of intellectuals occurred in Wenchow. The group of school teachers who began the Revolution there had initially decided that the new government should execute a Manchu to demonstrate opposition to the Ch'ing dynasty. They had already selected their victim, a minor *likin* official, but when he heard the news he visited one of the teachers and pleaded for his life. They all knew he was really a nice, harmless old man and so relented and allowed him to board an English ship bound for Shanghai. Ch'en Shou-yung, "Wen-chou hsiang-ying Wu-ch'ang ch'i-i ti chin-shen ching-li" (Personal experiences during the response to the Wuchang rising in Wenchow); in *KML,* 4:183, 185.

73. Sources for the Ningpo Revolution are Lin Tuan-fu, "Ning-po kuang-fu ch'in li-chi" (A personal chronicle of the Revolution in Ningpo), in *KML,* 4:174–180;

Hsin-hai ko-ming tzu-liao (Materials on the 1911 Revolution), *Chin-tai shih tzu-liao*, 1:543–548 (1961); *KSKF* 2:146–148; *NCH*, 101:289 (11/4/11); 101:359, 363 (11/11/11). Lists of members of the Society to Protect the Peace and of the revolutionary government appear in Lin Tuan-fu, pp. 178–180 and *KSKF*, 2:148.

74. The 42nd new army brigade was stationed outside of Ningpo and this was the only part of the province other than Hangchow where the new army played an important role.

75. The main source for the Huchow Revolution is Ch'iu Shou-ming, "Hu-chou kuang-fu hui-i" (Recollections of the Revolution in Huchow); in *KML*, 4:167–169.

76. Sources for the Kashing Revolution are Ma Chi-sheng as told to Tung Sun-kuan, "Chia-hsing kuang-fu chi-lüeh" (A summary of the Revolution in Kashing), *Chin-tai shih tzu-liao*, 2:67–68 (1958); *NCH*, 101:293 (11/4/11); 101:359, 367 (11/11/11); 101:446 (11/18/11); *HHKM*, 7:158.

77. Sources for the Wenchow Revolution are Ch'en Shou-ying, pp. 183–187; *NCH*, 101:440 (11/18/11); 101:511 (11/25/11).

78. Ch'en Fu-ch'en left Hangchow to protest the execution of the Manchu garrison's Colonel Kuei-lin. Possibly this is why the provincial government did not wish to see him head the Wenchow prefectural government, but I have no direct evidence on this point.

79. Ch'u Fu-ch'eng, p. 153.

80. *NCH*, 101:365 (11/11/11); 101:517 (11/25/11); 101:734 (12/16/11); Lü Kung-wang, p. 115.

81. Reports on Tsui appear in *NCH*, 101:517 (11/25/11); 101:654 (12/19/11); 101:734 (12/16/11); 102:98 (1/13/12); 102:178 (1/20/12); 102:711 (3/16/12); 103:307 (5/4/12).

82. Another example of peasant unrest occurred during March 1912 at the time of the early spring food shortage. A group of five hundred marched on a town in southern Taichow announcing they intended to depose the magistrate and demand contributions to enable them "to join the revolutionary forces." Gentry called out three thousand militia, which surrounded the protesters and forced them to disband. *NCH*, 102:711 (3/16/12).

83. On the Kinhwa Revolution see Tsou Lu, *Chung-kuo Kuo-min-tang shih-kao* (A draft history of the Kuomintang; Shanghai, 1938), p. 888; Kuomintang, Committee for the Compilation of Materials on the Party History of the Central Executive Committee, *Ko-ming hsien-lieh hsien-chin chuan* (Biographies of martyrs and forebearers of the Revolution; Taipei, 1965), p. 1026.

84. Shaohsing sources are Ch'en Hsieh-shu, "Shao-hsing kuang-fu shih chien-wen" (Experiences at the time of the Revolution in Shaohsing), *Chin-tai shih tzu-liao*, 1:105–108 (1958); Lu Hsün, *Selected Works*, 4 vols. (Peking, 1956), 1:415–418; Kuo Hsiao-ch'eng, "Che-chiang," p. 139; *NCH*, 102:300 (2/3/12); U.S. Department of State, Record Group 59, Decimal File, 893.00/1153.

85. Wang Chin-fa tried to purchase guns in Shanghai to use to keep order in Shaohsing, but was not allowed to do so. The official reason given was that weapons were needed for a northern expedition, but it is also possible that neither Ch'en Ch'i-mei nor T'ang Shou-ch'ien wished to arm a man known to be their enemy and a follower of T'ao Ch'eng-chang. *NCH*, 102:300 (2/3/12).

86. Chuchow sources are Chiang T'ien-wei, "Hsin-hai ko-ming hou Sung-yang ti i-t'zu chien-pien tou-cheng (A fight over queue cutting in Sung-yang after the 1911 Revolution), in *KML*, 4:203–204; Lü Yüeh-p'ing, "Hui-i Hsin-hai ko-ming shih-ch'i ti chi-chien shih ho Ch'u-chou kuang-fu ching-kuo" (Recollections of a few things of the period of the 1911 Revolution and experiences during the revolution in Chuchow), in *KML*, 4:199; Mao Hu-hou, "Hsin-hai ko-ming tsai Li-shui" (The 1911 Revolution in Li-shui), in *KML*, 4:201–202.

87. Ch'u Fu-ch'eng, p. 153.

88. *KSKF,* 2:151.

89. Kuo-wu-yüan yin-chu chü (Ministry of the Interior Printing Office), ed., *Chih-yüan lu* (Official register; Peking, 1913), 2.1: *Chung-i yüan* 4b–5a. Ch'en Fu-ch'en, president of the Chekiang provincial assembly before the Revolution was also elected to the national parliament. Among the leaders of the Revolution in the provinces who were elected were Chao Shu and Yü Feng-shao, the second military governor of Huchow.

90. Ma Hsü-lun, "Wo tsai hsin-hai che-i-nien," pp. 178–179; Ernest P. Young, "The Reformer as Conspirator: Liang Ch'i-ch'ao and the 1911 Revolution"; in Albert Feuerwerker, et al., eds., *Approaches to Modern Chinese History* (Berkeley, 1967), pp. 260–263.

91. Kuo Hsiao-ch'eng, "Che-chiang," p. 138.

92. Shen Chün-ju, p. 142; Ssu Tao-ch'ing, "Che-chün shih-pa nien ti hui-i lu" (Recollections of eighteen years in the Chekiangese army), *Chin-tai shih tzu-liao,* 2:82 (1957). During the first half of 1912 Chu Jui formed a "West Chekiang" clique of gentry and army officers who had been his fellow students. One of Chiang Tsun-kuei's supporters organized a counter-clique of "East Chekiang" natives and persuaded Chiang to organize a group of supporters in the army, especially from among graduates of the Chekiang Military Primary School and School for Noncommissioned Officers. Chiang still lost out in the ensuing power struggle, however, and resigned.

93. Ko Ching-en, pp. 122–123.

94. Wen Kung-chih, *Tsui-chin san-shih nien Chung-kuo chün-shih shih* (A military history of China during the past thirty years; Shanghai, n.d.), 1:190.

95. U.S. Department of State, Record Group 59, Decimal File, 893.02/73a.

96. Mao Hu-hou, p. 202.

97. Chiang T'ien-wei, pp. 203–204.

10. Conclusion

1. There are similarities between the behavior of the early twentieth-century Chinese students and radicals at the University of California at Berkeley and other American colleges in the 1960's despite differences in culture and issues. The American students displayed analogous individualism, moral indignation, self-righteousness, intellectual immaturity, and hope for sweeping solutions. They, too, demanded more influence in determining the course of their studies, used the weapons of strikes and demonstrations, and some withdrew to establish small schools reflecting their own educational ideas. Eventually some also turned to terrorism.

2. John Israel, *Student Nationalism in China, 1927–1937* (Stanford, 1966), p. 184, shares this view.

3. Robert Lifton, *Thought Reform and the Psychology of Totalism* (New York, 1961), pp. 376–387.

4. Cf. Walzer's characterization of the seventeenth-century English revolutionaries as "saints," "strangers," and "chosen men." Michael Walzer, *The Revolution of the Saints: A Study in the Origins of Radical Politics* (London, 1966), p. 317. A considerable portion of Walzer's model of radical politics based on the history of the seventeenth-century English Puritans can also be applied to the twentieth-century Chinese revolutionary intellectuals, and my analysis owes a considerable debt to his work. There are certainly also differences in the Chinese picture. Traditional Chinese society was not as far broken down as was that of seventeenth-century Britain and not as ready to yield to revolutionary pressure. Moreover, the Chinese revolutionary model was external (Western) rather than largely indigenous.

5. Lifton, pp. 377–378.

6. Joseph Levenson has analyzed the attitudes of Liang Ch'i-ch'ao (and by extension those of at least some other Chinese intellectuals) in terms of conflicting commitments to their history and to abstract value in the minds of men who were intellectually alienated from their tradition, but still emotionally tied to it. Joseph R. Levenson, *Liang Ch'i-ch'ao and the Mind of Modern China* (Cambridge, Mass., 1959), p. 1.

7. Maurice Meisner asserts that Li Ta-chao and others of his generation found nationalism and tradition compatible. Maurice Meisner, *Li Ta-chao and the Origins of Chinese Marxism* (Cambridge, Mass., 1967), p. 47. This seems also to have been at least partly true of many 1911 radicals.

8. Some examples of changes in local elite society were investment by gentry and scholars in modern industry and mining, which further obscured already hazy lines between merchants and gentry; the sincere interest in reform felt by some gentry; and the influence of moderate or even conservative returned students who came home to live fairly conventional lives, but who no longer thought quite the same way as did their fathers.

9. Chalmers A. Johnson, *Peasant Nationalism and Communist Power* (Stanford, 1962), p. 5.

10. Some revolutionary organizations had elaborate hierarchies, but usually these were purposely designed to appeal to secret societies. More typically, revolutionary groups had a fairly small number of officers whose authority was varyingly accepted. The individual's place in revolutionary history depended on his own deeds, not his party position.

11. The social flexibility of the local elite in China contrasts with the relative rigidity in Japan. The Japanese government was able to abolish samurai status, and once the samurai were deprived of their special position most were unable to maintain their old prestige. No similar attempt to abolish the gentry was made after the 1911 Revolution, although the traditional criteria of gentry status had already disappeared when the official examinations were abandoned. After a time gentry in the old sense died off. However, even if they had suddenly been robbed of their legal basis, the gentry already had alternative sources of power, wealth, and prestige. Many engaged in trade or industry, others were landlords, some had joined the constitutional movement or were members of new local associations. In 1911 the gentry were still a viable group and individuals could choose among many ways to make the relatively small adjustment necessary to maintain their influence after 1911.

12. Edgar Snow, *Red Star over China* (New York, 1939), pp. 123–127; Stuart Schram, *Mao Tse-tung* (New York, 1966), pp. 27–31. The comparison is with Mao and not with the Red Guard, whose roots do not so clearly reach back to the 1911 period.

13. Schram, p. 116.

Ai-tu-ko-ming-chün-che 愛讀革命軍者 (Chang Shih-chao 章士釗). "Tu *Ko-ming chün*" 讀革命軍 (Read *The revolutionary army*), *Su-pao* (June 9, 1903), in *Hsin-hai ko-ming ch'ien shih-nien chien shih-lun hsüan-chi*, 1.2:683–685.

"Ang-ko-lu So-sun jen-chung chih chiao-yü ping Chung-kuo chiao-yü chih fang-chen" 盎格魯索遜人種之教育并中國教育之方針 (The education of the Anglo-Saxon people is the prescription for Chinese education), *Che-chiang ch'ao*, no. 1, chiao-yü 教育 pp. 1–7.

Arendt, Hannah. *On Revolution*. New York, 1963.

Biggerstaff, Knight. *The Earliest Modern Government Schools in China*. Ithaca, 1961.

Boorman, Howard L., ed. *Biographical Dictionary of Republican China*, vols. 1 and 2. New York, 1967.

Brinton, Clarence Crane. *The Anatomy of Revolution*. New York, 1952.

Britton, Roswell S. *The Chinese Periodical Press, 1800–1912*. reprint; Taipei, 1966.

Brunnert, H. S. and V. V. Hagelstrom. *Present Day Political Organization of China*, tr. A. Beltchenko. Shanghai, 1912.

Buck, Pearl S., tr. *All Men Are Brothers*. New York, 1937.

Cameron, Meribeth. *The Reform Movement in China, 1898–1912*. New York, 1963.

CCC: Che-chiang ch'ao 浙江潮 (Tides of Chekiang). Tokyo, 1903.

Chang Chi 張繼. *Chang P'u-ch'üan hsien-sheng ch'üan-chi* 張溥泉先生全集 (The complete works of Chang P'u-ch'üan). Taipei, 1952.

Chang Ch'i-yün 張其昀. "Sun I-jang chih cheng-chih ssu-hsiang" 孫詒讓之政治思想 (The political thought of Sun I-jang), *Che-chiang hsüeh-pao* 浙江學報 (Chekiang studies), 1.1:1–8 (1947).

———*Chung-hua min-kuo shih-kang* 中華民國史綱 (An outline of the history of the Republic of China). 7 vols.; Taipei, 1954.

Chang Chung-li. *The Chinese Gentry*. Seattle, 1955.

Chang Hsiao-hsün 張效巡. "Che-chiang Hsin-hai ko-ming kuang-fu chi-shih" 浙江辛亥革命光復記事 (An account of the 1911 Revolution in Chekiang), in *Chin-tai shih tzu-liao*, 1:118–124 (1954).

Chang Hsing-yen 章行嚴 (Chang Shih-chao 章士釗). "*Su-pao* an shih-mo chi-hsü" 蘇報案始末記敘 (A complete narration of the *Su-pao* case), in *Hsin-hai ko-ming*, 1:387–390.

Chang Huang-ch'i 張篁溪. "Kuang-fu hui ling-hsiu T'ao Ch'eng-chang ko-ming shih" 光復會領袖陶成章革命史 (The revolutionary activities of Restoration Society leader T'ao Ch'eng-chang), in *Hsin-hai ko-ming*, 1:521–529.

———"*Su-pao* an shih-lu" 蘇報案實錄 (A true account of the *Su-pao* case), in *Hsin-hai ko-ming*, 1:367–386.

Chang Kuo-kan 張國淦. *Hsin-hai ko-ming shih-liao* 辛亥革命史料 (Historical materials on the 1911 Revolution). Shanghai, 1958.

Chang Ping-lin 章炳麟. "Cheng-ch'ou Man-jen" 正仇滿人 (The principal enemies are the Manchus), *Kuo-min pao* 國民報 (The China national), no. 4 (1901), in *Hsin-hai ko-ming ch'ien shih-nien chien shih-lun hsüan-chi*, 1:94–99.

———*Ch'iu-shu* 訄書 (Book of grievances), n.p., 1905.

———*Ch'iu-shu* (Book of grievances). Shanghai, 1958.

———"Po K'ang Yu-wei shu" 駁康有為書 (Letter disputing K'ang Yu-wei), in *Hsing-Chung hui*, 2:591–602.

———"Yü Wu Chih-hui t'an *Su-pao* an shu" 與吳稚暉談蘇報案書 (Letters to Wu Chih-hui discussing the *Su-pao* case), in *Hsin-hai ko-ming,* 1:398–400.

"Chang Ping-lin tzu-ting nien-p'u" 章炳麟自定年譜 (Autobiography of Chang Ping-lin), in *Hsing-Chung hui,* 2:635–639.

Chang Shih-chao 章士釗. "*Su Huang-ti hun*" 疏黃帝魂 (An explanation of *The Soul of Huang-ti*), in *Hsin-hai ko-ming hui-i lu,* 1:217–304.

Chang Wen-po 張文伯. *Chih-lao hsien-hua* 稚老閒話 (Chats about Wu Chih-hui). Taipei, 1952.

———*Wu Ching-heng hsien-sheng chuan-chi* 吳敬恒先生傳記 (A biography of Wu Ching-heng). Taipei, 1964.

Chao Chin-yü 趙金鈺. "Su-Hang-Yung t'ieh-lu chieh-k'uan ho Chiang-Che jen-min ti chü-k'uan yün-tung" 蘇杭甬鐵路借款和江浙人民的拒款運動 (The Shanghai-Hangchow-Ningpo Railway loan and the opposition to the loan by the people of Kiangsu and Chekiang), *Li-shih yen-chiu,* 9:51–60 (1959).

Chao Te-san 趙得三. "Chi kung-fen Che-chiang fu-shu chih i" 記攻焚浙江撫署之役 (An account of attacking and burning the Chekiang governor's yamen), in *Hsin-hai ko-ming hui-i lu,* 4:161–164.

Che-chiang ch'ao, see *CCC.*

Che-chiang chün ssu-i-chiu lü ssu-ling-pu 浙江軍四一九旅司令部 (Headquarters of the 419th brigade of the Chekiang army). "Che-chün Hang-chou kuang-fu chi" 浙軍杭州光復記 (An account of the Chekiang army in the Revolution at Hangchow), in Ko-sheng kuang-fu, 2:131–145.

Che-chiang hsüeh-pao 浙江學報 (Chekiang studies). Hangchow, 1947–1948.

Ch'en Hsieh-shu 陳燮樞 "Shao-hsing kuang-fu shih chien-wen" 紹興光復時見聞 (Experiences at the time of the Revolution in Shaohsing), *Chin-tai shih tzu-liao,* 1:105–108 (1958).

Ch'en Hsiung 陳雄, comp. *Min-tsu ko-ming wen-hsien* 民族革命文献 (Documents on the nationalist revolution). Taipei, 1954.

Ch'en Hsü-lu 陳旭麓. *Tsou Jung yü Ch'en T'ien-hua ti ssu-hsiang* 鄒容與陳天華的思想 (The thought of Tsou Jung and Ch'en T'ien-hua). Shanghai, 1957.

Ch'en, Jerome. "Secret Societies," *Ch'ing-shih wen-t'i* (Ch'ing Studies), 1.3:13–16 (1966).

Ch'en Shou-yung 陳守庸. "Wen-chou hsiang-ying Wu-ch'ang ch'i-i ti chin-shen ching-li" 温州響應武昌起義的親身經歷 (Personal experiences during the response to the Wuchang rising in Wenchow), in *Hsin-hai ko-ming hui-i lu,* 4:183–187.

Ch'en T'ien-hua 陳天華. *Ch'en T'ien-hua chi* 陳天華集 (A collection of writings by Ch'en T'ien-hua). Shanghai, 1946.

———*Ching-shih chung* 警世鐘 (A bell to warn the world), in *Hsin-hai ko-ming,* 2:112–143.

———*Meng hui-t'ou* 猛回頭 (About face!), in *Hsin-hai ko-ming,* 2:144–170.

Ch'en Wei 陳魏. "Kuang-fu hui ch'ien-ch'i ti huo-tung p'ien-tuan" 光復會前期的活動片斷 (Miscellany about activities preceding the founding of the Restoration Society), in *Hsin-hai ko-ming hui-i lu,* 4:127–130.

Cheng Ho-sheng 鄭鶴聲. *Chin-shih Chung-hsi shih-jih tui-chao-piao* 近世中西史日對照表 (Sino-Western historical calendar for the modern period). Shanghai, 1936.

Chi-tzu 季子. "Ko-ming chi k'o-mien hu" 革命豈可免乎 (Can revolution be avoided?), *Chiang-su* no. 4, in *Hsin-hai ko-ming ch'ien shih-nien chien shih-lun hsüan-chi,* 1.2:560–565.

Chia-t'ing-li-hsien-che 家庭立憲者. "Chia-t'ing ko-ming shuo" 家庭革命説 (On the family revolution), *Chiang-su,* 7:13–18.

Chiang Shen-wu 蔣慎吾 "Ai-kuo hsüeh-she shih-wai i-yeh" 愛國學社史外一頁 (A page out of the history of the Patriotic School); *Ta-feng pan-yüeh-k'an* 大風半月刊

(The typhoon magazine), no. 67, in *Hsing-Chung hui,* 2:369–375.

———"T'ung-meng hui shih-tai Shang-hai ko-ming tang-jen ti huo-tung" 同盟會時代 上海革命黨人的活動 (The activities of revolutionaries in Shanghai during the Revolutionary Alliance period), *I-ching* 逸經 (Unorthodox classics), 26:103–109.

Chiang Siang-tse. *The Nien Rebellion.* Seattle, 1954.

Chiang-su 江蘇 (Kiangsu). Tokyo, 1903–1904.

"Chiang-su jen chih hsin-kuei" 江蘇人之信鬼 (Belief in ghosts by Kiangsu natives), *Chiang-su,* 9–10:29–32.

"Chiang-su jen chih tao-te wen-t'i" 江蘇人之道德問題 (The question of the morality of Kiangsu natives), *Chiang-su,* 9–10:1–10.

Chiang T'ien-wei 江天蔚. "Hsin-hai ko-ming hou Sung-yang ti i-tz'u chien-pien tou-cheng" 辛亥革命後松陽的一次剪辮鬥爭 (A fight over queue-cutting in Sung-yang after the 1911 Revolution), in *Hsin-hai ko-ming hui-i lu,* 4:203–204.

Chiang Wei-ch'iao 蔣維喬. "Chung-kuo chiao-yü hui chih hui-i" 中國教育會之回憶 (Recollections of the Chinese Educational Association), in *Hsin-hai ko-ming,* 1:485–496.

Chien-kuo yüeh-k'an 建國月刊 (Reconstruction monthly). Shanghai and Nanking, 1929–1936.

Ch'ien Chi-po 錢基博. *Hsien-tai Chung-kuo wen-hsüeh shih* 現代中國文學史 (A history of modern Chinese literature). Shanghai, 1934.

———"Hsin-hai Chiang-nan kuang-fu shih-lu" 辛亥江南光復實錄 (A true account of the 1911 Revolution in southern Kiangsu), in *Hsin-hai ko-ming,* 7:38–56.

Ch'ien Chün-fu 錢均夫. "Hang-chou Ch'iu-shih shu-yüan 'Tsui-pien wen' an shih-mo chi-lüeh" 杭州求是書院罪辮文案始末記略 (A complete account of the "On abolishing the queue" case at the Hangchow Ch'iu-shih Academy), *Chin-tai shih tzu-liao,* 1:58–60 (1957).

Ch'ien Nan-yang 錢南揚. "Sun I-jang chuan" 孫詒讓傳 (A biography of Sung I-jang), *Che-chiang hsüeh-pao* 浙江學報 (Chekiang studies), 1.1:45–50.

Ch'ien Sheng-k'o 錢生可. *Ch'ing-hung pang chih hei-mu* 青紅幫之黑幕 (The black curtain of the Red and Green gangs). Shanghai, 1929.

"Chih-na fen-ko chih wei-chi" 支那分割之危機 (The danger of the partition of China), *Chiang-su,* 6:82–90.

Chih-na-tzu 支那子. "Fa-lü-shang jen-min chih tzu-yu ch'üan" 法律上人民之自由權 (The people's right of freedom under law), *Che-chiang ch'ao,* 10:33–40.

Chin-tai shih tzu-liao 近代史資料 (Materials on modern Chinese history). Peking, 1954–

Ching An 競盦. "Cheng-t'i chin-hua lun" 政體進化論 (On the evolution of political systems), *Chiang-su,* nos. 1 and 3, in *Hsin-hai ko-ming ch'ien shih-nien chien shih-lun hsüan-chi,* 1.2:540–547.

Ching-chung jih-pao 警鐘日報 (The alarm bell), photolithograph; Taipei, 1968.

"Ching-hsieh Chiao-yü hui" 敬謝教育會 (Respectful thanks to the Educational Association), *Su-pao* (June 19, 1903), in *Hsing-Chung hui,* 2:359–361.

Ch'ing-chen shang-t'uan 清真商團 (The Ch'ing-chen Merchant Volunteers). "Ch'ing-chen shang-t'uan chi-lüeh" 清真商團紀略 (A summary of the Ch'ing-chen Merchant Volunteers), in *Hsin-hai ko-ming,* 7:90–92.

Ch'iu Chin chi 秋瑾集 (The collected works of Ch'iu Chin). Shanghai, 1960.

Ch'iu Chin shih-chi 秋瑾史跡 (Manuscripts of Ch'iu Chin). Shanghai, 1958.

Ch'iu Shou-ming 邱壽銘. "Hu-chou kuang-fu hui-i" 湖州光復回憶 (Recollections of the revolution in Huchow), in *Hsin-hai ko-ming hui-i lu,* 4:167–169.

Ch'iu Ts'an-chih 秋燦芝 (Wang Ts'an-chih 王燦芝). *Ch'iu Chin ko-ming chuan* 秋瑾革命傳 (A revolutionary biography of Ch'iu Chin). Taipei, 1953.

Chou Ch'i-wei 周起渭. "Lo-ch'ing Hsin-hai ko-ming shih-liao" 樂清辛亥革命史料

(Historical materials on the 1911 Revolution in Lotsing), in *Hsin-hai ko-ming hui-i lu,* 4:188–196.

Chou Nan-kai 周南陔. "Shang-hai kuang-fu shih ti hsün-fang ying ho Wu-sung pao-t'ai" 上海光復時的巡防營和吳淞炮台　 (The Defense Forces and the Woosung forts at the time of the Shanghai Revolution), in *Hsin-hai ko-ming hui-i lu,* 4:38–41.

Chou Ya-wei 周亞圍. "Kuang-fu hui chien-wen tsa-i" 光復會見聞雜憶 (Miscellaneous recollections of the Restoration Society), in *Hsin-hai ko-ming hui-i lu,* 1:624–636.

Chow Tse-tsung. *The May Fourth Movement.* Cambridge, Mass., 1960.

Chu, Samuel C. *Reformer in Modern China: Chang Chien, 1853–1926.* New York, 1965.

Chu Te-shang 朱德裳. *Liu K'uei-i* 劉揆一. n.p., 1912.

Chu Tsan-ch'ing 朱贊卿. "Ta-t'ung shih-fan hsüeh-t'ang" 大通師範學堂 (The Ta-t'ung Normal School), in *Hsin-hai ko-ming hui-i lu,* 4:143–149.

Ch'u Fu-ch'eng 褚輔成. "Che-chiang Hsin-hai ko-ming chi-shih" 浙江辛亥革命紀實 (A record of the 1911 Revolution in Chekiang), in *Hsin-hai ko-ming,* 7:149–157.

Ch'ü T'ung-tsu. *Local Government in China under the Ch'ing.* Cambridge, Mass., 1962.

Chuan-chi wen-hsüeh 傳記文學 (Biographical literature). Taipei, 1961–

Chung-hua min-kuo k'ai-kuo wu-shih-nien wen-hsien, see *HCH, KSKF,* and *TMH.*

Chung K'an 重堪. "Tzu-chih p'ien" 自治篇 (On Self-government), *Che-chiang ch'ao,* 6: *she-shuo* 社説 1–10.

Chung-kuo jen-min cheng-chih hsieh-shang hui-i Hu-pei sheng wei-yüan hui 中國人民政治協商會議湖北省委員會 (Hupei Committee of the Chinese People's Political Consultative Conference), ed. *Hsin-hai shou-i hui-i lu* 辛亥首義回憶錄 (Recollections of the first rising of the Revolution of 1911). 2 vols.; Wu-Han, 1957.

Chung-kuo T'ung-meng hui, see *TMH.*

Chung Li-yü 鍾豐玉. "Kuang-fu Hang-chou hui-i lu" 光復杭州回憶錄 (Recollections of the Revolution in Hangchow), *Chin-tai shih tzu-liao,* 1:89–103 (1954).

CNL: Philosophical Society and Scientific Society of the Province of Hupeh, ed. *Hsin-hai ko-ming wu-shih chou-nien chi-nien lun-wen chi*　辛亥革命五十周年記念論文集 (Collection of articles commemorating the fiftieth anniversary of the Revolution of 1911). 2 vols.; Peking, 1962.

CSL-KH: Ta-Ch'ing li-ch'ao shih-lu 大清歷朝實錄 (Veritable record of the successive reigns of the Ch'ing dynasty). Kuang-hsü period.

Eastman, Lloyd. "Ch'ing-i and Chinese Policy Formation during the Nineteenth Century," *Journal of Asian Studies,* 24.4:595–611.

Elvin, Mark. "The Mixed Court of the International Settlement at Shanghai (until 1911)," *Papers on China,* 17:131–159. Harvard University, East Asian Research Center, 1963.

Emmet, Dorothy. *Function, Purpose, and Powers.* London and New York, 1958.

"Fa-lü kai-lun" 法律概論 (Summary of law), *Che-chiang ch'ao,* 3:33–40.

Fairbank, John K., ed. *Chinese Thought and Institutions.* Chicago, 1957.

"Fan-mien chih fan-mien shuo" 反面之反面説　 (On the opposite of the opposite), *Su-pao* (June 23, 1909), in *Hsin-hai ko-ming ch'ien shih-nien chien shih-lun hsüan-chi,* 1.2:698–701.

Fan Yin-nan 樊蔭南, comp. *Tang-tai Chung-kuo ming-jen lu* 當代中國名人錄 (Who's who in contemporary China). Shanghai, 1931.

Fang Chao-ying 房兆楹. *Ch'ing-mo Min-ch'u yang-hsüeh-sheng t'i-lu ch'u-chi* 清末民初洋學生題錄初輯 (A preliminary summary of Chinese students abroad during the late Ch'ing and early Republic). Taipei, 1962.

Fei Ching-chung 費敬仲 (pseud. Wu-ch'iu chung-tzu 沃丘仲子). *Tang-tai ming-jen hsiao-chuan* 當代名人小傳 (Brief biographies of contemporary famous men). 2 vols.; Shanghai, 1921.

Fei Hsiao-tung. *China's Gentry*. Chicago, 1953.

Fei-sheng 飛生 (Chiang Fang-chen 蔣方震). "Chen chün-jen" 真軍人 (Real military men), *Che-chiang ch'ao*, 3:65–72.

———"Chin-shih erh-ta-shuo chih p'ing-lun" 近時二大説之評論 (A critique of two current theories), *Che-chiang ch'ao*, nos. 8 and 9, in *Hsin-hai ko-ming ch'ien shih-nien chien shih-lun hsüan-chi*. 1.2:516–525.

———"Kuo-hun p'ien" 國魂篇 (On the national spirit), *Che-chiang ch'ao*, 1: she-shuo, 1–17; 7:31–40.

Fei-shih 匪石. "Che-feng p'ien" 浙風篇 (On the customs of Chekiang), *Che-chiang ch'ao*, 5:1–10.

———"Chung-kuo ai-kuo-che Cheng Ch'eng-kung chuan" 中國愛國者鄭成功傳 (A biography of the Chinese patriot Koxinga), *Che-chiang ch'ao*, 2:57–63.

Feng Tzu-yu 馮自由. *Chung-hua min-kuo k'ai-kuo ch'ien ko-ming shih* 中華民國開國前革命史 (A history of the Revolution prior to the founding of the Republic of China). 3 vols.; vol. 1, Shanghai, 1928; vol. 2, Shanghai, 1930; vol. 3, Chungking, 1944.

———*Ko-ming i-shih* 革命逸史 (Fragments of revolutionary history). 5 vols.; Shanghai, 1945–1947.

———*Chung-kuo ko-ming yün-tung erh-shih-liu nien tsu-chih shih* 中國革命運動二十六年組織史 (Twenty-six-years' organizational history of the Chinese revolutionary movement). Shanghai, 1948.

———"Su Man-shu chih chen mien-mu" 蘇曼殊之真面目 (The true face of Su Man-shu), *I-ching* 逸經 (Unorthodox classics), 21:1185–1187.

Feuerwerker, Albert. *China's Early Industrialization: Sheng Hsüan-huai (1844–1916) and Mandarin Enterprise*. Cambridge, Mass., 1958.

Field, Margaret. "The Chinese Boycott of 1905," *Papers on China*, 11:63–98 (1957). Harvard University, East Asian Research Center.

Franke, Wolfgang. *The Reform and Abolition of the Traditional Chinese Examination System*. Cambridge, Mass., 1960.

Gasster, Michael. *Chinese Intellectuals and the Revolution of 1911*. Seattle and London, 1969.

Hackett, Roger F. "Chinese Students in Japan, 1900–1910," *Papers on China*, 3:134–169 (1949). Harvard University, East Asian Research Center.

Han Chü 漢駒. "Hsin-cheng-fu chih chien-she" 新政府之建設 (Construction of a new government), *Chiang-su*, nos. 5 and 6, in *Hsin-hai ko-ming ch'ien shih-nien chien shih-lun hsüan-chi*, 1.2:579–593.

Han-chung-chih-chung-i-Han-chung 漢種之中之漢種. "Po ko-ming po-i" 駁革命駁議 (Arguing against opposition to revolution), *Su-pao* (June 12–13, 1903), in *Hsin-hai ko-ming ch'ien shih-nien chien shih-lun hsüan-chi*, 1.2:688–692.

Han-erh 漢兒. "Wei min-tsu liu-hsüeh Shih K'o-fa chuan" 爲民族流血史可法傳 (A biography of Shih K'o-fa, a man who shed blood for the nation), *Chiang-su*, 6:71–81.

Han Shih-shih 漢史氏. "Wu-sung Kuang-fu chün chi-lüeh" 吳淞光復軍紀略 (A summary of the Restoration Army of Woosung); in *Hsin-hai ko-ming*, 7:33–37.

HCH: Chung-hua min-kuo k'ai-kuo wu-shih-nien wen-hsien pien-tsuan wei-yüan hui 中華民國開國五十年文献編纂委員會 (Committee on the compilation of documents on the fiftieth anniversary of the founding of the Republic of China), ed. *Chung-hua min-kuo k'ai-kuo wu-shih-nien wen-hsien* 中華民國開國五十年文献

(Documents on the fiftieth anniversary of the founding of the Republic of China), vol. 1, pts. 9–10; *Ko-ming chih ch'ang-tao yü fa-chan* 革命之倡導與發展 (The beginning and development of the revolution). Vols. 1–2, *Hsing-Chung hui* 與中會 (The Society to Restore China's Prosperity). 2 vols.; Taipei, 1963.

HHKM: Chung-kuo shih-hsüeh hui 中國史學會 (Chinese Historical Association), ed. *Hsin-hai ko-ming* 辛亥革命 (The Revolution of 1911). comp., Ch'ai Te-keng 柴德賡, et al. 8 vols.; Shanghai, 1957.

Hinton, Harold. *The Grain Tribute System of China*. Cambridge, Mass., 1956.

Hirayama Shū (P'ing Shan-chou) 平山周. *Chung-kuo pi-mi she-hui shih* 中國秘密社會史 (A history of Chinese secret societies). tr. Commercial Press Translation Department. Shanghai, 1912.

Ho Chung-hsiao 何仲蕭. *Ch'en Ying-shih hsien-sheng nien-p'u* 陳英士先生年譜 (A chronological biography of Ch'en Ying-shih). Shanghai, 1946.

Ho P'ing-ti. *Studies on the Population of China, 1368–1953*. Cambridge, Mass., 1959.

Hobsbawm, Eric J. *Primitive Rebels: Studies in Archaic Forms of Social Movements in the 19th and 20th Centuries*. New York, 1965.

Hsi-pei yen-chiu she 西北研究社 (Northwest Research Society), ed. *Ko-lao-hui yü ch'ing-pang kai-k'uang* 哥老會與青幫概況 (General account of the Ko-lao hui and the Green Gang). 1941.

Hsia Yen 夏衍 (Shen Tuan-hsien 沈端先). *Ch'iu Chin chuan* 秋瑾傳 (A biography of Ch'iu Chin). Peking, 1961.

Hsiao I-shan 蕭一山. *Chin-tai pi-mi she-hui shih-liao* 近代秘密社會史料 (Historical materials on modern secret societies). 4 vols.; Peking, 1935.

Hsiao Kung-chuan. *Rural China: Imperial Control in the Nineteenth Century*. Seattle, 1960.

Hsiao P'ing 蕭平. *Hsin-hai ko-ming lieh-shih shih-wen hsüan* 辛亥革命烈士詩文選 (A selection of writings by martyrs of the 1911 Revolution). Peking, 1962.

Hsin-ch'ao she 新潮社 (The New Tide Society), ed. *Ts'ai Chieh-min hsien-sheng yen-hsing lu* 蔡子民先生言行錄 (A record of the words and deeds of Ts'ai Chieh-min). Peking, 1920.

Hsin-hai ko-ming, see *HHKM*.

Hsin-hai ko-ming ch'ien shih-nien chien shih-lun hsüan-chi, see *SLHC*.

Hsin-hai ko-ming hui-i lu, see *KML*.

Hsin-hai ko-ming tzu-liao 辛亥革命資料 (Materials on the 1911 Revolution), *Chin-tai shih tzu-liao*, no. 1 (1961).

Hsin-hai ko-ming wu-shih chou-nien chi-nien lun-wen chi, see *CNL*.

Hsin-lü wen-hsüeh she 新綠文學社, ed. *Ming-chia chuan-chi* 名家傳記 (Biographies of famous men). Shanghai, 1934.

Hsin-min ts'ung-pao 新民叢報 (The renovation of the people). Photolithograph; Taipei, 1966.

Hsing-Chung hui, see *HCH*.

Hsü Ping-k'un 許炳堃. "Hang-chou kuang-fu chih yeh ti i-t'zu kuan-shen chin-chi hui-i" 杭州光復之夜的一次官紳緊急會議 (An urgent meeting of officials and gentry on the eve of the Hangchow revolution); in *Hsin-hai ko-ming hui-i lu*, 4:165–166.

Hsü Shou-shang 許壽裳. *Chang Ping-lin* 章炳麟. Chungking, 1945.

Hsü Shuang-yün 徐雙韵. "Chi Ch'iu Chin" 記秋瑾 (Recollections of Ch'iu Chin), in *Hsin-hai ko-ming hui-i lu*, 4:205–222.

"Hsü-wu tang" 虛無黨 (The Nihilist party), *Su-pao* (June 19, 1903), in *Hsin-hai ko-ming ch'ien shih-nien chien shih-lun hsüan-chi*, 1.2:696–698.

Hsüeh Chün-tu. *Huang Hsing and the Chinese Revolution*. Stanford, 1961.

Hu Han-min 胡漢民. "Tzu-chuan" 自傳 (Autobiography), in *Ko-ming wen-hsien*,

3:373–442.

Hu Sheng-wu 胡繩武 and Chin Ch'ung-chi 金冲及. "Hsin-hai ko-ming shih-ch'i Chang Ping-lin ti cheng-chih ssu-hsiang" 辛亥革命時期章炳麟的政治思想 (The political thought of Chang Ping-lin during the period of the Revolution of 1911), in *Hsin-hai ko-ming wu-shih chou-nien chi-nien lun-wen chi*, pp. 323–353.

Hu Shih 胡適. *Ssu-shih tzu-shu* 四十自述 (Autobiography at forty). Hong Kong, 1957.

Huang Chung-huang 黃中黃 (Chang Shih-chao 章士釗). "Shen Chin" 沈藎, in *Hsin-hai ko-ming*, 1:287–303.

Huang Hua 黃華. "Chi T'ung-ch'eng Wu Chih-ying nü-shih"記桐城吳芝瑛女士(Recollections of Wu Chih-ying of T'ung-ch'eng), *Kuo-wen chou-pao* 國聞週報(Kuo-wen weekly, illustrated), 14.11:33–37 (Mar. 22, 1937).

Huang-ti hun 黃帝魂(The soul of Huang-ti). Photolithograph; Taipei, 1968.

Huang Tsung-yang 黃宗仰. "Ho Ai-kuo hsüeh-she chih tu-li" 賀愛國學社之獨立 (Congratulations on the independence of the Patriotic School); *Su-pao* (June 25, 1903); in *Hsing-Chung hui*, 2:354–365.

Huang Yen-p'ei 黃炎培. "Wo ch'in-shen ching-li ti Hsin-hai ko-ming shih-shih" 我親身經歷的辛亥革命事實 (Facts of the 1911 Revolution that I personally experienced), in *Hsin-hai ko-ming hui-i lu*, 1:60–69.

Huang Yüan-hsiu 黃元秀. "Hsi-hu pai-yün an yü Hsin-hai ko-ming chih kuan-hsi" 西湖白雲庵與辛亥革命之關係 (The relation of White Cloud Temple at West Lake to the 1911 Revolution), in *Hsin-hai ko-ming hui-i lu*, 4:150–151.

Hucker, Charles O. "The Tung-lin Movement of the Late Ming Period," in John K. Fairbank, ed. *Chinese Thought and Institutions*. Chicago, 1957, pp. 132–162.

Hummel, Arthur W., ed. *Eminent Chinese of the Ch'ing Period*. 2 vols.; Washington, D.C., 1943–1944.

I-ching 逸經 (Unorthodox classics). Shanghai, 1936–1937.

Israel, John. *Student Nationalism in China, 1927–1937*. Stanford, 1966.

Jansen, Marius B. *The Japanese and Sun Yat-sen*. Cambridge, Mass., 1954.

———ed. *Changing Japanese Attitudes towards Modernization*. Princeton, 1965.

Je-erh-wei-hun-chu 熱而末昏著 "Tu Chün-kuo-min chiao-yü hui chi-chüan ch'i" 讀軍國民教育會集捐啟 (On reading an appeal for contributions by the Society for the Education of a Militant People), *Su-pao* (June 6, 1903), in *Hsing-Chung hui*, 2:109–110.

Johnson, Chalmers A. *Peasant Nationalism and Communist Power*. Stanford, 1962.

Johnson, William R. "Revolution and Reconstruction in Yunnan: A Sketch," paper for Conference on the Revolution of 1911 in China, mimeo., 1965.

"K'ang Yu-wei" 康有爲, *Su-pao* (June 1, 1903), in *Hsin-hai ko-ming ch'ien shih-nien chien shih-lun hsüan-chi*, 1.2:680–682.

KMCC: Kuomintang, Committee for the Compilation of Materials on the Party History of the Central Executive Committee, ed. *Ko-ming hsien-lieh chuan-chi* 革命先烈傳記 (Biographies of revolutionary martyrs). Taipei, 1950.

KML: Chung-kuo jen-min cheng-chih hsieh-shang hui-i ch'üan-kuo wei-yüan hui wen-shih tzu-liao yen-chiu wei-yüan hui 中國人民政治協商會議全國委員會文史資料研究委員會 (Committee on written historical materials of the National Committee of Chinese People's Political Consultative Conference), ed. *Hsin-hai ko-ming hui-i lu* 辛亥革命回憶錄 (Recorded recollections of the Revolution of 1911). 5 vols.; Peking, 1961–1963.

KMWH: Kuomintang, Committee for the Compilation of Materials on the Party History of the Central Executive Committee, ed. *Ko-ming wen-hsien* 革命文献

(Documents on the revolution). Vols. 1–6; Taipei, 1953–1956.

Ko Ching-en 葛敬恩. "Hsin-hai ko-ming tsai Che-chiang" 辛亥革命在浙江 (The 1911 Revolution in Chekiang), in *Hsin-hai ko-ming hui-i lu*, 4:91–126.

Ko Kung-chen 戈公振. *Chung-kuo pao-hsüeh shih* 中國報學史 (A history of Chinese journalism). Peking, 1955.

"Ko-ming chih-tsao-ch'ang" 革命制造廠 (The factory of revolution), *Chiang-su*, no. 5, in *Hsin-hai ko-ming ch'ien shih-nien chien shih-lun hsüan-chi*, 1.2:576–578.

Ko-ming hsien-lieh chuan-chi, see *KMCC*.

"Ko-ming hua-seng Wu-mu" 革命畫僧烏目 (The revolutionary artist monk Wu-mu), *Chung-yang jih-pao* 中央日報 (June, 1948), in *Hsing-Chung hui*, 2:356–359.

Ko-ming wen-hsien, see *KMWH*.

Kotenev, A. M. *Shanghai: Its Mixed Court and Council*. Shanghai, 1925.

KSKF: Chung-hua min-kuo k'ai-kuo wu-shih-nien wen-hsien pien-tsuan wei-yüan hui 中華民國開國五十年文獻編纂委員會 (Committee on the compilation of documents on the fiftieth anniversary of the founding of the Republic of China), ed. *Chung-hua min-kuo k'ai-kuo wu-shih-nien wen-hsien* 中華民國開國五十年文獻 (Documents on the fiftieth anniversary of the founding of the Republic of China), vol. 2, *Hsin-hai ko-ming yü min-kuo chien-yüan* 辛亥革命與民國建元 (The 1911 Revolution and the construction of the Republic); pt. 4, *Ko-sheng kuang-fu* 各省光復 (The Revolution in the provinces). 3 vols.; Taipei, 1962.

Kuei Yün-chang 眭雲章, ed. *Ko-ming hsien-lieh shih-lüeh* 革命先烈事略 (Brief accounts of martyrs of the Revolution). Taipei, 1957.

Kung Fa-tzu 攻法子. "Ching-kao wo hsiang-jen" 敬告我鄉人 (Summoning our villagers), *Che-chiang ch'ao*, no. 2, in *Hsin-hai ko-ming ch'ien shih-nien chien shih-lun hsüan-chi*, 1.2:496–502.

"Kung-ssu p'ien" 公私篇 (An essay on the concepts of public and private), *Che-chiang ch'ao*, no. 1, in *Hsin-hai ko-ming ch'ien shih-nien chien shih-lun hsüan-chi*, 1.2:492–495.

K'ung Fan-lin 孔繁霖. *Ch'en Ying-shih* 陳英士. Nanking, 1946.

Kuo-feng pao 國風報 (The national spirit). Shanghai, 1910–1911.

Kuo Han-chang 郭漢章. "Lüeh-t'an Shang-hai kuang-fu chih i" 略談上海光復之役 (A short talk about the police in the Shanghai Revolution), in *Hsin-hai ko-ming hui-i lu*, 4:38–41.

Kuo Hsiao-ch'eng 郭孝成. "Che-chiang kuang-fu chi" 浙江光復記 (An account of the Revolution in Chekiang), in *Hsin-hai ko-ming*, 7:135–149.

———"Chiang-su kuang-fu chi-shih" 江蘇光復記事 (An account of the Revolution in Kiangsu), in *Hsin-hai ko-ming*, 7:1–33.

Kuo-min jih-jih-pao 國民日日報 (The China national gazette). Photolithograph; Taipei, 1965.

Kuo T'ing-i 郭廷以. *Chin-tai Chung-kuo shih-shih jih-chih* 近代中國史事日誌 (A chronology of modern Chinese history). 2 vols.; Taipei, 1963.

Kuo-wu-yüan yin-chu chü 國務院印鑄局 (Ministry of the Interior Printing Office), ed. *Chih-yüan lu* 職員錄 (Official register). Peking, 1912–1913.

Kuomintang, Committee for the Compilation of Materials on the Party History of the Central Executive Committee, ed. *Ko-ming hsien-lieh hsien-chin chuan* 革命先烈先進傳 (Biographies of martyrs and forebearers of the revolution). Taipei, 1965.

———*Ko-ming hsien-lieh hsien-chin shih-wen hsüan-chi* 革命先烈先進詩文選集 (Selected writings of departed martyrs of the revolution). 6 vols.; Taipei, 1965.

———*Kuo-fu nien-p'u ch'u-kao* 國父年譜初稿 (A preliminary draft of the chronological biography of Sun Yat-sen). 2 vols.; Taipei, 1958.

Lai Hsin-hsia 來新夏. "Shih-lun Ch'ing Kuang-hsü mo-nien ti Kuang-hsi jen-min ta ch'i-i" 試論清光緒末年的廣西人民大起義 (The great rising of the Kwangsi people in the last years of the Kuang-hsü period), *Li-shih yen-chiu*, 11:57–77 (1957).

Lai Wei-liang 來偉良. "Hsin-hai kung-ch'eng ying Hang-chou ch'i-i chi" 辛亥工程營杭州起義記 (A record of the engineers' battalion in the Hangchow rising of 1911), *Chin-tai shih tzu-liao*, 6:67–74 (1957).

Lee, Choong. "Chang Ping-lin and the *Su-pao* case," Harvard East Asian Regional Studies, January 1963.

Legge, James, tr. *The Chinese Classics,* vols. 1 and 2. 2nd ed.; Oxford, 1893, 1895.

Levenson, Joseph R. *Liang Ch'i-ch'ao and the Mind of Modern China.* Cambridge, Mass., 1959.

——"The Suggestiveness of Vestiges: Confucianism and Monarchy at the Last," in David S. Nivison and Arthur Wright, eds., *Confucianism in Action.* Stanford, 1959, pp. 244–267.

Li Chi-ku 李季谷. "Kuan-yü Hsü Hsi-lin lieh-shih" 關於徐錫麟烈士 (About Hsü Hsi-lin), *I-ching* (Unorthodox classics), 21:1182–1184.

Li Chiang-ch'iu 李江秋. "Ch'iu Chin hsün-nan chi" 秋瑾殉難記 (The death of Ch'iu Chin), in *T'ung-meng hui,* 3:238–242.

Li Chien-nung. *The Political History of China,* tr. Teng Ssu-yü and Jeremy Ingalls. New York, 1956.

Li Chu-jan 李竹然. *Hsin-hai ko-ming ch'ien ti ch'ün-chung tou-cheng* 辛亥革命前的群衆鬪爭 (The mass struggle before the 1911 Revolution). Peking, 1957.

Li-shih yen-chiu 歷史研究 (Historical research). Peking, 1954– .

Li Shih-yüeh 李時岳. *Hsin-hai ko-ming shih-ch'i Liang-Hu ti-ch'ü ti ko-ming yün-tung* 辛亥革命時期兩湖地區的革命運動 (The revolutionary movement in the Hunan and Hupei areas during the period of the 1911 Revolution). Peking, 1957.

Li Shu-hua 李書華. "Wu Chih-hui hsien-sheng ts'ung wei-hsin p'ai ch'eng wei ko-ming tang ti ching-kuo"吳稚暉先生從維新派成爲革命黨的經過(Wu Chih-hui's change from the reform to the revolutionary movements), *Chuan-chi wen-hsüeh,* 4.3:35–38; 4.4:40–43.

Li Wen-hai 李文海. "Hsin-hai ko-ming yü hui-tang" 辛亥革命與會黨 (The 1911 Revolution and the secret societies), in *Hsin-hai ko-ming wu-shih chou-nien chi-nien lun-wen chi,* 1:166–187.

Liang Ch'i-ch'ao. *Intellectual Trends in the Ch'ing Period.* tr. Immanuel C. Y. Hsü. Cambridge, Mass., 1959.

Lifton, Robert. *Thought Reform and the Psychology of Totalism.* New York, 1961.

Lin Tuan-fu 林端輔. "Ning-po kuang-fu ch'in-li chi" 寧波光復親歷記 (A personal chronicle of the revolution in Ningpo), *Hsin-hai ko-ming hui-i lu,* 4:174–182.

Liu Ch'i-chi 柳棄疾 (Liu Ya-tzu 柳亞子). *Nan-she chi-lüeh* 南社紀略 (An account of the Southern Society); Shanghai, 1940.

Liu Hou-sheng 劉厚生. *Chang Chien chuan-chi* 張謇傳記 (Biography of Chang Chien). Hong Kong, 1956.

Liu K'uei-i 劉揆一. *Huang Hsing chuan-chi* 黃興傳記 (Biography of Huang Hsing). Taipei, 1952.

Liu Lien-k'o 劉聯珂. *Pang-hui san-pai-nien ko-ming shih* 幫會三百年革命史(A history of the revolutionary activities of secret societies in the past three hundred years). Macao, 1940.

Liu Wu-chi 柳無忌. *Man-shu ta-shih chi-nien chi* 曼殊大師紀念集(A commemorative collection of Su Man-shu's works). Hong Kong, 1953.

Lo Kuan-chung. *Romance of the Three Kingdoms.* tr. C. H. Brewitt-Taylor. Rutland, Vt., 1959.

Lu Hsün, *Selected Works.* 4 vols.; Peking, 1956.

Lu Man-yen 陸曼炎. *Shih-hsien pieh-chi* 時賢別記 (Another record of contemporary worthies). 2 vols.; Chungking, 1943.

Lu Tan-lin 陸丹林. *Ko-ming shih t'an* 革命史譚 (Chats on revolutionary history). Chungking, 1946.

Lü Kung-wang 呂公望. "Hsin-hai ko-ming Che-chiang kuang-fu chi-shih" 辛亥革命浙江光復紀實 (An account of the 1911 Revolution in Chekiang), *Chin-tai shih tzu-liao*, 1:104–117 (1954).

Lü Yüeh-p'ing 呂月屏. "Hui-i Hsin-hai ko-ming shih-ch'i ti chi-chien shih ho Ch'u-chou kuang-fu ching-kuo" 回憶辛亥革命時期的幾件事和處州光復經過 (Recollections of a few things of the period of the 1911 Revolution and experiences during the Revolution in Chuchow), in *Hsin-hai ko-ming hui-i lu*, 4:196–199.

"Lun Shen Chin ts'an-ssu shih" 論沈藎慘死事 (On the cruel death of Shen Chin), in *Hsin-hai ko-ming*, 1:308–311.

Lust, J. "The *Su-pao* case," *Bulletin of the School of Oriental and African Studies, University of London*, 27:408–429 (1964).

Ma Chi-sheng 馬濟生 as told to Tung Sun-kuan 董巽觀. "Chia-hsing kuang-fu chi-lüeh" 嘉興光復記略 (A brief summary of the revolution in Kashing), *chin-tai shih tzu-liao*, 2:67–68 (1958).

Ma Hsü-lun 馬叙倫. "Kuan-yü Hsin-hai ko-ming Che-chiang sheng-ch'eng kuang-fu chi-shih ti pu-ch'ung tzu-liao" 關於辛亥革命浙江省城光復記事的補充資料 (Supplementary material on the 1911 Revolution in the provincial capital of Chekiang), *Chin-tai shih tzu-liao*, 1:47–57 (1957).

——"T'ao Ch'eng-chang chih ssu" 陶成章之死 (The death of T'ao Ch'eng-chang), in *Hsin-hai ko-ming*, 1:520.

——"Wo tsai hsin-hai che-i-nien" 我在辛亥這一年 (My experiences during the year 1911); in *Hsin-hai ko-ming hui-i lu*, 1:170–179.

Mao Hu-hou 毛虎侯. "Hsin-hai ko-ming tsai Li-shui" 辛亥革命在麗水 (The 1911 Revolution in Li-shui), in *Hsin-hai ko-ming hui-i lu*, 4:200–202.

Martin, W. A. P. *The Awakening of China*. New York, 1910.

Mei Lan-fang 梅蘭芳. "Hsi-chü chieh ts'an-chia Hsin-hai ko-ming ti chi-chien shih" 戲劇界參加辛亥革命的幾件事 (A few items about actors participating in the 1911 Revolution), in *Hsin-hai ko-ming hui-i lu*, 1:342–373.

Meisner, Maurice. *Li Ta-chao and the Origins of Chinese Marxism*. Cambridge, Mass., 1967.

Min-li pao 民立報 (The people's stand). Shanghai, October 1910–December 1911.

Min-pao 民報 (People's journal). Photolithograph; Peking, 1957.

Min-hsü jih-pao 民吁日報 (The people's sigh). Photolithograph; Taipei, 1969.

Min-hu jih-pao 民呼日報 (The people's cry). Photolithograph; Taipei, 1969.

"Nan-yang kung-hsüeh ti i-chiu-ling-erh nien pa-k'o feng-ch'ao ho Ai-kuo hsüeh-she" 南洋公學的一九〇二年罷課風潮和愛國學社 (The student strike at the Nan-yang Public Institute in 1902 and the Patriotic School); in *Hsin-hai ko-ming hui-i lu*, 4:63–77.

"Nan-yang kung-hsüeh t'ui-hsüeh-sheng i-chien shu" 南洋公學退學生意見書 (A letter expressing the views of the students who withdrew from the Nan-yang Public Institute); *Su-pao* (Nov. 25, 1902), in *Hsing-Chung hui*, 2:351–353.

NCH: North China Herald and Supreme Court and Consular Gazette. Shanghai, 1900–1912.

Nivison, David S. and Arthur Wright, ed. *Confucianism in Action*. Stanford, 1959.

North China Herald, see *NCH*.

O-shih ching-wen 俄事警聞 (Warnings on Russian Affairs). Photolithograph; Taipei, 1968.

P'an Kung-chan 潘公展. *Ch'en Ch'i-mei* 陳其美. Taipei, 1954.
Pao T'ien-hsiao 包天笑. "Hsin-hai ko-ming ch'ien-hou ti Shang-hai hsin-wen-chieh" 辛亥革命前後的上海新聞界 (Shanghai newspaper circles before and after the 1911 Revolution), in *Hsin-hai ko-ming hui-i lu*, 4:86–90.
P'eng Kuo-tung 彭國棟, ed. *Ko-ming hsien-che ku-shih ts'ung-shu* 革命先哲故事叢書 (A collection of stories about the foreknowers of the revolution). Taipei, 1957.
P'eng Tzu-i 彭子儀. *Ch'iu Chin* 秋瑾. Shanghai, 1941.
P'i-chih 辟支. "Hsien-cheng fa-ta shih" 憲政發達史 (A history of the development of constitutional government), *Che-chiang ch'ao*, 8:47–52.
Powell, Ralph L. *The Rise of Chinese Military Power, 1895–1912*. Princeton, 1955.
Pu-nan-tzu 不難子. "Chiao-yü hsüeh" 教育學 (A study of education), *Che-chiang ch'ao*, 2:49–56.

Rankin, Mary B., "The Tenacity of Tradition," in Mary C. Wright, ed., *China in Revolution: The First Phase, 1900–1913*. New Haven, 1968, pp. 319–361.
Romanov, B. A. *Russia in Manchuria, 1892–1906*. tr. Susan Wilbur Jones. Ann Arbor, 1952.
Ruhlmann, Robert. "Traditional Heroes in Chinese Popular Fiction," in Arthur Wright, ed. *The Confucian Persuasion*. Stanford, 1960, pp. 141–176.

Sakai, Robert K. "Ts'ai Yüan-p'ei as a Synthesizer of Western and Chinese Thought," *Papers on China*, 3:170–192 (1949). Harvard University, East Asian Research Center.
Scalapino, Robert A. "Prelude to Marxism: The Chinese Student Movement in Japan, 1900–1910," in Albert Feuerwerker et al., eds., *Approaches to Modern Chinese History*. Berkeley, 1967, pp. 190–215.
———and George T. Yu. *The Chinese Anarchist Movement*. Berkeley, 1961.
Schiffrin, Harold. "Sun Yat-sen's Early Land Policy," *Journal of Asian Studies*, 16:549–564.
Schram, Stuart. *Mao Tse-tung*. New York, 1966.
Schwartz, Benjamin. *In Search of Wealth and Power: Yen Fu and the West*. Cambridge, Mass., 1964.
"Shang-hai shang-t'uan hsiao-shih" 上海商團小史 (A short history of the Shanghai Merchant Volunteers), in *Hsin-hai ko-ming*, 7:86–90.
Shang-hai yen-chiu tzu-liao hsü-chi 上海研究資料續集 (Shanghai Research Section), comp. "Su-pao an shih-mo" 蘇報案始末 (An account of the *Su-pao* case), in *Hsing-Chung hui*, 2:529–540.
Shao Hsün-cheng 邵循正. "Hsin-hai ko-ming shih-ch'i tzu-ch'an chieh-chi ko-ming p'ai ho nung ti kuan-hsi wen-t'i" 辛亥革命時期資產階級革命派和農的關係問題 (The question of relations between the revolutionary strata of the bourgeoisie and the peasantry during the period of the 1911 Revolution), in *Hsin-hai ko-ming wu-shih chou-nien chi-nien lun-wen chi*, pp. 99–114.
Shen Chün-ju 沈鈞儒. "Hsin-hai ko-ming tsa-i" 辛亥革命雜憶 (Miscellaneous recollections of the 1911 Revolution), in *Hsin-hai ko-ming hui-i lu*, 1:138–142.
Shen Tieh-min 沈肤民. "Chi Kuang-fu hui erh-san shih" 記光復會二三事 (Recollections of two or three things about the Restoration Society), in *Hsin-hai ko-ming hui-i lu*, 4:131–142.
Shen Yen-kuo 沈延國. *Chi Chang T'ai-yen hsien-sheng* 記章太炎先生 (Recollections of Chang T'ai-yen). Shanghai, 1946.

Sheng Lang-hsi 盛郎西. *Chung-kuo shu-yüan chih-tu* 中國書院制度 (The system of Chinese academies). Shanghai, 1934.

Shu Hsin-ch'eng 舒新城. *Chin-tai Chung-kuo chiao-yü shih-liao* 近代中國教育史料 (Materials on the history of education in modern China). 4 vols.; Shanghai, 1928.

———*Chin-tai Chung-kuo liu-hsüeh-shih* 近代中國留學史 (A history of modern Chinese students abroad). Shanghai, 1929.

Shu Lou 書廔. "Chiao-yü hui wei min-t'uan chih chi-ch'u" 教育會爲民團之基礎 (The Educational Association is the basis for a militia), *Chiang-su*, no. 3; in *Hsin-hai ko-ming ch'ien shih-nien chien shih-lun hsüan-chi*, 1.2:547–550.

SLHC: Chang Nan 張枏 and Wang Jen-chih 王忍之, ed. *Hsin-hai ko-ming ch'ien shih-nien chien shih-lun hsüan-chi* 辛亥革命前十年間時論選集 (Selected essays on current events written during the ten years prior to the Revolution of 1911). 4 vols.; Peking, 1960, 1962.

Snow, Edgar. *Red Star over China.* New York, 1939.

Ssu Tao-ch'ing 斯道卿. "Che-chün shih-pa nien ti hui-i lu" 浙軍十八年的回憶錄 (Recollections of eighteen years in the Chekiangese army), *Chin-tai shih tzu-liao*, 2:76–93 (1957).

Su-pao 蘇報 (The Kiangsu journal; Feb. 27–May 26, 1903). ed. Wu Hsiang-hsiang 吳相湘 . Photolithograph; Taipei, 1965.

Su-pao (The Kiangsu journal; May 6-July 7, 1903). ed. Lo Chia-lun 羅家倫. Photolithograph; Taipei, 1968.

"*Su-pao* an" 蘇報案 (The *Su-pao* case), in *Hsin-hai ko-ming ch'ien shih-nien chien shih-lun hsüan-chi*, 1.2:775–780.

Su P'eng 蘇鵬. "Chi Chün-kuo-min chiao-yü hui" 記軍國民教育會 (Recollections of the Society for the Education of a Militant People), in *Hsing-Chung hui*, 2:100–101.

———"Wan Fu-hua tz'u Wang Chih-ch'un an yü-chung chi-shih" 萬福華刺王之春案獄中紀事 (An account in jail of Wan Fu-hua's attempt to assassinate Wang Chih-ch'un), in *Hsing-Chung hui*, 2:396–400.

Sun Te-chung 孫德中. *Ts'ai Yüan-p'ei hsien-sheng i-wen lei-ch'ao* 蔡元培先生遺文類鈔 (A topical selection of Ts'ai Yüan-p'ei's writings). Taipei, 1960.

Ta-Ch'ing li-ch'ao shih-lu, see *CSL-KH.*

Ta-wo 大我. "Hsin she-hui chih li-lun" 新社會之理論 (Principles of the new society), *Che-chiang ch'ao*, 8:9–21.

T'an Pi-an 譚彼岸. "O-kuo min-ts'ui chu-i tui T'ung-meng hui ti ying-hsiang" 俄國民粹主義對同盟會的影響 (The influence of Russian populism on the Revolutionary Alliance), *Li-shih yen-chiu*, 1:35–44 (1959).

T'ao Ch'eng-chang 陶成章. "Che-an chi-lüeh" 浙案紀略 (A brief account of the revolts in Chekiang), in *Hsin-hai ko-ming*, 3:3–111.

———"Lung-hua hui chang-ch'eng" 龍華會章程 (Regulations of the Dragon Flower Society), in *Hsin-hai ko-ming*, 1:534–544.

Teng Ssu-yü. *New Light on the Taiping Rebellion.* Cambridge, Mass., 1950.

———and John K. Fairbank, *China's Response to the West.* Cambridge, Mass., 1954.

T'ieh Lang 鐵郎. "Erh-shih shih-chi chih Hu-nan" 二十世紀之湖南 (Twentieth Century Hunan), in *Hsin-hai ko-ming*; 2:195–208.

TMH: Chung-hua min-kuo k'ai-kuo wu-shih-nien wen-hsien pien-tsuan wei-yüan hui 中華民國開國五十年文獻編纂委員會 (Committee on the compilation of documents on the fiftieth anniversary of the founding of the Republic of China), ed. *Chung-hua min-kuo k'ai-kuo wu-shih-nien wen-hsien* 中華民國開國五十年文獻 (Documents on the fiftieth anniversary of the founding of the Republic of China), vol. 1, pts. 11–16; *Ko-ming chih ch'ang-tao yü fa-chan* 革命之倡導與發展 (The beginning and development of the Revolution), vols. 3–8; *Chung-kuo T'ung-meng hui* 中國同盟會 (The Chinese Revolutionary Alliance). 6 vols.; Taipei, 1963–1965.

Ts'ai Yüan-p'ei 蔡元培. "Shih ch'ou-Man" 釋仇滿 (Explaining enmity to the Manchus), *Su-pao* (April 11–12, 1903), in *Hsin-hai ko-ming ch'ien shih-nien chien shih-lun hsüan-chi*, 1.2:678–680.

Ts'ai Yüan-p'ei as told to Huang Shih-hui 黃世暉. "Ts'ai Chieh-min hsien-sheng ti ch'ing-nien shih-tai" 蔡子民先生的青年時代 (The youth of Ts'ai Chieh-min), in *Hsin-Chung hui*, 2:362–367.

Ts'ao Ya-po 曹亞伯. *Wu-ch'ang ko-ming chen-shih* 武昌革命真史 (A true history of the Wuchang revolution). 3 vols.; Shanghai, 1930.

Tso Shun-sheng 左舜生. *Chung-kuo chin-tai shih ssu-chiang* 中國近代史四講 (Four essays on modern Chinese history). Hong Kong, 1962.

Tsou Jung 鄒容. *Ko-ming chün* 革命軍 (The revolutionary army). Shanghai, 1958.

Tsou Lu 鄒魯. *Chung-kuo Kuo-min-tang shih-kao* 中國國民黨史稿 (A draft history of the Kuomintang). Shanghai, 1938.

Tu Ch'eng-hsiang 杜呈祥. *Tsou Jung* 鄒容. Nanking, 1946.

Tu-li ts'ang-mang-tzu 獨立蒼芒子. "Tung-ching hsüeh-chieh kung-fen shih-mo kao hsiang-jen fu-lao hsing-hsüeh shu" 東京學界公憤始末告鄉人父老興學書 (A report on the public protest of students in Tokyo with the request that the village elders promote education), in *Hsin-hai ko-ming*, 2:127–134.

Tung-fang tsa-chih 東方雜誌 (The eastern miscellany). Shanghai, 1904–1912.

Tzu-jan-sheng 自然生 (Chang Chi 張繼). "Chu Pei-ching Ta-hsüeh-t'ang hsüeh-sheng" 祝北京大學堂學生 (Extolling the students at Peking University), *Su-pao* (June 6, 1903), in *Hsin-hai ko-ming ch'ien shih-nien chien shih-lun hsüan-chi*, 1.2: 682–683.

———"Tu yen-na liu-hsüeh-sheng mi-yü yu-fen" 讀嚴拿留學生密諭有憤 (Anger at reading the secret edict ordering the arrest of the returned students), *Su-pao* (June 10–11, 1903), in *Hsin-hai ko-ming ch'ien shih-nien chien shih-lun hsüan-chi*, 1.2:685–688.

U.S. Department of State. General Records (Record Group 59). Diplomatic Correspondence, Decimal File, 1901–1905.

———General Records. Central Files (1906–1929). Numerical File, 1906–1911.

Walzer, Michael. *The Revolution of the Saints: A Study in the Origins of Radical Politics*. London, 1966.

Wang I-sun 汪詒蓀. "Hsin-hai ko-ming shih-ch'i tzu-ch'an chieh-chi yü nung-min ti kuan-hsi wen-t'i" 辛亥革命時期資産階級與農民的關係問題 (The question of relations between the bourgeoisie and the peasantry during the period of the 1911 Revolution), in *Hsin-hai ko-ming wu-shih chou-nien lun-wen chi*, pp. 115–146.

Wang Kuei-fen 王桂芬, ed. *Ch'iu Chin nü-hsia i-chi* 秋瑾女俠遺集 (Posthumous collection of the writings of the heroine Ch'iu Chin). Shanghai, 1929.

Wang Shih-tse 王時澤. "Hui-i Ch'iu Chin" 回憶秋瑾 (Recollections of Ch'iu Chin), in *Hsin-hai ko-ming hui-i lu*, 4:223–232.

Wang Ts'an-chih 王燦芝. *Ch'iu Chin nü-hsia i-chi* 秋瑾女俠遺集 (A posthumous collection of Ch'iu Chin's writings). Shanghai, 1929.

Wang, Y. C. "Tu Yüeh-sheng (1888–1951): A Tentative Political Biography," *Journal of Asian Studies*, 26.3:433–455.

Wang Yün-wu 王雲五. "Chui-tao Ts'ai Chieh-min hsien-sheng t'e-chi" 追悼蔡子民先生特輯 (Special memorial issue on Ts'ai Chieh-min), *Tung-fang tsa-chih*, 37.8:1–4 (1940).

Washington Post, The. Washington, D.C., 1968.

Wei Chien-yu 魏建猷. "Hsin-hai ko-ming ch'ien-yeh ti Che-chiang hui-tang huo-tung"

辛亥革命前夜的浙江會黨活動 (Activities of Chekiangese secret societies on the eve of the 1911 Revolution), in *Hsin-hai ko-ming wu-shih chou-nien chi-nien lun-wen chi,* pp. 519–544.

Welch, Holmes. *The Practice of Chinese Buddhism.* Cambridge, Mass., 1967.

Wen Kung-chih 文公直. *Chung-hua min-kuo ko-ming ch'üan-shih* 中華民國革命全史 (A complete history of the Chinese republican revolution). Shanghai, 1929.

——*Tsui-chin san-shih nien Chung-kuo chün-shih shih* 最近三十年中國軍事史 (A military history of China during the past thirty years), vol. 1, Shanghai, n.d.

Werner, E. T. C. *A Dictionary of Chinese Mythology.* Shanghai, 1932.

Who's Who in China. 5th edition; Shanghai, 1936.

Wright, Arthur, ed. *The Confucian Persuasion.* Stanford, 1960.

——, ed. *China in Revolution: The First Phase, 1900–1913.* New Haven, 1968.

Wu Chih-hui 吳稚暉. "Wu Chih-hui shu Shang-hai *Su-pao* an chi-shih" 吳稚暉述上海蘇報案紀事 (Wu Chih-hui recounts the *Su-pao* case), in Feng Tzu-yu, *Ko-ming i-shih,* 3:174–182.

Wu Hsin-mu 吳欣木. "Hsin-hai ko-ming shih-ch'i ti Hsia-shih shang-t'uan ho kung-ping t'ieh-tao ta-tui" 辛亥革命時期的硤石商團和工兵鐵道大隊 (The Hsia-shih Merchant Volunteers and the laborers' railway brigade of the period of the 1911 Revolution), in *Hsin-hai ko-ming hui-i lu,* 4:170–173.

"Wu lieh-shih Yang-ku ko-ming shih" 吳烈士暘谷革命史 (A revolutionary history of the martyr Wu Yang-ku), in *Hsin-hai ko-ming,* 7:188–195.

Wu-min 吳民. "Chiang-su yü Han-tsu chih kuan-hsi" 江蘇與漢族之關係 (The relation between Kiangsu and the Chinese race), *Chiang-su,* 6:7–12.

Wu Tse-chung 吳則中. *Chih-hui hsien-sheng i-p'ien chung-yao hui-i* 稚暉先生一篇重要回憶 (Important recollections of Wu Chih-hui). Taipei, 1964.

Wu Yü-chang 吳玉章. *Hsin-hai ko-ming* 辛亥革命 (The 1911 Revolution). Peking, 1961.

Wu Yüeh 吳樾. "Ching-kao wo t'ung-chih" 敬告我同志 (A warning to my comrades), in Ch'en Hsiung, comp. *Min-tsu ko-ming wen-hsien* 民族革命文献 (Documents on the nationalist revolution. Taipei, 1954, pp. 288–289.

——"Tzu-hsü" 自序 (Personal introduction), in Feng Tzu-yu, *Ko-ming i-shih,* 3:199–202.

Ya Lu 亞盧 (Liu Ch'i-chi). "Chung-kuo ko-ming chia ti-i jen Ch'en She chuan" 中國革命家第一人陳涉傳 (A biography of China's first revolutionary, Ch'en She), *Chiang-su,* 9–10:107–118.

——"Chung-kuo li-hsien wen-t'i" 中國立憲問題 (China's constitutional question), *Chiang-su,* no. 6, in *Hsin-hai ko-ming ch'ien shih-nien chien shih-lun hsüan-chi,* 1.2:594–596.

Yamashita Yoneko 山下米子. "Shingai kakumei no jiki no minshū undō" 辛亥革命の時期の民衆運動 (The mass movement at the time of the 1911 Revolution), *Tōyō bunka kenkyūjo kiyō* 東洋文化研究所紀要 (Memoirs of the Institute of Oriental Culture), 37:111–218 (March 1965).

Yang-chou shih-fan hsüeh-yüan li-shih hsi 楊州師範學院歷史系 (History department of the Yangchow Normal School), ed. *Hsin-hai ko-ming Chiang-su ti-ch'ü shih-liao* 辛亥革命江蘇地區史料 (Historical materials on the 1911 Revolution in localities of Kiangsu). Nanking, 1961.

Yang Shou-jen 楊守仁 (Yang Yü-lin 楊毓麟). "Hsin Hu-nan" 新湖南 (New Hunan), in *Hsin-hai ko-ming ch'ien shih-nien chien shih-lun hsüan-chi,* 1.2:612–648.

Yang Yü-ju 楊玉如. *Hsin-hai ko-ming hsien-chu chi* 辛亥革命先著記 (The decisive steps of the 1911 Revolution). Peking, 1958.

Yen Tu-ho 嚴獨鶴. "Hsin-hai ko-ming shih-ch'i Shang-hai hsin-wen chieh tung-t'ai"

辛亥革命時期上海新聞界動態 (Shanghai newspaper circles during the period of the 1911 Revolution), in *Hsin-hai ko-ming hui-i lu,* 4:78–86.

Young, Ernest P. "Ch'en T'ien-hua (1875–1905): A Chinese Nationalist," *Papers on China,* 13:113–162. Harvard University, East Asian Research Center, 1959.

———"The Reformer as Conspirator: Liang Ch'i-ch'ao and the 1911 Revolution," in Albert Feuerwerker, et al., eds., *Approaches to Modern Chinese History.* Berkeley, 1967.

Yü Chao-i 于肇貽. *Ch'iu Chin* 秋瑾. Hong Kong, 1956.

———*Ch'iu Chin nü-hsia* 秋瑾女俠 (The heroine Ch'iu Chin). Hong Kong, 1961.

Yü I 余一. "Min-tsu chu-i lun" 民族主義論 (On nationalism); *Che-chiang ch'ao,* nos. 1 and 2, in *Hsin-hai ko-ming ch'ien shih-nien chien shih-lun hsüan-chi,* 1.2:485–492.

Yüan Sun 轅孫. "Lu-hsi-ya hsü-wu-tang" 露西亞虛無黨 (The Russian Nihilist party), *Chiang-su,* no. 4, in *Hsin-hai ko-ming ch'ien shih-nien chien shih-lun hsüan-chi,* 1.2:565–571.

Yüan Yün 願雲. "Ju-chiao-kuo chih pien-fa" 儒教國之變法 (Reform in a Confucian country), *Che-chiang ch'ao,* 10:19–23.

———Ssu-k'o cheng-lun 四客政論 (A political debate by four travelers), *Che-chiang ch'ao,* no. 7, in *Hsin-hai ko-ming ch'ien shih-nien chien shih-lun hsüan-chi,* 1.2:503–508.

———"T'ieh-hsüeh chu-i chih chiao-yü 鐵血主義之教育 (Iron and blood education), *Che-chiang ch'ao,* 10:63–69.

Yuji Muramatsu. "Some Themes in Chinese Rebel Ideologies," in Arthur Wright, ed., *The Confucian Persuasion.* Stanford, 1960, pp. 241–267.

Yün Wo 雲窩. "Chiao-yü t'ung-lun" 教育通論 (A general essay on education), *Chiang-su,* no. 3; in *Hsin-hai ko-ming ch'ien shih-nien chien shih-lun hsüan-chi,* 1.2:551–559.

Yung Meng-yüan 榮孟源. *Chung-kuo chin-pai-nien ko-ming shih-lüeh* 中國近百年革命史略 (An outline of the revolutionary history of China during the past hundred years). Peking, 1954.

Glossary

Because there are a very large number of Chinese names and terms in the text and notes, I have limited the glossary to those most pertinent to the subject of this book and those not easily available elsewhere. I have excluded most names for which characters are given in the bibliography, most names of persons, organizations, and books appearing in Arthur W. Hummel, ed., *Eminent Chinese of the Ch'ing Period,* and offices and titles appearing in H. S. Brunnert and V. V. Hagelstrom, *Present Day Political Organization of China*. I also have not included place-names and some special terms for which the characters are obvious from the romanization. Most traditional mythological figures and persons from earlier periods of Chinese history are not listed here, nor are a few of the best known revolutionaries and revolutionary organizations.

Ai-hua nü-hsüeh 愛華女學
Ai-kuo nü-hsüeh-hsiao 愛國女學校
Ai-li yüan 愛儷園
An-sha t'uan 暗殺團
Ao Chia-hsiung 敖嘉熊
Aoyama 青山

Chai-chiao 齋教
Chang Chao-t'ung 張肇桐
Chang Ch'eng-yu 張承槱
Chang Chu-chün 張竹君
Chang Ch'u-pao 張楚寶
Chang Chü-sheng 張菊生
Chang Ch'uan-pao 張傳保
Chang Jang-san 張讓三
Chang Jen-chieh 張人傑
Chang Kung 張恭
Chang Po-ch'i 張伯岐
Chang-yuan 張園
Chao Ching-nien 趙鏡年
Chao Feng-ch'ang 趙鳳昌
Chao Hung-fu 趙宏甫
Chao Shu 趙舒
Che-chiang lü-Hu hsüeh-hui 浙江旅滬學會
Che-hui 浙會
"Che-ku t'ien" 鷓鴣天
Ch'en Ch'eng 陳成
Ch'en Chi-fu 陳吉甫
Ch'en Ch'ü-ping 陳去病
Ch'en Ch'üan-ch'ing 陳泉卿
Ch'en Chung-i 陳仲彝
Ch'en Fan 陳範
Ch'en Fu-ch'en 陳黻宸
Ch'en Han-ch'in 陳漢欽
Ch'en Han-ti 陳漢第
Ch'en Hsieh-fen 陳擷芬
Ch'en Hsün-cheng 陳訓正
Ch'en Kuo-chieh 陳國傑
Ch'en Meng-hsiung 陳夢熊
Ch'en Po-p'ing 陳伯平
Ch'en Shao-pai 陳少白
Ch'en Shih-hsia 陳時夏
Ch'en Shu-ch'ou 陳叔疇
Cheng Ju-ch'eng 鄭汝成
Ch'eng-cheng hsüeh-t'ang 誠正學堂
Ch'eng I 程毅
Ch'eng Te-ch'üan 程德全
"Chi Hsü Chi-ch'en" 寄徐寄塵
Ch'i I-hui 戢翼翬
Chiang Chi-yün 蔣繼雲
Chiang Chih-yu 蔣智由
Chiang Chu-ch'ing 蔣著卿
Chiang Fang-chen 蔣方震
Chiang Lo-shan 蔣樂山
Chiang Tsun-kuei 蔣尊簋
Chien-hsing kung-hsüeh 健行公學
Chien-hu nü-hsia 鑑湖女俠
"Chien-ko" 劍歌
Ch'ien-jen hui 千人會

Ch'ien-t'ang 錢塘
Ch'ien Yün-sheng 錢允生
Chih-na wang-kuo erh-pai ssu-shih-erh
  chi-nien hui 支那亡國二百四十二紀念會
Chih-shuo 直說
Chin-ch'ien hui 金錢會
Chin I 金一
Chin-ling t'ung-wen kuan 金陵同文館
Chin T'ien-ko 金天翮
Ch'in Li-shan 秦力山
Ch'in Yü-liu 秦毓鎏
Ching-chin shu-chü 鏡今書局
Ching-chung jih-pao 警鐘日報
Ching K'o 荊軻
Ching-shih pao 經世報
Ching Yao-yüeh 景耀月
Ching-yeh hsün-pao 競業旬報
Ch'ing-chia 慶家
ch'ing-i 清議
Ch'ing-i pao 清議報
Ch'ing-nien hui 青年會
Ch'ing-pang 慶幫
Ch'ing pi-shih 清秘史
chiu-kuo 救國
chiu-shih 救世
"Ch'iu-feng ch'ü" 秋風曲
"Ch'iu-jih tu-tso" 秋日獨坐
Ch'iu-shih shu-yüan 求是書院
"Ch'iu-yen" 秋雁
"Ch'iu-yü ch'iu-feng ch'ou-sha jen" 秋雨
  秋風愁殺人
Chou Ch'eng-t'an 周承菼
Chou Hua-ch'ang 周華昌
Ch'ou-an hui 籌安會
Chu Jui 朱瑞
Chu-lin hsiao-hsüeh-hsiao 竹林小學校
Chu Shao-k'ang 竺紹康
Ch'u Fu-ch'eng 褚輔成
"Chü" 菊
Chü-O i-yung tui 拒俄義勇隊
Ch'ü Ying-kuang 屈映光
"Ch'un-t'ien ou-chan" 春天偶占
Chung Hsien-ch'ang 鍾憲鬯
Chung kuo chiao-yü hui 中國教育會
Chung-kuo jih-pao 中國日報
Chung-kuo kan-ssu-t'uan 中國敢死團
Chung-kuo kung-hsüeh 中國公學
Chung-kuo kung-pao 中國公報
Chung-kuo liu-hsüeh-sheng hui-kuan 中
  國留學生會館
Chung-kuo min-tsu chih 中國民族志
Chung-kuo min-tsu ch'üan-li hsiao-ch'ang

shih 中國民族權力消長史
Chung-nan hui 終南會
Chung-wai jih-pao 中外日報

En-shou 恩壽
Erh-shih shih-chi ta-wu-t'ai tsa-chih 二十
  世紀大舞台雜志

Fan-hua pao 繁華報
Fan Kuang-ch'i 范光啟
"Fan tung-hai ko" 泛東海歌
Fang Yü-ssu 方於筍
fei-k'o 匪窠
Feng Ching-ju 馮鏡如
Feng Hsü 瑪煦
Fu Hsiung-hsiang 傅熊相
Fu-hu hui 伏虎會
Fu Meng 傅孟
fu-pai 腐敗
Fu-pao 復報

Hai-chün kung-ch'eng 海軍工程
Hei-ch'i hui 黑旗會
Ho Mei-sheng 何梅笙
Ho Mei-shih 何梅士
Ho Pu-hung 何步鴻
Ho-t'ung 哈同
Hsia Ch'ao 夏超
Hsia Chu-lin 夏竹林
Hsiao-fan 筱帆
Hsiao-yu hui 校友會
Hsiao Tzu-t'ing 蕭紫庭
Hsieh Fei-lin 謝飛麟
hsien-chüeh 先覺
Hsin-ch'eng 信成
Hsin-i hui 信義會
hsin-min 新民
"Hsin-shan ko" 新山歌
Hsin shih-chi 新世紀
Hsin-wen pao 新聞報
Hsiung Ch'eng-chi 熊成基
Hsiung Yang-lü 熊暘履
Hsü Tzu-hua 徐自華
Hsü Wei 徐偉
Hsü Ching-wu 徐敬吾
Hsü Chung-ch'ing 許仲卿
Hsü Hsing-pin 許行彬
Hsü Pan-hou 徐班侯
Hsü Shao-chen 徐紹楨
Hsü Shou-shang 許壽裳
"Hsüeh-chieh feng-ch'ao" 學界風潮
Hsüeh-sheng chün 學生軍

Hsüeh-sheng shih-chieh 學生世界
Hsün-ch'i nü-hsüeh 潯溪女學
Hu Chang 胡璋
Hu-pei hsüeh-sheng chieh 湖北學生界
Hu Shih-chün 胡士俊
Hu Tao-nan 胡道南
Huang Fei-lung 黃飛龍
Huang Feng-chih 黃鳳之
Huang Fu 黃郛
Huang Han-hsiang 黃漢湘
Huang I 黃怡
Hui-lan shu-yüan 蕙蘭書院
Hung-ch'i hui 紅旗會

Jang-shu 攘書
Je-ch'eng hsiao-hsüeh 熱誠小學
Jen-ho mei-hao 人和煤號
"Jih-pen Suzuki hsüeh-shih pao-tao ko"
  日本鈴木學士寶刀歌
Jui-chün hsüeh-she 銳俊學社

Kao Chien-kung 高劍公
Kao Erh-teng 高爾登
Kao K'uei 高逵
Kao Ta 高達
Ko-ming chün ch'uan-ch'i 革命軍傳奇
Kōtō shihan gakkō 高等師範學校
K'o-fu hsüeh-pao 克復學報
K'o-hsüeh i-ch'i kuan 科學儀器館
k'o-min tsung-tung-shih 客民總董事
"K'o-ti k'uang-miu" 客帝匡謬
"K'o-ti lun" 客帝論
Ku-ch'eng hui 古城會
Ku-ching ching-she 詁經精舍
Ku Nai-pin 顧乃斌
kua-fen 瓜分
K'uai Kuang-tien 蒯光典
Kuan-ti hui 關帝會
Kuang-chih shu-chü 廣智書局
Kuang-fu chün 光復軍
Kuang Han-tzu 光漢子
Kuang-hsüeh hui 廣學會
Kuang-tung tu-li hsieh-hui 廣東獨立協會
Kuei-fu 貴福
Kuei-lin 貴林
kung-hsüeh 公學
Kung-ai hui 共愛會
Kung-fu-tzu chih hsin-kan 孔夫子之心肝
Kung-i she 公益社
Kung Pao-ch'üan 龔寶銓
Kuo Chen-ying 郭鎮瀛
Kuo-hsüeh she 國學社

Kuo-hui 國會
Kuo-min i-cheng hui 國民議政會
Kuo-min kung-hui 國民公會
Kuo-min pao 國民報
Kuo-min shang-wu fen-hui 國民尚武分會
Kuo-ts'ui hsüeh-pao 國粹學報

Lan T'ien-wei 藍天蔚
Li-chih 勵志
Li Chun 李準
Li Hsieh-ho 李燮和
Li I-chih 李益智
Li Jui-nien 李瑞年
Li P'ing-shu 李平書
Li T'ien-ts'ai 李天才
Li-tse hsiao-hsüeh-hsiao 麗澤小學校
Li-yung 利用
Liang-Che kung-hsüeh 兩浙公學
Liang Tun-cho 梁敦倬
Lin Hsieh 林懈
Lin Shu-ch'ing 林述慶
Liu Chi-p'ing 劉季平
Liu Chia-fu 劉家福
Liu Ch'eng-yü 劉成禺
Liu Fu-piao 劉福標
liu-hsüeh-sheng hui-kuan 留學生會館
Liu Hsün 劉洵
Liu Kuang-han 劉光漢
Liu Shih-fu 劉師復
Liu Shih-p'ei 劉師培
Liu Tao-i 劉道一
Liu Tung-hai 劉東海
Liu Yao-hsün 劉耀勳
Lo Chia-ling 羅迦陵
Lo-lan fu-jen 羅蘭夫人
Lo p'ing-kuo-wang 羅平國王
Lou Shou-kuang 樓守光
Lu-ch'en ts'ung-shu 陸沈叢書
Lu Ho-sheng 盧和生
Lu-shih hsüeh-t'ang 陸師學堂
Lu Yang 魯陽
Lü Chia-i 呂嘉益
Lü Chih-i 呂志伊
Lü Hai-huan 呂海寰
Lü Hsiung-hsiang 呂熊祥
Lü I-wen 呂翼文
"Lun Chung-kuo tang-tao chieh ko-
  ming-tang" 論中國當道皆革命黨
Lung Chi-chih 龍積之
Lung-hua hui 龍華會
Lung Tse-hou 龍澤厚

Ma Chün-wu 馬君武
Ma Fu-i 馬福益
Ma Tsung-han 馬宗漢
"Man-chiang-hung t'zu" 滿江紅詞
Min-chu pao 民主報
Min-hsü jih-pao 民吁日報
Min-hu jih-pao 民呼日報
Min-kuo tsa-chih 民國雜志
Min-li pao 民立報
Min-sheng ts'ung-pao 民聲叢報
Ming-chi p'i-shih 明季神史
Ming-ch'iang nu-hsüeh-hsiao 明強女學校
Ming-hua nü-hsiao 明華女校
Ming-te hsüeh-t'ang 明德學堂
"Mou kung-jen chuan" 謀宮人傳
mu-yu 幕友

Nan-ching lu-shih hsüeh-t'ang 南京陸師
 學堂
Nan-she 南社
Niu Yung-chien 鈕永建
Nü-chieh chung 女界鐘
Nü-pao 女報
Nü-tzu pei-fa tui 女子北伐隊

O-shih ching-wen 俄事警聞
Ōmori Taiikukai 大森體育會

Pai-ch'i hui 白旗會
Pai-hua pao 白話報
Pai-pu hui 白布會
Pai-tzu hui 百子會
Pan-k'u pan-hsiao lou shih 半哭半笑樓詩
P'an Ch'ing 潘慶
P'an-men 潘門
Pao-an hui 保安會
Pao-huang-hui 保皇會
"Pao-tao ko" 寶刀歌
Pao-ting 保定
Pien-mu hsüeh-t'ang 弁目學堂
P'ing-yang hui 平陽會
p'o-huai chu-i 破壞主義
p'o-ts'e 叵測
P'u Chen-sheng 濮振聲

Rikugun keiri gakkō 陸軍經理學堂
Rikugun shikan gakkō 陸軍士官學堂

Seijō gakkō 成城學校
Seika gakkō 清華學校
Seng chiao-yü hui 僧教育會
Seng-min hsüeh-t'ang 僧民學堂
Shang-t'uan kung-hui 商團公會

Shang-wu yin-shu kuan 商務印書館
Shao-nien she 少年社
Shen Chin 沈藎
Shen-chou jih-pao 神州日報
Shen-chou nü-pao 神州女報
Shen-ch'üan 神拳
Shen Chün-yeh 沈鈞業
Shen Hsiang-yün 沈翔雲
Shen Man-yün 沈縵雲
Shen-pao 申報
Shen Yung-ch'ing 沈榮卿
Sheng-wu chi 聖武記
Shih-chieh shih 世界社
Shih-jen t'uan 十人團
Shih-pao 時報
Shih-tzu hou 獅子吼
Shih-wu pao 時務報
Shimbu gakkō 振武學校
Shou-shan 壽山
Shuang-lung hui 雙龍會
Shuang-t'an 雙灘
Ssu-min tsung-hui 四民總會
Su Man-shu 蘇曼殊
"*Su-pao* an chi-shih" 蘇報安紀事
Sun Huan-ching 孫寰鏡
Sun I-chung 孫翼中
Sun Shih-wei 孫世偉
Sun Te-ch'ing 孫德卿
Sung P'ing-tzu 宋平子

ta-tu-tu 大都督
Ta-t'ung shih-fan hsüeh-t'ang 大通師範
 學堂
T'ai-p'ing-yang pao 太平洋報
T'an Jen-feng 譚人鳳
Tang-lu ts'ung-shu 蕩虜叢書
T'ang 湯
T'ang Erh-ho 湯爾和
T'ang Shou-ch'ien 湯壽潛
T'ao Chün-hsüan 陶濬宣
T'ao-hua ling 桃花嶺
T'ao Pao-lien 陶葆廉
T'ao Sen-chia 陶森甲
Ti-chu chiao 地主教
Ti Ch'u-ch'ing 狄楚青
ti-kuo 帝國
t'i-yü hui 體育會
"Tiao Wu lieh-shih Yüeh" 弔吳烈士樾
t'ien-chih 天職
T'ien-chu chiao 天主教
T'ien Hsin-shan 田鑫山
T'ien-i pao 天義報
t'ien-min hsien-chüeh 天民先覺

T'ien-pao chan 天寶棧
T'ien-t'ao 天討
T'ien-tsu hui 天足會
Ting Mu-han 丁慕韓
to-min 墮民
Ts'ai Ch'eng-hsün 蔡成勲
Ts'ai Chün 蔡鈞
Ts'ai-hui 菜會
Ts'ai Yüan-k'ang 蔡元康
ts'an-i hui 參議會
Ts'an shih-chieh 慘世界
tsao-fan 造反
tsei-Ch'ing 賊清
Tseng Shao-ch'ing 曾少卿
Tseng-yün 增韞
Tsu-tsung chiao 祖宗教
"Tsui-pien wen" 罪辮文
Ts'ui-hsin pao 萃新報
"Tu-tui" 獨對
"Tui-chiu" 對酒
Tui-O t'ung-chih hui 對俄同志會
Tung-hu chung-hsüeh 東湖中學
Tung-hu t'ung-i hsüeh-hsiao 東湖通藝
　學校
Tung Hung-wei 董鴻褘
Tung-ta-lu t'u-shu-chü 東大陸圖書局
Tung-Wu ta-hsüeh 東吳大學
Tung-yang 東洋
T'ung-ch'eng 銅城
T'ung-i tang 統一黨
T'ung Pao-hsüan 童保喧
"T'ung-pao k'u" 同胞苦
T'ung-shih 痛史
T'ung-wen Hu-pao 同文滬報
tzu-chih hui 自治會
Tzu-hsü 自序
Tzu-li hsüeh-she 自立學社
Tzu-yang shu-yüan 紫陽書院
Tzu-yu hsüeh 自由血

Wan-chiang chung-hsüeh 皖江中學
Wan Fu-hua 萬福華
Wan-kuo kung-pao 萬國公報
Wan-yün hui 萬雲會
Wang Chen 王震
Wang Chi-t'ung 王季同
Wang Chia-chü 王嘉榘
Wang Chih-ch'un 王之春
Wang Chin-fa 王金發
Wang Chin-pao 王金寶
Wang Chung-ch'i 王鍾麒
Wang Feng-tsao 汪風藻
Wang Ho-shun 王和順

Wang Hsi-t'ung 王錫彤
Wang Hsiao-hsü 王小徐
Wang Lien 王廉
Wang Ta-hsieh 王大燮
Wang Te-yüan 王德淵
Wang T'ing-chün 王廷鈞
Wang Wen-ch'ing 王文慶
Wang Wen-p'u 王文溥
Wang Yung-pao 汪榮寶
Wei Lan 魏蘭
Wen-ming shu-chü 文明書局
Wen-T'ai-Ch'u hui-kuan 温台處會館
Wu Chih-ying 吳芝瑛
Wu-chung kung-hsüeh-she 吳中公學社
Wu-hu chung-hsüeh 蕪湖中學
Wu-mu shan seng 烏目山僧
Wu Ssu-yü 吳思豫
Wu-tai hui 烏帶會
Wu T'ing-fang 伍廷芳
"Wu-yeh" 梧葉
Wu Yen-fu 吳彥復
Wu Yüan-chih 伍元芝

Yang-cheng shu-yüan 養正書院
Yang-chou shi-jih chi 楊州十日記
Yang P'u-sheng 楊譜笙
Yang Shan-te 楊善德
Yang Yü-lin 楊毓麟
Yao-tzu t'i-yü hsüeh-t'ang 耀梓體育學堂
Yao Wen-fu 姚文甫
Yao Yung-ch'en 姚勇忱
Yeh-chi ta-wang 野雞大王
Yeh Han 葉瀚
Yeh Hui-chün 葉惠鈞
Yeh Lan 葉瀾
Yeh Sung-ch'ing 葉頌清
Yen-shuo lien-hsi hui 演說練習會
Yin Jui-chih 尹銳志
Yin Wei-chün 尹維俊
yu-hsia 遊俠
Yu-hsüeh i-pien 游學譯編
Yü-ch'üan hui 玉泉會
Yü Feng-shao 俞鳳韶
Yü-hsüeh sheng 浴血生
Yü Lien-san 俞廉三
Yü Meng-t'ing 余孟庭
Yü Ming-chen 俞明震
Yü-ts'ai 育才
Yü Wei 俞煒
Yü Yu-jen 于右任
Yüan Shu-hsün 袁樹勛
Yüeh-wang hui 岳王會

Harvard East Asian Series